D0914107

THE BAIL BOOK

Mass incarceration is one of the greatest social problems facing the United States today. America incarcerates a greater percentage of its population than any other country and is one of only two countries that requires arrested individuals to pay bail to be released from jail while awaiting trial. After arrest, the bail decision is the single most important cause of mass incarceration, yet this decision is often neglected since it is made in less than two minutes. Shima Baradaran Baughman draws on constitutional rights and new empirical research to show how we can reform bail in America. Tracing the history of bail, she demonstrates how it has become an oppressive tool of the courts that disadvantages minority and poor defendants and shows how we can reform bail to alleviate mass incarceration. By implementing these reforms, she argues, we can restore constitutional rights and release more defendants, while lowering crime rates.

Shima Baradaran Baughman is Professor of Law in the S.J. Quinney College of Law, at the University of Utah.

The Bail Book

A COMPREHENSIVE LOOK AT BAIL IN AMERICA'S
CRIMINAL JUSTICE SYSTEM

SHIMA BARADARAN BAUGHMAN
University of Utah School of Law

CAMBRIDGE
UNIVERSITY PRESS

University Printing House, Cambridge CB2 8BS, United Kingdom

One Liberty Plaza, 20th Floor, New York, NY 10006, USA

477 Williamstown Road, Port Melbourne, VIC 3207, Australia

314–321, 3rd Floor, Plot 3, Splendor Forum, Jasola District Centre, New Delhi – 110025, India

79 Anson Road, #06-04/06, Singapore 079906

Cambridge University Press is part of the University of Cambridge.

It furthers the University's mission by disseminating knowledge in the pursuit of education, learning, and research at the highest international levels of excellence.

www.cambridge.org
Information on this title: www.cambridge.org/9781107131361
DOI: 10.1017/9781316443194

© Shima Baradaran Baughman 2018

First published 2018

Printed in the United Kingdom by Clays, St Ives plc

A catalogue record for this publication is available from the British Library.

Library of Congress Cataloging-in-Publication Data
Names: Baughman, Shima Baradaran, author.
Title: The bail book : a comprehensive look at bail in America's criminal justice system / Shima Baradaran Baughman, University of Utah School of Law.
Description: Cambridge, United Kingdom ; New York, NY, USA : Cambridge University Press, 2018. | Includes bibliographical references and index.
Identifiers: LCCN 2017042278 | ISBN 9781107131361 (hardback)
Subjects: LCSH: Bail—United States. | Bail—Social aspects—United States. | Arrest—United States.
Classification: LCC KF9632 .B38 2018 | DDC 345.73/056—dc23 LC record available at https://lccn.loc.gov/2017042278

ISBN 978-1-107-13136-1 Hardback

"We can't fix our broken criminal justice system until we take on the exploitative bail industry."

– Jay Z[1]

"Bail reform could save American taxpayers roughly $78 billion a year . . . [and] more important[ly], it would help restore Americans' faith in our justice system."

– Senators Kamala Harris and Rand Paul[2]

Contents

Acknowledgments

I would like to express my deep gratitude to all those who helped me during the last several years in completing this work. I would especially like to thank Dr. Frank McIntyre for his excellent empirical work that is relied on in this book. My grateful thanks are also extended to Madeline Aller, Mitchell Alexander Tate, Shelby Shaw, Clarissa West, Thomas Lingard, Matthew Grow, Sean Romney, Zachary Williams, Keegan Rank, Alexis Keiko Juergens, Amanda Ulland, Lauren Martinez, Curt Trickett, Helena Jordan, Justin Fouts, Marina Marisol Pena, Mary Martinez-Spainhour, Nina Kim, James Perry Sanders, Darrin McGill, Amylia Brown, Emily Mabey Swensen, Alexander Williams, and Marina Pena for excellent research assistance in this book. I am thankful for the excellent people at Cambridge University Press, including my editor, John Berger, who believed in the project from the start, and Lisa Sinclair and Abirami Ulaganathan, for their excellent work on this book. I am also grateful to Professors Mehrsa Baradaran, Carissa Byrne Hessick, Laura Appleman, Christopher Slobogin, David Harris, Amos Guiora, Andrew Ferguson, RonNell Anderson Jones, Andy Hessick, and Wayne Logan for their help in the early processes of preparing to write this book and throughout. Special thanks to Dean Robert Adler at the University of Utah for a Deans Scholar grant that helped facilitate my work.

I would also like to extend my thanks to the American Bar Association for the Restoring the Presumption of Innocence grant that has helped realize bail reforms I supported in several US jurisdictions. I am inspired by all of my great colleagues in the bail field for all of the amazing empirical and theoretical work they do: Douglas Colbert, Ronald Allen, Laura Appleman, Sandra Guerra Thompson, Sam Wiseman, Larry Laudan, Mark Miller, David Abrams, Jocelyn Simonson, Lauryn Gouldin, Sandra Mason, Megan Stevenson, Cherise Fanno Burdeen, Alec Karakatsanis, Tim Murray, Chris Griffin, Bryan Taylor, and Sturgeon Kennedy. And a special thanks to my

Judge and mentor, Judge Jay S. Bybee and Judge Alex Kozinski for introducing me to the pretrial world during my clerkship and to my co-clerk Lexie White for the great work she has done in the courts to support improvements in pretrial rights for the poor. I would like to thank Patti Beekhuizin, Baiba Hicks, and Angela Turnbow at the University of Utah law school for their excellent editing of this manuscript and general helpfulness in supporting my scholarly work.

Finally, I wish to thank Ryan Baughman for his love, support, and encouragement as well as his substantive help with "our" book, Kian Baradaran Robison, and Darian Baradaran Robison for their perpetual kindness, hard work, and independence that allowed me the time to complete this book, and Milo Baradaran Baughman for holding my hand in the last few months of drafting. Special thanks to Heather Pabst Ward, Kamla Fennimore, Katherine Jepsen, Brooke Clayton Boyer, Geidy Achecar, Gary, and Marilyn Baughman for their encouragement during this process and input on the book. I would also like to thank my parents, Narima and Asad Baradaran, and my siblings Mehrsa, Hediyeh, and Darius for their support and kindness during the drafting of this book.

This research was made possible, in part, through generous support from the Albert and Elaine Borchard Fund for Faculty Excellence at the S.J. Quinney College of Law, University of Utah.

Introduction

Bail is the temporary release of a person awaiting trial for a crime. This simple decision – to detain or release a defendant – is made all over the United States in courtrooms every day. It is a decision that often takes less than five minutes, does not require evidence, and usually only involves one lawyer and a judge. But what happens during those five minutes tells a significant story about criminal justice in America.

The story of bail is one that most heavily impacts poor individuals. Consider these three bail scenarios. James, a teenager, was accused of stealing a bus pass. After police arrested him, the court set a $1,500 bail that neither he nor his family could afford. He remained in jail until he could negotiate a plea with the prosecutor. Another teen, Kenny, was charged with receiving stolen property. The prosecution suggested her bail be set at $150, but the court set bail at $300. Kenny spent five days in jail awaiting trial since she did not have the money to be released.[1] A homeless man, Leslie Chew, who was living out of his car, was arrested after he walked into a convenience store and took four blankets to keep him warm on a cold night. Chew was arrested for theft and his bail was set at $3,500. A bail bondsman offered to cover it for $350, but Chew did not have enough even for that. Chew was in jail pending trial for eight months, costing Lubbock, Texas, taxpayers $9,210. Chew took a plea deal and pled guilty to felony theft.[2]

In contrast to these bail scenarios, consider three other very different ones.[3] A prominent foreign diplomat is released relatively quickly on bail and remained on house arrest after allegedly violently sexually assaulting a hotel maid. A wealthy husband and wife charged with brutally assaulting – including starving, beating, and torturing – two young maids are allowed their freedom on bail because they secure private bail guards. And finally, a well-known mob boss is released on $10 million bail, with an electronic bracelet, and remains in his extravagant mansion pending trial. These six real-world examples demonstrate that the inequities of bail are real. Poor defendants, who have committed minor, nonviolent crimes, are held in jail before trial while rich defendants charged with serious and sometimes violent crimes are released pending trial. Bail is not just a matter of abstract criminal justice policy, but a practice with real effects on real people. Indeed, these accounts demonstrate that the story of bail is one of poverty, inequality, and haste. It is also a tale of important constitutional rights lost and judicial discretion misused. And importantly, bail is the single most preventable cause of mass incarceration in America.

America is one of only two countries in the world that requires individuals to pay money to be released on bail awaiting trial. In most countries in the world, it is a constitutional right for most defendants to be released on bail awaiting trial. And even in America, the right to bail historically and constitutionally was available not just for the wealthy.

Bail rights should not be sold to the highest bidder but instead available for all of the accused. But today, average Americans struggle to meet bail and feel the repercussions and inherent inequity of the current bail system. Kenny and James are only 2 of the 27,000 juveniles held on bail in detention centers every day who cannot afford to be released.[4] In some areas, less than 10 percent of defendants can pay bail of less than $1,000. In New York, for instance, only 12 percent of defendants will make bail at their arraignment; the rest will remain incarcerated.[5] The cost of receiving freedom before trial results in many individuals sitting in jail before they are found guilty of any crime.

This volume provides a glimpse into the reality of bail and mass incarceration. It explores the inequities of bail for the poor, discusses racial and cost implications, and explains why bail is so important for a defendant's case. This book focuses on constitutional and empirical issues. In particular, it demonstrates that historically bail has been a constitutional right and that empirical evidence tells us judges could safely release up to 25 percent more defendants before trial. In short, this book shows how we can preserve bail as a constitutional right by releasing more defendants, without increasing crime rates.

From medieval times to the modern day, the concept of bail has been a mainstay of the law. Bail is the means through which accused criminals can obtain release from police or state custody before trial and after arrest. Traditionally, bail was some form of property (such as money) deposited or pledged to a court to persuade it to release the accused on the understanding that he will return for trial or forfeit the money. The principle of bail grounds itself in constitutional rights of liberty and due process. It also stems from the presumption of innocence that proclaims that all should be deemed innocent until proven guilty at trial. The presumption of innocence and the right to due process guarantee that a person will not be punished or lose their liberty before they face a trial. Therefore, every individual maintains a right to be free until a jury determines their guilt. And the Sixth Amendment of the US Constitution guarantees that a jury determines a person's guilt after a fair trial with evidence. These constitutional principles are deeply rooted in English and American law and preserve the constitutional right to bail.

The US criminal justice system has long recognized the constitutional importance of providing bail. The First Congress applied this broad protection to all noncapital offenses and left discretion to the judiciary for capital offenses.[6] Through the twentieth century until the 1950s, the Supreme Court protected the right to bail, even for communists who were the biggest national security threat at the time. For instance, when the government tried to prevent release for high-profile communists by demanding high bail amounts in *Stack v. Boyle*, the Supreme Court intervened, claiming that the government could not use expensive bails to deny individuals the constitutional right to release.[7] However, bail law started to shift with the first bail "reforms" of the 1960s. The Bail Reform Act of 1966, which still presumed release in noncapital cases, opened the door to individuals not receiving release on bail if a judge concluded they were likely to be found guilty. Then, the Bail Reform Act of 1984 further diluted the right to bail by allowing, for the first time, a defendant to be denied bail based on the likelihood of future criminality.[8] At the time, this new authority to detain individuals who were "dangerous" before trial was seriously controversial given the constitutional right to bail.

However, the Supreme Court quickly upheld this new requirement – future dangerousness – as a constitutionally valid reason for denying bail. The Court in *United States v. Salerno* held that "liberty is the norm," and detention before trial is the "carefully limited exception."[9] According to federal statutes, the norm is that people charged with a crime should be released before trial[10] and the government bears the burden of proving that a defendant should be detained pretrial.[11] Despite the supposedly limited nature of the 1984 bail reform policies, in the years since the 1984 reform, pretrial detention has become the norm rather than the exception.[12] It has become the norm not only in the federal system, but also in most states that have copied this bail scheme.

These significant changes in the latter part of the twentieth century are at odds with the long-standing principle that bail is a constitutional right. An oft-repeated value of US criminal justice is that all are innocent until proven guilty at trial. But our system has evolved into one where judges are allowed to predict which defendants are guilty and dangerous, and then to detain those people long before trial; and that detention ultimately results in the defendants being denied a real determination of guilt. Because most criminal cases involve a plea, if a person is denied bail before trial, they lose bargaining power with a prosecutor. The defendant feels pressure to plead guilty – even if they are innocent – and often receives a custodial sentence or time served. If a person is granted bail, they have more bargaining power and are much more likely to receive a noncustodial sentence. The denial of bail has led to a violation of formerly sacred constitutional rights for a defendant. Current bail practices allow predictions of guilt and weighing of evidence against defendants before trial since defendants' rights have lacked steady constitutional rooting. Without consistent protection of constitutional rights – including due process and Sixth Amendment rights – a defendant's constitutional rights have been watered down and applied inconsistently, resulting in unfairness for defendants. These protections are critical to preserving bail as a constitutional right.

Modern-day reductions in constitutional rights have had significant effects on incarceration in America. Prison statistics show that detention before trial increased after the 1984 reforms and has steadily increased since that time. Since the 1990s, pretrial detention rates have risen 72 percent,[13] with the number of unconvicted people in US jails having increased by 59 percent.[14] This contributes greatly to the astonishing incarceration rates in the United States and accounts for 99 percent of the total increase in the jail population.[15] To put this into the context of the broader incarceration problem, the United States has about 5 percent of the world's population, but incarcerates 25 percent of the world's prisoners – incarcerating a greater percentage of its population than any other country. In 2015, almost 11 million people were admitted into a jail in the United States.[16] And while the last seven years have seen a slight fall in incarceration rates, prison population rates increased in twenty-seven states in 2013,[17] twenty-one states saw a further increase in 2014,[18] and eighteen states had an additional increase in 2015.[19] But almost 700,000 of the 2.3 million American prisoners aren't convicts; rather, they are accused individuals awaiting trial.

According to recent data, over 60 percent of the nation's jail population consists of unconvicted detainees,[20] and like James and Kenny, 75 percent of those detainees have been charged with minor property crimes, drug offenses, or other nonviolent acts.[21] Since the 1980s, both federal and state detention rates have increased. Over the last two decades, local jails have housed more pretrial detainees than actual convicts.[22] In just a few short years, the United States has gone from releasing 56 percent of defendants to only 40 percent, without any complaint or even acknowledgment by scholars or policy advocates despite the serious impact on US incarceration rates. And according to the U.S. Bureau of Justice Statistics, 95 percent of the jail growth since 2000 has resulted from an increase in inmates held without bail.[23]

Besides arrest, bail is the most important criminal justice decision made today. The decision to deny or allow bail means more for a defendant's fate than any other decision besides arrest. This simple ability to afford bail determines whether the defendant loses her job or keeps it. Most criminal cases (95 percent or more) do not go to trial. In these cases, the decision to release someone from jail or detain them means everything for a case. If a judge denies a person bail, that person is more likely to lose their case and be detained for a longer period of time, simply based on whether they can pay bail or not. Defendants detained before trial are more likely to be convicted if they go to trial, four times more likely to be sentenced to jail, and three times more likely to receive prison sentences than similar people released pretrial.[24] Additionally, given their weak bargaining power with prosecutors while locked up, when jail or prison time is imposed pretrial detainees receive longer sentences regardless of the crime they are charged with and the evidence against them. In addition, their jail sentences are nearly three times as long, and prison sentences are more than twice as long.[25]

Detention leads to more detention, even among those who claim innocence. Consider the case of Shadu Green, who was arrested for speeding.[26] Officers claim that Green was belligerent and resisted arrest, but Green insisted that officers attacked him and proclaimed his innocence. The judge posted bail at $1,000, and a bondsman offered to cover it for a $400 fee. Green didn't have the money to pay bail and was sent to jail. The prosecutor offered Green sixty days in jail if Green pled guilty. Green maintained his innocence, he didn't want the charge to show up on his record, and wanted to assert his right to a trial by a jury of his peers. Green spent over half of the sixty days in jail before his girlfriend was able to pay the $400 fee for the bail bondsman.

When Green was interviewed after his experience in jail, he recognized that if his girlfriend had not been able to come up with the bail money he would have settled and pled guilty for a crime he did not commit. He had no leverage in negotiating a favorable agreement while he was detained. Because he made bail, he continued to assert his innocence, and he was eventually found not guilty at trial. This is not an uncommon scenario. Marty Horn, the commissioner of New York City's jails, reported that he had seen this kind of situation play out over and over: "Individuals who insist on their innocence and refuse to plead guilty get held . . . [b]ut the people who choose to plead guilty get out faster." Not only do defendants who cannot afford bail plead guilty to get out of jail faster, they also often receive and accept harsher punishments than those who are released before trial.

Poor jail conditions contribute greatly to a defendant's incentive to plead guilty to get out of jail. Jail conditions nationally are dreadful, unequivocally worse than prison conditions, and individuals denied bail go directly to jail. The jail environment is often "chaotic" because resources are scarce, staff often lack adequate training, classification of inmates is random, and turnover is quick.[27] Despite some efforts at reform, there are countless stories of jail abuse, gang rapes, illness, overcrowding, and other unsafe and abusive conditions nationwide. Jails are often older structures and sometimes contain mold contamination, poor ventilation, lead pipes, and asbestos. Furthermore, although serious illness is common in local and county jails, these facilities often have only minimal health services.

Jurisdictions across the country have been unable to cope with the financial costs of such high pretrial detention rates. As pretrial detention has become routine, overcrowding is now a problem for many jails and prisons. The financial strain appears to have compounded the poor conditions in jails, leading to horrible treatment in certain locations. For instance, LA County Jail inmates sleep on dirty floors and are allowed only one opportunity to go outside in a week.[28] In Maricopa County, Arizona, inmates sleep outdoors in military tents without air conditioning in over 100° temperatures, and are fed 15-cent meals only twice a day to cut costs.

And while dire jail conditions are enough reason to question current bail practices, what is worse is that it is actually a tool used by the government. Detention before trial is one of the prosecution's favorite tools for getting rid of a case. A prosecutor knows that detention before trial increases the likelihood that a defendant will accept a plea bargain. Shadu Green's case illustrates the pressure felt by defendants who cannot make bail. A prolonged stay in jail nearly broke Green's resolve to maintain his innocence to the point where he almost accepted a plea deal.[29] This pressure is felt most acutely by defendants who are risk averse and who do not have the financial resources to mount a defense.[30] Not only are defendants more likely to plead guilty if detained, but the prosecution is also more likely to prevail if the case is against a detained defendant at trial than against a defendant who is released on bail. That is because an individual who is detained often faces practical difficulties in attempting to prepare her case.

Prosecutors certainly know that once bail is denied a defendant is much more likely to plead guilty to get out of jail, even if she did not commit the crime. And they likely know that defendants who opt for trial are less capable of preparing an effective defense. For instance, a defendant who is in jail does not have the ability to investigate her case, line up witnesses, or do other necessary background work that busy lawyers often rely on clients to do.

As a result, prosecutors have an incentive to ask for high bails to ensure that defendants will remain behind bars.

In addition to the difficulties of negotiating with prosecutors while detained, an important constitutional concern is that defendants have little to no access to their lawyers while held without bail. Indeed, recent news accounts demonstrate the difficulty of defendants in communicating with counsel while in jail before trial. Busy attorneys who cannot visit their clients often must resort to discussing case matters over the phone or email. Those modes of communication are not secure, resulting in prosecutors gaining access to these privileged exchanges. When a defendant in pretrial detention is unable to communicate openly with her attorney, she is also less able to assist in her own defense. This inability to assist in the preparation of trial deprives defendants of important constitutional rights of due process, access to counsel, and the right to a fair trial. Some jails who used to screen lawyer emails and letters as attorney–client privileged claim they no longer have resources for screening and end up reviewing them all and disclosing the attorney information to prosecutors. Defendants are at a severe disadvantage when prosecutors have a sneak peek into their case before they reach court. There have even been instances in Brooklyn, New York, where prosecutors have read communications between defense attorneys and the accused and presented them against defendants in court.[31]

Defendants often lack access to any lawyer during this key pretrial period. About half of the local jurisdictions in this country do not provide counsel for indigent defendants at pivotal bail hearings. Bail hearings take one of two different forms. In some of these jurisdictions, a judicial officer presides with neither a prosecutor nor defense counsel present. Others have a judicial officer presiding and prosecutor participation, but no defense counsel.[32] In these jurisdictions, the defendant has no one to speak on their behalf. A recent study found that defendants who were provided counsel at bail hearings fared significantly better than a similar group of defendants who were not provided with counsel. Additionally, defendants who had counsel reported greater satisfaction with the bail process, including a sense that they were treated respectfully by the judge, and that the judge considered a great deal of information when making the bail decision.[33] Since pretrial detention has such serious and negative consequences for people in terms of the criminal justice outcomes at sentencing, defendants should have access to an attorney to preserve their constitutional right to bail.

The costs of incarceration, in general, and bail, in particular, are also a great burden on society. Spending on incarceration has increased dramatically over the last several decades. Over the past three decades, between 1979–80 and 2012–13, state and local expenditures for corrections quadrupled from $17 to $71 billion[34] – and spent an estimated $9 billion just on housing pretrial detainees.[35] According to William Stuntz, even when adjusted for inflation, spending on corrections from 1971 to 2002 rose 455 percent. Institutions of higher learning and prisons compete for state funds, and prisons are winning. This burden caused by pretrial detention has serious consequences in many states, like California, that spend more on prisons than schools. In California, for example, 10 percent of the state general fund went to higher education and 3 percent went to prisons thirty years ago. In 2010, 11 percent went to prisons and 7.5 percent to higher education.[36] Today, per-inmate spending in the state is $70,836,[37] compared with per-student spending of $18,050.[38] And other states are not too far behind with current statistics showing that even when population changes are factored in twenty-three states increased per capita spending on corrections at more than double the rate of increases in per-pupil educational spending.[39] In sum, the costs of incarceration for individuals not released on bail are a massive burden on many state and local economies.

The individual costs of not obtaining release on bail are also significant. Individuals who are held on bail are often not convicted later and pose no danger to the public, but simply lack the funds to get out on bail. Consider the case of Perchelle Richardson, a seventeen-year-old high school student who, after the devastating impact of Hurricane Katrina, was a year behind in school.[40] When Perchelle allegedly took an iPhone from her neighbor, she was arrested, charged with felony burglary, and sent to jail. At her arraignment, the Judge issued a $5,000 personal surety, assuming Perchelle would be released from detention the following morning. However, New Orleans has a $200 administrative fee for all personal sureties. Perchelle's family was not able to raise the $200, and as a result this young high school student remained in jail pretrial for 51 days. Perchelle's family, who relied on Perchelle for childcare, had to find alternative living arrangements for the other children. Perchelle fell behind in her studies and spent her pretrial detention detached from family and friends and among individuals who were charged with serious crimes.

After fifteen days, the prosecutor simply dropped the charges. Perchelle was never convicted. She spent fifty-one days in pretrial detention, at immense personal costs and costs to her family, simply to have the case dropped. Perchelle is not alone, her case highlights an extremely common problem of individuals facing serious personal and financial consequences because they cannot afford bail. The city of New Orleans alone pays $10 million each year to hold pretrial detainees. These individuals take up almost half of the jail beds and place a significant strain on the infrastructure. Between 2010 and 2011, in New Orleans, 95 percent of the people booked into jail were never sent to prison, and 75 percent of felony defendants will be found innocent, given probation, or placed in rehabilitation facilities. New Orleans is certainly not an isolated example as many defendants detained pretrial never serve prison time and are eventually released. The overwhelming majority of the time individuals held on bail can safely be released pending trial, but are often not.

Inequality in bail is not just a problem of those who can afford bail and those who cannot afford to pay bail. Inequality exists among jurisdictions because judges often rely on their gut instinct in determining who and how many defendants to release. While some defendants are able to pay their bail and go free, most cannot. This is because many judges, lacking firm insight into what types of prisoners are too dangerous to release, set high bail amounts knowing the accused can't afford them. Though some of these defendants will eventually be found not guilty and go free, keeping individuals incarcerated before their trial creates a burden on the prison system. There is no national consistency on which defendants are held on bail and which are released. And in many jurisdictions, I discovered in my research that because there is no guidance on release before trial, and no reliance on evidence-based practices, judges detain more than 90 percent of defendants before trial.[41] But in other jurisdictions, there is less concern for public safety and judges release over 95 percent of defendants. There is also no consistency in the types of defendants that are held or released, even though it is clear from the empirical data that is revealed here that judges are primarily focused on preventing violent crime on release. Most judges and even attorneys are not aware of this stark disparity between jurisdictions and lack of consistency in the bail decision.

Another layer of inequity comes with the unfair burden bail creates for minorities. Commentators over the years have acknowledged race discrimination in the bail decision, evidenced by more blacks being detained pretrial compared to whites charged with the same crimes. The bail decision is an obvious source of potential bias as 41.6 percent of black defendants are detained pretrial while only 34.4 percent of white defendants are. Also, black and Hispanic defendants are more than twice as likely to be unable to make bail than white defendants. African-Americans are more likely to pay higher bail amounts when charged with the same crimes as white people. In addition, national criminal justice data from the Department of Justice concluded that African-Americans and Latinos were twice as likely as white defendants to be held in pretrial detention for failure to pay bond amounts.[42] And even when charged for the same crimes, black and Hispanic defendants often pay higher bail amounts than white defendants. Some have blamed the police and judges who make arrest and release decisions based on predictions of whether defendants will commit future crimes. They claim that prediction leads to minorities being treated unfairly. Others complain that racism results from misused discretion. This book explores where racial bias enters the criminal justice system through an empirical analysis that considers the impact of race in the bail decision.

Bail is the hidden key to cutting mass incarceration in America. Individuals have the constitutional right to release but yet are caged like criminals before conviction, leading to mass incarceration in our jails. As Judge Kozinski points out, and we often forget, pretrial detainees "are ordinary people who have been accused of a crime but are presumed innocent."[43] The decision of whether to release a person on bail has immense consequences for an individual as well as for society. This important decision calls for a more empirically rooted decision-making mechanism. And one that takes into account the evidence, costs – and more importantly the constitutional implications – of incarcerating millions of people who have not been convicted. With firm constitutional grounding and consideration of empirical methods, this book traces a path for future bail reform that explains how jurisdictions can take a few simple steps to reduce incarceration pretrial while cutting pretrial crime.

The chapters that follow discuss several important issues surrounding bail. They cover a brief history, explain the bail process and the constitutional rights surrounding bail – including due process, and the Sixth Amendment and Eighth Amendment rights in detail. In addition, this volume lays out empirical evidence about prediction in the pretrial context, racial bias in bail decisions, and the costs of detention to society and a defendant. Other chapters cover an international perspective on bail, consider how pretrial detention is handled for terrorism crimes, and explore the unique challenge of money bail. The final chapter concludes with the important principles for an optimal bail system and describes practical changes that jurisdictions can make to achieve it. A brief description of each of these chapters follows.

CHAPTER 1: HISTORY OF BAIL IN AMERICA

With firm constitutional grounding and consideration of empirical methods, this book traces a path for future bail reform that explains how jurisdictions can take a few small simple steps to reduce incarceration pretrial while cutting pretrial crime. Chapter 1 traces the history of American bail, beginning with its roots in the Magna Carta and continuing through to the British common law and finally US cases and statutes. Bail determinations historically served the purpose of ensuring that the defendant appeared at trial, not preventing additional crimes from being committed, as is the case today. And there were no decisions about guilt *before* trial as guilt was properly determined *during* trial. Under the common law, the entire purpose of bail was to ensure that a criminal defendant would appear for trial. Early US law largely followed English law by requiring bail to be presumed for all but capital defendants, where there was significant proof that the person committed the alleged crime. The guarantee of returning to court did not provide any sort of protection against the defendant committing other crimes, as this was not the focus of bail. The focus of bail changed, starting in the 1940s and particularly in the 1960s–1980s, as the presumption of bail was often not respected and judges were allowed to weigh evidence against defendants in determining whether to release them and consider additional factors in determining whether to release a defendant on bail. This chapter traces these historical changes to highlight the changes that have led us to the current bail model, which aims to prevent danger a defendant may pose to the community.

CHAPTER 2: BAIL AS A CONSTITUTIONAL RIGHT

Chapter 2 lays the theoretical groundwork for the book by tracing the changes in constitutional case law that allowed for major changes in American bail. The theoretical argument underlying this book is that the right to release on bail was historically respected as a constitutional right and it should maintain this status. Due process principles and the presumption of innocence demanded a guarantee of bail for all defendants. One of the most familiar maxims in criminal justice is the presumption of innocence: the principle that a person is innocent until proven guilty by a court of law. This goes hand in hand with the principle of due process that prohibits punishing a person or taking their liberty without proper court processes. Establishing a constitutional and theoretical basis for a defendant's release before trial is important in demonstrating that bail is a right for all defendants.

CHAPTER 3: THE BAIL PROCESS: HOW PRETRIAL RELEASE OPERATES AND THE TYPES OF RELEASE BEFORE TRIAL

After establishing a background of historical and constitutional changes in bail, Chapter 3 traces the typical process of bail in America. In order to understand the current system of bail in America, or even begin discussing reform of the current system, it is important to understand how bail typically operates and the different types of pretrial release that are typically available. This chapter explains the current process and goals of pretrial release, defines bail (or pretrial release), and discusses the types of release that are available in the US criminal justice system. It briefly describes each type of release and discusses the procedures for obtaining release on bail in America. The various types of pretrial release discussed include release on recognizance, supervised release, money bail, property bail, conditional release, surety bail, and deposit bail. It highlights how the different types of release respect a defendant's constitutional right to bail.

CHAPTER 4: BAIL AND PREDICTION OF CRIME

After an understanding of how American bail currently works, Chapter 4 focuses how judges try to use the bail decision to predict which defendants are likely to commit crimes while released. In essence, judges attempt to release individuals who do not pose a threat to public safety and detain individuals who they believe will commit additional crimes. But what do judges look at in deciding which defendants to release on bail? Is it possible for judges to actually know which defendants will commit a crime when released? This chapter focuses on the answers to these questions based on my empirical research and reveals that judges can predict which defendants will commit crimes with some accuracy, and exposes what factors they focus on in deciding who to release. The biggest concern for judges in releasing defendants is whether the defendant is dangerous or will commit a violent crime.

This chapter also examines how judges determine who will commit a violent crime if released and whether they are doing a good job with this decision. It also considers the current release rate of defendants nationally and considers how judges may be able to release more defendants without an increase in violent crime – which is the biggest concern for judges in deciding bail. My empirical research based on the last fifteen years of pretrial detention practices reveals that judges are often releasing and detaining the wrong groups of people. The data suggest that about half of those detained are less likely to commit a violent crime pretrial than many of the people released. If this data were taken into account with my proposed model, judges could make more efficient decisions and increase the number of people released pretrial, without increasing danger to the public.

CHAPTER 5: INDIVIDUAL AND SOCIETAL COSTS
OF PRETRIAL DETENTION

After examining the data on bail and pretrial violent crime, Chapter 5 focuses on the costs of bail and violent crime to society. Over the past few decades, the amount of money expended on the administration of the criminal justice system has skyrocketed. Specifically, the amount spent on pretrial detention calls out for reform. On top of detention costs, there are large costs to victims and society when more crimes are committed while an individual is released. The costs of murder, rape, burglary, robbery, and other violent crimes are tremendous both financially and in other intangible ways. This chapter explores how to make the pretrial release decision with consideration of costs to defendant and the costs to society. Relying on my own research and on data aggregated from prior studies, I quantify the costs and benefits of pretrial detention and compare those to the costs of pretrial release. I ultimately find that in the realm of violent felonies judges maximize economic savings when they detain a relatively low number of defendants – those statistically most likely to pose a danger to society. I demonstrate that only detaining the most dangerous defendants could save US jurisdictions up to $78 billion. At a minimum, considering the costs and benefits of pretrial detention is helpful for policy-makers hoping to increase efficiency in criminal justice and reduce expanding criminal justice budgets.

CHAPTER 6: RACE AND BAIL IN THE CRIMINAL JUSTICE SYSTEM

Chapter 6 provides an in-depth analysis of race and bail. Despite the efforts to create equality in criminal laws, blacks are imprisoned at far higher rates than whites before trial. Indeed, one in every three black males can expect to go to prison during their lifetime compared to one in six Latino males and one in every seventeen white males, with current incarceration trends.[44] This chapter provides an analysis of race and the bail decision and whether racial bias enters the decision to detain minority defendants over white defendants. With a close look at the numbers and consideration of factors ignored by others, my research confirms some conventional wisdom but also makes several surprising findings. This chapter confirms through an empirical analysis of pretrial data of the 75 largest US counties what many commentators have suspected – that police arrest black defendants more often for drug crimes than white defendants. However, judges, who are often blamed for racial bias in the bail decision, actually detain white defendants pretrial *more* than similarly situated black defendants for all types of crimes. However, this chapter also discusses the bias against minority defendants who pay higher bail amounts and receive less favorable release options before trial for similar crimes than white defendants.

CHAPTER 7: BAIL AND THE SIXTH AMENDMENT RIGHTS
TO COUNSEL AND JURY TRIAL

Chapter 7 discusses how release on bail can be restored as a constitutional right
by rejuvenating the Sixth Amendment, which guarantees the right to a jury trial
and access to counsel for a criminal defendant. These two Sixth Amendment
rights are critical to protecting the constitutional right to bail. The first part
of this chapter explains the importance of the right to a jury after trial, and
that facts should not be determined before trial. Currently, judges decide facts
before trial in the bail decision and "weigh evidence" against defendants. In
recent years, the Supreme Court has reinvigorated the importance of the jury
in the sentencing phase, stopping judges from making important factual determinations related to punishment, and instead reserving these decisions for the
jury. This part argues that because the role of judges is limited they should not
be deciding facts about a defendant's guilt before trial, and this should be left
to the jury after trial. This rationale has not been applied to judges deciding
important pretrial facts, like bail, but the same rationale should apply to reju-
venate the Sixth Amendment right pretrial. The second part of this chapter discusses the importance of providing counsel to defendants in their bail hearing,
a right that should also be guaranteed by the Sixth Amendment and is critical
to a defendant's constitutional right to bail. Providing counsel to the accused at
a bail hearing will also increase pretrial release generally, so more individuals
have the opportunity to prepare their case outside of jail. Overall, rejuvenating
the Sixth Amendment will increase rights for defendants before trial and better
respect the constitutional right to bail.

CHAPTER 8: PRETRIAL DETENTION AND TERRORISM
IN POST-9/11 AMERICA

Chapter 8 discusses how in the wake of the September 11 attacks on the World
Trade Center the basic guarantee of American justice, "innocent until proven
guilty," has transformed into "guilty until proven guilty" for suspected terrorists. The world of pretrial detention after 9/11 has changed dramatically. So
much so that it is difficult to discuss modern bail rights without comparing the
various differences in detention for suspected terrorists with average criminal
defendants. National security interests have led to indefinite detention without bail for terror suspects, while some cry foul at the abuse of human rights.
The key question with the increased suspicion of homegrown terror after 9/11
is what are the rights to pretrial release of suspected terrorists? In other words,
should suspected terrorists be granted the right to release before trial or do

they pose a danger too great to be released? This chapter demonstrates that suspected terrorists do not have a constitutional right to pretrial release. Bail laws applicable to other dangerous defendants prohibit suspected terrorists from obtaining pretrial release. But there are a handful of other federal laws (Special Administrative Measures, Patriot Act, etc.) that also provide justification to detain suspected terrorists pretrial and to limit their communication and rights vis-à-vis the outside world. Some terrorism suspects have been detained in military centers, like Guantanamo, and while these detentions have been criticized greatly, detaining these individuals safely on US soil presents substantial budgetary and security challenges. As a whole, however, after detention, terrorism suspects have been tried successfully in federal and military courts, with greatest success in federal courts, given the plethora of federal statutes available to charge defendants.

CHAPTER 9: INTERNATIONAL BAIL

Chapter 9 provides a comparative perspective on how pretrial detention is handled across the globe. Unfortunately, the situation for pretrial detainees outside of the United States is often worse in some ways than conditions in the United States. Internationally, individuals lack access to release before trial, much like in the United States, but often for longer periods. About one-third of inmates internationally are held in pretrial detention and are not convicted criminals. While each country maintains individual pretrial release standards or practices, international law requires that people receive release before trial unless there is a danger the individual might flee or if they will disrupt the opportunity for a fair trial. Individuals must only be detained in the first place if there is a reasonable belief that they committed the alleged crime. Countries that mirror international standards often release individuals in a short amount of time. Those countries that lack adequate standards for judges or processes for pretrial detention allow defendants to suffer from excessive periods of detention. Many countries lack appropriate lack of counsel before trial, allow forced confessions, corrupt practices, and other abuses and poor conditions for inmates. Internationally, there are reports of inmate illness and death, lack of access to healthcare, food, water, and time out of a jail cell, and other inhumane treatment.

CHAPTER 10: MONEY BAIL

Chapter 10 focuses on the uniquely American money bail problem. America is one of only two countries in the world that requires a defendant to pay money to be released before trial. To make matters worse, the commercial money bail system requires a defendant to pay a fee to be released and never refunds the money to defendant. And despite the fact that pretrial release is a time-honored and constitutionally protected right of a defendant, money bail has grown dramatically in the last twenty years such that it is now the most popular pretrial release option. Money bail discriminates against poor people who cannot obtain release simply because they cannot afford to pay even less than $500 bail. It also leads to increased detention for poor people and allows higher-risk wealthy defendants obtain release while lower-risk poor defendants remain in jail. This chapter discusses the history of money bail and how it became commercial. It discusses constitutional challenges to money bail – including recent Eighth and Fourteenth Amendment challenges that have led to abolishing money bail in some cities nationwide. The harms money bail imposes on defendants are significant and states are beginning to take steps to mitigate the harmful effects. Some states and cities have out-right banned money bail and others have introduced legislation favoring other release options, like pretrial release and risk assessments. There is an active struggle between the money bail industry and the criminal justice community as states are constantly proposing pretrial reforms, and the bail industry is constantly fighting to retain its lucrative claim on criminal justice.

CHAPTER 11: OPTIMAL BAIL: USING CONSTITUTIONAL AND EMPIRICAL TOOLS TO REFORM AMERICA'S BAIL SYSTEM

And finally, Chapter 11 focuses on the way forward for American bail reform in an age of mass incarceration. Bail "reform" in America has typically resulted in locking more people up and reducing rights for defendants, but true bail reform is needed to address the bloated and expensive US jail system. The Bail Reform legislation of the 1960s and 1980s resulted in judges obtaining more legitimate reasons to keep someone behind bars pretrial. For this reason, this chapter discusses what "optimal bail," or bail reform in the modern age, should look like. Optimal bail, in contrast to "bail reform," focuses on correct constitutional principles to govern bail as well as a focus on releasing as many defendants safely while cutting incarceration costs. It identifies three principles that federal and state courts and legislatures should apply to ensure that all defendants have this right and that the public remains safe. The first principle of optimal bail is that pretrial restraints of liberty should be limited to only what is necessary and only where there is a proper legal basis. The second principle is that there should be no pretrial determination of guilt without access to counsel and no bail hearing without counsel. And the third principle is that a defendant's pretrial release should not be contingent on wealth or ability to pay a bail. After introducing these three principles, this chapter highlights state efforts – often backed with empirical data – that exemplify optimal bail and serve as a guide for the rest of the country.

This volume serves as an empirical and constitutional guide for improving the US criminal justice system through a hidden key: bail. The changes in bail recommended by this book can lead to dramatic improvements in the rights of defendants, help reduce jail overcrowding, and allow for a more efficient and just criminal justice system.

1

History of Bail in America

But this imprisonment [on bail], as has been said, is only for safe custody, and not for punishment: therefore, in this dubious interval between the commitment and trial, a prisoner ought to be used with the utmost humanity: and neither be loaded with needless fetters, or subjected to other hardships than such as are absolutely requisite for the purpose of confinement only.

—William Blackstone (1765)[1]

Understanding the history of bail in America provides perspective on the challenges of the current system and helps to highlight the need for further reform. From medieval times to the modern day, the concept of bail has been a mainstay of the law. Bail is the means through which accused criminals can procure pretrial release from police or state custody. Traditionally, bail is some form of property (such as money) deposited or pledged to a court to persuade it to release the accused on the understanding that he will return for trial or forfeit the bail. The principle of bail grounds itself in the presumption of innocence and the principles of due process. It is a principle that has a rich history in English and American laws.

This chapter traces a very brief history of American bail, beginning with its roots in the Magna Carta, continuing through to the British common law, and concluding with recent US cases and statutes. While it is in no way comprehensive, it does provide insight into the changes in bail standards that have allowed for the modern-day bail standards. Bail determinations historically served the purpose of ensuring that the defendant appeared at trial and there were no decisions about guilt, as guilt was properly determined at trial. Early US law largely followed this purpose by requiring bail to be presumed for all but capital defendants where there was significant proof that the person committed the alleged crime. The guarantee of returning to court did not provide any sort of protection against the defendant committing other crimes as this was not the focus of bail. However, the focus of bail changed, starting in the 1940s and particularly in the 1960s–80s, as the presumption of release was often not respected and judges were allowed to weigh evidence against defendants in determining whether to release them and consider additional factors in determining whether to release a defendant on bail. The result is a bail system whose central focus is preventing further crime, a far departure from its original purpose.

1.1 EARLY BAIL HISTORY PROTECTS RIGHT
TO RELEASE BEFORE TRIAL

In seventeenth-century England, there was a presumption of release for non-capital cases and a guarantee that guilt would not be determined before a trial. A defendant had the constitutional right to be released before trial after she was arrested and charged. While there was some discretion and bail was not always allowed for every alleged crime, it was generally presumed for all accused of noncapital crimes. Part of this was because an important piece was that English common law clearly respected the right to liberty before trial. English bail law presumed that defendants would be released and discussed the "bail decision" as though it were a decision of *how* to release the defendant, not *if* he would be released. To deny bail to a person who is later determined to be innocent was thought to be far worse than the smaller risk posed to the public by releasing the accused.

In the early nineteenth century, US state and federal courts unanimously agreed that the constitution entitled the accused to pretrial release except in cases where the crime charged was a capital offense. Bail was presumed in most cases. In capital cases, the court reserved discretion to determine whether the accused should receive bail. The rationale was that in capital cases the death penalty may be imposed and a defendant would have a serious incentive to flee before trial. In noncapital cases, bail was generally presumed for the accused.

Bail historically served the sole purpose of returning the defendant to court for trial, not preventing her from committing additional crimes. Indeed, English judges set bail with only one purpose: to ensure the defendant's appearance in court. Early state courts very rarely weighed the evidence against defendant pretrial, mentioned concerns for safety of the community, or considered dangerousness of the defendant – even to dismiss them as improper justifications for denying bail.[2] Under US law, the purpose of bail was to ensure the appearance of a defendant to "submit to a trial, and the judgment of the court" and not to prevent future crimes.

1.1.1 *Early English Bail Protects Presumption of Innocence*

Early English law followed the maxim that it was far worse to deny bail to a person later determined to be innocent than to release someone who was actually guilty of a crime. Some ancient English law went so far as to ban pretrial detention in all criminal cases. Although sheriffs initially had wide discretion to deny bail, English law began to restrict that discretion via the Statute of Westminster the First in 1275, which established lists of bailable and nonbailable crimes. Traditionally, nonbailable offenses included those involving homicide as well as "offenses in the forest and other offenses customarily non-bailable." Several subsequent reforms followed, including the Habeas Corpus Act of 1679, which allowed prisoners to force the Crown to set bail, and the Bill of Rights of 1689, which stated that "excessive bail ought not to be required." Each of these developments and limitations on denying bail led to a historical presumption in favor of granting bail for all noncapital cases and guaranteed that a determination of guilt, or even a determination of the likelihood of guilt, would not occur before trial.[3]

The British American colonies also enacted provisions strengthening the right to bail. The Massachusetts Body of Liberties, passed in 1641, "declared that all crimes were bailable except capital crimes, contempt in open court, and cases in which the legislature expressly denied bail." Similar provisions were passed in the Pennsylvania, New York, and Virginia colonies. In addition, the Northwest Ordinance of 1787, passed prior to the ratification of the constitution, provided that "all persons shall be bailable, unless for capital offences, where the proof shall be evident, or the presumption great." Overall, in early English law, a strong right to bail prevailed.[4]

1.1.2 *Early American Law Presumes Bail*

Early American bail followed the English law and presumed bail for all noncapital offenses. Shortly after the ratification of the constitution, the First United States Congress passed the Judiciary Act of 1789. The act echoed the Massachusetts Body of Liberties, stating that "bail shall be admitted, except where the punishment may be death."[5] Note, though, that a greater number of crimes were punishable by death at this time. In capital cases, judges were to "exercise discretion" and take notice of "the nature and circumstances of the offence, and of the evidence, and the usages of law."[6] Throughout the nineteenth century, American courts operated under the standard for bail set forth by the act. Denying bail in noncapital cases was largely seen as a violation of the presumption of innocence.

In addition to presuming bail, early American law dictated that the purpose of the pretrial period was simply to compel the defendant to appear in court, not to punish the defendant or determine her guilt. In the Supreme Court case of *Ex parte Milburn*, the court recognized that the purpose of bail was to "compel[] the party to submit to the trial and punishment, which the law ordains for his offence."[7] In essence, bail was meant to ensure the return of the defendant to court for trial, not to prevent her from committing additional crimes or as punishment, as is often presumed.[8] In *Hudson v. Parker*, the Supreme Court also made clear that "[t]he statutes of the United States have been framed upon the theory that a person accused of crime shall not, until he has been finally adjudged guilty in the court of last resort, be absolutely compelled to undergo imprisonment or punishment."[9] Courts could consider the nature of the crime, but generally were not allowed to detain defendants based on their guilt or innocence. Guilt was to be determined at trial, not before trial, because of the protections provided by the Due Process Clause of the Constitution and the presumption of innocence. These principles guided American courts throughout the nineteenth and early twentieth centuries, but change was on the horizon.

1.2 BAIL REFORM MAKES IT MORE DIFFICULT TO OBTAIN RELEASE

US bail law historically required release on bail for noncapital crimes due to a defendant's constitutional right to due process. A defendant only had to establish that she would not flee in order to receive release on bail. However, changes to laws in the 1940s altered the bail landscape in America. For the first time in 1944, Federal laws allowed courts to consider other factors – besides flight – in determining whether to release people before trial. In 1944, Federal Rule of Criminal Procedure 46 allowed courts to take into account several factors in setting a bail amount to ensure the defendant's appearance at trial, including "the *weight of the evidence against him*." This went beyond previous laws that allowed judges to consider the weight against an individual only in capital cases, expanding this consideration to all cases. This change opened the way for later, more expansive determinations of defendants' guilt before a jury trial. This contradicted both the presumption that all noncapital defendants deserve release and the requirement that guilt not be determined until trial.

Changes in state and federal laws between the 1960s and 1980s went even further to demonstrate a shift in bail. From the late 1960s on, courts considered various factors, including the weight of the evidence against an individual and how her release would impact the safety of the community. These changes in statutory laws attempting to "reform" bail from the 1960s to the 1980s opened the door to increased detention by allowing judges to make predictions about defendants' guilt and future proclivity to commit crime. Under current US laws upheld by the Supreme Court in *United States* v. *Salerno,* bail is no longer presumed in most cases and judges are given a greater ability to consider additional factors in determining whether to release a person on bail. The pretrial bail decision became *whether* to release a person on bail rather than *how* to release the person on bail. And ironically the two bail "reforms" of the 1960s and 1980s justified more detention pretrial. These changes are not in line with fundamental constitutional standards, as demonstrated by Chapter 3.

1.2.1 *Opening the Way to Restricting Bail Rights*

Several legal changes in the 1940s and 1950s opened the way to restricting access to bail for Americans. With bail, often the federal government passed laws and often states would mirror those laws with state statutes. In 1944, the Supreme Court enacted the Federal Rules of Criminal Procedure. Rule 46 provided that courts could take into account several factors in setting a bail amount to ensure the defendant's appearance at trial. Among these factors were "the nature and circumstances of the offense charged, *the weight of the evidence against him,* the financial ability of the defendant to give bail and *the character of the defendant.*"[10] The consideration of "the weight of the evidence" essentially allowed a judge to make a quick determination of the likelihood of guilt before trial. This consideration, along with that of "the character of the defendant," opened the way for later, more expansive determinations of defendants' guilt before a jury trial. This standard spread in states as well as federal courts.

During this period, immigration officials tasked with fixing bail for aliens facing immigration charges were allowed to consider more factors than judges and were even afforded discretion to deny bail.[11] These officials were allowed to take into account "the probability of the alien being found deportable, the seriousness of the charge against him, if proved, *the danger to the public safety of his presence within the community,* and the alien's availability for subsequent proceedings if enlarged on bail."[12] Nevertheless, courts reassured that "[t]he denial of bail [was] not intended as punishment."[13] However, consideration of public safety and danger of a defendant was still not permitted for garden variety bail cases.

As denial of bail became more common, the Supreme Court was forced to answer the question of whether the Eighth Amendment grants a right to bail in addition to forbidding excessive bail. A pair of companion cases illustrates the difficulties the Court had in making this determination. First, in *Stack* v. *Boyle,* four defendants were charged with violations of an act that set criminal penalties for advocating the overthrow of the US government as a result of alleged Communist activities.[14] Bail was at $50,000 per defendant. The defendants argued that the amount was excessive. The government, without introducing any specific evidence, sought to have the bail amounts upheld on the nature of the offenses charged. The Court rejected the government's contentions, stating that it was arbitrary to set a high bail based on an indictment alone. Accordingly, the court ruled that bail must be based on standards that relate to assuring that the defendant appears for trial. And Justice Jackson, in his concurring opinion, made clear that bail is not a device for keeping persons in jail upon mere accusation, but on the contrary, the spirit of the procedure is to enable them to stay out of jail until (or unless) a trial has found them guilty. *Stack* thus restricted detention before trial to the standards of Rule 46 and based on whether the accused would show up for trial.

The second case, *Carlson v. Landon*,[15] took a markedly different tack. *Carlson* also involved alleged Communists, but the *Carlson* defendants were also resident aliens. The defendants sought relief from their being held without bail pending deportation hearings. The Court rejected their contention that the Eighth Amendment required that they be granted bail. In so doing, the Court noted that there was no right to bail in all cases but simply provided that bail should not be excessive when it is proper. According to the court, if the framers had intended to make all arrests bailable, they could have done so, but they did not. Although *Carlson* dealt with aliens, the Court left open the possibility of denying bail in some cases where the defendants were dangerous to release.

Thus, where *Stack* certainly rejected a focus on the defendant's accused crimes for purposes of bail determinations, the *Carlson* Court appeared, at least implicitly, to condone this consideration. *Carlson* also introduced the idea that denial of bail might be justified if it could be shown to have been done for "non-punitive" purposes. This reasoning expanded in the 1960s–1980s, moving even further away from exclusively considering a defendant's likelihood to return to court in determining bail.

1.2.2 *The First Wave of Bail Reforms and Expansion of Pretrial Detention*

In an effort to expand pretrial release and reduce the use of bail, Congress enacted the Bail Reform Act of 1966.[16] Unfortunately, bail "reform" leads to more denials of bail, not less. Under the Bail Reform Act, persons charged with noncapital crimes were required to be released before trial unless the judge "determine[d], in the exercise of his discretion, that such a release [would] not reasonably assure the appearance of the person as required." In such cases, the act empowered judges to take several steps to restrict a defendant's release, up to and including the complete denial of release. In making decisions as to whether a defendant's appearance could be reasonably assured, judges could consider "the nature of the offense charged, the weight of the evidence against the accused, family ties, employment, financial resources, character and mental condition, the length of [the defendant's] residence in the community, his record of convictions, and his record appearance at court proceedings." Notably, the act explicitly allowed judges to weigh the evidence against defendants, which was typically a function reserved for the jury at trial.

Initially, courts interpreting the 1966 Act recognized its limitations on the power of judges to order detention. The Second Circuit noted that while trial judges have the discretion to revoke bail during trial, that "power *does not extend to revocation of bail before trial.*"[17] Courts also continued to recognize the constitutional limitations placed on a court's authority to refuse bail. For example, in *Gerstein* v. *Pugh*,[18] the US Supreme Court held that any "extended restraint of liberty following arrest" must be accompanied by "a judicial determination of probable cause."[19]

However, changes came in 1979 when the Supreme Court issued a decision that appeared to greatly expand the authority of courts to deny bail. *Bell* v. *Wolfish* involved a challenge to certain restrictive confinement practices in a federally operated jail for pretrial detainees.[20] Justice Rehnquist, writing for the majority, framed the question as one of "whether [the jail's] conditions amount to punishment of the detainee." The court determined that if a condition of pretrial detention is "reasonably related to a legitimate governmental objective" then "punishment" does not exist. Although *Bell* dealt with the conditions of detention and not detention itself, the logic of the case seemed to indicate that such detention was widely available under the constitution, provided that it is necessary to secure the safety of a facility. *Bell* thus echoed the detention justifications presented earlier in the immigration context in *Carlson* and showed that the court wanted to start considering "safety" in determining bail.

In the next major case on bail, *Schall* v. *Martin*,[21] the Supreme Court took this rationale to its next logical step. *Schall* involved a challenge to the constitutionality of New York's juvenile pretrial detention scheme. The Supreme Court upheld the scheme, and Justice Rehnquist, again writing for the majority, noted that "[t]he legitimate and compelling state interest in protecting the community from crime cannot be doubted." Thus, the pretrial detention scheme satisfied the test set out in *Bell*.[22] This purpose, combined with the statute's emphasis on speedy dispositions and the relatively benign conditions of confinement, satisfied the Court in its decision that this detention of juveniles was permissible, rather than punitive. *Schall* thus paved the way for the justification of pretrial detention on a larger scale and for the purposes of protecting community safety.

1.2.3 *The Second Wave of Bail Reform: Bail Reform Act of 1984 and the Current Standard*

Within months of the Court's decision in *Schall*, an emboldened Congress passed the Bail Reform Act of 1984.[23] This act, although only applicable to federal courts, influenced many states who passed copycat laws and matched the federal standard. The act contained much of the language of the 1966 Act, which provided that a defendant should be released if his presence at trial could be reasonably guaranteed. However, the 1984 Act went a step further and provided that judges making bail decisions could, for the first time, take into account "the nature and seriousness of the danger to any person or the community that would be posed by the person's release." Thus, the act explicitly allowed the "dangerousness" inquiry that had before only been implicitly condoned in other contexts since at least *Carlson*.

The 1984 Act also provided certain categories that subject a person to a presumption of detention: those charged with "a crime of violence"; those charged with "an offense for which the maximum sentence is life imprisonment or death"[24]; those charged with drug offenses that carry a maximum sentence of greater than ten years; repeat felony offenders; or defendants who pose a "serious risk" of flight, obstruction of justice, or "threaten, injure, or intimidate" a witness or juror.[25] A judge will hold a hearing to determine whether the defendant fits within these categories. If the judge determines that the defendant fits within these categories – based on a standard of probable cause – then a presumption of dangerousness is created. The judge must then establish by "clear and convincing evidence" that "no condition or combination of conditions [of release] will reasonably assure the safety of any other person 'and the community' or 'the appearance of the [defendant].'"[26] This is accomplished by taking into account the following factors:

(1) the nature and circumstances of the offense charged, including whether the offense is a crime of violence or involves a narcotic drug;
(2) the weight of the evidence against the person;
(3) the history and characteristics of the person, including
   (A) the person's character, physical and mental condition, family ties, employment, financial resources, length of residence in the

community, community ties, past conduct, history relating to drug or alcohol abuse, criminal history, and record concerning appearance at court proceedings; and

(B) whether, at the time of the current offense or arrest, the person was on probation, on parole, or on other release pending trial, sentencing, appeal, or completion of sentence for an offense under federal, state, or local laws; and

(4) the nature and seriousness of the danger to any person or the community that would be posed by the person's release.[27]

The court has the following options at the detention hearing: (1) release the defendant on personal recognizance or execution of an unsecured appearance bond (the defendant agrees to appear at a later date), (2) release the defendant with nonmonetary restrictions, (3) release the defendant based on an unsecured written agreement to forfeit property of a particular value upon failing to appear, (4) release the defendant based on execution of a bail bond with sureties who can pay the bond, or (5) deny bail and detain the defendant.[28] Bail is denied in many federal cases and has increased substantially over the last twenty years. In 1995, only about 40 percent of federal defendants were denied bail, and in 2010 over 80 percent of defendants were denied bail.[29] The causes of this ballooning of federal pretrial detention include increased numbers of drug and weapons defendants (both presumptively dangerous and held without bail) and increases in cases filed and large increases in the immigration docket.

Finally, as part of a detention order denying bail, the magistrate must make a written statement of findings of fact and state the basis for his decision to detain.[30] This written statement is very important, and judges can overturn a bail determination without a statement in support. In *U.S. v. King*, the eleventh Circuit Court of Appeals overturned a district court's decision to deny bail because the judge failed to include "written findings and written reasons supporting [his] decision."[31]

After the Bail Reform Act of 1984 was passed, many courts began to weigh in on how to apply the act. One of the most widely cited cases even today is *U.S. v. Jessup.*[32] The court held that the presumption of detention created under the act (if the defendant is charged with certain crimes) is constitutional, and that once a presumption is created, the burden of production of evidence shifts to the defendant (i.e., the defendant must bring evidence showing that she is not a flight risk or does not pose a danger to the community).[33] Even if the defendant produces evidence and satisfies that burden, however, the judge will still "keep the presumption in mind when making a decision." Thus, it has become very difficult for federal defendants to obtain release when they are charged with a crime that comes with a presumption of detention.

By the 1990s, the recognized purposes of bail had evolved from ensuring the defendant's presence at trial to the more explicit public safety justifications of preventing danger to the community. This justification is made clear by the language of the 1984 Act. Though the 1984 Act also made it clear that release before trial is a constitutional right. And after the 1984 Act, there are a certain category of crimes that, if charged, lead to a presumption of detention for a defendant. However, it is important to note that the presence of other procedural guarantees, such as the requirement of establishing probable cause prior to detention, still limits the scope of federal pretrial detention. Many states did not create presumptive categories for detention but most now allow judges to consider the evidence against defendants and community safety in the detention decision. Other constitutional rights still apply as well in protecting against bail abuses, as discussed in detail in Chapter 2.

1.3 CONCLUSION

With changes in bail standards, although the presumption should still be release of a defendant, judges now try to decide which defendants are guilty or dangerous and detain those defendants before trial. After finding that a defendant poses a danger to an individual or the community, forty-five states and the District of Columbia permit either pretrial detention or release subject to restrictive conditions to prevent potential danger to the community. While most states provide defendants with some procedural safeguards with a hearing before detention, there are no precise legal standards for judges to predict dangerousness and these methods are not carefully scrutinized. From the early English common law until the present, our system of bail has moved from one where release is presumed for most defendants with no flight risk to one where only certain defendants get released if they can demonstrate that they are unlikely to be guilty.

The purpose of bail has evolved from a guarantee of the defendant's presence at trial to a way to predict the criminal defendant's guilt and prevent danger she may pose to the community. The presumption that most defendants should be bailed is weaker now that judges can legally predict dangerousness and weigh the evidence against defendant pretrial. What is more, and what has helped contribute to the demise of the presumption of release, is that bail has become a forgotten constitutional right. The next chapter deals with the changes in constitutional rights surrounding bail.

2

Bail as a Constitutional Right

But in criminal cases it is for the interest of the public as well as the accused that the latter should not be detained in custody prior to his trial . . . Presumptively they are innocent of the crime charged, and entitled to their constitutional privilege of being admitted to bail.

—*United States* v. *Barber* (1891)[1]

Giving the government free rein to grant conditional benefits creates the risk that the government will abuse its power by attaching strings strategically, striking lopsided deals and gradually eroding constitutional protections.

—*United States* v. *Scott*, 450 F.3d 863 (9th Cir. 2005)
Chief Justice Kozinski

This chapter lays the theoretical groundwork for the book and traces the changes in constitutional case law that allowed for major changes in American bail. The theoretical argument underlying this book is that the right to release on bail was historically respected as a constitutional right and should maintain this status. Due process principles and the presumption of innocence demanded a guarantee of bail for all noncapital defendants. One of the most familiar maxims in criminal justice is the presumption of innocence: the principle that a person is innocent until proven guilty by a court of law. This goes hand in hand with the principle of due process that prohibits punishing a person or taking their liberty without proper court processes, including a jury trial. Establishing both a constitutional and a theoretical basis for a defendant's release before trial is important to demonstrating that bail is a right for all defendants.

This chapter traces US cases discussing the Due Process Clause and the presumption of innocence to demonstrate that these constitutional principles guarantee liberty before trial. Historically, release on bail was closely guarded by constitutional principles – not just statutory law as demonstrated by Chapter 1. The presumption of innocence and due process required a legal determination at trial to punish a defendant for a crime. Early US law recognized the importance of bail rights due to the presumption of innocence. Due process demanded that a person maintain liberty and not be imprisoned or punished without appropriate legal action. Also, since the sole purpose of bail was to ensure defendants' presence at trial, due process principles did not allow a judge to detain defendants in noncapital cases because they were likely to commit a crime while released or to weigh the evidence against defendants before trial.

However, as discussed in the last chapter, in the 1960s–1980s, constitutional case law changed in determining that detention before trial was not punishment and did not violate due process. And during the 1980s in *Salerno*, the court confirmed that due process and the presumption of innocence were not violated when courts preventatively detained people to protect the public from danger. The changes in the right to bail have accompanied a weakening of the pretrial constitutional right to the presumption of innocence. Case law upholding the presumption of innocence prevented judges from punishing a defendant or deciding whether a defendant committed a crime before a trial. With changes in state and federal case law, now state and federal judges often deny bail based upon the nature of the crime, the weight of the evidence, past conduct, and dangerousness. Thus, judges are essentially predicting guilt in detaining defendants who they deem to pose a danger in the interest of public safety. They are also determining guilt in weighing the evidence against defendants before trial. As such, bail has lost its status as a constitutional right.

The constitutional right to bail is founded on several principles, including the Fifth and Fourteenth Amendments' guarantee of due process and right to liberty – including the presumption of innocence; the Sixth Amendment's right to a speedy and fair trial and the right to counsel; the Eighth Amendment's protection from excessive bail; and the Thirteenth Amendment's right to be free from involuntary servitude. This chapter will explore all of these constitutional rights, except the Sixth Amendment. The Sixth Amendment right to a speedy and fair trial and right to counsel will be explored in Chapter 7.

While historically it is clear that bail was a constitutional right, today states protect the right to bail constitutionally at varying levels. States can be grouped into one of three categories: states without a constitutional right to bail, states with a broad right to bail, and states with a conditional right to bail.[2] Nine state constitutions fall within the first category, remaining silent on the right to bail.[3] Nineteen state constitutions fall within the second category by enumerating

an explicit and broad right to bail.[4] These constitutions typically mirror the
language found in the Alabama Constitution, which guarantees that "all persons shall, before conviction, be bailable by sufficient sureties, except for capital offenses, when the proof is evident or the presumption great."[5] Finally,
twenty-two state constitutions are in the third category.[6] These constitutions
are similar to the second category, in that they guarantee the right to bail;
however, they include a range of offenses under which a judge can refuse bail.
For example, the California constitution guarantees the right to bail except
in capital cases, violent or sexual felonies, and felonies where the defendant
poses a likely threat to another individual.[7]

Some state statutes, however, weaken constitutional rights to bail in other
ways. For example, at first glance, Utah's constitution seems to protect the
right to bail in a majority of circumstances: "All prisoners shall be bailable by
sufficient sureties, except for capital offenses when the proof is evident or the
presumption strong."[8] However, it severely weakens the right by creating an
exception for "persons charged with any other crime, designated by statute as
one for which bail may be denied."[9] The extent of this exception is obvious
when looking at Utah's bail statute, which allows a judge to deny bail to a
defendant charged with any felony if it is determined that the defendant is
a danger to the community or is likely to flee.[10]

Before moving to the substance of constitutional rights in this chapter, it
is important to consider the consequences of being denied the constitutional
right to bail. Is it a constitutional violation to be put in jail before trial? In
many cases, a detention feels like a punishment. Consider the case of Kalief
Browder, an African-American boy who was arrested at the age of sixteen
while walking home in the Bronx.[11] He was accused of stealing a backpack
and charged with robbery. His mother was unable to pay his bail, which was
set at $3,500.[12] As a result, Browder remained incarcerated while he awaited
his trial. Sixteen-year-old Browder was incarcerated at Rikers Island Prison in
New York. Rikers Island, designated one of the ten worst prisons in the United
States, is notorious for abuse and neglect of prisoners.[13] In Browder's case, this
description proved to be accurate. Browder was badly beaten by numerous
inmates (captured on camera), stomped on, and hit with weapons by correction officers.[14] Browder described his experience at Rikers as "hell on Earth."[15]
Three years passed while Browder awaited his trial. He spent two of these
years in solitary confinement. Browder never saw his day in court because
the charges against Browder were dropped. So, Browder, charged for a minor
robbery, awaited trial for three years in horrendous conditions but was never
found guilty of any crime and, according to constitutional principles, should
not have faced any punishment.

2.1 DUE PROCESS, LIBERTY, AND THE PRESUMPTION OF INNOCENCE

The Fifth and Fourteenth Amendments to the US Constitution guarantee that "[n]o person shall . . . be deprived of life, liberty, or property, without due process of law."[16] Relying on the Fifth and Fourteenth Amendments, pretrial detention deprives a person of their liberty and, without sufficient basis, is a constitutional violation.[17] At the cornerstone of our nation's criminal justice system lays the principle that you are presumed innocent until proven guilty.[18] This presumption of innocence reflects a fundamental principle in our society that it is far worse to convict an innocent man than to let a guilty man go free.[19] Contrary to a presumption of innocence, denial of bail and liberty results in unconstitutional punishment.

The United States Supreme Court requires that a right that is fundamental to due process must be "deeply rooted in this Nation's history and tradition" and "fundamental to *our* scheme of ordered liberty."[20] The right to bail is both fundamental to liberty and deeply rooted in this nation's history and tradition, satisfying both standards. The right to bail has been formally acknowledged and utilized in our judicial system for over 200 years since Congress ensured the right to bail in the US territories with the Northwest Ordinance of 1787.[21] From the passage of the Judiciary Act of 1789 to the present Federal Rules of Criminal Procedure,[22] federal law has provided that a person arrested for a noncapital offense should be admitted to bail. This traditional right to freedom before conviction allows for the unhampered preparation of a defense and serves to prevent punishment before a conviction.[23] Unless this right to bail before trial is preserved, the presumption of innocence would mean nothing.[24] Also, the right to bail is deeply rooted in this nation's history and tradition because the concept of bail can be traced back to English tradition, from the time of the Magna Carta,[25] because the English form of bail was adopted by the settlers in America and because, as declared by the court itself in 1971, "[b]ail, of course, is basic to our system of law."[26] Thus, a guarantee to bail is fundamental to the right of due process.

The Fourteenth Amendment also guarantees the right to liberty. Prolonged or unnecessary pretrial detention is an explicit infringement on an individual's right to liberty. And without a conviction, this infringement is unconstitutional. While the government can detain defendants before trial, pretrial detention must not constitute punishment because punishment can only occur after conviction. Following the Court's holding in *United States v. Salerno*,[27] there is an argument that pretrial detention *regulates* instead of *punishes*, and therefore does not impede an accused's due process right.[28] Following this logic, there is a compelling government interest in preventing crime that is more important than an individual's due process interest. But when an individual can be released safely with some supervision or restrictions, then incarceration is just serving as punishment and should not be required. And when there is excessive delay between arrest and trial, and thus a long period of detention, the distinction between pretrial detention and punishment is merely a facade. There are several examples of defendants waiting substantially long periods of time – including many years in detention – without seeing their day in court. For instance, former police officer Adam Torres, who had no criminal record, was incarcerated almost three years after being denied bail while he was awaiting trial for shooting a man who allegedly was in his home threatening him with a gun.[29] Another such example is Warren McClinton, charged with sexual assault, who waited in jail for three years for a trial, then three more years before a conviction.[30] Certainly there is a constitutional violation of due process when individuals are deprived of liberty for long periods of time without a trial or conviction. There is also arguably a due process violation when individuals are deprived of liberty for even short periods of time, where there is no legal justification. The appropriate justifications for denying release to a defendant are discussed in Chapter 11.

2.2 THE EIGHTH AMENDMENT "EXCESSIVE BAIL" PROTECTIONS

The Eighth Amendment states that "[e]xcessive bail shall not be required" and is the only mention of bail in the constitution.[31] "Excessive bail" under the Eighth Amendment is not merely bail that is beyond one's means, rather, it is bail greater than necessary to achieve purposes for which bail is imposed.[32] The purpose for which bail is imposed is to ensure that the accused will appear in court for trial. Therefore, bail amount should reflect an amount that will ensure that a defendant will appear for trial and should not reflect a punishment to the defendant. Bail amounts that are set higher than what would ensure that a defendant appear for their trial may be considered excessive. Usually, to constitute excessive bail in violation of the Eighth Amendment, the excess must be greater than a trivial amount.[33]

Excessive bail can be reflected in monetary terms or in other limitations on the defendant's freedom such as curfews, house arrests, limits on employment, or electronic monitoring.[34] Bail amount is decided by the court, and the excessive bail clause requires reasonableness in fixing the amount. If the accused is able to pay the bail amount to the court, then she will be released until trial. However, if the accused is unable to furnish the bail amount, she will remain detained until trial.[35]

The Supreme Court has struck down excessive monetary bail under the Eighth Amendment. In *Stack* v. *Boyle*, four defendants were charged with violations of an act that set criminal penalties for advocating the overthrow of the US government as a result of alleged Communist activities in the 1950s.[36] Bail was at $50,000 per defendant. The defendants argued that the amount was excessive and violated the Eighth Amendment and even "submitted statements as to their financial resources, family relationships, health, prior criminal record, and other information" as proof of excessiveness. The government, without introducing any specific evidence, sought to have the bail amounts upheld on the nature of the offenses charged. The Court rejected the government's contentions that the fact of indictment alone does not dictate an unusually high bail amount. The Supreme Court rejected an excessive bail amount set for the purpose of preventing defendants from receiving bail.

While the Supreme Court defended the historic meaning of bail in *Stack*, it adopted a looser interpretation of the Eighth Amendment in the 1980s. Under this new definition, bail was not ensured as long as detention was not excessive. The court explained in *United States* v. *Salerno* that the function of bail is limited neither to preventing flight of the defendant prior to trial nor to safeguarding a court's role in adjudicating guilt or innocence.[37] "[W]e reject the proposition that the Eighth Amendment categorically prohibits the government from pursuing other admittedly compelling interests through regulation of pretrial release." Instead, "the only arguable substantive limitation of the Bail Clause is that the government's proposed conditions of release or detention not be 'excessive' in light of the perceived evil." Thus, the court found that arresting individuals charged with serious felonies who after a hearing are found to "pose a threat to the safety of individuals or to the community which no condition of release can dispel" satisfies this requirement.[38] In other words, the court held that the Excessive Bail Clause did not ensure a right to bail in all cases, upholding the constitutionality of pretrial detention so long as the detention was not "excessive" given the crime charged and the threat posed by the individual.

Excessive bail can have as significant an effect on defendants as a denial of bail. Some courts have held that the setting of an excessive bail is the functional equivalent of setting no bail at all.[39] But since *Salerno*, the Eighth Amendment has not been a fruitful constitutional provision with which to challenge bail.[40] The Court has failed to define "excessiveness."[41] This creates an undefined area within which attorneys are left to navigate for lower bail for their clients. But this has left the Excessiveness Clause as a narrow and nearly abandoned source of constitutional rights.[42]

Despite the vague "excessiveness" clause standard, one Michigan court struck down bail as excessive under the Eighth Amendment. In 2008, the Michigan Supreme Court publically censured a judge for setting "grossly excessive" bail in multiple cases.[43] The first allegation against Judge Norene Redmond involved a case where a woman was arrested for misdemeanor domestic violence, resisting arrest, and obstruction of justice.[44] Judge Redmond initially set her bail at $5,000.[45] After the bail hearing, the accused's son called Judge Redmond an asshole outside of the courtroom.[46] When Judge Redmond heard about the comment, she went back on record and raised the mother's bond to $25,000 cash.[47] Even after the son apologized in open court, the judge refused to change the bond.[48]

The second allegation against Judge Redmond involved two defendants accused of overbilling an elderly woman for a paint job. The two defendants had taken $800 in cash from the lady and gave her an inflated estimate for painting her house.[49] They were charged with the felonies of embezzlement from a vulnerable adult and larceny in a building.[50] Judge Redmond set the bail for one defendant who had no criminal record at $750,000, and the other defendant who had a minimal criminal record at $1,000,000.[51] In a rare case, the Michigan Supreme Court censured Judge Redmond for violating the Eighth Amendment with excessive bail.

A problem many criminal defendants face is that they cannot afford to post bail when it is excessive. For these individuals, their options are to either plead guilty or wait in jail until their trial. Both options present defendants with hardships. If a defendant pleads guilty, they will have a criminal record and will be responsible for payment of any fines or other punishments they are sentenced to. If a defendant waits in jail until their trial, they are left to the mercy of the judicial system. That defendant may suffer as a result of missing work, missing payments, or missing time at home for as long as it takes the judicial system to hear their case. This begs the question as to why defendants even have to pay at all to obtain what was formerly a free constitutional right. More on this discussion appears in Chapter 10. It is a given though that when judges set excessive bail even more defendants find themselves unable to afford their freedom.

2.3 THE THIRTEENTH AMENDMENT AND THE RIGHT TO BAIL

The Thirteenth Amendment's connection to the right to bail is not readily apparent, but at least one court has recently determined that detention before trial violates the Thirteenth Amendment. The Thirteenth Amendments guarantees that "neither slavery nor involuntary servitude, except as a punishment for crime whereof the party shall have been duly convicted, shall exist within the United States, or any place subject to their jurisdiction."[52] In 2008, Finbar McGarry was arrested by Vermont police on charges stemming from a domestic dispute. He was denied bail and sent to the Chittenden Regional Correctional Facility (CRCF) until June 2009 when all charges against him were dropped.[53] While detained at the CRCF, McGarry was required to work in the prison laundry over his repeated objections. McGarry was told that his refusal to work would result in his being placed in either administrative segregation or "in the hole," which involves isolation for 23 hours a day and the use of shackles. McGarry was also informed that if he refused to work he would receive an Inmate Disciplinary Report (DR) and that even minor DRs affect when sentenced inmates are eligible for release. McGarry was forced to work long hours, sometimes 14-hour shifts, in the prison laundry in hot, unsanitary conditions. Even though McGarry was required to handle other inmates' soiled clothing, he was not provided with gloves or access to hand-cleaning products. In *McGarry* v. *Pallito*, the appellate court found that since McGarry was threatened by physical and legal coercion to work as a pretrial detainee his Thirteenth Amendment right to be free from involuntary servitude was violated.[54] This recent opinion could have implications for other pretrial detainees who are forced to work in a jail environment. Before conviction, a defendant is entitled to the presumption of innocence and protected from involuntary servitude under the Thirteenth Amendment.

2.4 CONCLUSION

In addition to inflicting severe individual hardship, pretrial detention denies millions of people vital constitutional rights. Due process is violated when a defendant is denied his right to liberty before trial, violating the Fifth and Fourteenth Amendments. This denial of liberty has serious consequences for a defendant who is hampered in his ability to prepare a legal defense. The Thirteenth Amendment is sometimes violated when an innocent individual is placed behind bars and forced to work. Bail is often set at excessive amounts, violating the Eighth Amendment. As the individuals highlighted in this chapter have demonstrated, defendants often cannot afford to pay bail. Kalief Browder could not even afford his relatively small bail of $3,500 after being accused of stealing a backpack.[55] As a result, he suffered in Rikers prison for three years.[56] Like Kalief, other poor defendants are unable to pay bail for minor offenses and thus bail can be excessive to them even at a few hundred dollars.

Excessive bail and the denial of bail have serious implications because if a defendant cannot pay bail their options are to plead guilty or wait in jail until their trial. Both options present defendants with significant hardships. If a defendant pleads guilty, they will have a criminal record and will be responsible for payment of any fines or jail time. If a defendant waits in jail until their trial, they are at the mercy of the judicial system. That defendant will suffer economic, physical, and mental harms as a result of being incarcerated, missing work, missing payments, or missing time at home. That defendant will suffer these harms for as long as it takes the judicial system to hear their case. As the story of Kalief Browder demonstrates, some defendants, even minors, can sit in dangerous jails for years on end and be denied liberty before they are even found guilty. From the day Kalief Browder was arrested, he never received a presumption of innocence, but rather prolonged and punitive punishment. Ultimately, this detention inflicts physical, emotional, and economic hardships that are discussed more fully in Chapter 5.

Pretrial detention without legal justification violates constitutional rights and challenges the principle that an accused is presumed to be innocent until proven guilty. Today defendants are routinely denied the presumption of innocence and instead suffer a presumption of punishment. As we are starting to see with the few individuals highlighted in this chapter, incarceration results in economic, physical, and emotional hardships. On top of these hardships – and the most offensive to due process and the presumption of innocence – is the pressure to plead guilty when a defendant is innocent to avoid the threat of pretrial detention for an unknown duration. Such hardships are devastating for the life of an individual – not to mention devastating to a constitutional judicial system – and should not be taken lightly. Indeed, constitutionally, our system is still founded on the maxim that it is far worse to convict an innocent man than to let a guilty man go free. And quoting Chief Justice Frederick Moore Vinson: "Unless the right to bail is preserved, the presumption of innocence, secured only after centuries of struggle, would lose its meaning."[57] It is vital to our constitutional criminal justice system that the right to bail be reinvigorated. Chapter 11 provides some suggestions to effectuate these constitutional rights in today's system of bail.

3

The Bail Process: How Pretrial Release Operates and the Types of Release Before Trial

The object of bail is to secure the appearance of the one arrested when his personal presence is needed; and, consistently with this, to allow to the accused proper freedom and opportunity to prepare his defense. The punishment should be after the sentence.

—*Hampton v. State* (1884)[1]

The federal courts have traditionally held . . . [that] the only relevant factor [with the bail decision] is the likelihood that the defendant will appear for trial.

—*Hunt v. Roth* (1981)[2]

In order to understand the current system of bail in America, or even begin discussing reforming it, it is important to understand how bail operates and the different types of pretrial release that are typically available. Bail is typically defined as the process a court takes to determine if a person charged with a crime should be released before trial or should be detained in jail pending trial. It also determines what conditions may be required in order to obtain release from jail. If a defendant is released – with or without conditions – this is referred to as "pretrial release." If a defendant is detained before trial, this is called "pretrial detention."

The bail process is the procedure that governs the front end of criminal justice – what happens after a person is arrested but before they receive a trial. Although historically the presumption was release before trial for all but capital defendants unless the individual posed a flight risk, this has changed substantially. According to the Bureau of Justice, the number of people held before trial has increased from around 275,000 in 1995 to nearly 500,000 in 2008 and has hovered only slightly below that number since 2008.[3] There are almost twice as many unconvicted inmates in our jails than convicts.[4] Between 2008 and 2010, only 36 percent of federal defendants were released before trial.[5] And in the state system between 1990 and 2004, 62 percent of felony defendants in state courts in the seventy-five largest counties were released before trial.[6] And there is a strong relationship between pretrial detention and the likelihood of conviction. Pretrial release can discriminate against defendants without the means to secure bail.

Several different types of pretrial release are available. The one with the least conditions is "release on recognizance." This is where the defendant is released with no conditions and told to return for their court date. Alternatively, a defendant is released on "supervised release" usually with a pretrial services agency – typically a government-funded agency or nonprofit that supervises the defendant on release and ensures that they appear for their court date. The other most common type of release is surety bail – where a person or company assures the court that the defendant will return to court. They will put property or money down with the court to guarantee the individual's return for their court date. The most common type of surety bail is commercial money or cash bail. This is where a defendant pays a sum of money to a commercial bail agent (usually 10 percent of the amount of bail set by a judge) and the bail agent promises to ensure that the defendant will return for her court date. If the defendant does not return, then the bail agent should pay the full bail amount to the court. Money bail is controversial and will be discussed at length in Chapter 10. The other types of surety release discussed include property bail and deposit bail. Conditional release, which is very popular, allows a defendant to obtain release after agreeing to various conditions related to their alleged crime. For instance, a defendant would agree not to leave the state and abstain from alcohol or drugs in order to obtain release before trial.

Between 1990 and 2004, just over half of state court defendants were released on nonfinancial conditions, including recognizance (agreeing to voluntarily return to court), conditioned release, and unsecured bond.[7] Just under half of the defendants were released with financial conditions, including surety bonds, deposit bonds, full cash bonds, and property bonds.[8] In the federal system, the two most common forms of pretrial release in the federal system were unsecured bond and release on personal recognizance, which together accounted for 71 percent of defendants released pretrial in the federal courts.[9] Defendants requiring a financial bond accounted for 27 percent of all federal pretrial releases, with 12 percent posting a deposit bond, 8 percent using a surety bond (i.e., bail bondsman), and 7 percent using a collateral bond. The state system relies on financial release options much more than the federal system, but they also release more defendants before trial.

This chapter explains the current goals of pretrial release and discusses various types of release that are available in the US criminal justice system. It will briefly describe each type of release and the procedures for obtaining release on bail in America. The various types of pretrial release discussed include release on recognizance (ROR), supervised release, surety bail (including money/cash bail, unsecured bond, property bail, deposit bail), and conditional release. This chapter highlights how the different types of release respect a defendant's constitutional right to bail and briefly discusses their effect on detainees. Chapter 5 more specifically lays out the challenges for defendants of not being able to afford bail or obtain release as well as the costs to society of releasing individuals on bail.

3.1 TYPES OF PRETRIAL RELEASE

To understand and compare the various types of pretrial release, it is important to understand the bail process or the steps by which courts determine whether to detain suspects or release them. Once arrested, suspects are taken to jail. Once suspects are in jail, the question becomes whether or not courts should hold alleged criminals in jail until they are charged with a crime or found innocent and accordingly released.[10] Usually a defendant is brought to court in 24, 48, or 72 hours (if arrested on a weekend). Courts typically choose between two options. First, the court may decide that the suspect should not have the option of leaving jail before trial based on how likely the prisoner is to flee and not show up for trial, or how likely that prisoner is to commit a crime if released.[11] Second, a court could determine that the suspect can leave jail and then return on their court date, but only if the suspect can meet certain conditions. This is an important decision for the defendant because remaining in jail will often involve a detention period of a few weeks or more, where the defendant would most likely lose their job. Remaining in jail also makes it more difficult for the defendant to meet with counsel or prepare a defense.

To make matters worse, this important bail decision is often made in less than 5 minutes.[12] In some jurisdictions, including in Philadelphia and Texas, this important decision happens in 1–2 minutes, and often without defense counsel – or even a prosecutor present.[13] Because of the sheer number of arrests in America, courts are overcrowded. In 2012 alone, the US criminal system processed 12 million people.[14] This volume of arrests encourages judges to rush pretrial decisions. Ralph Barry's experience shows how a quick pretrial decision can ruin the life of an individual. Barry, a black man from the Bronx, was arrested in 2010 and sent to Rikers Island jail, one of the worst prisons in the United States,[15] for a murder he didn't commit.[16] Because Barry couldn't afford bail and refused a plea deal, he was forced to wait for his trial in jail.[17] A few days after Barry was sent to prison, police officers discovered DNA evidence that proved Barry could not have committed the murder.[18]

However, because of the vast number of people in courts in the Bronx, known locally as the "traffic jam," Barry spent three years in jail waiting for his trial.[19] Barry's experience is unfortunately not uncommon – prisoners in the Bronx sometimes wait up to five years to go to trial.[20]

In most US jurisdictions, the court determines whether a defendant should be released based on money bail. As demonstrated later, bail is one of the tools courts use to ensure that suspected criminals stay within their jurisdiction and show up to their court hearings.[21] This is how it works. The court sets a "bail" amount that defendants can pay in order to be released from jail until trial. If the defendant pays a percentage of that bail amount (usually 10 percent) to a commercial bail bondsman (which is the most common approach in most US jurisdictions), the defendant does not obtain her bail money back, even if she appears for her court date. If the defendant does not appear for his trial, the court could request the full bail amount from the bail company. In some jurisdictions, a suspect is permitted to pay a percentage of the bail to the court and will typically get the bail payment back if they appear for trial – whether she is found guilty or innocent. This is called deposit or percentage bail because the bail money just serves as a deposit when paid to the court. However, typically, with commercial (or surety) bail, the money is paid to a bail bondsman and is never returned to the defendant, regardless of whether they appear for court. However, those who can't afford to pay bail and prisoners who aren't given the option to pay bail must wait for their court date in their jail cells irrespective of how serious their crime was, how innocent they are presumed to be, and how likely they are to flee. In fact, up to 60 percent of all jail inmates in the United States are simply waiting for their court date and haven't been charged with a crime.[22]

To determine whether to set bail or to deny release altogether, a judge will consider whether a defendant is likely to commit a crime while released or whether they are likely to flee the jurisdiction before their trial. To determine this, they look at various factors that differ somewhat between US jurisdictions.[23] Generally, however, judges consider how severe the crime is; the weight of the government's case against the defendant; the defendant's criminal history (particularly interested in convictions for violent crime); whether the defendant has missed court hearings in the past; the defendant's ties with the jurisdiction; whether the prisoner is employed and is in a good financial situation; and health-related information, like how healthy the defendant is, how mentally stable the defendant is, and whether the suspect is using illegal drugs.[24]

In many states, the bail decision is not even made by a judge. Some jurisdictions delegate pretrial decisions to nonjudges and nonlawyers.[25] In Maine, for example, bail determinations are made by a bail commissioner appointed by the chief judge of the state district court. These bail commissioners are required to complete an "eight hour training course within a year of appointment (though they can begin making bail determinations before they complete the training course)."[26] Some jurisdictions deem making pretrial decisions as "minor administrative proceeding task[s]."[27] The unfortunate lack of attention that some jurisdictions pay to pretrial detention and bail seems inconsistent with what the Supreme Court of the United States has called "perhaps the most critical period of [criminal] proceedings[.]"[28]

How courts gather a suspect's background information and then predict the likelihood of a defendant fleeing or committing another crime while waiting for their trial also varies depending on the jurisdiction. Some jurisdictions, like the District of Columbia, prepare a pretrial report for each defendant.[29] A pretrial report provides the judge with specific information about the prisoner's criminal background, economic status, community ties, health, and where the prisoner is living.[30] Pretrial reports are extremely helpful to provide an independent assessment to evaluate how likely a prisoner is to flee or commit a crime if released. In the District of Columbia, these reports have been considered quite successful at predicting the risk of releasing any given defendant. In fact, in 2011, 88 percent of those released pretrial were not arrested again, and 88 percent of those released showed up to their court hearings.[31] Federal pretrial release also has similarly high rates of success in returning defendants to court.

Many other jurisdictions, however, simply allow judges to use a list of factors to predict each defendant's risk and determine whether they are eligible for pretrial release. Often judges are not provided additional information so they rely on the defendant to answer questions, without any independent verification of information. Judges then rely on their own sense of whether a defendant is being honest, which is often wrong. Scholars argue that without adequate information about defendants judges make arbitrary or racially biased decisions that are often left unquestioned because judges wield total discretionary power in bail determinations.[32] In such jurisdictions, judges "are forced to make 'quick and dirty' decisions, relying solely on their 'gut instincts.'"[33] Indeed, a Connecticut judge admitted that "[u]ntil challenged, a judge could justify almost any bond . . . certain judges will assess certain cases differently. You can assemble a room full of judges and the range of bail for the same crime can vary from $5,000 to $250,000."[34] And indeed, there is such disparity on bail amounts set for similar crimes within jurisdictions and throughout the country.

Another issue in the bail process is the length of time a defendant remains in pretrial detention before a trial. When enacting the Federal Bail Reform

Act, Congress chose not to limit the length of time a defendant could spend in pretrial detention. Instead, it relied on the Speedy Trial Act to restrict the period of confinement for a pretrial detainee to ninety days. However, the Speedy Trial Act contains eighteen exclusions from its time limits and thus has not effectively restricted the period of pretrial detention.[35] Because of this, defendants facing federal criminal charges have been incarcerated without bail for as long as thirty-two months awaiting trial.[36] The courts have further promulgated this issue by upholding the constitutionality of the act. Despite the clear concerns regarding the length of pretrial detention, the Third Circuit ruled that, in relying on the Speedy Trial Act, Congress had a "rational scheme for limiting the duration of federal pretrial detention."[37]

However, a number of circuits have developed a test to determine whether or not a detainee's pretrial detention has been too long, and in some cases have determined that due process was violated. One such Second Circuit case, *United States* v. *Ojeda Rios*,[38] describes a test that determines if the defendant has been unnecessarily detained and her due process rights violated required considering "(1) the length of detention that has occurred and the non-speculative nature of future detention; (2) the extent to which the prosecution bears responsibility for the delay in starting trial; and (3) the facts concerning the risk of flight."[39] At this point the defendant in *Ojeda Rios* had been held for over two years pending trial and was likely to be detained for nearly another year before the trial would be complete. In this case, the court held that many of the delays were caused by the defense, but found that the government's unwillingness to sever the case also contributed to the excessive period of detention. Because of this finding, the defendant's right to due process was, in fact, violated. However, the court did hold that this was a close call because of the above balance. The consideration of "the extent to which the prosecution bears responsibility for the delay in starting trial" however seems unfair. A defendant should not be detained for wanting to present the best case possible. Indeed, a defendant should not have to choose between constitutional rights – a speedy or fair trial. A defendant should maintain the right to prepare an appropriate defense, without having to be detained for a long period of time, if at all possible.

Overall, the bail process is a quick one. A judge (or other appointed person) often decides in a couple of minutes whether and how to release a defendant, but the defendant may remain in detention for a long time. In most jurisdictions, the judge has no information on the suspect and determines whether the defendant is safe to release and will return based on her own common sense. In the majority of cases, the judge will set money bail based on the crime charged (though the amounts set will vary tremendously by judge or jurisdiction, unless the jurisdiction has set a uniform bail schedule by crime). In a minority of cases, a judge will choose one of the other release options. As discussed in detail in Chapter 10, commercial money bail is the worst option for a defendant because the defendant loses the bail money no matter what. A consideration of the various pretrial release options follows.

3.2 RELEASE ON RECOGNIZANCE

Release on recognizance remains one of the most common types of pretrial release. Release on recognizance is the process by which a defendant appears before a judge after arrest and the judge determines that the defendant should be released without any payment or other conditions if he promises to return to court for his court date. The defendant is simply released to return to his home and job with the promise that he will return to court.

Release on recognizance is often referred to as unsecured bail because it does not create any financial or other conditions for a defendant's release. Release on recognizance provides an assurance to judges that certain defendants will not be held in pretrial detention. This assurance cannot be guaranteed with any other form of release because of the economic standing of many defendants. Even a financial bail as small as $200 has proven too difficult for certain defendants to pay. Some states have enacted a presumption in favor of ROR, while other states have attempted to limit its application. Utah law, for instance, allows a judge discretion by law to ROR in any case where bail could be assigned to the defendant.

Another type of unsecured bail is an unsecured bond. An unsecured bond is where a defendant is released after he contracts to appear before the court on a specified date and promises to pay a set bail amount later if he fails to appear. The defendant pays nothing and puts no deposit or property down in order to obtain release, and only pays the bond if he does not appear in court. Unsecured bail, like secured bail, requires a defendant to contractually agree to appear for trial. While ROR requires no contract or security before releasing a defendant, an unsecured bond requires a contractual agreement and deposit. Federally, ROR and unsecured bonds are the two most popular release options.

3.2.1 *Benefits of ROR*

Release on recognizance can be an effective tool in decreasing incarceration rates. Since the 1980s, federal prisons have grown by nearly 800 percent.[40] Approximately 450,000 people in the United States are held awaiting trial on any given day.[41] As a result, overcrowding and human rights are now a concern in some holding centers. Some jurisdictions have shifted to increase ROR to alleviate a growing prison population. One example is Texas. Between 1980 and 2005, the Texas prison population grew by 308 percent, with a significant number of the prisoners who qualified for ROR – or release before trial without any conditions or money. Texas courts reviewed their bail policies, and in response to the inmate crisis, chose to favor ROR. Kentucky has also seen success by implementing similar changes. The state altered criminal laws and penal codes to require "low risk" defendants to be released on recognizance or an unsecured bond.[42] Since 2011, the state has seen a 10 percent decrease in defendants arrested and a 5 percent increase in the overall release rate, with nonfinancial releases increasing from 50 percent to 66 percent.[43] Texas and Kentucky are good examples of the ability to reduce jail numbers through ROR.

Release on recognizance is as effective as paid forms of release and the best type of release to avoid discrimination against poor or minority defendants. Nondiscriminatory and presumptive pretrial release is rooted in both national and state-level legislation. The Bail Reform Act of 1984,[44] echoing the Bail Reform Act of 1966, retains a presumption for ROR and a directive to release defendants on the least restrictive conditions possible. Sixteen states have sustained this directive by adding their own legislation requiring judges to impose the "least restrictive requirements" on defendants in bail sentencing.[45] The actions taken through the Bail Reform Act, as well as state legislatures, encourage judges to permit ROR when possible. Because of this legal precedent, the American Bar Association's policies specifically recommend that ROR should be the default type of pretrial release in federal and state courts. A study by the Pretrial Justice Institute found that ROR is as effective as secured bonds at protecting public safety and ensuring court appearance by the defendant.[46] ROR also avoids the economic and racial disparities that are inherent in secured bonds. And many believe that an increase in the use of ROR would alleviate the current inequalities in the American bail system. Furthermore, as courts rely more frequently on unsecured bail, the high costs associated with pretrial detention, such as overcrowding and sanitation issues in jails, will likely decline. Release on recognizance is the legally preferred method of release pretrial and leads to less discrimination but some challenges are inherent in deciding who to release before trial.

3.2.2 *Challenges in Administration of ROR: Risk Assessments*

Even with the presumption of ROR, states want a uniform way to determine who to release before trial. For this purpose, states increasingly rely on risk assessment tools. Fifteen states currently require risk assessment results prior to determining bail conditions.[47] New Jersey, in an effort to reduce its incarceration rate, recently enacted both legislative and constitutional changes to its state bail system.[48] A key component of the reform was a legislative bill that shifted New Jersey's bail system from a money-based system to a risk-based system, ensuring that every arrestee will be evaluated to determine if there is any risk that the defendant might flee, intimidate witnesses, or commit future crimes with trial pending.[49] Under the new system, defendants deemed to be low-risk offenders are released on their own recognizance, while those who pose moderate risks are released, but will be subject to curfews, travel restrictions, or electronic monitoring.[50] Only the highest risk defendants may have the option of bail denied to them entirely.[51]

Risk assessment tools help jurisdictions avoid unnecessary detention and pretrial misconduct (that defendant will be arrested or fail to appear in court). This prevents jurisdictions from operating on release dichotomies based on charge rather than on the spectrum of risk involved with each defendant. States that determine the risk of pretrial misconduct based on subjective factors are, according to a study, more than twice as likely (56 percent compared to 27 percent) to have an excessive jail population than programs that assess risk exclusively through an objective risk assessment instrument.[52] In addition to New Jersey, many states have successfully implemented risk assessment tools. The first comprehensive statewide risk assessment tool was formulated by Marie VanNostrand in Virginia in 2003.[53] Virginia Pretrial Risk Assessment (VPRAI) relies on pending charges, employment status, drug use, criminal history, and other objective factors to help judicial officers determine bail. Perhaps the best-known evidence-based risk assessment tool can be found in the District of Columbia. Under the DC system, defendants are classified as high, medium, or low risk according to points on a thirty-eight-factor instrument. Since 1969, this system has lowered dependence on secured bail by 69 percent while still ensuring an 88 percent court appearance rate. In Kentucky, mandate requires pretrial officers to conduct an interview and investigation of all persons arrested on bailable offenses within 24 hours of arrest. In addition, many states are attempting, or already have, standardized screening tools and other bail-oriented legislation at the state level.[54]

Unfortunately, even with risk assessment technology, pretrial detention rates in some states continue to rise. In Delaware, courts are mandated to use an objective risk assessment tool when making pretrial release determinations of defendants.[55] Despite the reform and a declining violent crime rate, however, the pretrial detention of Delaware rose by 20 percent from 2012 to 2014.[56] This phenomenon demonstrates that although important, risk assessment tools are not always enough to reduce pretrial detention. Risk assessments still allow for the possibility that a defendant may be required to pay a secured bond (or cash bail) that they cannot afford instead of ROR. The next section explores the challenge of cash bail.

3.3 CASH (OR MONEY) BAIL

Cash bail is currently the most common pretrial release method.[57] Cash bail is a type of secured bond, a form of bail that, unlike ROR, requires defendants to meet a financial obligation before they can be released. At a defendant's arraignment hearing, if the defendant is eligible for release, a judge can choose to set an amount of money the defendant must pay before she can be released. If defendant is able to pay the full amount of bail, the court returns that amount to her when she returns for her court date. However, if a defendant cannot pay the full bail amount, either the court allows her to pay 10 percent of this amount to the court (which is called percentage bail), or more commonly, she pays a fee to a commercial bail agent (or bail bondsman) or bail bonds company (usually 10 percent of the bail) to act as her surety with a promise that she will return for her court date. If the bail bondsman does not return the defendant to court, the bondsman is then responsible for the full bail amount to the court. When a defendant hires a bail agent, the defendant does not have any money returned to them and they lose the fee. Often, as discussed in further detail in Chapter 10, because of lobbying by the bail industry, the bail bondsman does not even have to pay the full amount of bail to the court if the defendant fails to appear to court.

The use of cash bail has increased in the United States. About half of the defendants were released on cash bail in 1990, and this number jumped to two-thirds in 2004.[58] The increase in cash bail is concerning as economic and racial disparities are inherent in the application of cash bail, and indigent defendants are prejudiced by cash bail in the criminal justice system. Defendants who are not able to raise their bail amount are detained pretrial. In New York City, a recent study over a one-year period identified over 11,000 defendants charged with misdemeanor offenses who were detained because they could not raise bail amounts as small as $100.[59]

3.3.1 *Determining Cash Bail*

States have taken a variety of approaches to determine cash bail in court. Some jurisdictions have established a general rubric to assist judges in determining how much money bail to set for a particular defendant. Judges are not deprived of the authority to deviate from the rubric or guidelines. These guidelines typically include factors such as a defendant's criminal history and the criminal classification of the charged offense. In some counties (including in California, Utah, and Wisconsin), the information is placed into a sentencing matrix that will establish the exact amount of money bail a judge should assign to a defendant. In what is called a "uniform bail schedule," this matrix assists judges in setting comparable bail amounts for similarly situated defendants. This is heavily criticized because when there is a set dollar amount of bail assigned to a certain crime money bail arguably becomes the default method (and easiest method) of pretrial release, even though it is not favored under federal or state law.

Some states have implemented legislation to ensure that money bail is not ordered if ROR can occur safely. For example, based on a recent change in law in Kentucky, a judge is required to consider five factors prior to issuing a money bail condition: (1) the nature of the offense charged, (2) the amount necessary to ensure compliance with conditions of release, (3) whether the conditions are oppressive, (4) past criminal acts and reasonably anticipated future acts, and (5) a defendant's ability to pay.[60] Additionally, all defendants charged with a crime that carries a presumptive probation are automatically released on their own personal recognizance.[61] The results of Kentucky's law have included an 8 percent increase in the number of low-risk defendants released on recognizance and a 7 percent increase for moderate-risk defendants.[62] And as far as timing of release, defendants who are released on money bail are not necessarily released more quickly than those released on recognizance as the time from their arrest to release for money bail ranges from a mean of eight to twenty-two days or more.[63]

3.3.2 *Challenges of Cash Bail*

By and large, the studies comparing cash bail to other release options seem to indicate that it does not reduce rearrest rates or failure to appear, may exacerbate recidivism, and increases financial burdens on indigenous defendants. Some data demonstrate that defendants released on cash bail have the same failure to appear rates and engage in similar amounts of new criminal activity as defendants released on their own recognizance. Alternative data show, however, that defendants on financial release are more likely to attend all scheduled court dates.[64] One study by Arpit Gupta et al. in Philadelphia and Pittsburgh found that assigning money bail increases the likelihood of conviction by 12 percent and increases recidivism by 4 percent.[65] Another study by Megan

Stevenson, also focused on Philadelphia, reported that defendants detained due to their inability to pay money bail face up to a 30 percent increase in convictions, primarily driven by an increase in guilty pleas. Indigent defendants who cannot afford money bail may also face an additional eighteen months of incarceration compared to those who are able to afford it, at a taxpayer cost of about $14,000 per person.[66] Finally, the Prison Policy Initiative recently found that most individuals who are unable to meet bail fall into the poorest third of society, with the median bail bond amount in the United States representing eight months of income for the typical detained defendant.[67] These studies and others like them suggest that cash bail may not allow access to pretrial release for many Americans and places high burdens – with negative impacts – on poor defendants. Chapter 10 on money bail discusses the challenges of cash bail in more detail.

3.3.3 *Surety Bonds and Commercial Bail Bonds*

A popular type of cash bail is called a surety bond or commercial bail. A surety bond refers to the assumption of responsibility by a third party for a defendant's bail. This can be with cash or property. Commercial bail – using a bail bondsman – is the most popular vehicle of the surety bond, but it is not the only form it takes. A defendant can also have a surety who is not a bail bondsman. In some cases, a defendant's family member or friend can act as a surety and pay a percentage of the bail fee to the court and be responsible for the full amount (like a bail bondsman) if the defendant does not appear. Historically, the third party was often a friend or family member of the defendant. This allows defendants to be released into the custody of a third party, who would assume liability for the bail amount if the defendant violated the terms of their release or failed to appear in court. While this option is available in some jurisdictions, it constitutes a very small percentage of people who receive a surety bond. Over time bail bondsmen have replaced other third-party sureties, and bail bondsmen are the dominant form of surety bonds. This shift in custom led many jurisdictions to preclude the possibility of third-party sureties. As a result, many low-income defendants, who are unable to raise the fees for a bondsman, are unable to obtain their constitutional right to release.

The shift from third party to commercial bondsman has taken power out of the hands of defendants and their families, and given private businessmen the power to choose their clients and prices. This shift – that has continued to take place even in the last twenty years – is constitutionally troubling but also has practical implications on the American criminal justice system.

3.3.3.1 Role of Bail Bondsmen

The primary mechanism of a surety bond currently is a bail bondsman. Bondsmen set a nonrefundable fee that defendants must pay to use the services. When a defendant has paid the necessary fees, a bondsman will post bail to the court and the defendant will be released. If states do not establish a statutory maximum as to the fees a bail bondsman can charge a defendant, bail bondsmen enjoy a significant amount of latitude. Occasionally, however, a state defines a limit to the percentage a bondsman can charge, and four states – Oregon, Wisconsin, Illinois, and Kentucky – have abolished commercial bail bonding for profit outright.[68] In Kentucky, commercial bail bonding has been outlawed for forty years. Likewise, Wisconsin recently rejected a bill attempting to reinstate the commercial bail bond industry, and a Wisconsin Court of Appeals ruling cautioned "that a mandatory condition or release based solely on the nature of a charged crime without considering a defendant's individual circumstances constitutes an erroneous exercise of discretion in setting bail conditions."[69] However, the vast majority of states not only allow bail bondmen to act as sureties for defendants, but rely on commercial sureties as their primary method of pretrial release.

If a defendant fails to appear in court, the bondsman becomes liable for the full value of the defendant's bail. In order to secure a return of that money, a bondsman is given broad power to find and capture the defendant and return him to the state's custody. This authority is controversial, and there have been reported abuses of this "bounty hunter" authority.[70] This authority was affirmed by the Supreme Court when it held that bondsmen hold wide discretion in their power to return a defendant to the jurisdiction in which they stand accused. Many scholars have called for limitations on the power given to private commercial bondsmen, who in many ways now have more power than state actors to arrest and detain defendants. Some legislatures have addressed these criticisms by restricting the fees bondsmen can charge and by limiting the actions a bondsmen can use to pursue a defendant.

3.3.3.2 Benefits and Challenges of Commercial Bail

While Chapter 10 deals more specifically with the benefits and challenges of money bail – and focuses largely on commercial bail – it makes sense to mention the major issues here. Commercial bonds come with a significant benefit for some defendants. Defendants who would not be able to raise the full value of their bail can be released through the help of commercial bail. Courts and legislatures have noted this important role that bondsmen play in our current system. Significantly, the service of bondsman is at no cost to the state since it's a commercial enterprise so it decreases the burden on taxpayers if it reduces the rate at which defendants fail to appear in court or decreases rearrest rates. At least one study shows that defendants released via a commercial bond are significantly more likely to make appearances in court compared to attorney bonds, cash bonds, and pretrial services bonds.[71]

Obviously the benefits of surety bonds must be carefully weighed against harms to both courts and defendants. The nonrefundable upfront fees a defendant must pay a bond company severely limit the class of people who are able to use a bondsman's services. To pay bond fees, many low-income defendants must sacrifice what little financial resources they have, inhibiting those funds from contributing to needed living expenses. Often these sacrifices place an extraordinary strain on the defendant and their family. In addition, when commercial bail is the primary release method, many low-risk poor defendants do not obtain release, leading to substantial costs to the taxpayer of housing these individuals who can't afford bail in jail. This is not even considering the constitutional harms suffered in a system that relies primarily on money bail and does not guarantee release to defendants as historically required. All of these harms are discussed in greater detail in Chapter 10.

3.3.4 *Percentage Bail*

Percentage bail is a financial (secured bond) option that offers an affordable alternative to surety bonds from a commercial bondsman. Percentage bail requires a defendant to pay a portion of the total bail in order to be released. The defendant also contractually agrees to pay the entire bail if he violates the conditions of his release or fails to appear in court. Defendants who do not violate any conditions of their release and appear in court will be refunded the percentage they deposited with the court. Judges often have wide discretion for the percentage of the total bail required; however, jurisdictions vary on the degree to which they rely on percentage bail. This alternative does not eliminate all of the disparities inherent in secured bonds. However, it does provide an alternative for those defendants who can raise the funds necessary for a deposit, but do not want to lose a nonrefundable fee paid to a bondsman.

3.3.4.1 Ten Percent Bail

State legislatures will occasionally establish a percentage rubric for a judge to rely on, but many jurisdictions have adopted a 10 percent bail. Under bail reform legislation passed in 2007, Kansas courts received the discretion to grant both personal recognizance bonds and 10 percent bonds.[72] However, the conditions permitting a defendant to pay only 10 percent bail are limited to lower-level offenses and only if the defendant meets several conditions, including having a low criminal history score, residency in Kansas, and no history of failing to make court appearances.[73]

In an analysis of appearance rates, defendants who were given a 10 percent bail were at least as likely to make their appearance as defendants who received a surety bond. This study indicates that percent bails can achieve the same desired outcome as surety bonds without the involvement of commercial bondsmen. In comparison to surety bonds, percentage bonds result in a positive economic advantage for low-income defendants. Despite the relative benefits of percentage bails, many policymakers maintain that all forms of secured bond are less effective and fair than unsecured bail.

3.4 PROPERTY BAIL

Property bail is a secured bond as well as a type of surety bond. Rather than requiring a defendant to meet a monetary obligation, courts allow a property surety to put property down as collateral to meet a defendant's financial obligation. If a judge allows a property bail, a defendant may apply the value of their property to satisfy the bail amount. Often a court will hold the deed or title to a defendant's property until the defendant appears for their trial, but alternatively, the court may also choose to place a lien on the property until the defendant appears for their trial. Some courts allow property bail for personal property. To accurately ascertain the value of the property a defendant wishes to use as surety, a defendant must "justify by affidavit" the value of the property. A magistrate will then evaluate the affidavit and make the final valuation for the property.

3.4.1 *Challenges of Property Bail*

Many advocates of property bail have argued that it is beneficial because it provides an alternative means for defendants to ensure their release. However, some courts have attempted to fully or partially eliminate property bails.[74] Courts trying to eliminate the practice of property sureties have issued cash-only bails. The Ohio Supreme Court, for example, has held that cash-only bail is constitutional.[75] Defendants have argued that a court's denial of property bail violates their rights under the US Constitution. Defendants who would otherwise be unable to raise the necessary sums of cash or who would have to rely on high fees from bondsman can use their property (or a surety's property) to meet the financial conditions imposed by bail. Property bail is not usually done with the use of a commercial surety, but a private one. When determining the effectiveness of property bail, the likelihood a defendant who lacks the funds to post bail will also lack sufficient property to meet their bail is a consideration. And the most disadvantaged defendants often do not have property resources that would allow them to take advantage of property bail. For this reason, many of the same problems that plague cash bail and percentage bail result from property bail as well.

3.5 CONDITIONAL RELEASE

Conditional release is often a combination of the forms of release listed earlier. It may include a secured bond with financial conditions, but most often it includes certain nonfinancial requirements. The magistrate judge often sets conditions for release based on the needs of a defendant, the severity of the charges against them, and the laws of the jurisdiction within which they are sentenced. Sometimes with conditional release judges may choose to apply nonfinancial conditions such as mandatory drug testing or substance abuse programs, counseling, or admittance to a rehabilitation facility. A court must ensure the conditions of a defendant's release are sufficient to guarantee their appearance in court, prevent direct contact with victims or witnesses, and ensure the safety of the public. For instance, for a drunk driving offense, the defendant may obtain conditional release upon the condition that she not be permitted to drive, except to and from work, until her court date. Beyond these considerations, broad discretion is left to the court for the number and the nature of any conditions. A defendant may be required to continue or initiate employment or education by court-established conditions. Other precautions that may be considered with conditional release include electronic monitoring, where a defendant's travel is monitored to ensure that either he does not leave the jurisdiction or avoids certain prohibited locations. Risk assessment programs, mentioned previously in this chapter, can assist in creating meaningful and appropriate conditions of release that do not overcondition low-risk offenders or undercondition high-risk offenders. Overall, conditional release is considered a low-cost option for releasing individuals pretrial, with tailored precautions to ensure the safety of the public.

3.6 ELECTRONIC MONITORING

Electronic monitoring may be an extremely effective low-cost pretrial alternative as it allows officials to closely monitor defendants while allowing them freedom to work, meet with attorneys, and remain with family. There have not been studies to demonstrate its effectiveness, but it arguably fits the demand of many jurisdictions that the means of detention pretrial not be any "broader than necessary to achieve [the government's] interest."[76] Many states have been experimenting with lower-cost pretrial alternatives, including electronic monitoring, and the federal government has been using electronic monitoring since 1991.[77] There are several types of electronic monitoring programs. One type requires home monitoring where the defendant is assigned to remain at home during certain hours and the government can track whether the individual has complied with this requirement and whether the equipment has been tampered with. Since 1989, Cook County, Illinois, has used electronic monitoring – with a radio signal and home monitoring for 250,000 defendants, some released pretrial.[78] Another type of electronic monitoring requires periodic check-in through voice verification or another means of proving location. Finally, more recently, counties use Global Positioning System (GPS) tracking devices to track a defendant's movements so they are not bound to the home for any certain period of time. Federal Pretrial Services uses radio and GPS tracking devices that send a signal to a receiver attached to the defendant's phone. Several jurisdictions use GPS tracking technology including Mesa Arizona, and Strafford County, New Hampshire and New Jersey, after new legislative changes in 2014.[79]

Electronic monitoring can be an important pretrial tool, often used with other methods to reduce pretrial costs and recidivism. Vermont undertook an initiative involving electronic monitoring in a package with other important pretrial services. In 2007, Vermont launched its Justice Reinvestment initiative, hoping to reduce its high and unsustainable rate of prison population growth. The state reduced probation terms, established community treatment services, and used electronic monitoring for pretrial release and ultimately closed one prison facility and converted another into a therapeutic work camp. As of January 2013, Vermont's prison population, which was expected to rise by more than 20 percent, dropped by nearly 5 percent. Indeed, combined with supervision and other programs, electronic monitoring can be a very important and cost-effective tool to allow defendants to remain employed and at home while being monitored to ensure the safety of witnesses and others in a case.

In the federal context, electronic monitoring has proven highly effective, particularly when combined with supervision.[80] Unfortunately, there is little research in the state pretrial context to demonstrate the effectiveness of electronic monitoring, so it has not been validated there. And while concerns remain that defendants can circumvent technologies and block tracking, for the most part, the average criminal defendant who cannot afford bail is often not in a position to employ technologies toward this effort. It also seems to better fit the constitutional goal of allowing a defendant to maintain the presumption of innocence through the least restrictive means available, while also keeping criminal justice costs in check.

3.7 PRETRIAL SUPERVISION

Pretrial services are entities created to supervise the release of a defendant prior to trial and help judges determine how to safely release an individual. A pretrial services program is usually funded by the state or federal government to help defendants avoid pretrial detention by working to manage the risk that some defendants will fail to appear for scheduled court events. While the federal government has established pretrial services in all judicial districts, at the state level, pretrial services programs are not available in most jurisdictions.[81] There are approximately 10 percent of jurisdictions (or states) that have pretrial release programs.[82]

Pretrial services obtains information and recommends release or detention, and release conditions to a judge. The first step is that pretrial services interviews defendants and conducts an investigation for risk factors.[83] Research has shown that there are specific objective elements of a defendant's past and current behavior that are valid predictors of a defendant's danger to the community.[84] While it is inevitable that some defendants who are released pretrial will jeopardize the safety of the community, risk assessment before release substantially lowers that risk. This investigation determines whether pretrial services will recommend release and sometimes other requirements like periodic supervision, daily reporting, or other methods to ensure their appearance at trial. For instance, in Kentucky, pretrial services (under a program called Monitored Conditional Release) creates a risk reduction plan and supervision strategy using a matrix to match supervision level with level of risk and defendant needs.[85] The standard by which the government imposes pretrial release conditions is the least restrictive measure required to ensure safety of the community and respect for the rights of the defendant.[86] Indeed, research has found that supervision that is not calibrated to a defendant's level of risk can result in an increase in failure to appear and recidivism rates. In other words, oversupervising a low-risk defendant can actually lead to increased failure to appear and pretrial crime rates.[87]

Sometimes, pretrial services imposes conditions with the broader goal of avoiding criminal conviction by making positive changes in a defendant's life and preventing any future criminal behavior. Their primary focus is to make sure the defendant appears for her court date. Likely, the method with the lowest cost, in reference to effectiveness of ensuring a defendant returns to court, is to simply remind them of their court date. This type of reminder can be done through a manual or automated telephone call or through the mail. This simple reminder substantially reduces failure to appear rates, which in turn helps the defendant to avoid a warrant, rearrest, and additional court appearances. In studies involving Nebraska, Oregon, Arizona, Colorado, Washington, and New York, it was found that actually speaking with the defendant on the phone, as little as one time, decreased failure to appear rates to as low as 5.9 percent.[88] Some pretrial services programs aim to reduce criminal behavior by the defendant. Pretrial services sometimes makes diversion programs available to defendants (particularly someone without a criminal record), allowing a defendant to avoid jail time in exchange for completing education, community service, restitution, or treatment programs.[89] According to a study from the Pretrial Justice Institute, electronic monitoring and substance abuse programs are generally more effective for defendants to avoid criminal activity than limitations on driving or reminder calls.[90]

3.7.1 *Benefits of Pretrial Supervision*

The primary benefit of pretrial services is providing monitoring of a defendant to comply with release conditions and assistance in locating and returning defendants who fail to appear in court.[91] Overall, failure to appear and rearrest rates for defendants released to a pretrial release program and those released through a money bailbond are comparable. However, defendants released on their own recognizance have a higher rate of failure to appear in court than those on pretrial supervision. One study in Baltimore, Maryland, found that among supervised defendants 96 percent were not arrested on new charges and 94 percent made all court appearances. New York City spends $2.50 per day per person monitoring released supervisees versus $100 per day per person to have individuals incarcerated while awaiting trial. Thus, in Queens County, the New York City Criminal Justice Agency introduced an experimental supervised pretrial release program that released specific types of nonviolent felony defendants to community supervision, rather than monetary bail. 87.4 percent of participants were successful, and, when convicted, only 10.2 percent of successful participants were sentenced to imprisonment.[92] In other jurisdictions, where pretrial supervision used a risk matrix that calculated the risk of each defendant and made decisions based on this, they reduced detention rates.[93] For instance, Santa Cruz County, California, developed a supervision program and reporting rules for those released pretrial. They found that 92 percent did not reoffend, and 89 percent made all court appearances. This saved ninety jail beds per day or a 25 percent reduction in daily population, leading to a pretrial detention rate of 56 percent.[94] Most of the costs attached to pretrial services are minimal and far less expensive than fees for money bail. In addition, pretrial services can reduce the monetary burden on a jurisdiction by reducing high pretrial detention rates. These findings suggest that by implementing a pretrial supervision program more defendants can be released, with even less convictions, at lower costs to the public.[95]

Pretrial release programs typically include the costs of supervision, alternative residential arrangements or treatment programs, and the cost of recovering defendants who have fled the jurisdiction. Pretrial release programs vary dramatically in cost, usually due to variations in demographic and jurisdiction size.[96] In 2009, about 26 percent of pretrial programs in the United States reported an operating budget of less than $200,000 annually. On the other hand, in that same year, about 25 percent of the jurisdictions reported costs of at least $1.5 million for criminal justice administration.[97] Thus, in comparison, the costs for pretrial programs are minimal compared to the costs of criminal justice in general.

3.8 DIVERSION PROGRAMS

An alternative for certain defendants on pretrial release is a diversion program. Often, with pretrial diversion, a defendant who is arrested is not charged with a crime and instead is supervised with various services depending on their particular alleged crime. In the investigation that occurs pretrial (usually by pretrial services), screening should occur for special needs, such as drug or alcohol abuse, mental illness, or disabilities. Diversion aids in providing low-risk supervision and simple follow up (for instance, for misdemeanor defendants), streamlining treatment and testing for drug abuse, immediate placement in in-house treatment programs, placement in half-way houses for the homeless or for those with no community ties, job placement, mental health treatment, behavior modification, and outpatient therapy.[98] There are a few main types of diversion programs – misdemeanor diversion, judicial diversion – including drug diversion, all discussed later.

3.8.1 *Misdemeanor Diversion*

Misdemeanor diversion programs are typically reserved for first-time misdemeanor defendants. With these programs, rather than receiving charges, a misdemeanor defendant can choose to go through education or provide community service in exchange for having any potential charges dropped. These individuals will not be incarcerated either. One common example is a driving misdemeanor defendant can choose to attend drivers' education courses rather than receive a driving-related misdemeanor on their record. Diversion programs assist in reducing overall costs by minimizing trial docket caseloads. Though more costly in their utilization of community resources than other pretrial supervision programs that may only require simple supervision, misdemeanor diversion programs allow resources to be allocated to more serious cases. Additionally, these programs decrease recidivism rates among the successful graduates of the program and increase volunteer hours contributed by diversion clients at nonprofit, charitable, and public agencies.[99]

3.8.2 *Judicial Diversion: Drug Court and Mental Health Court*

Another type of diversion is judicial diversion – with the most common types being drug court or mental health court. Drug diversion is discussed in more detail in the next section. Judicial diversion programs aim to funnel participants into treatment, and are typically reserved for higher-risk defendants or defendants charged with a felony. For this reason, they are one of the most expensive supervision programs.[100] The majority of the expenses, approximately 77 percent, comes in the form of treatment services, such as residential detoxification, outpatient detoxification, short-term rehabilitation, long-term inpatient, day treatment, methadone, and intensive outpatient treatment.[101] While these diversion programs are expensive, they may result in a net benefit to taxpayers. Defendants in judicial diversion programs use fewer criminal justice system resources – that would be involved with prosecution – and spend fewer days on probation, in jail, and in prison. In a 2013 New York study comparing costs associated with defendants in a judicial diversion program to defendants who were not admitted to a judicial diversion program, New York realized a net benefit of over $18 million per year.[102] The savings include net investment costs, recidivism costs, and victimization costs. The overall cost savings, however, were reduced in future years, but five years after the implementation of the study, the accumulated financial benefit resulted was nearly $77 million. Although treatment costs are high and there is a high treatment investment per participant, there is an overall net benefit for judicial diversion participants. However, for many US jurisdictions, funding has not been available for pretrial services or diversion programs, and ROR remains the only alternative to detention.[103]

3.8.3 Drug Treatment Diversion

A type of judicial diversion is drug treatment for defendants battling drug addiction. Research shows that treatment is much less expensive than incarceration for substance-abusing offenders. According to a U.S. Department of Health and Human Services report, treatment costs range from $1,800 per client to approximately $6,800 per client.[104] Brooklyn, New York, has implemented a Drug Treatment Alternative to Prison program, which enables alcohol- or drug-addicted defendants to plead guilty to an offense and then live in a treatment community system for a term of up to two years as an alternative to a prison sentence. The program was found to be highly successful in reducing recidivism and drug use, increasing the defendant's likelihood of finding employment and saving money from avoiding incarceration.[105]

Maryland has also saved a substantial amount of money using treatment as an alternative to incarceration. Maryland's programs focus on assigning treatment after some prison time has been served, or similar to New York, offering treatment as an alternative to incarceration altogether. The program includes treatment centers, day reporting, intensive supervision, home detention, and harsher punishment for program failures. Assessing the programs together, Maryland's Sentencing Commission concluded that the state had reduced the annual cost of housing an offender from $20,000 down to $4,000.[106]

Drug treatment (rather than incarceration) for suspects pretrial becomes a more viable option as society's attitudes toward drug offenders has shifted. In 2013, the Pew Research Center poll reported that two-thirds of Americans want to see drug offenders enter programs that focus on rehabilitation rather than incarceration. The poll consisted of telephone interviews with 1,821 adults, and from this survey, only 26 percent of the interviewees believe jail time is the best solution.[107] Drug treatment is an alternative that not only benefits a defendant, but also decreases the overall costs to society.

3.9 CONCLUSION

This chapter discussed the different types of pretrial release – including money bail, pretrial supervision, electronic monitoring and diversion, property bail, percentage bail, and ROR. It has also briefly highlighted some of the benefits and challenges of each type of release. Release on recognizance provides assurance to a judge that a defendant will not be held in pretrial detention, and it is does not discriminate against indigent defendants. Money bail is the most common type of bail in the United States, but there are deep-rooted economic and racial disparities in cash bail practices, not to mention constitutional flaws in its denial of release to large swaths of eligible individuals. Surety bonds offer important benefits to defendants who cannot raise the full value of their bail; however, these bonds discriminate against individuals who do not have large bank accounts or contacts with people with large financial means. Percentage bail is an affordable alternative to surety bonds and typically offers courts a lot of discretion, but is not commonly used. Property bail has many of the same problems as cash bail, if a defendant cannot post bail, the defendant will likely lack sufficient property to satisfy bail. And pretrial release and diversion – while superior in every measure as it reduces pretrial crime and costs – is only used in 10 percent of American counties. Electronic monitoring is used in conjunction with supervision in the federal context and is growing in states as GPS monitoring becomes cheaper and more accessible. It is important to study the effectiveness of the types of pretrial release used in this country in considering how to reform the current system. It is important to remember that the traditional right to freedom before trial allows the unhampered preparation of a defense and serves to prevent the infliction of punishment prior to conviction.[108] And realizing the stakes for defendants and the implications of denying a defendant release, and aiming to provide the least restrictive alternative is vital to pretrial reform.

4

Bail and Prediction of Crime

All guarantees of liberty entail risks, and under our Constitution those guarantees may not be abolished whenever government prefers that a risk not be taken.
— *United States v. Melendez-Carrion* (1986)[1]

Given the historical and constitutional changes in bail discussed previously, the pretrial release decision is now one that determines which defendants pose a danger to the public. While constitutionally suspect (as discussed in Chapter 2), predictions of whether defendants will commit a crime on release are foremost in pretrial release. In essence, judges attempt to release individuals who do not pose a threat to public safety and detain individuals who they believe will commit additional crimes – not just individuals they believe may be a flight risk. Recognizing the reality in which current bail decisions are made, this chapter attempts to at least educate pretrial decision makers to make better predictions on which defendants will be dangerous on release, while appreciating that all defendants should have the right to release with the most limited restrictions. As far as prediction, this chapter considers what factors should be considered in deciding which defendants to release on bail.

Every day, both federal and state judges decide whether to release defendants based on whether they are dangerous or safe, relying on various factors. The decision to release a defendant on bail is one that weighs heavily on a judge's mind. Judges are nervous to release an individual who will commit a crime and hope to avoid that by making the right decision for release. The implications of releasing an individual charged with a crime are critical to public safety, and thus guidance on this decision is extremely helpful. For instance, in September 2016, Officer Betty Jo Shelby fatally shot Terrence Crutcher as Crutcher walked away from his vehicle with his hands raised.[2] This is but one of many high-profile shootings of black citizens by police officers in recent years.[3] Oklahoma prosecutors charged Shelby with first-degree manslaughter, stating that Shelby shot Crutcher in the heat of passion due to fear.[4] Twenty minutes after booking into the Tulsa County Jail, Shelby was released on $50,000 bail.[5] While Shelby was released after being charged with murder, other defendants are often not released when charged with manslaughter or there is great public outrage when they are released.[6] But the larger question is, who is safe to release pretrial and who should be detained? Is it possible for judges to determine that? Are judges more concerned with flight risk or dangerousness of defendants? These questions are all answered in this chapter.

The biggest concern for judges in releasing defendants is whether the defendant is dangerous or will commit a violent crime. This chapter examines how judges determine who will commit a violent crime if released and whether they are making good decisions in this area. It also considers the current release rate of defendants nationally and considers how judges may be able to release more defendants while not increasing crime rates. This research also finds that based upon current pretrial detention practices judges are often releasing and detaining the wrong groups of people. The data suggest that about half of those detained are less likely to commit a violent crime pretrial than many of the people released. Relying on this data, this chapter proposes guidance for judges to make more efficient decisions and increase the number of people released pretrial, without increasing danger to the public.

To begin, I briefly review general statistics about pretrial release and rearrest rates to provide context on increases in detention rates over the years and an explanation of the types of defendants released and detained. Next, I will explore past and current practices of pretrial prediction, including the statistical methods used in crime prediction research to demonstrate that early on there were many doubts about the effectiveness of pretrial prediction and the growth now of empirical methods to predict crime. The next section discusses in detail some key factors in pretrial crime prediction and the importance of risk instruments in this process. Finally, this section concludes with some suggestions for best practices in pretrial prediction, which include a largely objective assessment that retains judicial discretion for a limited subjective analysis.

4.1 PRETRIAL RELEASE AND REARREST STATISTICS

Basic to the understanding of pretrial crime prediction are statistics concerning release and rearrest rates. This section will examine those figures while making note of relevant outliers and trends. Unfortunately, data concerning misdemeanant defendants is largely unavailable. Most information presented here relates to felony defendants.

4.1.1 *How Many Are Released Pretrial?*

Before bail reform, there were some state jurisdictions that released less than 30 percent of defendants.[7] After the Bail Reform Act of 1966, which aimed to increase pretrial release, state pretrial release rates significantly increased through the end of the 1970s.[8] By 1980, release rates were close to 62 percent in some state courts.[9] These release numbers have remained consistent in states as between 1990 and 2004, 62 percent of felony defendants in state courts were released before trial. However, there is a lot of variability in release of state defendants nationwide. Some counties report as low as a 30 percent release rate, and others release up to 90 percent of those arrested.[10]

Until recently, federal detention rates were not well recorded, but a 1982 study of ten federal districts found release rates of close to 90 percent between 1978 and 1980.[11] The Bail Reform Act of 1984 began a shift toward higher detention rates.[12] Between 1980 and 2004, the federal release rate dropped to 40 percent.[13] Thus, federal release rates are extremely low, and since the 1980s, overall, the release rate in many state jurisdictions also remains low.

4.1.2 *Who Is Rearrested Pretrial?*

Overall, a small percentage of people released before trial are rearrested. In the largest study looking at rearrest rates of pretrial defendants over a fifteen-year period, the data Frank McIntyre and I considered shows relatively low rearrest rates overall.[14] In this study, of all defendants released, only 16 percent are rearrested for any reason, 11 percent are rearrested for a felony, and only 1.9 percent are rearrested for a violent felony. In other words, 80 percent of defendants released have less than a 3 percent chance of being rearrested for a violent crime. And for almost all crimes, the average rearrest rates are only about 1–2 percent for a pretrial violent crime.[15] Indeed, the rearrest rate for murder defendants is almost zero.[16] Rape and assault is much higher at around 14 percent,[17] and robbery defendants have extremely high rearrest rates at 24 percent.[18] And in general, rearrest for individuals with property offenses was high at 17 percent, though their violent crime arrests are extremely low.[19] Drug offenders (trafficking and possession) had overall rearrest rates of 16 percent,[20] but had extremely low rates of violent crime averaging less than 2 percent.[21] The data gathered from pretrial release programs is consistent with the data found in my study, showing rearrest rates range between 10 percent and 21 percent for most crimes.[22]

A factor that highly predicts rearrest is a defendant's criminal justice status at the time of arrest. Those who had been released pending a prior case were rearrested 30 percent of the time.[23] Those without an active criminal justice status were rearrested only 12 percent of the time.[24] Those on probation were rearrested at 26 percent and those on parole at 25 percent.[25] These staggeringly high rates support the argument that risk assessments should heavily rely on pending criminal charges to determine whether to release a defendant.[26]

To summarize, overall, rearrest rates are relatively low for pretrial defendants. Murder, fraud, and driving-related defendants have much lower rearrest rates than average for all offenses.[27] Robbery and burglary defendants have a significantly higher rearrest rate than the overall average.[28] Having a current charge while arrested increases the risk of rearrest. It is important for judges to consider the overall risk of rearrest – particularly for violent crime – in determining release rates if "dangerousness" is relied upon in determining release. On this point, defendants charged with fraud, public order offenses and drug defendants have extremely low rearrest rates for violent crimes. To help judges make these determinations, risk assessment programs have been developed that consider many factors to determine dangerousness.

4.2 DEVELOPMENT OF PRETRIAL PREDICTION

The year after completing his felony probation for criminally assaulting singer Rihanna, Chris Brown was arrested on charges of assault with a deadly weapon.[29] Mocking the police on Instagram during the standoff prior to his arrest, Brown stated, "Y'all gonna stop playing with me . . . like I'm going crazy."[30] Brown posted a $250,000 bail and was released shortly after being booked.[31] Despite his charge of a violent offense, Brown's release matches current trends of releasing defendants on bail based on financial means with an unreliable emphasis on prior criminal history.

Historically, bail was guaranteed for all but capital offenders, and later evolved to hold defendants that posed a flight risk.[32] Judges were expressly prohibited from considering the danger posed by the defendant in determining whether they should be released. With the bail reform movement, particularly the Bail Reform Act of 1984, and similar state laws, judges began to justify holding defendants they deemed dangerous or a threat to public safety.[33] Judges received the charge to determine if a defendant was a flight risk or dangerous, and while release was (and is) still a constitutional right, it became acceptable to hold defendants pretrial for a variety of reasons.[34] One of these reasons is if the defendant is likely to pose a danger while released. The Bail Reform Act of 1984 was challenged numerous times on many grounds, and the bill passed muster on each occasion.[35] Following Supreme Court approval, judges received authorization to detain defendants on a finding of flight risk *or* dangerousness, which opened the door to judges predicting which defendants are dangerous and which are safe to release.

The question is, can judges predict who will commit a crime while released? Perfect prediction is unachievable due to natural variances and aberrations of human behavior. Indeed, some scholars assert that predicting pretrial crime will never be accurate or scientific.[36] But modern empirically based prediction tools provide impressively accurate results. Early on, however, the jury was out on whether pretrial prediction was accurate.

4.2.1 *History of Pretrial Crime Prediction*

For many years, there was a debate whether it was possible to predict pretrial crime. In 1969, the National Bureau of Standards conducted a study,[37] which for the first time in US history permitted defendants be held pretrial if they were found to be a danger to the community.[38] The bureau used ten characteristics to attempt to predict which defendants were most likely to commit crime.[39] The study concluded that "none of the ten characteristics were accurate predictors, because criminal law is a 'chancy process'."[40] Some of those factors have since been found to hold significant predictive value.

Shortly after the bureau study, a Harvard study found similar results, examining, among others, the same ten characteristics of the bureau study.[41] While the Harvard study generally found few helpful correlations between particular factors and pretrial crime, there were some correlations with higher recidivism. However, the sample size was too small to properly differentiate between indicators.

Though research and academic critique was abundant through the 1980s, little work of importance occurred in the 1990s. In the past fifteen years, pretrial practice research has regained momentum. In 2001, The Urban Institute (UI) examined data from defendants processed by the DC Pretrial Services Agency.[42] After attempting to predict failure-to-appear and safety risks based on twenty-two factors related to criminal history and the current charge, the UI concluded that "most of the variation across people lies in factors not captured by the data."[43] Thus, again the UI confirmed earlier studies finding that pretrial crime was not reliably predictable. These studies illustrate the difficulty of identifying predictive factors and highlight what prior research confirmed – that predicting pretrial crime will never be accurate or reliable.[44] However, empirical methods have improved greatly since the early prediction studies, and now several studies have shown effective prediction of pretrial crime.

4.2.2 *Future of Pretrial Crime Prediction*

Bail and crime prediction research has expanded in the past fifteen years as empirical methods have improved and financial stresses have created demand for more efficient pretrial systems. Most advancement of bail and crime prediction is occurring through the development and research of pretrial risk assessments. This section will explore the current field of prediction research including logistic regression models, pretrial risk assessments, random forest modeling, and, finally, the continued reliance on human intuition in predicting crime.

4.2.2.1 Logistic Regression as a Prediction Tool

A commonly used method, logistic regression modeling, statistically examines data to produce predictions of the probability of rearrest based on individual factors. As discussed earlier, prior empirical studies have disagreed whether judges could predict which defendants would commit crimes while released pretrial. However, with logistic regression and other empirical modeling, my recent study answers this question conclusively based on data from a nationally representative sample of over 116,000 covering the seventy-five largest counties in the United States from 1990 to 2006.[45] The conclusions of this study reveal important information about bail and pretrial crime. First, and most importantly, this study reveals that judges can predict with a high level of accuracy which defendants are likely to commit violent crimes while released pretrial. According to our empirical data, it appears that judges can determine which defendants are likely to commit a crime on release by considering the crime the defendant is charged with and their previous convictions. It also demonstrates that when judges purportedly consider flight risk *and* dangerousness in releasing defendants (the two main factors judges consider), judges consider dangerousness almost five times more heavily than flight risk in most states. Therefore, judges in deciding which individual to release consider how dangerous the defendant is much more than whether the person is likely to flee. So it is important that judges use the tools to accurately determine which defendants are more likely to pose a danger to society. These tools are available with new empirical research and risk assessments that help implement this data and give judges this information before trial. Results from logistic regression models are extremely beneficial in developing risk prediction formulas for pretrial risk assessments, which are discussed in the next section.

4.2.2.2 Pretrial Risk Assessments

As a whole, pretrial risk assessments are the most heavily studied aspect of pretrial crime prediction. The backbones of these assessments are their risk prediction formulas, which are created by compiling and analyzing logistic regression models. Compilations of multiple factors result in the formula used to predict crime and create a generalized risk assessment. Assessment developers must assign each factor a weight; any additional weight given to one factor lessens the weight of other factors.[46] This effectively limits the number of relevant factors used in a reasonably accurate model.[47] Once the formula is established, the release officials interview a defendant or look at the defendant's record to fill out a short, objective questionnaire. Once inputted with the defendant's information, the risk assessment outputs a risk factor predicting the likelihood of failure for the defendant. The release official then uses the risk factor to aid in his release determination.

The Laura and John Arnold Foundation has developed a comprehensive pretrial risk assessment that they argue is applicable across the country.[48] This risk assessment was developed from over 1.5 million cases originating in over 300 jurisdictions.[49] It is an open-source project and offered free of charge to local jurisdictions.[50] The Arnold Foundation's risk assessment has been used in over twenty-nine jurisdictions, including three statewide programs: Arizona, Kentucky, and New Jersey.[51]

Before the Arnold Foundation's significant research and development in the area, many different pretrial risk assessments have been developed across the country. Some states, like Ohio, have developed their own risk assessment program.[52] The federal government also has an empirically based tool used nationwide.[53] Studies of these risk assessments produce much of the most contemporary research of crime prediction available.[54]

Though they vary significantly across jurisdictions, the basic structure of most risk assessments is the same. Research shows that pretrial risk assessments should be objective, empirically based, and locally validated.[55] Local demographics vary and exact factors and their applied weights should be tailored to each jurisdiction. However, local jurisdictions should not necessarily develop their own pretrial risk assessment models since many are less effective than their statewide counterparts.[56]

4.2.2.3 Random Forest Modeling as a Pretrial Prediction Tool

Another potential prediction tool in the pretrial area is random forest modeling. In Philadelphia, Richard Berk is using a statistical method known as random forest modeling to create recidivism risk assessments, as measured by rearrest rates after release from jail.[57] Though Pennsylvania uses it in a probation setting, some believe it is applicable in other areas, including pretrial services.[58] Los Angeles also has a predictive computer program used for prediction in the arrest context.[59]

Random forest modeling's complete operation is quite complex, but essentially it functions by running hundreds of risk assessment scenarios based on predictive factors, and then averaging the predictors into a risk assessment. Discussing this method's advantages, researcher Geoffrey Barnes explains, "It allows for the inclusion of a large number of predictors, the use of a variety of data sources, the expansion of assessments beyond binary outcomes, and taking the costs of different types of forecasting errors into account."[60]

Random forest modeling allows the use of a large number of predictors.[61] Regardless of how many predictive factors are included, the algorithm self-regulates each time it is run to give appropriate weight to each factor used.[62] A factor that has a low predictive value will not have a strong effect on the prediction.[63] Unlike logistical regression equations, random forest modeling allows room for inclusion of factors that have low predictive but high political or social value without loss of accuracy.[64] Still, for the model to identify the factors as important, researchers must input them.

Another benefit of forest modeling is its ability to accurately account for non-linear variables.[65] For example, the younger a probationer is, the higher their risk of recidivism. Risk drops precipitously through the twenties and then slowly levels out as age increases past thirty, presenting a curved relationship between age and risk.[66] Forest modeling will identify and adjust based on this curve, whereas regression modeling inaccurately treats the relationship as linear.[67] As such, forest modeling provides a more accurate prediction for probationers whose age falls between the inaccurate linear progression and the more accurate curved relationship.[68]

Forest modeling also allows the developer to adjust the cost ratio.[69] Researchers suggest jurisdictions place a higher cost on false negatives, than false positives, because releasing a dangerous defendant is more costly than detaining a low-risk defendant for a period of time.[70] This has tremendous political and social appeal.

Naturally, such a thorough modeling and prediction system is costly and labor intensive. Many of the same difficulties exist with random forest modeling as with other types of prediction using empirical methods. The constitutional soundness of large-scale detention as is occurring in federal and state courts is questionable alone, and this is worsened by using an algorithm to detain individuals. And while random forest modeling has not expanded to the pretrial decision, since it is being used in arrest, it is possible that it will expand to the bail context. Using a model to predict crime, pretrial or otherwise, is a tricky business, both practically and politically. The next section discusses how pretrial crime prediction functions in the bail context and some of the policy issues that surround these decisions, including the challenges of risk assessment.

4.3 CONTEMPORARY CRIME PREDICTION USING DATA

Understanding how and whether to predict crime is still a controversial issue in criminal justice. Jurisdictions use a variety of objective and subjective factors to determine whether to release individuals. Electronic tracking of cases and large databases provide researchers immense caches of material to find correlations, patterns, and outliers. Yet, this data must meet careful analysis to provide useful results. Most practical crime prediction and research is now provided by risk assessment tools. To create a risk assessment, a judge or pretrial services enters defendant information into a questionnaire. Using a formula including correlations developed by statisticians, the risk assessment tool calculates the likelihood of the defendant failing to appear or being rearrested. Reliance on or compliance with the risk assessment tool to make release decisions raises public policy concerns.

4.3.1 *Factors to Consider Before Releasing an Individual Before Trial*

The factors judges rely upon to determine whether to release a defendant vary across jurisdictions, but a summary exploration is provided next. Some factors judges use to determine pretrial detention are more universally accepted than others. Though flight risk is still very relevant in bail decisions, the primary focus of judges is on dangerousness.[71] Many state statutes do not explicitly define dangerousness, but each state (except New York and New Jersey) provides some method for determining it.[72] Furthermore, many states begin the list with an "including but not limited to" clause indicating that judges may consider any factor they feel appropriate.[73] Most recently, courts and legislatures are attempting to mechanize a part of this process through risk assessments based on demographic statistics. This is discussed in the next section. Factors are split into two general categories: objective and subjective.

4.3.1.1 Objective Pretrial Factors

Historically, few objective factors were considered apart from the present offense charged, but post Bail Reform Act, the majority of pretrial assessment programs consider objective factors, which are particularly predictive.[74] Some risk assessments rely on objective factors and have completely eliminated defendant interviews.[75] While somewhat controversial, the present offense charged has had, and continues to have, a strong impact on bail determinations; a strong majority of jurisdictions include some aspect of the present offense charged.[76] Similarly, a majority of states permit some review of a defendant's past conduct, where a defendant's past conduct refers to prior criminal acts.[77] The most predictive element in most risk assessments is prior criminal activity, particularly prior violent crimes if dangerousness is the key consideration.[78] An individual with three or more past violent crimes is much more likely to commit a violent crime if released pretrial.

Many other objective factors are used in various ways across jurisdictions. No consensus exists as to exactly which factors should or should not be used, or precisely how predictive all of these factors are. These objective factors include residential address, marriage status, record of appearances or history of flight, outstanding warrants at time of arrest, pending charges at time of arrest, active criminal justice status at time of arrest (pretrial, probation, parole), having a telephone, age, prior arrests, prior convictions, property owner, age at first charge, length of years since prior first charge, and prior jail days.[79] Certainly the research has shown that considering the crime charged and previous convictions are predictive of future crime. And prior flight risk is predictive of future flight risk, and an active criminal justice status is predictive of a rearrest if a defendant is released.

4.3.1.2 Subjective Pretrial Factors

Subjective factors or assessments are also strongly considered in a majority of jurisdictions when considering bail decisions. In states without pretrial assessments, apart from consulting the money bail schedule, nearly the entire release decision is a subjective assessment of the risk of the defendant. Factors vary but can include finances, family situation, character and reputation, community ties, gang involvement, propensity for violence, general attitude and demeanor, history of depression, and treatment of animals.[80] Even comments from the arresting officer or the victim are considered in about a third of pretrial programs surveyed.[81]

Furthermore, this subjective category includes judicial discretion and intuition, a traditional and respected aspect of bail determinations. Subjective judicial discretion provides the release official essentially an open door for a finding of dangerousness based on aggravating circumstances that objective risk assessments may not capture. Some of this can include the demeanor of the defendant and the "gut instinct" of the judge about a particular person. Witnesses, arresting officers, prosecuting attorneys, release officials, and many others introduce discretion and intuition, yet a review of both historical and modern research illuminates the overall failure of intuition in professional judgments as a whole as well as in accurately predicting pretrial crime.[82] All current research shows that intuition coupled with an objective actuarial tool creates more accurate predictions than subjective assessments alone.[83] In the end, subjective intuition should be reduced to a minimal part of pretrial crime prediction. There are times when a defendant has demonstrated some indicia of dangerousness that an assessment will not detect. In these instances, detention is merited based on these observations. Yet, these determinations should not be based simply on intuition but on observable fact. However, even objective-only risk assessments typically allow for judicial override.[84] It is unavoidable to have some subjective consideration in the bail decision.

4.3.1.3 More on Risk Assessments

Since the passage of the Pretrial Service Act of 1982, risk assessment programs have existed in federal district courts. There are also at least 300 state jurisdictions that already utilize risk assessment programs in lieu of using money-based bail.[85] This only constitutes approximately 10 percent of jurisdictions nationwide.[86] Risk assessments are informative, but not definitive, allowing a judge to override the determination of the assessment. However, some courts mandate the release of low- or moderate-risk defendants, based on the assessment.[87]

Many risk assessments use both subjective and objective factors, while a minority attempt to only use objective factors. These factors may include the present charge, criminal history, age, employment situation, housing situation, and family status. No jurisdictions have removed judicial discretion, so there is always a subjective determination in bail decisions, even where risk assessments dominate.[88] However, no matter how the defendant is assessed, there are still strong policy concerns about pretrial behavioral prediction. The next section describes the challenges associated with the process of making a pretrial prediction of crime.

4.3.2 Policy Considerations of Risk Assessments

Crime prediction is plagued with policy questions that reach beyond simply the accuracy or reliability of the predictions made. Rather, the key question is: what to do with those predictions? And of course, the answer depends on the goal of the predictions. Is it to reduce jail populations? Is it to reduce rearrests to as close to zero as possible? If some risk is allowed, how much is appropriate? And, importantly, are risk assessments constitutional or fair?

4.3.2.1 Considering Risk and the Cutoff for Release

At the end of the day, the most critical decision in pretrial crime prediction is what to do with information provided by a risk assessment. Some relevant questions help explore these issues without clear answers.

For one, where should the cutoff be set to determine which defendants are high risk? For moderate risk? Should violence-prone offenders be treated differently than felony or misdemeanor defendants? Some risk assessments appear to accurately flag violent offenders as high risk.[89] Should this flagging alone warrant detention? In reality, the cutoff is usually dictated by the jurisdiction's pretrial services or jail capacity. Resources for supervision programs and the number of jail beds limit what percentage of defendants can be labeled moderate or high risk and provided these services. However, rather than an ad hoc approach to risk assessments that depends on jail or pretrial services space, it makes sense for jurisdictions to carefully consider the level of risk they are prepared to handle in releasing defendants.

Another important policy question is whether risk assessments should be made available to the public. The best practice here is that the risk assessment instrument itself should be available to the public. But a particular individual's risk assessment information should not necessarily be made available to the public during sentencing or trial.[90] The interest is to protect the privacy and due process rights of the defendant, while enabling development, critique, and review of the system. These policy concerns apply to all aspects of pretrial crime prediction.

4.3.2.2 Constitutionality of Crime Prediction

There has been at least one court that has weighed in and determined a risk assessment to pass constitutional muster. The American Civil Liberties Union (ACLU) sued Virginia, arguing that its risk assessment tool was unconstitutional.[91] The ACLU argued that risk assessment violates the Equal Protection Clause of the Fourteenth Amendment by imposing punishment based on demographic characteristics, including age, sex, and education level.[92] Second, the ACLU argued that punishment based on "status" is in violation of the cruel and unusual punishment clause.[93] Finally, the ACLU argued that the risk assessment violated due process and "fundamental fairness in criminal proceedings."[94] However legitimate, these concerns are simply concerns, at least according to the Virginia Court of Appeals, which dispatched the appeal in less than one page.[95] The court concisely explained that the guidelines are not binding, but only a tool to help assist the judge in making a decision.[96] Release officials can rely upon the authorization provided by the Supreme Court in *U.S. v. Salerno* of pretrial detention based on a finding of dangerousness.[97] Thus, it is unlikely that risk assessments will be invalidated on constitutional grounds. It is true that constitutional and historical due process principles are offended by the factors considered by risk assessments, particularly dangerousness and present crime charged. And a constitutionally faithful pretrial system would allow release for the majority of defendants and only detain those who would interfere with the possibility of a fair trial if released. That said, a judicial decision relying on an objective risk assessment based on objective factors and sound empirical data is certainly better than one considering problematic factors and relying on gut instinct. In other words, given the current state of pretrial prediction, risk assessment instruments may be the most fair approach to determine who is safe to release pretrial.

4.3.2.3 Gender and Race Bias in Crime Prediction

One consideration in modern criminal prediction is the racial and gender biases found in the application of risk assessments. The fact is men are much more likely to be rearrested pretrial than women,[98] but risk prediction tools typically leave gender out of their formula.[99] For constitutional reasons, most jurisdictions do not allow judges to consider gender in determining release.

The racial bias is more hidden. It is a secondary effect revealed only by examining the factors that make up many risk assessments. Essentially, risk assessments can be racially inequitable by giving more weight to certain factors that, although unrelated to race per se, are racially disparate. For example, research indicates that African-Americans are arrested for drug use at higher rates than whites.[100] Other factors that may lead to racial bias include living in certain zip codes, education levels, job history, income, marriage status, and housing. So some of these factors may not need to be included in the risk assessment because they introduce racial bias. For instance, homeownership or marital status may not be necessary and may introduce racial bias. The difficulty here is that some factors linked to race are relevant. For instance, black defendants often have higher risk factors for dangerousness, including previous convictions for violent crime. While race is not an appropriate factor to consider, previous violent crime convictions must be considered if judges are to determine dangerousness with any level of reliability.[101] So to balance the important factors here, we cannot remove all potentially unequal factors as it reduces the predictive ability of the assessments, but some factors linked to race can be considered if relevant to future dangerousness. Balancing race and constitutional rights are challenges with risk instruments; however, there are other difficulties to overcome in developing crime prediction tools.

4.3.2.4 Methodological Difficulties in Crime Prediction Tools

Developing and validating crime prediction methods is complicated and methodologically challenging. Predicting human behavior is an inherently complex goal. There are endless contributing factors, and attempting to isolate the effect of one in particular is tremendously difficult, as many researchers candidly admit.[102] The pretrial time period is limited and rearrest rates are low, making the event of rearrest statistically rare.[103]

Validating crime prediction tools is also difficult. Establishing effectiveness of models requires a blind or randomized study. A blind study is not possible as crime prediction models must be consulted by the applicator. Randomization is possible and has been done at least once,[104] but the burdensome logistics of such studies have prevented their widespread use.[105] This is concerning.

Another difficulty faced by researchers is the lack of standard definitions. What exactly constitutes pretrial failure? Do traffic tickets count as new criminal activity? Is a conviction required or does any arrest mean failure? These ambiguities mean different jurisdiction's metaphorical measuring sticks are different lengths. In an effort to promote uniformity, the National Institute of Corrections published a monograph of recommended outcome and performance measures, which suggests standard definitions and metrics.[106] Ideally more jurisdictions will adhere to these standard definitions and data will become more uniform. In addition to these methodological challenges, there are also practical hurdles of applying predictions.

4.3.2.5 Practical Hurdles of Pretrial Crime Assessment Tools

In many counties, pretrial services are extensive operations. Adopting a risk assessment instrument requires cooperation of the judicial and legislative branches, which can be a slow process, often fraught with resistance. To begin with, the state legislature must be on board with the use of crime prediction instruments. This may require education, money, and public support to both spur the change and to implement the system. Next, a program must be put into practice, requiring selection and development of the necessary tool.[107] The courts must hire and train staff on its use.[108] Ideally, though not necessary, the jurisdiction creates pretrial services to provide information about defendants to judges and helps to obtain the information on the risk instrument. Once in use, there must be some follow-up to validate that the system is working.[109] Validation alone, as discussed earlier, can be difficult to accurately measure. Despite these hurdles, jurisdictions have reported great success in using crime prediction as part of their pretrial services.[110] Some of the lessons learned from those jurisdictions are summarized in the next section as best practices (and science) for pretrial prediction.

4.3.3 *Best Practices for Pretrial Prediction and Assessment*

At this point, what is most clear is how complex predicting pretrial crime is. There is continued growth with new empirical methods like logistic regression and random forest modeling. We are still evaluating risk assessments in an effort to determine how effective they are, now using randomized controlled trials.[111] After decades of research, legislation, and review, there is a consensus that the best predictions combine both subjective and objective (data-driven) assessments and that models should be developed locally. What role crime prediction plays in criminal justice will likely remain disputed, however, as a policy matter. And convincing judges and jurisdictions to adopt risk assessments and rely on data is another challenge altogether. Despite these challenges, the research demonstrates empirical support for the factors discussed next being relevant in predicting pretrial crime.

Release determinations and crime prediction efforts are shaped by reliance on objective and subjective factors. As of the latest survey in 2009, most pretrial services programs use a combination of both.[112] Time and repetition have revealed the most reliably predictive objective factors, which include defendant's age, prior jail stays, prior arrests, current charge, pending criminal actions, active warrant, prior violent crime, and failure to appear.[113] For instance, people convicted of three or more prior violent crimes are statistically more likely to commit a violent crime if released before trial.[114] And those with three or more prior failures to appear are more likely to fail to appear in the future.[115] Older defendants are safer to release as pretrial arrests decrease after age 40. Those with prior arrests, jail stays, and pending criminal actions are more likely to be arrested if released. Judges and pretrial risk assessments should consider this data in their considerations.

Subjective factors also play a role in pretrial crime prediction. Given the data, there is little room to argue that subjective factors alone are effective or provide accurate predictions of who is safe to release. Indeed the consensus is that data-driven, objective assessment outperforms subjective human assessments nearly universally.[116] Yet, there is an appropriate role for subjective crime predictions. Judicial discretion should remain available to protect society in instances where there are indicia of danger that the risk assessment would omit in its calculation. Judges should certainly not abandon discretion altogether in favor of even the best data-driven tools.

In the end, the best practice for release officials is to combine an objective, actuarial risk assessment with a limited subjective assessment. The objective assessment should consider the empirically supported factors provided earlier to produce a risk ranking. The judge's discretion should be limited to overriding the risk prediction with a legitimate and supported concern of flight risk or dangerousness. Using a risk assessment is a way to achieve this goal.

4.4 CONCLUSION

Though the field of pretrial crime prediction is still integrating new technology, research developments and pressure provided by large jail populations are spurring it toward reform. Electronic abilities facilitate larger-scale, more accurate research. Practitioners and policymakers are beginning to see the need and potential for effective improvement. Jail populations can be reduced. More defendants can be released without increasing crime rates. Indeed, judges are making substantially mistaken judgments on which defendants and how many defendants to release pretrial. This chapter provides data from a large comprehensive study of the seventy-five largest US counties to determine what factors, if any, are relevant in predicting "dangerousness" pretrial and what percentage of defendants can be released safely before trial. Prior work in this area disagrees as to whether judges can accurately predict which defendants are dangerous and the extent of pretrial crime. My empirical work, with Frank McIntyre, reveals that out of all of the state felony defendants released, only 1.9 percent are rearrested for a violent felony. And even repeat offenders, those with four prior convictions, are still only committing pretrial violent crime in about one in thirty instances.[117] This data demonstrates that judges are detaining way too many defendants and can release a lot more defendants overall.

If the goal is to prevent crime, judges often detain the wrong defendants. With the empirical evidence provided in this chapter, judges can both release more defendants pretrial and cut crime in America. If judges considered the data, they could release more of the accused population (and less of others) without increasing the risk of violent crime or total pretrial crime rates. About half of those detained have less chance of being rearrested pretrial than many of the people released. Judges would be able to release 25 percent more defendants while decreasing pretrial crime levels if they released defendants using an evidence-based model. The data demonstrates that judges may safely release more older defendants, people with clean prior records, and people who commit fraud and public order violations, without increasing danger to the public. All of these groups are at extremely low risk for violent crime. In addition, and contrary to current law expectations, judges can also release more defendants charged with drug possession and trafficking as these defendants are among the safest to release pretrial. To cut violent crime rates and decrease the risk of danger, judges can release more drug defendants, older defendants, defendants with clean records, and those charged with fraud and public order defenses. In addition, individuals with an active criminal justice status and prior arrests and jail time are generally at a higher risk for committing crimes if released.

Detention of high-risk individuals where appropriate is the goal. Better risk assessment based on empirically backed studies can improve prediction accuracy. While all judges seek to avoid pretrial crime, many judges lack information available through risk assessments and empirical data. These tools are better than judicial common sense or gut instinct in helping judges predict the likelihood of pretrial crime. With data-driven decisions, judges can actually reduce pretrial crime, while releasing more defendants and cutting incarceration rates. Decisions based on data-driven factors could also minimize reliance on money bail. All of this is possible with a slow, deliberate adoption of modern, data-driven pretrial crime prediction. Significant policy questions still must be addressed, but there is hope of transforming pretrial prediction into a more equitable and efficient system.

5

Individual and Societal Costs of Pretrial Detention

It's almost like trusting an altimeter on an airplane. You can't see the ground, but you've got to trust your instrument because there is so much you can't see.

— Chief Judge Joseph McGraw, Chair of Illinois Conference of Chief Judges
(speaking of the difficult balancing by judges in determining bail)[1]

Over the past few decades, the amount of money allocated to the criminal justice system has skyrocketed. According to the Washington State Institute of Public Policy, in 1975, it costs an individual taxpayer $200 to pay for his or her part of the criminal justice budget. By 2000, the annual cost rose to $1,200 per taxpayer, while crime rates have remained about the same.[2] To look at it another way, in 2012, state taxpayers spent $52 billion on corrections – 300 percent more than 25 years ago[3] – and spent $9 billion dollars just on housing pretrial detainees.[4] Much of this spending goes toward housing pretrial detainees – individuals held without bail based on some perceived level of dangerousness or flight risk – who now make up the majority of jail inmates nationwide. The US pretrial detention system calls out for reform.

On top of detention costs, there are large costs to victims and society when more crimes are committed. The costs of murder, rape, burglary, robbery, and other felony offenses are tremendous both in immeasurable human costs and also financially. Certainly, there are risks in releasing individuals who have been charged with a crime as they sometimes commit crimes on release. This risk of crime is a cost to society that we bear when respecting the constitutional right to release before trial. On the other hand, there is a cost to defendants in being detained before trial and the financial and other losses they face. This is the difficult balance that judges face when determining whether and how to release an individual before trial. This chapter provides a cost–benefit analysis of the costs to society and to defendants for a fuller consideration of the bail balancing act.

In this chapter, I discuss the potential value of a cost-based method of pretrial detention decision-making. Relying on my own research and on data aggregated from prior studies, I quantify the costs and benefits of pretrial detention and compare those costs to the costs and benefits of pretrial release. I ultimately find that in the realm of felony defendants, judges maximize economic savings when they detain a relatively low number of defendants – those statistically most likely to pose a danger to society. These tend to be individuals charged with violent crimes with three or more previous convictions. I demonstrate that detaining the defendants most likely to pose a danger to society could save US jurisdictions up to $78 billion. At a minimum, considering the costs and benefits of pretrial detention is helpful for policy-makers hoping to increase efficiency and reduce expanding criminal justice budgets.

5.1 COST OF PRETRIAL DETENTION BORNE BY SOCIETY

Society's highest direct cost associated with pretrial detention is the cost of imprisonment. This includes facility maintenance, prison staff, administration officials, meals, rehabilitation, education programs, and other jail costs. One study has estimated that the annual cost to detain one inmate is $22,650,[5] although individual states, most notably New York and California, spend more than twice as much on imprisonment.[6] Other monetary costs to society include a reduction in gross domestic product (GDP) from wages that the defendant would have otherwise earned,[7] as well as lost tax revenue.[8] Society also bears the expenses incurred to administer court proceedings and the cost of providing counsel for indigent defendants.[9]

Pretrial detainees also often deprive their children of financial and emotional support,[10] and because of this, these children are much more likely to develop antisocial behaviors and engage in future criminal activity themselves.[11] Likewise, they are significantly more likely to drop out of school, costing society $260,000 per child in the long term[12]; and given that these children are more likely to receive public assistance, creating a potential for future costs to society as well.[13] Crime also imposes further costs on society, such as reduced housing prices,[14] and reduction in local business activity.[15] Indeed, the costs to society are significant and snowball when a crime is committed. However, as demonstrated by this chapter, these costs do not compare with the high costs of incarceration from detaining low-risk defendants unnecessarily.

5.1.1 The Rise of Incarceration Rates and the Costs of Imprisonment

As incarceration rates have risen, so has spending on prisons. According to one study, spending on corrections from 1972 to 2002 rose 455 percent (adjusted for inflation).[16] Institutions of higher learning and prisons compete for state funds, and prisons are *winning*. Thirty years ago in California, 10 percent of the state's general fund went to higher education and 3 percent went to prisons. In 2010, the Governor of California reported that 11 percent of the annual budget was allocated to prisons and only 7.5 percent to higher education.[17] Today, per-inmate spending in the state is $70,836,[18] compared with per-student spending of $18,050.[19] In 2013, the Independent Budget Office released a study showing that New York City paid $167,731 to feed, house, and guard each inmate that year. Multiplying this by approximately 12,287 inmates who rotate through the city jails, the cost of imprisonment is significant. In 2012, the Vera Institute of Justice's study found that the aggregate cost of prisons in 2010 in 40 states was $39 billion. This breaks down to costing the annual average taxpayer in these states $31,286 per inmate. New York State was the most expensive with an average cost of $60,000 per prison inmate.[20] With incarceration rates being as high as they are, costs of incarceration cannot lessen unless some sort of reform is implemented.

Much of this correctional spending contributes to housing pretrial detainees, individuals who are held without bail based on some perceived level of dangerousness or flight risk. These individuals are who now make up the majority of jail inmates nationwide.[21] As the law has evolved in this area, judges have been charged with deciding which defendants can be safely released and which should be held in jail before trial. The current balancing process that judges use to make pretrial release and detention decisions are full of individual biases and ad-hoc heuristics that make these decisions unpredictable. We see this reflected in the fact that some counties release less than 5 percent of defendants, whereas others release more than 90 percent of defendants charged with exactly the same crimes.[22] Overall, incarceration costs are crippling many state budgets and reducing costs by releasing low-risk individuals is one way to improve this situation.

5.1.2 Individuals Released and Detained Pretrial and the Ultimate Costs to Society

As compared to pretrial detention, pretrial release generates relatively minimal direct costs. For example, in the federal system, pretrial release programs cost $3,000 to $4,000 per defendant, depending upon the degree of flight risk and comparative dangerousness of the defendant. However, the decision to release a defendant pretrial gives rise to other costs, which, though indirect, are heavy. The largest cost is a potential crime committed while an individual is released.[23] When crimes are committed, there are huge costs to victims as well as increases in law enforcement and court costs.[24] Crime also imposes further costs on society, such as reduced housing prices and reduction in local business activity. However, detention also may create costs, such as an increase in recidivism and criminal behavior even if people are only detained a few extra days. Given the high costs of violent crime to society, and of course the costs of incarceration and costs to the individual defendant, I ultimately conclude that detaining a lower number of defendants – those statistically most likely to pose a danger to society – provides the best cost–benefit solution to bail.

5.1.2.1 Costs of Crime on Society

Society pays a high cost when defendants commit crimes that would not have been committed but for the pretrial release of dangerous defendants. This leads to an increase in law enforcement costs, court costs, and the costs borne by victims. It can also result in reduced housing prices and reduced local business activity. Research indicates that a very small number of defendants are being released pretrial, and of those defendants released, a very small fraction of them actually commit new crimes. Although many pretrial detainees are considered low-risk defendants, there are a small number of defendants who are considered "high-risk" defendants who should be detained pretrial in order to protect the community from additional crimes, specifically violent crimes.[25] The District of Columbia's Pretrial Services Agency released statistics stating that of the 1,351 defendants who were released with GPS ankle bracelets to track their movements, 110 were arrested and charged with new crimes. This is roughly 8 percent. Nearly a dozen of the crimes committed were violent, including armed robbery, assault, and attempted child sex abuse. In the past years, a few defendants in the program have even been charged with murder and rape. Javon Hale, an eighteen-year-old, was charged in two shootings and a kidnapping over a three-day period that left one man dead and two others badly wounded. This incident occurred while Hale was on the District's electronic monitoring program. He had been released from jail one month earlier and was awaiting his trial for a killing in 2010.[26]

Hale's arrest brings high scrutiny of pretrial release and highlights the fear judges face when considering whether to release an individual pretrial. After Hale's arrest, one DC Superior Court judge said, "It's one of my biggest fears.

No judge wants to release someone and have that person commit a violent crime while on release." This is a serious decision, in which judges have wide discretion. They may release the defendants who are awaiting trial to help the overcrowded jails and backlogged court dockets, while keeping track of defendants' whereabouts with GPS supervision. Nevertheless, situations like Hale's come up, making it more difficult for judges to accurately assess a defendant's risk potential and making an emotional decision more likely.[27]

This data only further suggests that whether or not a defendant should receive pretrial detention is a question that should be carefully evaluated case by case. A majority of defendants are low risk enough to be released pretrial, while a minority of defendants are unsafe to release and should be detained before trial. Society bears the cost of unnecessarily detaining these defendants pretrial and creating circumstances that may lead these defendants to reoffend.

5.1.2.2 Pretrial Detention Increases Crime and Recidivism

It turns out that release of an individual is not the only risky decision. Detention can also lead to more crime for defendants and a lower likelihood of appearing in court. There is evidence that low-risk defendants become high risk if detained for longer periods of time pretrial. In other words, detaining an individual even a few extra days pretrial increases the risk that they will be arrested for a crime pretrial. Even for short periods of pretrial detention, defendants held 2–3 days pretrial were 17 percent more likely to commit another crime within two years after case disposition. Defendants held 4–7 days had a 35 percent increase in recidivism rates, while defendants held 8–14 days were 51 percent more likely to recidivate than defendants who were held for less than 24 hours.[28] Additionally, data shows that defendants held before trial have a higher probability that they will commit violent or drug-related crimes later in their lives because they were exposed to criminals and criminal behavior while detained.[29] Another study, analyzing records of over 60,000 defendants arrested in Kentucky, found strong correlations between the length of pretrial detention and the likelihood of defendants to reoffend in both the short- and long-term after release. Even for minor charges, defendants who were detained for longer periods of time pretrial were more likely to commit additional crimes within the pretrial period.[30] The Kentucky records from 2009 and 2010 showed that low-risk defendants, detained for more than 24 hours, were more likely to commit new crimes while their cases were pending and even years later. Interestingly, these defendants were also more likely to fail to appear in court.

Research has shown that failure to appear rates follow the same pattern. Defendants held for 2–3 days were 22 percent more likely to fail to appear in court than similarly situated defendants who were held for less than 24 hours. Defendants held for 15–30 days had a 41 percent failure to appear rate, while defendants who were held for more than 30 days had a 31 percent failure to appear rate.

There are both significant risks and costs to detaining defendants unnecessarily and potential risks to releasing defendants. The risk of release is always the chance that the defendant commits another crime or fails to appear at court for their trial. These risks can be mitigated by careful risk assessments that are extremely accurate now in predicting which defendants are low or high risk. However, the risk of detention it turns out can also be great as new studies demonstrate that sometimes detaining low-risk individuals before trial can actually increase pretrial crime and increase failures to appear. In addition to the societal costs associated with detention, pretrial detainees also shoulder individual costs, as discussed in the next section.

5.2 PRETRIAL DETENTION'S COSTS TO A DEFENDANT

Pretrial detention imposes significant costs to a defendant. It harms an individual's chance of defending a successful case and increases the likelihood of a conviction. It significantly reduces an individual's ability to strike a successful plea bargain, which is the most common way to resolve a criminal case. It often results in economic harm, like a defendant losing her job and home, and puts a financial strain on their families. Detention also makes it more likely for an individual to commit more crimes when released, even if detained just a few days. Detention can also lead to a defendant suffering harsh jail conditions such as abuse, health hazards, and other violence. The section below discusses these topics in greater detail.

5.2.1 *The Most Crucial Moments: The Time Leading Up to Trial*

Perhaps the most critical period of criminal justice proceedings is the time between arrest and the decision to plead or take a case to trial because of the consultation, investigation, negotiation, and motion filing that can all take place at this time.[31] It is not overstating the fact to say that pretrial detention decreases the chance of a defendant getting a fair shake in criminal proceedings. For example, preparing one's case is much more difficult when the defendant is in jail than if the defendant were immediately released. The Supreme Court has even acknowledged that it is much more difficult for a defense attorney to prepare a case on behalf of a pretrial detainee because it is harder for pretrial detainees to stay in touch with their lawyers, provide attorneys with evidence, and give input on whom they should call as witnesses.[32] Indeed, the disadvantage is so great that some scholars go so far as to say that a denial of bail is equivalent to a conviction – that is just how hard it is to prepare a solid case while the prisoner is in jail.[33]

Assume that a defendant has a few alibi witnesses for a crime he has been charged with. However, the defendant does not know the alibi witnesses' names. The defendant, detained pretrial, will not be able to look for the witnesses and is therefore unable to contact the witnesses and ask them to testify on his behalf. Or assume that there is critical evidence in favor of a defendant's acquittal, yet the defendant cannot search for it because she is being held pretrial.[34] Public defense attorneys have a difficult time tracking down witnesses and evidence, even if they have the time or resources to investigate a case. It is virtually impossible for indigent defendants to successfully plead their case without an ability to investigate.

Many studies have shown that pretrial detention causes increased conviction rates. So with two similarly situated defendants, if one is released, she has a higher likelihood of not being incarcerated after trial than a defendant who is detained. In the 1950s, Caleb Foote found a strong correlation between pretrial detention and subsequent conviction, in comparing accounts of bailed and jailed defendants. Of defendants charged with violent crimes, 67 percent of released defendants were acquitted, while only 25 percent of jailed defendants were acquitted. Of those charged with property crimes, 49 percent of released defendants were acquitted, while a mere 7 percent of jailed defendants were acquitted.[35] Similarly, more recent studies show that there is a higher proportion of defendants being incarcerated pretrial than are actually convicted.[36] A state court study found that individuals detained for the entire period before their trial were over four times more likely to be sentenced to jail and over three times more likely to be sentenced to prison than defendants who were released at any point before trial. The study also showed that pretrial detainees' sentences were significantly longer. Their sentences were almost three times as long in jail, and more than twice as long for those sentenced to prison. Another study found that the federal system also had similar results.[37]

Whether a defendant is deemed guilty may depend on whether they are released or held before trial. Indeed, from 1990 to 2004, 78 percent of pretrial detainees were eventually convicted, but only 60 percent of alleged criminals released were convicted of a crime.[38] A 2013 study showed that judges are almost four and a half times more likely to convict and sentence pretrial detainees when compared with otherwise similarly situated alleged criminals who were not subjected to pretrial detention.[39] Pretrial detainees that are considered "high risk" are three times more likely to go to jail than high-risk alleged criminals who did not have to spend time in pretrial detention.[40] Even pretrial detainees whom judges conclude are low risk are almost five and a half percent more likely to be sent to jail than their otherwise equal counterparts who did not spend time in pretrial detention.[41] Additionally, the jail time for pretrial detainees is almost three times that of alleged criminals who avoided pretrial detention.[42] Overall, scholars argue that justice is much more attainable from outside of a prison cell. With pretrial detention being utilized far too often, this ultimately leads to defendants being incarcerated for a far longer time, costing society considerably more money than is necessary and often costing a defendant his freedom in the long term.

5.2.2 *Plea Bargaining Impact on Detention before Trial*

The most alarming effect of pretrial detention is on plea bargaining which is the way more than 95 percent of state and federal criminal cases are determined. Because the US criminal justice system relies on plea bargains, an individual loses any kind of leverage or bargaining power that may come with evidence gathering when they are detained before trial. A study in England showed that close to 55 percent of prisoners who are released end up pleading guilty to their crime while nearly 85 percent of pretrial detainees plead guilty.[43] It is commonly known among prosecutors and defense attorneys that "given enough time in custody . . . most individuals . . . will eventually plead guilty to something."[44] Even for prisoners in pretrial detention who are innocent, accepting a plea bargain for time served is very tempting because they just want to leave jail and return to their families and jobs. If inmates accept a plea deal, their guilt is forever marked on their criminal record. But if they do not take the plea deal, the prosecutor could increase the charges and a jury could still find them guilty, both of which would likely result in more jail time, and their guilt would appear on their criminal record regardless.

Victor Rivera's case demonstrates the dilemma faced by many charged with a crime who cannot obtain release. For example, Victor Rivera was placed in pretrial detention after he was arrested for allegedly threatening a police officer. Rivera was detained before trial after he was unable to pay the $25,000 bail bond. Even though he adamantly denied the charges, after eleven months in pretrial detention, Rivera decided to take the plea deal because he knew that he would have to spend at least four more months in pretrial detention before his case was resolved. Rivera was immediately released for time served, but by accepting the plea deal, his conviction will be on his record permanently.[45]

The next section deals with another key issue for most defendants – an inability to afford bail.

5.2.3 *The Inability to Afford Bail: The Indigent Defendant's Demise*

Most defendants are not released before trial because they cannot afford to pay bail, rather than because they are unsafe to release. In states, a much larger percentage simply cannot afford bail than those who are prohibited from release by a judge. Even in cases where judges set a minimal bail of $500, many defendants cannot afford this and thus remain in jail until their case has been closed. On average, out of every 100 people who have a bail set at $500 or less, only 19 make bail at their arraignment, while the rest go to jail.[46] Indeed, in 2008 in New York City, approximately 17,000 people accused of misdemeanors could not make bail of $1,000 or less.[47] Most of these individuals were accused of nonviolent crimes, such as possession of marijuana or jumping a subway turnstile to avoid paying the subway fare, and they spent an average of 16 days in jail.[48] The bail system, in effect, rewards the wealthy by allowing them to escape punishment with payment and punishes the poor because they are not able to make the payment.

For example, Raul Hernandez was arrested for a misdemeanor drug possession charge after an officer accused him of dropping an empty plastic bag containing heroin residue. Hernandez asserts that he did not commit a crime that day. He turned down an offer of seven days in jail in exchange for pleading guilty and the judge set his bail at $500. Hernandez could not afford this, so he spent nine days in jail. When he appeared at court to argue his case, the officer who allegedly witnessed the crime was off that day and was unavailable to testify. Hernandez had to make the choice of either maintaining his innocence and staying in jail or pleading guilty and going home. Hernandez, like many other poor defendants, plead guilty simply to get out of jail.[49]

In the nation's seventy-five largest counties, 37 percent of felony defendants are held on bail until their cases are settled. It is very rare to see wealthy defendants in pretrial detention because they are most often able to afford their bail, even when their bail amounts are extremely high. John "Junior" Gotti was accused of racketeering, and was able to post a $2 million bail. Sonny Franzese, accused of extortion, was able to post a $1 million bail. On the other hand, many people accused of low-level offenses, such as possession of marijuana, lack the means to post their bail and thus remain in jail until their court date.[50]

Indigent defendants remain in jail pending trial over miniscule amounts of bail money. For instance, Thomas Layzell received a ticket for failure to observe a traffic light in Montana and due to his refusal to appear in court, he was arrested a few months later. He received a second ticket for rolling through a stop sign. When Layzell was arrested, the court set his bail at $300, knowing he only had $47 to his name. The court denied both Layzell's requests for a court-appointed counsel and reductions in his bail.[51] This pretrial detention resulted in the loss of the only job he had been offered in a long time and he ultimately spent thirty days in jail after being released on his own recognizance.[52] The circumstances that Hernandez and Layzell were in are, unfortunately, not uncommon. The fact that these defendants are imprisoned simply due to their lack of money further shows that a major reform within bail needs to take place.

5.2.4 *Economic Costs of Pretrial Detention on an Individual*

Pretrial detention imposes direct economic costs on detainees along with more difficult to quantify costs to an individual. For example, society loses economic contributions and tax revenue on a defendant detained pretrial and, in turn, a detainee's inability to work causes lost income.[53] If pretrial detainees lose employment, they often simultaneously suffer reduced wages. Serving time also reduces hourly wages for men by approximately 11 percent, annual employment by nine weeks, and annual earnings by 40 percent.[54] Furthermore, when properties (either apartments or rented homes) are lost, as occurs in 23 percent of cases, extra funds are expended on a subsequent housing search. In addition, one-third of detainees report having their property stolen upon detention and thereafter,[55] which amounts to losses of about $370 per incident of larceny.[56] Indeed, economists can quantify the actual costs borne by defendants being detained rather than released before trial.

While these costs are difficult to define, economists have put numbers on some of the intangible losses to defendants for the purpose of considering costs and benefits. Other significant, yet difficult-to-quantify, costs include the loss of liberty, dignity, damaged reputation, community standing,[57] and disruptions to family life and other relationships.[58] Detainees are often victims of humiliation, rape,[59] and other violent acts while incarcerated, and as a result also suffer added anxiety, stress, suicide,[60] and a lower quality of life.[61] Despite the extreme stress and anxiety caused by incarceration, there is little to no mental care for pretrial detainees, even juveniles and those who have no experience with the justice system. For instance, when Brian Warner, a nineteen-year-old, was sent to jail for repeatedly shoplifting, the judge assigned him a cash bond of $50,000. Because he could not post bail, he was detained. The morning after he was arrested, jail guards found him dead – he had committed suicide by strangling himself with his bed sheet.[62] While it is unclear whether Warner had previous mental problems, prisoners who do have mental problems and ask for assistance are often ignored.

Additionally, and very importantly, pretrial detention may be the crucial factor leading to a conviction or the direct cause of prison sentences.[63] All told, the value of lost freedom to detainees may range from $800 for the most dangerous defendants to $6,770 for the least dangerous defendants, both subsets of which may be detained before trial.[64] In this section, I delve into what kinds of costs detainees face when it comes to detention. It is also important to take note that many of the costs that detainees face also overlap with some of the societal costs already discussed.

5.2.5 *The Result of Pretrial Detention: Lost Income,*
Employment, and Property

While in pretrial detention, many defendants lose their jobs. If they lose employment, they often simultaneously encounter reduced wages. Then, if and when they find new employment, their hourly wages may be reduced due to the fact that they served time. Some defendants even lose their property and then need extra funds to find new housing.

Shadu Green, a twenty-five-year-old, was charged with a series of misdemeanors after getting pulled over in his car. The judge granted release if he could provide a $1,000 cash deposit. A bondsman offered to post the money for him for a $400 nonrefundable fee. Green did not have $1,000 for the court, $400 for the bondsman, or even 44 cents to mail a letter to his mother asking for bail money. At this point, Green could either sit in jail waiting for his trial or plead guilty, take the sixty-day sentence prosecutors offered him, and then go home. Green asserted his innocence as to the charges and he did not want to plead guilty because he knew it would reduce future job prospects. Almost done with half of the 60 days already, Green struggled in deciding what to do. He had a daughter at home and her mother was unable to pay the bills without his income. He eventually chose to fight his case, because he had already lost his apartment and his job. After Green had been in jail for about eight months, his baby's mother was finally able to scrape together the last of $400 to pay the bail bondsman, and he was released. Green was free, but he had no money, no job, and no place to live. Green was an innocent man who spent eight months in jail for minor driving violations and had to pay $400 to receive his right to a jury trial.[65] His experience demonstrates the domino effect of not being able to afford bail which results in jail time and a loss of a job, income, and even a home.

On average, incarceration reduces more than half the earnings a white man would otherwise have earned by age 48, and about 41–44 percent of earnings for Hispanic and Black men. This is an expected earnings loss of almost $179,000 for people who have been incarcerated. In analyzing economic mobility – the extent to which individuals are able to move up the ladder relative to their peers – individuals who have previously been incarcerated were more disadvantaged than those who had never served time. In 2006, out of the formerly incarcerated who had earnings in the bottom fifth percentile, two-thirds remained at the bottom of the earnings ladder after 20 years. By comparison, only one-third of the men who were not incarcerated remained stuck at the bottom of the ladder. Offenders had a 2 percent chance of moving from the bottom of the earnings to the very top, while those who had not served any time had a 15 percent chance.[66] Unfortunately, incarceration has far too heavy of an impact on future employment, wages, and economic mobility.

5.2.6 Children with Incarcerated Parents: Costs to the Defendant, Their Family, and Society

Children with incarcerated parents suffer grave consequences that may not cause immediate harm, but carry long-lasting effects. Harm to children burdens both defendants and society. Society suffers many indirect costs when resorting to the use of pretrial detention, specifically with defendants who are parents. Pretrial detention often deprives detainees' children of financial and emotional support and as a result, children with incarcerated parents are much more likely to develop antisocial behaviors, engage in future criminal activity themselves, and drop out of school.

The number of children with an incarcerated parent has increased by almost 80 percent since 1991, and the number of children with a mother in prison has more than doubled during that time.[67] One in eight children who are victims of parental maltreatment had a parent who was arrested within six months of the reported child abuse,[68] and at least one in three children in contact with the child welfare system has had a primary caregiver arrested at some point in their lives.[69]

One study found that parental incarceration may be more harmful to children's health and behavior than divorce or even death of a parent compared to children of similar demographic, socioeconomic, and familiar characteristics.[70] It found that these children are more likely to have behavioral problems and conditions such as attention deficit hyperactivity disorder, learning disabilities, speech or language problems, and developmental delays.

As for the indirect costs of detention, when a sole wage-earning parent is incarcerated, this restricts parents from providing adequate economic support to their families. One study examining the financial wellbeing of children before, during, and after incarceration of a father found that during the period that the father was incarcerated, the average family income fell 22 percent. In the year after release, the family's income increased a bit, but was still 15 percent lower than the year before incarceration.

For instance, consider the case of Dorothy Gaines, a middle-aged widow and a mother of three. Dorothy was convicted of conspiracy to deliver crack cocaine and was sentenced to nearly twenty years in prison. Even though the police never found any evidence of drugs in her home, she served six years in prison before President Clinton finally commuted her sentence in 2000.[71] Before her arrest, Ms. Gaines was a nurse technician with a good salary. At the time of Ms. Gaines's arrest, her son, Phillip, was eight years old, her daughter, Chara, was ten years old, and her eldest daughter, Natasha, was eighteen years old.[72] After being released from prison, Ms. Gaines tried to piece her life together, but her drug conviction essentially blocked every avenue she had to becoming economically self-sufficient and taking her place at the head of her family again. With a drug conviction, Ms. Gaines could not live in public housing, receive welfare, or obtain food stamps. In an interview, Ms. Gaines expressed her frustrations:

> When you come out, where are you supposed to go? There's nothing for a person when they come out of the system: no housing, no jobs. You go to fill out a job application and the first thing on it says, "Are you a convicted felon?" They don't want to hire you. If you lie and they find out about it, it's not just that you're not hired. [U]nder your parole, those are grounds for terminating your probation and sending you back to prison.[73]

Once an incarcerated parent is released, their inability to get a job, food stamps, or public housing assistance seriously strains the parent–child relationship and leaves thousands of children uncared for.[74] These tensions that are commonly the result of incarceration not only harm the defendant but also ultimately cost society.

5.3 CONSIDERING COSTS AND BENEFITS OF DETENTION TOGETHER TO DETERMINE OPTIMAL PRETRIAL RELEASE

As covered above, there are various costs and benefits to an individual and society of detention. In my empirical research on the costs and benefits of detention, I quantified some of the most important costs above to determine the optimal level of detention.[75] The average cost of detention exceeds the cost of release by approximately $20,000. Detaining a defendant typically results in $40,300 in direct costs, while the average cost of releasing a defendant pretrial is just $19,500. In considering the costs to society of release, I account for the potential costs of crimes committed on bail. This section considers these costs and benefits together and concludes with a recommendation for optimal release given the risks posed by individuals before trial. After considering the risks, optimal release means that it is more cost-effective to release some defendants and to detain others.

There are some important factors to consider in this cost–benefit calculation. As discussed more completely in Chapter 4, there are ways for judges to know which defendants are more likely to pose a threat pretrial. In short, the individuals who pose a greater risk are those who pose a higher risk of violent crime because the costs to society for violent crimes are the greatest. For instance, according to my research and other studies, the tangible and intangible cost of a murder to society is $10,754,332 and for rape it is $266,332.[76] On the other side, it is cost-effective to release nonviolent defendants because the costs of property and drug crimes are much lower if committed on bail. For instance, the average cost of theft is $3,906.[77] The way to save money through a cost–benefit analysis is by classifying defendants into categories, aggregating costs of releasing and detaining these individuals, and presenting this information to judges as part of a risk calculation. Judges can then consider the costs and risk associated with releasing each type of defendant and use this information in making their determination.

To be more exact, my research finds that by considering the higher risks posed by some individuals and detaining them, jurisdictions can save $78 billion dollars while detaining 28 percent fewer defendants. In other words, judges can release significantly more defendants without increased crime while also saving state and federal governments' money. This cost–benefit analysis reveals six factors that have the greatest influence on costs of releasing an individual:

(1) original arrest for a violent crime,
(2) four or more prior arrests,
(3) prior incarceration,
(4) a prior failure to appear,
(5) an active criminal justice status, and
(6) aged nineteen or younger.

In analyzing these factors, I learned that releasing an individual with any one of these six traits results in costs of $159,519.[78] And considering state data, judges on average released 30 percent of defendants with these risk factors. If judges decided *not* to release *any* individuals with these six factors, it would result in an average cost of only $4,181 per defendant. Still, state judges nationwide still detained 18.6 percent of these defendants. Given the number of felony arrests per year, pretrial-detention policies that consider these factors in the release decision could save billions per year. In fact, even a simple policy, where judges detained all defendants who were under the age of 24 who were arrested for a violent felony and released all other defendants, results in lower costs than what judges are doing right now. This policy would save an average of $7,624 per defendant relative to judges' actual detention decisions.[79] If this simple policy were adopted, 28 percent fewer defendants would be incarcerated and the increased savings nationally given all of the felony arrests would be 78 billion dollars. I am by no means suggesting that judges should abandon discretion and simply detain all defendants under 24 arrested for a violent felony. However, I am suggesting that if judges carefully considered the costs of detaining the defendants they chose to detain, they may be able to increase public safety while reducing incarceration.

I am not suggesting that a cost–benefit analysis should supercede or fail to consider the important constitutional and human rights at play in the detention decision. Indeed, equity, due process, and justice can all be legitimate critiques of any cost–benefit analysis. However, given that there is no perfect decision in pretrial detention, and judges are largely doing a quick uninformed cost–benefit determination in each bail decision anyway, a proper consideration of these costs and benefits is in order.

5.4 CONCLUSION

The United States spends billions to detain more than 500,000 suspects every day. While these detentions are arguably constitutionally problematic, there are also important costs incurred by society and by the individual that are highlighted in this chapter. The costs of incarceration for defendant include reduced success at trial and in plea bargaining, loss of job, home, and property, harm to children, and additional harms of abuse during incarceration. Costs to society of detention include high incarceration costs and increased likelihood of recidivism, decreased taxes, and increased burden of supporting the family of the defendant. While it is clear that defendants suffer in pretrial detention and society pays incredible costs, quantifying and comparing these costs have never been done in a methodical way. My empirical research – the first conducting a cost–benefit analysis of the pretrial detention – considers the risk posed by each group of defendants and considers the costs to release defendants including the costs of crimes that they may commit on society.[80] It then considers the costs of detention to the defendant and to society including incarceration costs, loss of income, and other personal and family costs. Considering these costs and benefits, using the model in my research, courts could release 28 percent more defendants at an estimated cost savings of $78 billion in the last decade.[81] Given the high costs of violent crime to society, and of course the costs of detention and costs to an individual, I ultimately conclude that detaining a lower percentage of defendants – those who are statistically most likely to pose a danger to society – provides the best cost–benefit solution to both society and the defendant.

6

Race and Bail in the Criminal Justice System

Discrimination on the basis of race, odious in all aspects, is especially pernicious in the administration of justice.

— Justice Anthony Kennedy[1]

More black defendants are detained before trial than white defendants. Despite the efforts to create equality in criminal laws, blacks are imprisoned at far higher rates than whites. Indeed, one in every three black males can expect to go to prison during their lifetime compared to one in six Latino males and one in every seventeen white males, with current incarceration trends.[2] Many scholars and political leaders denounce racism as the cause of disproportionate incarceration of black Americans. Commentators over the years have denounced race discrimination in the detention decision, evidenced by more blacks being detained pretrial compared to whites charged with the same crimes. The bail decision is an obvious source of potential bias as 41.6 percent of black defendants in states are detained pretrial while only 34.4 percent of white defendants are. And black and Hispanic defendants often pay higher bail amounts for the same crimes charged as white defendants. Indeed, the majority of studies from the last fifty years have almost uniformly concluded that blacks receive unfavorable disparate treatment specifically in bail and pretrial detention determinations.[3] For example, one of the most comprehensive reports on bail analyzed twenty-five studies from 1975 to 2002 and concluded that "racial disparities are remarkably stable."[4] Another study, conducted in 2011, echoed earlier conclusions and found that African-American defendants face higher bail amounts than white arrestees with similar criminal charges and criminal histories.[5] Some argue that judges often compensate for their lack of information about the prisoner's background and their lack of time by relying on their own individual evaluation of the prisoner's race to guide their pretrial detention and bail decisions.[6]

Some commenters have blamed the police, prosecutors, and judges who make arrest, charging, and release decisions based on predictions of whether defendants will commit future crimes. Others complain that racism results from media and bad legislation. All of these factors are explored by this chapter. This chapter explores where racial bias enters the criminal justice system through an empirical analysis that considers the impact of race in the bail decision. It also closely considers how police decisions and courts may allow racial bias in the bail context. With a close look at the numbers and consideration of factors ignored by others, my research confirms some conventional wisdom but also makes several surprising findings. This chapter confirms through an empirical analysis of pretrial data that police arrest black defendants more often for drug crimes than white defendants. Judges discriminate against black and Hispanic defendants by granting less favorable release options and more expensive bails than white defendants. However, judges, who are often blamed for racial bias in the bail decision, actually detain white defendants pretrial more than similarly situated black defendants for all types of crimes. Despite the fact that more black defendants are detained and incarcerated, judges actually are acting in a biased way against *white* defendants, not black defendants, and black communities. The important and surprising findings in this chapter challenge long-held conventions of race and help mitigate racial disparity in the bail decision.

6.1 RACIAL BIAS IN THE ADMINISTRATION OF CRIMINAL JUSTICE

Most academic commentators and casual observers would agree that racial bias exists in the US criminal justice system. This chapter begins exploring racial bias in the criminal justice system generally by examining the impacts our laws have on minorities, the presence of racial bias in police officers' decisions to arrest, the existence of racial bias among judges, and the media's role in perpetuating racial bias. This introductory section is meant to give broader context for the challenges discussed later in this chapter with bail, given general racial dynamics like higher arrests and less diversion of their sentences. Later, this chapter considers how racial bias impacts the bail decision.

Without first acknowledging that racial bias exists in the US criminal justice system, it would be difficult to explain the fact that blacks in 2014 comprised 33 percent of all prisoners, even though they only made up 12 percent of the national population.[7] Or that together African-Americans and Hispanics comprised 58 percent of all prisoners in 2008, even though African-Americans and Hispanics make up approximately one-quarter of the US population.[8] In 2014, black males had an imprisonment rate that was nearly six times higher than white males.[9] The arrest rate is even more alarming concerning drug offenses: African-Americans were sent to prison for drug offenses at ten times the rate of whites.[10] Indeed, many consider the alarming racial disparity in US prisons as one of the greatest racial problems today, some going so far as to claim that it is the modern way of "reimposing Jim Crow."[11] While criminal law academics note that racial discrimination is generally not purposeful, it is impossible to ignore alarming statistics that demonstrate that racial bias is alive and thriving in many aspects of the US criminal justice system. Indeed, media influences, legislators, police officers, judges, and prosecutors can and often do contribute to the racial bias problem that our criminal justice system is facing. The following sections will discuss the propensity of each of these groups to contribute to racial bias.

6.1.1 Media Influences on Racial Bias

The media plays a critical role in allowing racial bias to enter the criminal justice system. According to a study conducted in 2011, African-Americans, and African-American males in particular, are underrepresented in positive images and attributes and overrepresented in negative imaging, such as criminality, unemployment, and poverty.[12] Another study from 2011 conducted by the Pew Research Center found that 43 percent of newspaper stories involving black men were crime stories and the most frequent topics of television news stories were sports (43 percent) and crime (30 percent).[13] Such distorted media representations "can be expected to create attitudinal effects [including] general antagonism toward black men and boys."[14]

The media is also influential in creating perceptions about crime and the relative threats posed by African-Americans. The crack epidemic is a perfect case study of this phenomenon. A large part of what allowed for the Reagan-era draconian laws against crack in the 1980s – which disproportionately impacted and continues to impact inner-city blacks – was the media. Media in the 1980s devoted disproportionate amounts of airtime and print to "America's drug crisis."[15] Indeed, "in July 1986 alone the three major TV networks offered seventy-four evening news segments on drugs, half of these about crack."[16] And the vast majority of these featured blacks in inner cities, when crack usage rates were similar among black and white Americans during this time.[17] Meanwhile, the perception of the problem created by the media did not follow reality as Congress and the media overlooked government data that demonstrated that drug use in America peaked in 1978 and 1979 and declined steadily through 1984.[18] Despite the drop in drug usage rates in the 1980s, due to media influence, public perception solidified that drugs were the major problem in America and that drugs were strongly linked to black violent crime.[19] In fact, in 1986 (years after the steep decline in crack usage, but before the media barrage of drug crisis propaganda), drug use was viewed as the most important problem facing the nation by only 3 percent of the population, but due to the help of the media campaign, that number soared to 64 percent in three short years.[20] Indeed, when Americans were legislating harsh laws against crack use because of the fear of inner-city black crime, crack usage in America had long since declined. The perception created by the media led to laws (discussed later) that are still disproportionately affecting black Americans today.

6.1.2 *Legislative Impact on Racial Disparity and Bias*

Though most members of Congress would immediately strike down legislation that explicitly endorsed racist policies, it is important to note that American law and racism developed together in a somewhat "symbiotic existence."[21] And even though laws in the United States are not racist on paper, some are in effect. It is important to examine all criminal legislation to make sure it does not have an unintended disproportionate impact on racial minorities. Mandatory minimum sentences and other tough-on-crime legislation, like California's three strikes law, have disproportionately affected minority defendants.[22] In addition, some legislation requires a consideration of criminal history for sentencing. This type of legislation can also disproportionately impact minorities since they are more likely to be arrested than whites committing the same crimes.

To use a high-profile example of legislative disparity, Congress until recently punished possessing and distributing crack cocaine 100 times more severely than powder cocaine. Indeed, people who get caught selling 5 grams of crack cocaine spend just as much time in jail as people who get caught selling 500 grams of powder cocaine despite the fact that they are simply two varieties of the same exact drug.[23] Though on its face such a law is not racist, it effectually has made it so blacks are punished 100 times more severely than whites because blacks comprise 90 percent of those who have been found guilty of drug crimes that involve crack cocaine, while they only make up 20 percent of those found guilty of possessing or distributing powder cocaine.[24]

Draconian drug laws have impacted blacks at dramatically higher rates than whites, partially because blacks are arrested more frequently for drug crimes – even though whites and blacks use drugs at similar rates. Indeed, the ACLU estimates that blacks are four to five times more likely to be convicted for drug possession, even though whites use drugs at higher rates. One example of the disparate impact laws can have on minorities is the story of Tonya Drake. Tonya, a young African-American woman, was asked by a man she barely knew to send a package for him. He offered to give her $100 to cover the shipping cost, and as payment, he would allow her to keep the change. Even though Tonya thought the package contained drugs, she sent it anyway because she was a struggling twenty-five-year-old mother of four on welfare who desperately needed the money to provide for her family. Because the package contained crack cocaine, Tonya was sentenced with the mandatory minimum of ten years in jail even though her only prior offenses were traffic violations. After the judge sentenced her, he said, "This woman doesn't belong in prison for 10 years for what I understand she did. That's just crazy, but there's nothing I can do about it." If the package had contained powder cocaine, Tonya would have been guilty of a crime with no minimum prison sentence.[25] By amplifying the punishments typically given to crack-using blacks, Congress has effectually made it so whites receive a less severe punishment than blacks for essentially the same criminal act. Because of recent legislation, this disparity between crack and cocaine has improved, though the disparity is still there.[26]

6.1.3 Police, Arrest Rates, and Racial Bias

Legislation is not the only explanation for racial bias in the US criminal justice system. Studies show that police officers, purposefully or not, are also racially biased in enforcing the law. For example, police officers are more than thirteen times more likely to arrest black drug offenders than white drug offenders even though whites and blacks commit drug crimes proportionally.[27] While arrest disparity is the worst with drug crimes, blacks are often arrested more for other crimes than whites. The racial disparity can be even more alarming in certain areas. In Madison, Wisconsin, for example, African-Americans make up about 7 percent of Madison's population, but account for 45 percent of arrests[28] and were nearly ten times as likely to be arrested than whites in 2012.[29] And because police arrest more minorities, those minorities are subject to the bail decision more often than whites.

Michael A. Lawson's story is especially illustrative of the adverse effects that racially biased police strategies have on blacks. After graduating from Harvard Law School, Michael, a black man, started working as an associate at one of the most prestigious law firms in the country. One of his fellow associates offered to give Michael a ride back to the office in her Mercedes SLC coupe from a social event sponsored by the firm. As their route took them through the Bronx, a police officer pulled them over. The officer said that Michael's friend was speeding and asked some odd questions. Eventually, the police officers let them go with just a warning. Michael's friend was sure she wasn't speeding and wondered why the officer pulled them over. Michael, however, was convinced that the police officer pulled them over because she was driving with a black man. Initially, she didn't think Michael was correct, but later learned that the New York Police Department (NYPD) was instructed to pull over black men driving with white women in nice cars in the Bronx based on the suspicion that they were drug dealers.[30] The NYPD gained national notoriety for its racial profiling in stop-and-frisk tactics that stopped and searched disproportionately more minority defendants with little justification, as few individuals had any weapons or contraband.[31] Other jurisdictions, like New York, have demonstrated through real data that their racial profiling rates of minorities are much higher than whites.[32] Police racial bias is exacerbated by the fact that there is little accountability and few adequate checks on police.[33]

The effect of racial bias in police arrests is compounding. When law enforcement makes more minority arrests in urban environments, more blacks are represented in our criminal justice system. As law enforcement dedicates more of its resources to patrolling and investigating blacks in urban areas, the resulting arrest population is not a proportional representation of all offenders, but rather disproportionately represents black citizens. Whether a person obtains a criminal record (and the size of that record) is related to both criminal activity and race. Thus, more blacks are represented in the arrest population, and this overrepresentation self-perpetuates and is increasingly aggravated as law enforcement officers and judges rely on arrest and prison data to determine who is more likely to commit crimes in the future. This in turn exaggerates the public and police perception that blacks commit more crimes, as well as the association between being black and being a criminal. Prior arrests and convictions are also a factor on who obtains release on bail, so black defendants are more likely to be at high risk for a crime and less likely to receive release pretrial.

6.1.4 *Judicial Implicit and Explicit Racial Bias*

Race plays a role in the US criminal justice system even after police officers arrest perpetrators because, like legislators and police officers, judges are not immune from potential implicit or explicit bias.[34] Sometimes judges make decisions arbitrarily, and it disproportionately harms minority defendants. When judges make bail decisions informed by gut instinct rather than a risk assessment, bias is much more likely to infect the decision. Consider Tyriel Simms's experience with a bail decision. After Simms was arrested, the judge initially offered him the option to pay $150,000 bail, but later changed his mind because he said "he was in a bad mood," and Simms was denied the option to obtain release from trial.[35] This similar variation has allowed for racial bias.

Generally, judges do not purposefully discriminate against minorities. Usually the bias is implicit or based on a lack of experience.[36] However, there are some exceptions. A few judges have expressed their racial biases privately and, in some cases, even publicly. For example, in 2013, a judicial ethics complaint was filed against Edith H. Jones, a judge on the Fifth Circuit Court of Appeals, for saying in a public speech at a law school event that "blacks and Hispanics [are] more prone than others to commit violent crime" and that a death sentence was a service to defendants because it allowed them to make peace with God.[37] And a US district court judge in Montana resigned in 2013 after a judicial review panel found hundreds of emails "that showed disdain for blacks, Indians, Hispanics, women, certain religious faiths, [and] liberal political leaders."[38]

Whether judges are racially biased purposefully or subconsciously, studies support the notion that racial bias exists among judges. For example, once arrested for possession or use of illegal drugs, judges are ten times more likely to imprison blacks than whites.[39] Additionally, African-Americans serve virtually as much time in prison for a drug offense (58.7 months) as whites do for a violent offense (61.7 months).[40] Even when blacks are accused of committing crimes that are not drug related, the results of some criminal proceedings tend to indicate a racial bias in the judicial system.

Consider, for example, Millie Simpson's interaction with a judge in New Jersey. Millie was a black woman who worked for a white suburban family. One of her son's friends took her car and was involved in a hit-and-run accident. Because he was driving Millie's car, the judge thought she had committed the crime. The first time she appeared in court, the judge declared that Millie was not guilty based on the fact that her son's friend took her car without permission. The second time she appeared in court, it was in front of a different judge. Because the first judge already had deemed Millie not guilty, she did not repeat her story to the second judge, who she assumed already knew the details of her situation. However, the second judge pronounced her guilty without hearing any evidence and without her public defense lawyer present. For her sentence, she had to pay $300, give up her driver's license for an entire year, and had to do fifteen hours of community service. Millie's white employer heard the story and hired an attorney on Millie's behalf, who explained Millie's situation to the second judge. The judge then declared that Millie was not guilty and dismissed all charges against her. Millie's employer concluded that "[t]o get justice, the poor black woman needs a rich white lady."[41] While Millie's judicial interaction may provide an instance of implicit – rather than explicit – bias, these difficulties are reported by black defendants in courts throughout the country with regularity.

6.1.5 *Prosecutors, the Charging Decision, and Racial Bias*

Some argue that racially biased prosecutors affect the outcome of criminal matters more than racially biased judges. Because prosecutors have more unreviewable power than any other decision maker in American criminal justice,[42] the discretion afforded prosecutors can greatly impact black defendants if a prosecutor is racially biased.[43] Indeed, a recent study by Sonja Starr found that federal prosecutors are twice as likely to initially charge black men with crimes that have a minimum sentence requirement than equally situated white men,[44] which results in blacks facing prison sentences that are 10 percent longer than similarly situated white males.[45]

While prosecutors statistically demonstrate bias against minority defendants, it is a rare case where the bias appears on the record. Such a rare instance appeared recently at the United States Supreme Court. Justice Sotomayor reproached a federal prosecutor for trying to use racist assumptions about blacks and Hispanics to prove his case during a trial.[46] The defendant in that trial, Bongani Charles Calhoun, a black man, had accompanied some of his friends, who were black and Hispanic, on a road trip. It turned out that his friends were going on this road trip to buy a large amount of cocaine. To their surprise, the drug dealers were two Drug Enforcement Agency agents, who arrested Calhoun and his friends when his friends tried to buy cocaine from them. To charge Calhoun with possessing cocaine with the intent to distribute, the prosecutor had to show that Calhoun went on the road trip with the knowledge that his friends were planning to buy cocaine. If Calhoun adequately demonstrated that he was "simply along for the ride," then he likely wouldn't be guilty.[47] The night before Calhoun and his friends departed on the road trip, Calhoun noticed that his friends had a large bag full of money. Therefore, to prove that Calhoun knew that his friends embarked on their road trip to buy drugs, the prosecutor asked Calhoun: "[Y]ou've got African-Americans, you've got Hispanics, you've got a bag full of money. Does . . . a light bulb [go] off in your head and say, this is a drug deal?"[48] Though the United States Supreme Court chose to not hear Calhoun's case, Justice Sotomayor wrote specifically to condemn the prosecutor's racial bias. She said the Court's decision not to hear Calhoun's case "should [not] be understood to signal our tolerance of a federal prosecutor's racially charged remark."[49]

She went on to say that the prosecutor's "conduct diminishes the dignity of our criminal justice system . . . We expect the Government to seek justice, not to fan the flames of fear and prejudice. In discharging the duties of his office in this case, the [prosecutor] missed the mark . . . I hope never to see a case like this again."[50] Like police, prosecutors face little accountability for racism in their charging practices. In fact, even worse than with police, there is little transparency in prosecutorial decision-making, such that the public often has no knowledge of the racial make-up of the individuals prosecutors choose to charge and those they decline to charge.[51]

The role of prosecutors, police, legislators, and the media all come together to help contribute to racial bias in the criminal justice system. The next section focuses more specifically on racial bias in the bail decision.

6.2 RACIAL BIAS IN PRETRIAL RELEASE AND BAIL AMOUNTS

Having established a framework with which to view race in the criminal context, the remainder of this chapter will focus on the role of racial bias in the bail system. The 6.2.1 examines how race affects whether arrestees are given the option of bail. The 6.2.2 discusses how race affects bail amounts, with black defendants being assigned higher amounts of bail. The final section discusses empirical data from my work with Frank McIntyre on whether race plays a role in judges' decisions in determining bail. Racial bias certainly exists in the bail context, particularly in whether defendants are offered bail and the type of bail they are offered. Whether judges express bias in which defendants are released is a more complicated question, however, as discussed in this section.

6.2.1 Racial Bias and Minority Bail Decisions

Although race is not a permissible factor that judges use to determine whether a prisoner should have the option to pay bail, race nevertheless plays a role. Indeed, one empirical study found that judges are 25 percent more likely to deny bail to blacks when compared with whites,[52] and 24 percent more likely to deny bail to Hispanics when compared with whites.[53] As discussed in Chapter 4, nonfinancial release options are better for defendants than cash-based bonds since the defendant is never returned a money bond paid to a commercial bail bondsman. While over 70 percent of bail bonds are money bonds,[54] courts give prisoners other types of nonfinancial release options. Blacks, when compared to whites, are 12 percent less likely to receive nonfinancial release options, while Hispanics are 25 percent less likely to be released without a money-based bail agreement.[55] So not only are minority defendants more likely to not be released on bail, but they are also more likely to obtain a less-favored money bond.

Consider two similar cases that demonstrate how differently a judge treated a white man and a black man with respect to what kind of bail each would receive. Richard Davis, a white man from Cherry Hill, New Jersey, worked as a car salesman. Police officers arrested Davis for drunk driving. The court noted that Davis had previously been arrested for drunk driving and set his bail amount at $300. However, Davis, instead of spending time in prison for pretrial detention, went home that night because the judge let him sign his own bail bond, "which meant he could walk out of the door" because he had signed "a written promise to pay the bail himself if he didn't show up for trial."[56]

A week later, another man was arrested for drunk driving. The two men were very similar: both had jobs, were in the middle class, had lived in their respective cities for a long time, were in their mid-thirties, and were married with children. However, the second man, Alex Horne, was black. Horne was an insurance salesman from West Philadelphia. Like Davis, Horne had previously been arrested for drunk driving. However, instead of assigning Horne a $300 bail amount, the judge set bail at $500. The judge also did not allow Horne to sign his own bail bond, which meant that either Horne had to immediately pay $500, call a bondsman to pay his bail amount for him for a charge, or wait in jail until his trial. The prosecutor in Horne's case asked the judge "whether Horne or his family could post the bond or pay a bondsman so late at night."[57] The judge responded: "I can't do anything about that . . . They give 'em each one phone call. If he gets through, fine. Next case." The prosecutor then approached the judge and talked to him in private. When the prosecutor asked the judge why he did not allow Horne to sign his own bail bond, the judge said that Horne "could be dangerous, driving home drunk like that, and it wasn't his first time."[58] The prosecutor then brought up Davis's case and explained how similar their circumstances were, including the facts that they had both been charged with driving while drunk and both had prior drunk driving charges. The judge justified his decisions by saying that Davis "wouldn't hurt anybody."[59] The prosecutor then reasoned that "it might hurt just as bad to be run over by a drunk car salesman from Cherry Hill as a drunk insurance salesman from West Philadelphia."[60] Though the prosecutor did not directly accuse the judge of making a racially biased decision, he later recalled, "[W]e both knew at that point that the only difference between the cases was the race of the defendants."[61] The judge treated Davis, the white man, as a "friend or a member of [his] family"[62] and assumed he was a harmless person who had just made a mistake by drinking and driving. However, the judge treated

Horne, the black man, as an outsider, and his bail decision was "dominated by fear."[63]

Some commentators argue that in the pretrial detention context judges are more likely to use their own racial bias when, in their mind, the stereotype of the race of the prisoner corresponds with the crime the prisoner has allegedly committed. As explained in the last section, due to media and other implicit biases, the US public, including judges, associates blacks with violence and danger. Indeed, one study found that a judge is 33 percent more likely to deny bail to black prisoners if their crime is associated with violence when compared to similarly situated white prisoners.[64] Furthermore, while judges are 12 percent less likely to grant black prisoners a nonfinancial bail option, that percentage jumps to 21 percent when the black prisoner is accused of a violent crime.[65]

Consider sixteen-year-old Kalief Browder, a black teenager arrested because he was accused of a violent crime. Even though he didn't have a previous criminal record, Browder did not receive a nonfinancial release option. Police officers stopped and confronted Browder on his way home from a party. A man who was riding with the police officer told the police officers that Browder was the person who had stolen his backpack and punched him in the face. Browder was arrested immediately. The judge set bail at $10,000, and because neither Browder nor his family could pay that amount of money, Browder was forced to wait in jail for his trial. Before this incident, Browder did not have a criminal record. He was offered a plea deal that would have allowed him to walk out of jail immediately, but Browder refused to take it because he didn't feel comfortable admitting to a crime he knew he did not commit, even if it meant that he would have to wait longer in jail for his trial, or worse, risk being found guilty of his crime and being sentenced to fifteen years in prison. Browder eventually was released after spending three years in pretrial detention. During those three years, he spent 400 days in solitary confinement. He was also subject to physical abuse and mental neglect, which prompted him to attempt suicide on six separate occasions. Had Browder received a nonfinancial release, or a smaller bail amount, he would have avoided the mental and physical anguish that accompanied his prison time.[66]

Minorities are not only portrayed as violent in the media, but there is a strong perception that blacks and Hispanics are associated with illegal drugs.[67] Indeed, while judges are typically 25 percent more likely to deny bail to black prisoners, when the prisoner's crime is drug related, judges are 80 percent more likely to deny black prisoners bail.[68] Hispanics are also often associated with illegal drugs.[69] Therefore, while judges are 24 percent less likely to give Hispanic prisoners the option of bail, when compared to similarly situated white prisoners, judges are 67 percent more likely to deny Hispanic prisoners bail if they have allegedly committed a drug crime.[70] It may be that Hispanic defendants are most affected by racial bias because, as one study found, Hispanics, when compared to all other races, are least likely to be released pretrial because they receive the highest bail amounts and are the least likely to be able to pay those amounts. [71]

Consider the case of Juan Delgado Perez. Perez, a man of Hispanic descent from Las Vegas, who was arrested for a drug-related crime and denied bail. After spending fifteen days in pretrial detention, the trial judge set bail at $3,000, and then inexplicitly raised it to $1 million. Perez could not afford either amount.[72] While it is unclear why the judge decided to raise the bail amount so drastically, the record revealed that during a hearing Perez said that he needed "to get another lawyer," and the judge responded saying, "[W]ith an attitude like that, you can sit in jail." The Supreme Court of Nevada eventually reversed the trial judge's harsh and unjustified bail determination.[73]

In the release decision, judges release black and Hispanic defendants less often than white defendants and with less preferable release methods. Often minority defendants receive financial bail options and are often denied more favorable nonfinancial options. The cultural perception that Hispanics and blacks are more violent or associated with drugs does not help either as this is a factor judges use to justify detention of minority defendants. Informing judges and other criminal justice actors of these race disparities may help these actors exercising implicit bias to be more aware of this problem.

6.2.2 *How Race Affects Money Bail Amounts*

Many minorities are subject to pretrial detention because they cannot pay high bail amounts to obtain release. In New Jersey, 5,000 pretrial detainees – about 39 percent of the whole state's jail population – were incarcerated solely because they could not pay bail.[74] Even more startling is the fact that in New Jersey 12 percent of pretrial detainees who were assigned a bail amount of $2,500 or less were in prison only because they could not afford to pay.[75] Even small bail amounts prevent defendants from obtaining release before trial. And this disproportionately impacts indigent defendants, who in some jurisdictions are more likely to be minorities. Bail amounts are increasing, and this disparately impacts minority defendants, who often receive higher bails anyway. From 1992 to 2006, the average bail amount increased more than $30,000,[76] a finding that seems excessively high considering that 75 percent of charges against pretrial detainees are minor, nonviolent offenses.[77]

Besides rising bails, there are also disparities in bail amounts given to minority defendants. Indeed, studies also show that blacks receive substantially higher bail amounts when compared to similarly situated whites.[78] For example, a 2010 study found that the average bail for blacks charged with violent crimes is just under $36,000, about $7,000 above the average bail assigned to whites charged with these crimes.[79] And the disparity is close to $12,000 with blacks charged with drug crimes.[80] Based on varying bail amounts of blacks and white prisoners, one study found that judges value a black prisoner's day of freedom $64 less than a white prisoner's day of freedom.[81]

To make paying bail even harder for financially distressed families, non-financial bonds are becoming more and more rare. While in the past non-financial bail options were the most common method of release, now judges are more likely to assign a prisoner a money bond than a nonfinancial release option and do so in 70 percent of all criminal cases.[82] Money bonds are non-refundable, and unlike nonfinancial options, a suspect who cannot pay is unable to be released regardless of how compliant he is with conditions or any court instructions.

Bail trends nationally are especially harmful to minority defendants. Bail amounts are increasing across the board as money bail has become the norm nationwide. This overall increase in the amounts of bail that defendants have to pay harms minorities most because not only are they more likely to be disadvantaged financially, but judges also often assign them higher bail amounts in the first place. Indeed, in Philadelphia, Megan Stevenson found that minority defendants from low-income neighborhoods are less likely to post even the same bail amounts as white or wealthier defendants.[83] Minorities are more likely than whites to receive money bail as the preferred option for release and are less likely to be able to pay even small amounts of money bail. Whether judges explicitly or implicitly disfavor minorities when it comes to bail amounts, it is important to understand the disparate impacts their pretrial decisions have had on minority defendants.

6.2.3 Judges' Racial Bias in Pretrial Detention

As this chapter has demonstrated, there are certainly disparities between minority and white defendants in pretrial detention. Particularly in the last two sections, it is clear that judges express bias in the types of bail and bail amounts they offer to minority and white defendants. Some judges also demonstrate implicit bias in their treatment of minority defendants, releasing them at lower rates. The research over the last fifty years has also demonstrated that judges as a whole detain more black defendants than white defendants before trial.

This is also assumed to be as a result of racial bias. However, a recent study I conducted with economist Frank McIntyre demonstrates that it is a lot more complicated than statistics look at first glance.

In my research, Frank McIntyre and I examined over 100,000 pretrial defendants between the years 1988 and 2006 and examined whether judges released them, considering their record. Given that judges in most jurisdictions are permitted to consider the defendant's current charge and previous convictions, we considered the defendant's likelihood to commit a violent crime while released in determining whether a judge released or detained the individual. Judges across the United States are much more interested in whether a defendant is likely to commit a violent crime on release than whether they are a flight risk.[84]

My study, like many others, found that blacks are arrested and spend time in pretrial detention more than whites. However, importantly, we found that when judges determine whether or not to offer suspects the option of release, judges primarily focus on whether the suspect is accused of a violent crime and how likely the prisoner is to commit another violent crime if released, rather than the prisoner's race.[85] To determine whether the suspect is likely to commit a violent crime on release, we considered the number of previous convictions for a violent crime on the defendant's record. Additionally, judges are less concerned about drug crimes (or rearrests for drug crimes) and are unlikely to make detention decisions based on an increased risk for committing a drug crime.

Second, the study showed judges actually hold whites in pretrial detention more often than blacks when their threat to society is equal for both drug crimes and violent crimes.[86] Essentially, judges release more black defendants than they should, given the determinations they are asked to make in the bail decision. In other words, our study, unlike others, took into account how at-risk prisoners were to commit violent crimes if released; as a result, the racial disparities in pretrial detentions disappeared. We concluded that as far as the release decision is concerned, once pretrial risk for violent crime is accounted for, the racial disparity between black and white defendants is reversed. The cause for this disparity is unclear. It may indicate that judges are less sensitive to violent crime in black communities than white communities as they are more likely to release violent black defendants than violent white defendants. It could also indicate that judges detain whites more often than blacks because judges recognize that whites are less likely to be caught for their criminal behavior than blacks.[87] This is supported by the fact that black defendants are arrested more often than whites, particularly for drug crimes. Regardless, judges' decisions discriminate against both races by detaining white suspects more often than black suspects, and releasing more black defendants pretrial who pose a violent crime risk.[88] Indeed, a closer look at the release statistics reveals a more complicated picture than simply judges discriminating against black defendants in the pretrial decision.

6.3 CONCLUSION

Racial bias certainly exists in the US criminal justice system. Specifically, legislators, police officers, judges, prosecutors, and the media can, and often do, contribute to this problem. The media and legislatures have worked together to create perceptions that black defendants pose criminal risks that may not necessarily fit with reality. Prosecutors and police demonstrate racial bias in arrests and charging decisions and judges have been known to set higher bail amounts for similarly situated minority defendants and offer them less preferable money bail more often than nonfinancial bail options. There is certainly implicit racial bias at some level given these disparities in bail – and even sometimes explicit racism against minority defendants by judges and other criminal justice actors. Another consideration is that more white defendants are released before trial than black defendants. While this seems to also point to implicit bias, it turns out that this racial gap is not explained by simple bias. My recent study, with Frank McIntyre, challenges long-held conventions that judges are simply expressing racial bias against black defendants in determining who to release before trial. Indeed, the pretrial release decision is more complicated, and once risk of violent crime is considered (which is the most important consideration for judges in deciding who to release before trial), judges actually detain white defendants more than similarly situated black defendants for all types of crimes. Judges may be expressing a bias against white defendants in being more sensitive to their risk of violent crime, or expressing a bias against black communities by expressing less sensitivity to the risk of violent crime posed by black defendants. Either way, it is important that judges are aware of their decisions and how they impact both defendants and communities who may suffer due to pretrial violent crime. Improving the US bail system will certainly involve an awareness of the disparities in pretrial release between white and minority defendants. Part of this will certainly include eliminating the role that implicit and explicit racial bias plays. Another part involves a careful consideration of the bias that exists and how it impacts defendants and communities. A full consideration of reforming bail in America is contained in Chapter 11.

7

Bail and the Sixth Amendment Rights to Counsel
and Jury Trial

In all criminal prosecutions, the accused shall enjoy the right to a speedy and public trial, by an impartial jury of the state and district wherein the crime shall have been committed, which district shall have been previously ascertained by law, and to be informed of the nature and cause of the accusation; to be confronted with the witnesses against him; to have compulsory process for obtaining witnesses in his favor, and to have the assistance of counsel for his defense.

— Sixth Amendment of the US Constitution

Amidst the recent police brutality controversy that swept the nation, there were demonstrations, riots, looting, protests, and widespread media coverage exhibiting the outrage of the American people. One such demonstration occurred over the death of unarmed Freddy Grey in Baltimore. During these April 2015 riots, a twenty-nine-year-old black man named Dominick Torrence was arrested and charged with disorderly conduct for allegedly throwing bricks and other items at a fire truck.[1] Torrence's bail was set at $250,000, ironically the same amount as the officers charged with the murder of Freddy Grey.[2] Dominick Torrence was not able to make bail, nor was he able to come up with 10 percent ($25,000) of the $250,000 to use a bail bondsman.[3] Unable to pay bail, or a bondsman, Dominick had to spend thirty days in jail. This resulted in his girlfriend losing $18,000 in student loans because she had to quit her job to stay home with her two sons, a job Dominick usually did, and was subsequently forced to drop out of cosmetology school. If that wasn't enough, the charges against Torrence were eventually dropped, essentially meaning that the time spent in jail, the loss of the $18,000, and his partner's lost educational opportunity were for nothing.

Torrence's situation is unfortunately a common one. But the question remains as to why a defendant with no history of violence being charged with nonviolent misdemeanor should have the same bail amount set as two people involved in a high-profile murder case? The answer is likely because Torrence did not have an attorney to represent him at his bail hearing. Research shows that defendants who have representation at their bail hearings are two and a half times more likely to be released on their own recognizance,[4] meaning bail money does not need to be paid at all. Furthermore, defendants who are represented by attorneys are over *four times* more likely to have their bail reduced.[5] If Torrence had an attorney at either his bail hearing or bail review hearing, is it possible that this series of life challenges could have been prevented? Almost certainly. Furthermore, the right to trial by jury before punishment should have prevented his thirty-day pretrial detention in the first place. If the Sixth Amendment guarantees an indigent defendant an attorney, why didn't Torrence have one at his bail hearing?

Unfortunately, many Americans have a vague understanding of the rights afforded to them under the Sixth Amendment of the US Constitution. Supreme Court Justice Black explained pointedly that "[t]he right of one charged with [a] crime to counsel may not be deemed fundamental and essential to fair trials in some countries, but it is in ours."[6] It was the 1963 landmark case of *Gideon* v. *Wainwright* that granted indigent defendants the right to appointed counsel under the Sixth Amendment, and *Miranda* soon after that made it mandatory that every defendant be informed of this when in custody.[7]

Even though each suspect in custody has the right to counsel, the Sixth Amendment does not typically kick in at the time of arrest. In fact, in most states, not only does a defendant *not* get an attorney immediately upon arrest, but she does *not* retain the right to an attorney at her first appearance in front of a judge.[8] Recently, this issue has become a larger concern to the broader American public. While this concern may seem novel, legal scholars have been researching and criticizing bail practices for decades, dating back to the Manhattan Bail Project in 1961.[9] Unfortunately, their arguments have not gained enough traction to promulgate reform in all fifty states. With this rejuvenated interest in America's bail system, it is important to understand why providing attorneys to indigent defendants at bail hearings would drastically improve the criminal justice system.

This chapter focuses on the important Sixth Amendment right and its pretrial implications. The Sixth Amendment of the US Constitution guarantees the right to a jury trial and access to counsel for a criminal defendant. These two rights are critical to protecting the constitutional right to bail. This chapter discusses the importance of rejuvenating the Sixth Amendment to apply pretrial and is broken up into distinct parts. The first part discusses the importance of the right to a jury as a fact finder, and that facts should not be determined before trial. Currently, judges decide facts before trial in the bail decision and "weigh evidence" against defendants. In recent years, the Supreme Court has reinvigorated the importance of the jury in the sentencing phase, stopping judges from making important factual determinations related to punishment, and instead reserving these decisions for the jury. This rationale has not been applied to judges deciding important pretrial facts, like bail, but the same rationale may apply. This part argues that because the role of judges is limited – and excludes fact finding – they should not be deciding facts about a defendant's guilt before trial, and this should be left to the jury after trial. The second part of this chapter discusses the importance of providing counsel to defendants in their bail hearing, a right that should also be guaranteed by the Sixth Amendment and is critical to a defendant's constitutional right to bail. Providing counsel to the accused at a bail hearing will also increase pretrial release generally, so more individuals have the opportunity to prepare their case outside of jail. Overall, rejuvenating the Sixth Amendment will increase rights for defendants before trial and better respect the constitutional right to bail.

7.1 BAIL AND THE JURY: FACTUAL DETERMINATIONS SHOULD BE BY JURIES AT TRIAL

Juries have always determined the guilt of a defendant and defendants should only be punished after this determination. Due process and the presumption of innocence have required this historically. However, bail customs have evolved against this constitutional requirement such that judges currently weigh factual evidence to determine release before trial.

Recent changes by the Supreme Court are important for restoring bail as a constitutional right. For years, academics have bemoaned the encroachment made by judges on the right to a jury trial. However, the Supreme Court has, at least in the sentencing stage, turned meaningfully back toward the original conception of due process and the right to jury trial. This Sixth Amendment shift in the role of judges can potentially help stop improper judicial determinations in the bail decision as well.

Historically, the role of the judge has been to determine questions of law, with fact finding reserved for the jury. These rights had been lost over time with judges often determining facts, especially in sentencing. However, landmark Supreme Court decisions in *Apprendi* v. *New Jersey* (2000) and *Blakely* v. *Washington* (2004) hold that juries must find facts and that judges should not usurp the power of the jury. Now, the right to a fair trial includes a jury finding facts, not a judge, in the sentencing phase of trial. The following sections discuss *Apprendi* and its progeny and how the important rationale in these sentencing cases applies in the pretrial context as well.

7.1.1 *Presumption of Innocence and Due Process Demand Application of the Sixth Amendment Before Trial*

At the outset, it is important to consider the importance of the presumption of innocence and the jury trial right as potential triggers for the Sixth Amendment jury right pretrial. The presumption of innocence is the starting point where the judge and jury should consider the acts of the defendant.[10] As discussed in Chapter 1, the history of the presumption of innocence and due process is linked. And the entire American legal system is based upon due process. The concept of due process, in its simplest form, is communal justice – no person should be punished without being found guilty by her peers.[11] Bail is an instrument used to ensure one's right to the due process of law by form of security. The concept of bail dates back to 1628 England where the English Petition of Right was written by the legislature: "[N]o man, of what estate or condition that he be, shall be put out of land or tenements, nor taken, nor imprisoned, nor disinherited, nor put to death, without being brought in answer by due process of the law."[12] This notion of due process included a jury decision on guilt – before any sort of punishment was imposed. And this understanding of due process was eventually brought from England to the American colonies. In colonial bail law, individuals involved in capital cases (historically murder and treason) were the exception to this English Petition of Right.[13] These individuals were not guaranteed discharge from imprisonment until trial, whereas those who allegedly committed noncapital offenses were ensured that right.[14] However, currently, these due process ideals are not being met. What we see in our current bail system is that *everyone* who is unable to make bail is kept in jail while awaiting trial, not just those accused of capital offenses.

Indeed, now at initial hearings, prosecutors present information about the crime defendant is charged with, some evidence regarding these charges, and whether bail should be set or, in some cases, why bail should not be offered at all. The information offered is generally regarding the accused's guilt or innocence involving the case at hand. This is information that should not be offered this early on in the trial – where usually defense counsel is not even present – and because it ultimately eliminates a defendant's constitutional right of a presumption of innocence. When a judge decides to enforce a high bail amount or refuses bail altogether based on this out-of-place evidence, he or she has basically deemed the defendant guilty before trial has even commenced. This results in the elimination of the defendant's long-held right to the due process and promise to be deemed innocent until proven guilty by a jury of one's peers. So while due process requires that the right to release is respected before trial, now the majority of defendants are held on bail and denied access to the right to a jury before a determination of guilt.

7.1.2 *Role of Juries in Finding Facts, Weighing Evidence, and Determining Guilt*

Juries are a fundamental part of the judicial system, dating back to the twelfth century and later observed in the Magna Carta and the US Constitution. The responsibility of the jury has traditionally been to find facts and determine if a defendant is guilty of a crime before any punishment is inflicted. Whereas the role of a judge has always been narrowly restricted to ascertaining the law.[15] In ancient courts, juries were the most important players, and "judges were functionaries of only secondary importance."[16] For a judge to provide punishment, a jury had to find a defendant guilty.

Through the 1960s–1980s, the role of a judge expanded to allow fact finding before trial. The 1960s bail reform allowed judges to "weigh the evidence" against a defendant in determining whether a defendant should be released before trial, without a jury. Further, the 1984 Bail Reform Act enabled judges to detain defendants based on the defendant's "risk of danger" to the community. Within this act, the definition of what was constituted as "dangerous" was never defined.[17] The act was upheld after a Supreme Court challenge in the 1987 case, *U.S. v. Salerno*. The Court held that pretrial detention does not constitute punishment, but the decisions made by judges pretrial are simply based on public safety.[18] With the authority granted by the 1984 Bail Reform Act and *U.S. v. Salerno*, judges are now deciding facts and weighing evidence in pretrial hearings to determine dangerousness and decide whether or not bail will be offered to a criminal suspect. This evidence presented by the prosecutor at a bail hearing revokes a defendant's presumption of innocence and is improperly weighed by a judge, not a jury. This ultimately results in the violation of a person's Sixth Amendment rights and therefore should not be permissible.

In order to trigger the Sixth Amendment right to trial by jury, pretrial incarceration must be considered punishment. As Laura Appleman has articulately explained: "[T]he combination of inhumane and degrading conditions, a corrupt and unregulated system of bail surety, bail bondsmen, and bounty hunters, and rising numbers of detainees, with the general absence of criminal due process in the pretrial realm, has resulted in a criminal justice system that punishes before it convicts."[19] Additionally, "[m]uch of pretrial detention, whether based on fears for community safety or flight risk, has an effect virtually indistinguishable from punishment."[20] Given these conditions, courts could certainly find that pretrial detention, in some contexts, constitutes punishment. The argument that pretrial detention can be considered punishment has been made numerous times.[21] When pretrial detention is considered punishment, this would prompt a Sixth Amendment right to trial by jury arguments.

7.1.3 *Juries Should Weigh Evidence at Trial, Not Judges Before Trial*

The Sixth Amendment admonishment that no punishment should be allowed without a factual determination by a jury was recently affirmed by the Supreme Court in the sentencing context. These cases have important pretrial implications that may change the considerations of *Salerno* and help the court determine that pretrial determination of guilt by judges (rather than juries) violates the Sixth Amendment.

The Sixth Amendment of the US Constitution prohibits punishment before a conviction by a jury, "[i]n all criminal prosecutions, the accused shall enjoy the right to . . . trial, by an impartial jury."[22] Moreover, in *Apprendi* v. *New Jersey*, Justice Scalia declared that "all the facts which must exist in order to subject the defendant to a legally prescribed punishment must be found by the jury."[23] Recently, the Supreme Court has brought attention to the right to trial by jury issue in the *Apprendi-Blakely* line of sentencing cases. First, *Apprendi* v. *New Jersey* held that facts regarding a sentencing enhancement that increase a sentence beyond the statutory maximum constitute punishment that needs to be determined by a jury beyond a reasonable doubt. As a result, increased punishment that is contingent upon the finding of facts is to be decided by a jury – not a judge. *Blakely* v. *Washington* followed, suggesting that the community should decide all punishment to be inflicted upon a criminal defendant,[24] and held that a judge may only escalate a sentence based on a sentencing factor if he or she does so without any additional facts.[25] Likewise, *Southern Union Company* v. *United States* depended on the historical nature of the Sixth Amendment right to find that a jury must decide guilt by evaluating each element of a crime beyond a reasonable doubt.[26] The Court extended the right to trial by jury to everything from indictment to criminal fines.[27] Collectively, these cases provide good fodder to advocate that the right to trial by jury, along with the jury being the only arbiter of facts and punishment, should be applicable to pretrial hearings.[28] Judges regularly engage in much more egregious fact finding in bail hearings where they are permitted to weigh evidence to determine how likely it is that a defendant committed a crime. This falls squarely in the jury's historic role, particularly as preserved in the *Apprendi* line of cases.

Taken together, the *Apprendi* line of cases are immensely instructive on the role that due process plays in ensuring a full and fair jury trial, as well as limiting judges to their traditional role as interpreters of law, rather than as triers of fact. The *Apprendi* logic also applies to fact finding pretrial and helps fix the constitutional problem with bail. Under the Sixth Amendment and due process principles, the jury, and not the judge, is the body charged with finding facts. But judges in most jurisdictions in the United States are weighing evidence against defendants before trial in order to determine whether to release them on bail. This pretrial weighing of evidence is often sanctioned by statute in many jurisdictions. The irony that defendants appear to have greater due process rights after they have been found guilty of a crime than before they are even tried for that crime is striking. Applying the principles required by the Sixth Amendment and prohibiting judges from finding facts and applying punishment before trial can resolve this inconsistency – not just *after* the trial is over, but arguably more importantly, *before* it even begins. Applying the Sixth Amendment principles prohibiting judges deciding facts before trial will help restore bail as a constitutional right.

7.1.4 *Proof Beyond a Reasonable Doubt Is Required to Prove Guilt*

For someone to be deprived of his or her liberty, the US Constitution declares that a jury must determine beyond a reasonable doubt (the highest standard of proof) that *every component* of an alleged crime has been proven by the prosecution. *In re Winship* held, "[t]he reasonable-doubt standard plays a vital role in the American scheme of criminal procedure. It is a prime instrument for reducing the risk of convictions resting on factual error."[29] So the hurdle to overcome to place someone in prison after trial is beyond a reasonable doubt.

Pretrial detention is a different story. If a court finds by clear and convincing evidence "that no condition or combination of conditions will reasonably assure the safety of any other person and the community,"[30] a criminal suspect is deemed dangerous and can be detained before he or she is convicted. That law therefore establishes that punishment can be inflicted upon a defendant using less than a reasonable doubt standard before trial. This lower standard to allow pretrial detention – which is a form of punishment – particularly for those who simply cannot be released because they cannot afford a bail payment, is offensive to the Constitution. *Salerno* further supports the idea that the clear and convincing standard is not constitutionally enough to impose punishment. But *Salerno* states that pretrial detention is regulation as opposed to punishment.[31] The Court was careful not to label pretrial detention as punishment, knowing that, if it did, the requirement would then be proof beyond a reasonable doubt. The decision to incarcerate a defendant pretrial should be determined by a jury using the beyond a reasonable standard, anything less violates the guaranteed rights of the Sixth Amendment.

Justice Blackstone wrote, "[A]cts that trammel upon the due process right to trial by fact-finding jury contradict our constitution and must be viewed with a wary and watchful eye." [32] In order to abide by the dictates of the Constitution and prevent the extinction of the presumption of innocence, we must ensure that the only rightful fact finder in criminal cases are members of the community that come together to form a jury and those jury members must only use the highest standard of proof to determine the guilt of a criminal defendant.

7.2 BAIL AND ACCESS TO COUNSEL BEFORE TRIAL

The Sixth Amendment of the US Constitution and most state constitutions guarantee access to counsel for every person accused of a crime. The Sixth Amendment also guarantees a defendant the right to counsel at all critical stages of the criminal proceedings, including pretrial.

The Supreme Court in *Rothgery v. Gillespie County* held in 2008 that the constitutional right to counsel attaches at the initial hearing held within 48 hours of an individual's arrest. This would usually require counsel at the bail determination hearing, but the opinion has been interpreted to allow assignment of counsel soon after this point. The reality of the right to counsel is that it is not universally provided by all states to indigent defendants before their bail hearing. Judges most often set bail for defendants while charges are pending before counsel has been appointed. The problem this provides is that defendants without counsel have a substantially lower chance of being released before trial (two times less likely), obtain more expensive bails ($500 more in one study), and obtain a less favorable trial outcome. And defendants who cannot afford bail must remain incarcerated before trial, even if they are charged with a minor crime and pose little safety risk to the public. This section analyzes the current law in the fifty states on providing access to counsel before trial to determine how we are doing in the goal of providing access to counsel to defendants at their initial bail hearing. Indeed, honoring the Sixth Amendment right to counsel at a bail hearing is critical to honoring bail as a constitutional right.

7.2.1 *Bail Hearing Requires Access to Counsel*

It is important to review the exact process after a person is arrested to understand when counsel should be appointed. Generally, after a person is arrested, they are taken to jail for booking. Under due process of law, a defendant has the right to be brought in front of a judge to review charges, determine if probable cause was established for the arrest, and set bail. This hearing must occur in a "timely manner," which has been defined by the Supreme Court to mean within 48 hours of arrest.[33] These hearings have different names depending on which jurisdiction one is in and if they are combined with another hearing. Some common terms used within this realm of bail are bail hearing, arraignment, pretrial release hearing, and initial appearance. The bail hearing is the first time the defendant appears in front of a judge with the opportunity to be released while awaiting trial. Like the other stages of criminal proceedings, an attorney has a greater ability to represent a defendant at a bail hearing due to their knowledge of the law, experience, and training.

Without counsel, a defendant at a bail hearing is severely disadvantaged. "An accused standing alone is virtually defenseless, disadvantaged, and often silenced when a judicial officer orders an unaffordable financial bond as a condition of pretrial release."[34] Indeed, one teenage defendant, Darian Watson, who was denied counsel spent a year in pretrial detention without any access to a lawyer.[35] In his own words, "[A]s soon as I knew that I was denied bail, it just set in: well, you're not going anywhere. No Chance. It was really devastating for my immediate family, . . . especially for my mother . . . There was no hope[.]"[36] Defendants without counsel lack the knowledge, skill, experience, and training required to obtain pretrial release on their own recognizance or achieve an affordable bail. In addition, they are in large part completely incognizant of the safeguards available to them by state law and the US Constitution.

Without defense counsel present at a bail hearing, there is no one to challenge the prosecutor's recommendation to the judge. Criminal defense attorneys are the only people who are able to ensure bail is not being indecorously used by judges and prosecutors. In some states, upon booking for certain crimes, judges adhere to what is called a "bail schedule." A bail schedule is a guideline set by that particular state that provides the amount of bail to be paid. Without defense counsel, a judge may set bail according to a schedule and not consider the means a defendant has to pay the bail amount. At hearings, defense lawyers are able to advocate for their client's release by understanding and promoting the arguments that judges are receptive to in making bail decisions.

7.2.2 *Importance of Attorney at Bail Hearing*

When it comes to the effect that lawyers have at bail hearings, there have been two major projects that have outlined the exact effects attorneys have on their clients' cases when they are present at bail hearings. Understanding the circumstances and results of these projects is helpful in understanding the importance of the pretrial Sixth Amendment right to counsel.

7.2.2.1 Manhattan Bail Project and Pretrial Rights

Louis Schweitzer was a chemical engineer[37] and prosperous New York businessman[38] with no legal training. He was outraged when he found that one's mere inability to post bail caused so many people to await trial in prison. He became informed about the bail system, specifically about the duration of imprisonment that ranged from months to over a year and the fact that oftentimes the charges brought against these prisoners were dropped. This alarming information inspired him to investigate bail in New York City in the 1960s. Louis Schweitzer was soon introduced to Herbert Sturz, a journalist,[39] through a mutual friend and soon discovered that they had a shared interest in criminal justice reform.[40] Following their meeting, Schweitzer and Sturz visited a Manhattan prison and noticed many people held there because they were unable to make bail.[41] In response to their findings, Schweitzer created the Vera Foundation and appointed Sturz as the director in order to investigate and mitigate unjust bail practices.[42] After much research, Sturz determined that the best solution would be to release defendants on their own recognizance. Schweitzer agreed and pitched the idea to Robert Wagner, the New York Mayor, who also supported it.[43] With the help of the New York University School of Law and the Institute of Judicial Administration, the Manhattan Bail Project was born in 1961.[44]

New York University law students, research associates, and secretaries began the quest of providing judges with corroborated background, financial, and personal information about defendants in order to make an informed bail decision. The volunteers reviewed cases of charged defendants who did not have counsel but excluded those charged with prostitution, certain sex crimes, and crimes linked to narcotics due to the lack of roots the typical offender of these crimes had with the community.[45] Researchers distributed questionnaires where defendants provided information regarding criminal history, employment history, duration of residency, family ties, etc. This information was confirmed and then used to determine if a defendant was likely to show up for trial. From this information, researchers suggested that release on one's own recognizance was best suited for those defendants who were likely to attend future court hearings.[46] In order to properly track the results of the Manhattan Bail Project, some defendants qualified for the program were separated into a control group. In this control group, the judge decided on bail without any interference from the project. This way the control group results could be compared with the experimental group, with whom the project made suggestions.[47]

The Manhattan Bail Project achieved outstanding results and was an overwhelming success: "[F]rom October 16, 1961, through April 8, 1964, out of 13,000 total defendants, 3,000 fell into the excluded offense [ineligible for bail] category, 10,000 were interviewed, 4,000 were recommended [release on recognizance] and 2,195 were paroled. Only 15 of these failed to show up in court, a default rate of less than 7/10 of 1 percent."[48] Additionally, at the start of the study, 28 percent of defendants interviewed were recommended for release and that increased to 65 percent by the end. And judges' agreement with recommendations went from 55 percent to 70 percent. Significantly, the District Attorney's office, which initially agreed with about half of Vera's recommendations, by the end of the study agreed with almost 80 percent.[49] In just the first year of the project, release recommendations allowed four times as many people to be released than previously.[50]

The Manhattan Bail Project also carefully tracked the outcomes of defendant's cases. The results were a resounding success as 60 percent of the recommended defendants were acquitted or had their cases dismissed compared with only 23 percent of the control group.[51] And out of the project group, of the 40 percent who were found guilty, only one out of six was sentenced to prison. In contrast, 96 percent of the convicted defendants in the control group were sentenced to serve jail time.[52] The Manhattan Bail Project demonstrated early on that with pretrial advocacy provided on behalf of defendants more people can be released before trial – and return for their court dates. It also significantly demonstrated that providing information to judges helps defendants avoid jail time and conviction. The Manhattan Bail Project did not provide counsel to defendants, but its results were similar to later studies comparing defendants with or without counsel at bail hearings. The next project is such an example.

7.2.2.2   Colbert's LAB project and Access to Counsel Pretrial

Roughly thirty-seven years later, Professor Douglas Colbert followed in the footsteps of the Vera Foundation to improve pretrial rights.[53] While managing a program where law students served as counsel for indigent defendants suspected of committing misdemeanors, he became aware of the injustices that were occurring in regards to pretrial release and representation. Specifically, he noticed that attorneys were not present for any bail hearings of indigent defendants, the overwhelming majority of whom were African-Americans charged with nonviolent offenses. Where there was no legal counsel present,[54]

Colbert found that bail was reaffirmed for 85–90 percent of cases.[55] Colbert was under the impression that attorneys were mandated to appear and represent defendants at bail and bail review hearings under the Sixth and Fourteenth Amendments.[56] He was shocked to find his assumption to be completely incorrect in practice. In fact, very few municipalities in Maryland actually required counsel at an initial hearing. This was not a rare case that was only seen within Maryland, but unfortunately it was (and is) the case in the majority of states across the United States.[57] Because no legal counsel attended the poor incarcerated defendants' hearings, defendants were forced to sit in jail for thirty to forty-five days until their next court date.[58] Colbert initially hoped to find attorneys to attend pretrial release hearings, but he learned that the public defenders did not have sufficient funding or staff to provide attorneys at bail hearings.[59] Colbert decided that law students could represent indigent defendants at pretrial release hearings. With the help of Judge Mary Ellen Reinhardt, school approval, and later funding, the Access to Justice Clinic began in the spring of 1998 at Maryland Law School and later became the Lawyers at Bail Project (LAB).[60]

The Lawyers at Bail Project started in August 1998, consisting of three paralegals and twenty attorneys who had an office in the District Courthouse.[61] In an effort to prove LAB's efficacy, the project hired social scientists to administer an empirical experiment on the effect of counsel at bail hearings. The study was controlled and randomized by appointing attorneys to 175 of the 300 defendants who were predetermined to qualify for LAB based on their purported crime being nonviolent. Those suspects who were randomly assigned attorneys served as the experimental group ("LAB clients") and 125 qualified defendants that were not assigned attorneys served as the control group ("non-LAB clients"). Law students attended the pretrial hearings and interviewed defendants and gathered data about the cases along with their results.

Similar to the Manhattan Bail Project, the results showed that LAB was a success. Five main areas were examined, including release on own recognizance, bail reduction, amount of bail reduction, bail reduction to $500 or less, and amount of time spent in jail. The average original bail set for the experimental group (with attorneys) was $3,357 and $3,178 for the control group (without attorneys).[62] Following a bail review hearing, 34 percent of LAB clients were released on their own recognizance compared to 13 percent of non-LAB clients; those defendants with attorneys were more than two and a half times more likely to be released on their own recognizance than those without attorneys.[63] When students provided judges with verified personal information about their client, a total of 70 percent were discharged. This was because their bail was minimized to an amount they were actually able to pay or they were released on their own recognizance.[64] Indeed, bail was reduced by 59 percent for LAB defendants and bail was only lowered for 14 percent of non-LAB defendants. This resulted in the LAB defendants being over four times more likely to have their bail amount reduced.[65] Of those who were able to get their bail lowered, the ones with lawyers had theirs lowered dramatically more than those without. LAB suspects had their average bail reduced from $3,357 to $2,441, a $916 difference (and 33 percent decrease). Whereas non-LAB bail average went from $3,178 to $3,012, only a $166 difference (and an only 5 percent decrease).[66]

A secondary effect measured by LAB was how much time clients were spending in jail. The median time spent in jail for a LAB defendant was two days as opposed to nine for non-LAB clients, showing that arrestees without attorneys spent seven more days behind bars than their LAB counterparts. Also, defendants that had attorneys at their bail review hearings were left feeling more satisfied than those who did not have attorneys.[67] The client's perception of fair treatment is important because if they believe the hearing was fair they are more likely to "express an intention to comply with the bail decision."[68]

The positive results from both the Manhattan Bail Project and the Lawyers at Bail Project are undeniable. The benefits of having an attorney present at bail and bail review hearings include, but are not limited to being, more likely to be acquitted or have their case dismissed, less likely to serve jail time if convicted, more likely to be released on recognizance, more likely to have their original bail decreased by a larger amount, and more likely to be given affordable bail. There is no question that legal counsel has a substantially positive effect at pretrial release hearings. And ultimately, Sixth Amendment rights to counsel are better protected when a defendant is represented at their initial bail hearing. However, as discussed in more detail later, over fifty years have passed since the Manhattan Bail Project and almost twenty since LAB and the majority of states still do not mandate counsel at pretrial release hearings.

7.2.3 *State of Pretrial Sixth Amendment Law*

The Sixth Amendment of the US Constitution declares, "[I]n all criminal prosecutions, the accused shall enjoy the right . . . to have the Assistance of Counsel for his defense."[69] An indigent defendant's right to a lawyer at an initial hearing under the Sixth Amendment applies when two conditions are satisfied: First, the right to counsel must "attach." This right attaches at "the first formal adversarial proceeding against the defendant, even if that procedure does not involve a prosecutor."[70] Then, "once attachment occurs, the accused at least is entitled to the presence of appointed counsel during any 'critical stage' of the post attachment proceedings."[71] Critical stages are defined as "proceedings between an individual and agents of the State whether 'formal or informal, in court or out,' that amount to 'trial-like confrontations,' at which counsel would help the accused 'in coping with legal problems or . . . meeting his adversary.'"[72]

The Supreme Court's holding in *Rothgery* v. *Gillespie County, Texas* made progress for explicitly guaranteeing an indigent defendant the right to an attorney at their bail hearing.[73] In 2002, Walter Rothgery, the defendant, was arrested for possessing a firearm as a felon, even though he had never actually been convicted of a felony. This mistake was due to a computer glitch showing he had been convicted, when in reality his felony arrest had been dismissed.[74] He then attended a pretrial hearing without an attorney, where a $5,000 bail was set. If Walter Rothgery had an attorney at the bail hearing, he could have proved that he never was convicted of a felony. Instead, Rothgery's wife posted bail for him and he was released. He repeatedly tried to get an attorney assigned to him through oral and written requests because he could not afford one, but his efforts were refused. And due to his unresolved felony charge, he was unable to get a job.[75] M. Patrick Maguire, Rothgery's attorney, described, "[N]o one wanted to hire someone they thought was a prior felon who now faced a new felony of carrying a loaded gun and allegedly making threats."[76] With no job to provide reliable revenue, Walter and his wife were incapable of paying their rent and subsequently lost the home they had been renting. Luckily, they found a landlord willing to trade Rothgery's work for a place to live.

However, that luck soon ran out when he was indicted by a grand jury and consequently arrested again, after being out on bail for six months. To make matters worse, his bail was tripled to $15,000. Unable to pay the bail, he went to jail for three weeks and was moved to a facility where his wife was unable to visit.[77] His request for an attorney was finally granted at this point despite his prior six months of requests and denials. Rothgery's lawyer got his bail reduced and was able to prove that Walter had never even been convicted of a felony by simply speaking to a probation officer. The documentation showing Walter was not convicted of a felony was given to the prosecutor and a judge dismissed the charge an entire nine and a half months after Walter had been initially arrested.

Rothgery then filed a lawsuit against Gillespie County declaring that his Sixth Amendment right to counsel was violated by Gillespie County's practice of not providing attorneys to released indigent defendants until an indictment or entry of information. Furthermore, he claimed if he had been given an attorney at that time, he never would have been arrested the second time nor subsequently been imprisoned because he could have proved he was never convicted of a felony in the first place.[78] The Court agreed with Rothgery, holding that "a criminal defendant's initial appearance before a judicial officer, where he learns the charge against him and his liberty is subject to restriction, marks the start of adversary judicial proceedings that trigger attachment of the Sixth Amendment right to counsel" and "what makes a stage critical is what shows the need for counsel's presence."[79]

Rothgery's holding is significant, but just how significant has proven to be the problem. *Rothgery* recognizes the crucial importance of an indigent defendant's right to counsel following an initial appearance. However, the ruling was very limited. The court did pinpoint when adversary judicial proceedings begin, which is at the initial hearing, but *Rothgery's* holding only casually mentioned the idea that an attorney could be assigned in a "reasonable time" following the initial hearing.[80] Justice Alito explained, in his concurrence, that even though the holding states that the right to counsel "attaches" at the initial hearing, the court did not declare that a lawyer had to be appointed to an indigent defendant when attachment occurs. Thus, the law still does not *mandate* appointment of counsel specifically for the initial appearance, leaving indigent defendants to fend for themselves when their liberty is at stake at the critical bail hearing and enabling circumstances like Rothgery's to continue to occur.[81]

In order to constitutionally require that states provide an attorney to defendants at the initial hearing, the initial appearance will have to be deemed to be a "critical stage." According to *United States* v. *Wade*, a critical stage is any time during prosecution, formal or informal, where there is a potential substantial prejudice to the defendant's rights.[82] This was recently refined by *Bell* v. *Cone*, which deemed a critical stage as a "step of a criminal proceeding . . . that h[olds] significant consequences for the accused."[83] In addition, *Rothgery* holds that when there is potential substantial prejudice there is a need for counsel.[84] If initial appearances are deemed as a "critical stage," it would essentially guarantee an attorney to be present during initial hearings.

7.2.4 *Access to Counsel for Bail Hearing: How the Fifty States Stack Up*

If *Rothgery* taught us anything, it exposed that the Supreme Court knows little to nothing about state court bail practices, making it vital to inform them about the realities of how unjust and dysfunctional the status quo genuinely is.[85] Douglas Colbert, of the LAB project, believes that when the time comes to address this issue in the Supreme Court, the key will be educating the justices on how states and counties handle the appointment of counsel. To prepare for this, Colbert sent 900 surveys to public defenders in 2008–2009. This survey demonstrates an array of practices in appointing counsel at the initial appearance including a majority of states who do not require council at an initial bail hearing.[86] Where counsel is not provided at bail hearings, a defendant will wait in jail at a minimum of seven days, but usually a month or more before returning to court to meet his assigned counsel.

According to Colbert's survey, only ten states and the District of Columbia actually guarantee poor defendants the right to an attorney at the initial bail hearing. Those ten states include California, Connecticut, Delaware, Florida, Hawaii, Maine, Massachusetts, North Dakota, Vermont, and Wisconsin.[87] Further, in Minnesota, Montana, Oregon, and Washington, approximately three-quarters of the municipalities require an assigned attorney advocate for poor suspects at their first appearance.[88] In contrast, ten states outright deny counsel to suspects who cannot afford defense counsel at the initial hearing: Alabama, Kansas, Maryland, Michigan, Mississippi, New Hampshire, Oklahoma, South Carolina, Tennessee, and Texas.[89] The majority of states, thirty to be exact, are "hybrid" states. In these states, the county where the arrest takes place ultimately determines if the right to counsel is guaranteed at the initial hearing. Hybrid states are split into two groups; the first group consists of "majority hybrid" states, which favor representation by appointing an attorney at the initial appearance in the majority of the state's local courts. The twelve "majority hybrid" states are Idaho, Kentucky, Louisiana, Minnesota, Montana, New York, Ohio, Oregon, Rhode Island, Utah, Virginia, and Washington – with Kentucky, Minnesota, Montana, New York, Oregon, Rhode Island, Utah, and Washington having "considerably better odds for an indigent defendant gaining early representation in most locations within the statewide jurisdiction."[90] The second group are "minority hybrid" states, where less than half of the localities, frequently only one or two, require an appointed lawyer's appearance at initial bail hearings for poor suspects. The following states fall into that "minority hybrid" category: Alaska, Arizona, Arkansas, Colorado, Georgia, Illinois, Indiana, Iowa, Missouri, Nebraska, Nevada, New Jersey, New Mexico, North Carolina, Pennsylvania, South Dakota, West Virginia, and Wyoming.[91] The overall picture that 2008–2009 survey data illustrates is that about *half* of the country has practices where indigent defendants attend their bail hearing in front of a judge without a lawyer by their side to advocate on their behalf.

7.2.5 *Guaranteeing Attorneys for Bail Hearings*

As demonstrated in the last section, only about half the counties in the country require representation for defendants. There are several reasons that jurisdictions should mandate counsel for defendants at initial hearings where bail is decided. Defendants benefit in several ways from having counsel present. With the help of counsel, defendants often receive release on recognizance more often, smaller bail amounts if bail is set, less jail time before trial, and a lower likelihood of conviction. Without representation, there are also risks of substantial prejudice and significant consequences for the accused. Some of these risks include the self-incrimination of *pro se* defendants, a substantial prejudice to a defendant's right to liberty, an obstructed ability to assist with their own defense, the possibility of defendants pleading guilty just to be released from jail, and the danger of receiving a harsher sentence in general. Lack of access to counsel negatively impacts a defendant's right to a fair trial under the Sixth Amendment.

7.2.5.1 Self-Incrimination Is Likely Without Counsel

First, defendants without counsel are unable to advocate effectively and the absence of counsel at bail hearings usually leads to defendants incriminating themselves. Without counsel, suspects are prone to speak freely in an effort to secure their release, not knowing that what they say will be used against them at trial. Also, they are unable to take advantage of the rights and opportunities afforded to them due to their lack of knowledge about the law and inability to advocate for themselves.

For instance, Donald Fenner, an indigent defendant, was charged with the distribution of cocaine and conspiracy to distribute cocaine for a $50 drug transaction.[92] At his bail hearing, when asked by the judge, "[I]s there anything you'd like to tell me about yourself, sir?" Instead of choosing to remain silent or answering appropriately, he unknowingly and voluntarily incriminated himself in a lengthy monologue stating, "[Y]our Honor, this is just for me to make ends meet, to make money for me to be able to get by. They never caught me that (indiscernible) amount of drugs on me. You know what I'm sayin'. I mean I'm not denying what happened but when they caught me, they didn't catch me with nothing but that $50." To which the judge replied, "Sir, you need to have a lawyer just as soon as you can."[93] Fenner's admission and failure to invoke his Fifth Amendment right to remain silent was likely an attempt at honesty in hopes of ensuring release; however, it almost single-handedly ended up leading to his ultimate conviction and twenty-year sentence.[94]

7.2.5.2 Obstructed Ability to Assist with Own Defense

Although the Sixth Amendment promises the right of the accused to assist in his or her own defense,[95] when held in jail, they are severely limited in doing so. Specifically, the communication that occurs between attorneys and their imprisoned clients becomes extremely difficult and oftentimes there are restrictions on what prisoners can receive via mail.[96] This is problematic due to discovery that requires the exchange of various documents that need to be reviewed by the defendant. Furthermore, the duration and scheduling of visitation time and telephone calls impede the frequency and quality of attorney–client conversations. Additionally, detained suspects cause the investigation process to become extended and convoluted. An investigator is forced to spend precious time jumping through hoops to obtain necessary information and materials (such as names, addresses, phone numbers, documents) that could have been effortlessly provided by the client had him or her not been locked up.[97] Lastly, law books and internet resources are often inaccessible, inadequate, or nonexistent, making it essentially impossible for defendants to ascertain legal knowledge and aid in their own research. These factors contribute to the delay in case building and result in inadequate preparation of a defense, ultimately creating substantial prejudice and damaging consequences for the accused.

Moreover, the jail setting compromises confidentiality for visitation, mail, and phone calls. It is rare for visitation to be truly private due to bystanders; mail is often opened despite the "legal mail" label and telephone correspondence is recorded. For instance, inmates in federal prison are constantly having their emails read by Bureau of Prisons staff, and it often is passed on to opposing counsel, despite the emails to lawyers clearly marked as "attorney–client" communications.[98] So unless state and federal jails institute new communications systems (which would be extremely expensive),[99] it is nearly impossible for indigent defendants to receive the benefit of the help of counsel while in jail.

7.2.5.3 People Unable to Afford Bail Plead Guilty Just To Be Released from Jail

Incarcerated defendants are more likely to plead guilty just to be released from jail. A major dilemma many criminal defendants face when they are unable to post bail is deciding between the options of pleading guilty to a crime they did not commit or waiting in jail a lengthy amount of time for trial to prove their innocence. Pleading guilty to a crime an individual did not commit may sound unlikely, but for many it is a viable option to preserve life as they know it. Defendants may spend up to a year in jail awaiting trial, and the repercussions of awaiting trial in jail are devastating. Being removed from society causes many to face eviction, deportation, forfeiture of child custody, and the loss of their job, along with a decreased ability to obtain a new one. Scott Hechinger, a senior trial attorney with Brooklyn Defender Services, knows all too well about the effects jail time can have on indigent defendants. He described the predicament well in the *New York Times*:

> Our clients work in service-level positions where if you're gone for a day, you lose your job. People in need of caretaking – the elderly, the young – are left without caretakers. People who live in shelters, where if they miss their curfews, they lose their housing. Folks with immigration concerns are quicker to be put on the immigration radar. So when our clients have bail set, they suffer on the inside, they worry about what's happening on the outside, and when they get out, they come back to a world that's more difficult than the already difficult situation that they were in before.[100]

When faced with these grave consequences, many feel as if they have no other choice but to plead guilty and get back to their daily responsibilities.

One unfortunate example is William Cedric Wheeler, who was placed in this exact predicament in 2009 after being charged with stealing on the job.[101] Despite having no prior convictions and maintaining his innocence, he decided to plead guilty out of fear of being separated from his six children. Part of his plea deal required him to pay $3,069.80 of restitution to his former employer. Pleading guilty resulted in his life circumstances becoming significantly worse. The conviction of theft made it near impossible for him to find a decent job, which subsequently resulted in Wheeler getting his tax refund withheld, falling behind in child support payments, and only being able to put $1,000 toward the restitution he owed. After some time, Wheeler was able to secure a reliable job and started to get his life back on track. Unfortunately, soon thereafter, he had a stroke. Medical bills piled up, along with the remaining $2,069.80 restitution he owed. He was arrested for not paying the restitution in full, could not afford to make bail, and spent a month and a half in jail. Everything he had hoped to avoid in the first place by pleading guilty came to fruition. Mr. Wheeler had his car repossessed, lost his job, lost his home, and lost countless possessions. He, his wife, and his children ended up staying in motels and living out of a minivan, which held everything they owned.[102]

7.2.5.4 More Likely to Get Convicted, Receive Jail Sentence, and Receive a Harsh Sentence

Those who are incarcerated awaiting trial are much more likely to be convicted, receive a custodial sentence, and receive a harsher jail sentence than those who obtain pretrial release. This is all linked back to the effects lawyers have at bail hearings.[103] The time spent in jail is relevant because the more time a defendant spends imprisoned, the more likely she is to be convicted. In fact, a report based on ten years of bail research in New York City shows that those who are incarcerated prior to trial are convicted at a much higher degree than those who are not. When it comes to nonfelony charges, 50 percent of defendants who were not incarcerated before trial were convicted, as opposed to 92 percent of defendants who were imprisoned until resolution.[104] Spending time in jail dramatically increases whether a defendant will obtain a custodial sentence. Demonstrating to a judge that the defendant has maintained their job and home after arrest, in contrast, makes judges feel a lot more comfortable imposing a sentence of community service or probation.

As this section demonstrates, there are substantial risks and significant consequences that occur based simply on the outcome of a bail hearing. The consequences of not obtaining counsel for a bail hearing include self-incrimination, a less successful defense and higher likelihood of conviction, and a likelihood of pleading guilty simply to be released and a harsher sentence. Because of this, only an attorney's training and experience is able to mitigate these risks, clearly exhibiting that bail hearings require the need of counsel's presence, ultimately qualifying this as a "critical stage." Considering the potential risks that defendants encounter when it comes to facing substantial prejudice to a fair trial and the probable consequences to the accused that arise from initial hearings, the fact that attorneys are not yet mandated at indigent defendant's bail hearings is wholly unacceptable.

7.3 CONCLUSION

In the United States, at any given time, approximately 450,000 people, many of whom are accused of nonviolent offenses, are incarcerated as pretrial detainees because they are denied bail or cannot afford to pay the amount of bail that is set.[105] These people suffer behind bars for days, weeks, even months, and ultimately lose much more than just their freedom. As a direct result of pretrial incarceration, many lose their jobs, homes, possessions, and custody of their children. This appalling reality occurs in part because these individuals lacked legal representation at their bail hearings. Only about half of indigent Americans have access to counsel at their initial bail hearings, even though the Sixth Amendment guarantees defendants counsel for every critical stage of their proceedings.

This chapter demonstrates that the initial bail hearing is a critical stage of a judicial proceeding. Studies over the years have demonstrated that having an attorney advocate for defendants at bail hearings significantly improves the accused's probability of being released on her own recognizance, having their bail reduced (and by a larger amount), having bail set affordably, and spending less time in jail. In addition, not having counsel at a bail hearing often results in self-incrimination, increased incarceration, inability to prepare an adequate defense, and additional pressure to plead guilty despite innocence. Because of this, the right to counsel must be extended to the pretrial phase for defendants nationally in order to combat the injustices of current bail practices.

On top of that, judges are infringing upon the Sixth Amendment right to trial by jury in determining facts at the bail hearing. The presumption of innocence guaranteed to criminal defendants loses its meaning when judges are deciding matters of guilt or innocence at the pretrial phase. The only way to safeguard an accused's presumption of innocence is to leave all issues of guilt and innocence up to a jury. Judges are constitutionally barred from making such determinations because of the right to a jury trial. When judges make factual determinations, they are using an unacceptable and unconstitutional standard of proof which is less than beyond a reasonable doubt. The only standard by which criminal matters should be judged is beyond a reasonable doubt. The importance of the jury as the finder of fact has only begun to be revisited pretrial – as it has been in the sentencing context with *Apprendi* and its progeny – and it is imperative that judicial actions pretrial are examined under a Sixth Amendment lens for this right to be lawfully expanded to bail hearings.

The extension of the rights to counsel to all defendants pretrial and respect of the right to trial by jury at bail hearings will ensure criminal defendants receive the rights explicitly afforded to them by the Sixth Amendment of the Constitution. By all accounts, this is a step in the right direction for achieving "justice for all."

8

Pretrial Detention and Terrorism in Post-9/11 America

[T]he rules of war mark the minimal constraints that we must respect in our dealings with other human beings, whatever they have done. So even if we cannot or should not see some terrorist groups as criminals who should be subjected to (and so also protected by) the normal criminal process, we should minimally see them as enemies whom we should treat with the minimal respect and decency required by the rules of war.

—Antony Duff[1]

In the wake of the September 11 attacks on the World Trade Center, the basic guarantee of American justice, "innocent until proven guilty," has transformed into "guilty until proven guilty" for some suspected terrorists.[2] The world of pretrial detention after 9/11 has changed dramatically. So much so that it is difficult to discuss modern bail rights without comparing the differences in detention for suspected terrorists and average criminal defendants. National security interests have led to indefinite detention without bail for terror suspects, while some cry foul at the abuse of human rights.[3] The key question with the increased suspicion of homegrown terror after 9/11 is what are the rights to pretrial release of suspected terrorists? In other words, should suspected terrorists be granted the right to release before trial or do they pose a danger too great to be released? Does it matter if the terror suspect is an American citizen or resident or a foreign alien? And do suspected terrorists have the right to a federal trial or can they be detained indefinitely in military tribunals? All of these important questions have been considered in the last fifteen years and are discussed in this chapter.

This chapter starts by discussing some of the legal justifications for the denial of bail to terrorism suspects. These justifications include the Eighth Amendment and ordinary denials under the flight risk standard. It then lays out the specific federal laws allowing the denial of bail for terrorism suspects – including the Patriot Act and Special Administrative Measures (SAMs). Next, it compares the courts used to charge terrorism suspects, which include military courts and civilian federal courts. Finally, it briefly discusses the law of war and the impact of classifying a terrorist as a civilian, combatant, or enemy combatant on how they are treated in the courts.

Overall this chapter demonstrates that suspected terrorists do not maintain broad pretrial release rights. Bail laws applicable to other dangerous defendants prohibit suspected terrorists from obtaining pretrial release. But there are a handful of other federal laws (SAMs, Patriot Act, etc.) that also provide justification to detain suspected terrorists pretrial and to limit their communication and rights vis-à-vis the outside world. Some terrorism suspects have been detained in military centers, like Guantanamo, and while these detentions have been criticized greatly, detaining these individuals safely on US soil presents substantial budgetary and security challenges. As a whole, however, after detention, terrorism suspects have been tried successfully in federal and military courts, with greatest success in federal courts, given the plethora of federal statutes available to charge defendants.

8.1 LEGAL JUSTIFICATIONS FOR THE DENIAL OF BAIL TO TERRORISM SUSPECTS

Courts have found several ways to deny pretrial release to suspected terrorists. In that sense, suspected terrorists are worse off under the law than garden-variety defendants. While the Eighth Amendment was used historically to prohibit courts from setting excessive bail for suspected communists, modern courts post-9/11 have had no problem with setting high bails to avoid the release of suspected terrorists pretrial. Courts have also relied on flight risk – and foreign ties – as a justification to detain suspected terrorists before trial. In federal court, several laws discussed allow presumptive detention of suspected terrorists and limit the rights of these defendants while they are held.

8.1.1 *Eighth Amendment and Flight Risk as Justification for Denying Bail*

The Supreme Court has historically made clear that setting a high bail amount simply to keep a defendant behind bars before trial violates the Eighth Amendment. The Eighth Amendment prohibits the setting of excessive bail. However, modern-day judges have set extremely high bail amounts to prevent defendants from release before trial. The handling of the communist scare in the 1950s gives us an interesting parallel in considering bail for suspected terrorists today. In the early 1950s, while Senator McCarthy and many in the country warned of a severe threat of communist spies, the Supreme

Court ruled in the case *Stack* v. *Boyle* that bail is guaranteed for all but capital offenders and should not be excessive under the Eighth Amendment.[4] *Stack* involved a case where a judge set an extremely high bail for suspected communists. The Supreme Court upheld release rights even for suspected spies against the country, where excessive means greater than that usually set for crimes with similar penalties.[5] Indeed, the Court made clear that bail is conditioned upon adequate assurance that the defendant will stand trial and submit to the judgment and sentence passed, and should not be used as a tool to keep a defendant detained.[6] Thus, the 1950s Supreme Court favored granting a standard bail to suspected communists unless there was a proven flight risk. Current bail standards have dramatically shifted from this standard and are not so generous for suspected terrorists today.

Terrorism suspects are rarely granted bail rights due to federal laws discussed later. However, in some cases, a judge will grant a suspected terrorist an extremely high bail that it would be impossible for him to afford rather than denying bail altogether. For instance, in 2014, Abdirahman Mohamud exchanged communications with his brother Abed, who died while engaging in violent jihad in Syria.[7] Mohamud expressed desire to join the war and allegedly attended a terrorist training camp with Abed in Syria.[8] Mohamud returned to the United States just days after his brother died, with instructions from a cleric to carry out an act of terrorism.[9] Federal authorities arrested Mohamud after a Federal Bureau of Investigation (FBI) investigation concluded his intent to commit an act of terrorism.[10] Although prosecutors requested a $2.5 million bail, arguing national security, the state magistrate judge set bail at $1 million, an amount Mohamud still could not afford.[11] Mohamud's bail begs the question of why the court even bothered to set a bail since only the most wealthy defendants could even afford such a high bail. Given Mohamud's serious foreign ties, why did the judge not simply state that Mohamud was a flight risk and could not be guaranteed to return to his trial. Under current standards, the judge could have also expressed a concern for public safety if he were released.

In other terrorism cases, judges have relied on flight risk as the rationale for denying bail. Flight risk is a natural reason to detain terrorism suspects before trial since many have foreign passports and foreign connections, allowing possibilities to escape US trial. In 2003, Deputy Attorney General Larry D. Thompson testified before Congress that a Hezbollah supporter charged with providing material support to a terrorist organization was released on bail. Before his trial date, the supporter fled the United States and was living in Beirut at the time of the court date.[12] Thompson used this story to help argue in favor of presumptive detention of terrorists. If Thompson was correct, then

Mohamud's excessive bail (which was effectively a denial of bail) is arguably consistent with the Court's decision in *Stack*, because the required reassurance that he will appear before trial will not be met if he is released on bail. However, the better way to deny bail to terrorism suspects is based on flight risk, rather than an excessively high bail that arguably violates *Stack* v. *Boyle*.

In some circumstances, the required assurance is met, and courts have released terrorism suspects before trial. For example, Abdullahi Yusuf, a teenager living in Minnesota, was stopped from fleeing the country at the Minneapolis airport in 2014.[13] Yusuf was charged with "conspiracy to provide material support to a foreign terrorist organization." The prosecutors argued against his release, claiming he was a flight risk, even though he was living with his parents at the time. The judge, deciding Yusuf was not a flight risk, released him to a halfway home with a GPS bracelet and limited internet and communication privileges.[14]

The Eighth Amendment provides powerful precedent to prevent judges from setting high bails in order to detain a terrorist before trial. However, it has not been compelling to modern-day judges. Current bail standards are determined in large part by the events surrounding the September 11, 2001, attacks on the World Trade Center. Judges have continued to set high bail amounts to prevent terrorists from obtaining release or deemed terrorism suspects a flight risk under modern-day standards. In addition, a series of changes in federal law allow judges to presumptively detain terrorism suspects before trial. The next section will discuss the four major avenues of federal law available for obtaining detention without bail: the Intelligence Reform and Terrorism Prevention Act (IRITPA), SAMs, the Patriot Act, and the Bail Reform Act.

8.1.2 *Federal Standards for Pretrial Detention Without Bail*

Individuals charged with crimes of terrorism are treated differently in the US criminal justice system. Most of these individuals are charged in federal court or military court, rather than in state court. The vast majority that are brought to trial in federal court are subject to the four federal laws discussed later. The laws as a whole allow a rebuttable presumption of detention for terrorism suspects, restrict terrorists while detained with limits on communication and isolation, and even more broadly permit temporary and even indefinite detention for aliens posing a threat of terrorism.

8.1.2.1 Intelligence Reform and Terrorism Prevention Act (IRITPA)

In federal court, one way to detain a defendant before trial is through legislation called the IRITPA. This act provides a rebuttable presumption of detention without bail before trial for a variety of crimes and was expanded to include terrorism in 2004.[15] The act (18 USC § 3142) expanded the crime classified as terrorism, which was already listed as a crime justifying detention, and provided a probable-cause standard for detention without bail.[16] This presumption of detention is similar for individuals charged with drug crimes (where the drugs they are carrying are greater than a certain amount), and those charged with certain acts of violence. IRITPA was not without opposition, but supporters considered it "bizarre" that drug offenders could be detained without bail, but not terrorists.[17] Justified with similar arguments, the SAMs discussed in the next section were introduced for drug offenders and appropriated into the terrorism sphere.

8.1.2.2 Special Administrative Measures

Even before 9/11, in 1996, federal officials obtained the power to invoke SAMs for terrorism suspects.[18] SAMs authorize the government to take "reasonably necessary" steps to prevent disclosure of confidential information if the disclosure would threaten national security.[19] The measures may include severely limited communication privileges and contact with the outside world.

Reasonably necessary steps may be quite harsh. Syed Fahad Hashmi was arrested in 2006 in London on charges of providing material support to Al-Qaeda. Hashmi was denied bail. Then, after five months of imprisonment, Attorney General Eric Holder enacted SAMs on Hashmi. Despite Hashmi's substantial ties to New York and nonexistent criminal record, Holder justified SAMs because of Hashmi's "proclivity for violence." Hashmi was placed under strict surveillance, with no privacy for bathing or the bathroom. Additionally, he could only hand-write a letter to his family once a week and was allowed one visit by one parent every two weeks, which was often denied at the prison for administrative reasons.[20]

The use of SAMs for terrorism suspects raises serious constitutional concerns. SAMs limits due process, the right of access to counsel, and free speech. Solitary confinement like Hashmi's has negative mental health consequences and may be a form of cruel or unusual punishment.[21] Some scholars argue for increased reviewability, consistency, and transparency in their application.[22] However, similarly restrictive measures are available for garden-variety criminal defendants, such as the Special Housing Unit in federal court.[23] Despite the use of similar measures for common criminals, SAMs still represent a significant limitation on the right to pretrial release. In addition to SAMs, aliens face the decision of deportation or detention under the Patriot Act, discussed in more detail later.

8.1.2.3 Patriot Act and Pretrial Detention

The Patriot Act allows detention, without pretrial release, of any alien who constitutes a threat to the United States.[24] The Attorney General makes this threat determination using the less-than-exacting standard of "reasonable grounds to believe."[25] To do this, the Attorney General determines whether there is a threat – even though as the prosecutor, she is not neutral in terrorism trials. This power has one limited check; the Attorney General must file criminal charges or begin deportation hearings shortly after detention.[26] However, proceedings can take a long time, and the Attorney General may detain individuals without a criminal charge in six-month increments.[27] These six-month periods can continue indefinitely as long as a criminal charge has been filed.

While indefinite detention is not within the norms of American law or even military law, it is acceptable within the confines of the laws of war.[28] In justifying America's stance on the indefinite detention of terrorists, Senators Lindsey Graham and John McCain stated: "Under the law of war, the idea that an enemy combatant has to be tried or released is a false choice. Rather, it is well-established that combatants can be held off the battlefield as long as they present a military threat."[29] This pervasive justification is the common excuse for denying aliens common constitutional rights guaranteed to all citizens, so long as national security is threatened. Given that the common view on responses to acts of terrorism is that they are strategies in a larger, "war on terror," judges have applied the Patriot Act to detain aliens who are terrorism suspects indefinitely. The next section discusses specific provisions in the Bail Reform Act that target individuals who are unlawfully in the United States.

8.1.2.4 Bail Reform Act and Terrorism

In addition to the specific laws given earlier targeting terrorism suspects, the Bail Reform Act provides specific procedures for criminal defendants who are unlawfully present in the United States. If a terrorism suspect is an alien who is illegally in the United States, there are special detention restrictions under the Bail Reform Act. However, these restrictions apply to simple garden-variety aliens, as well as terrorism suspects. Under the Bail Reform Act, if the judicial officer determines that a criminal defendant who is not lawfully present in the United States is likely to flee or pose a danger to the community, the judicial officer may order detention of the criminal defendant for up to ten days and direct the government to notify the appropriate Immigration and Naturalization Service Official.[30] If immigration officials do not take custody of the defendant during that ten-day period, the defendant is subject to the other provisions of the Bail Reform Act.[31] These bail determinations concerning aliens being detained by immigrations officials pending removal proceedings under the Immigration and Nationality Act are unreviewable by federal courts.[32]

However, the federal courts have repeatedly reviewed the constitutionality of different aspects of this detention scheme. The Supreme Court upheld the constitutionality of the provision that makes bail unavailable to certain criminal aliens for relatively short periods.[33] But later, at least one federal circuit court held that to avoid a due process violation the statute implicitly requires that aliens convicted of certain crimes and aliens who are not entitled to admission to the United States receive bail hearings after six months of detention.[34] Though, typically if there is an immigration hold on a defendant, a defendant is unlikely to be released before trial. If the defendant was released on bail in this situation, Immigration and Customs Enforcement would most likely take the defendant into custody, which would interrupt the criminal case.

This section has focused on rights of defendants charged with terrorism in federal court. These four federal laws as a whole restrict the ability of individuals charged with terrorism to obtain release before trial. The Patriot Act limits aliens who pose a threat to national security to be detained indefinitely before trial. SAMs allow major restrictions in detention, including limits on communication with the outside world and isolation. IRITPA allows a rebuttable presumption of detention for all individuals charged with crimes of terrorism. And the Bail Reform Act allows detention for illegal aliens for at least ten days, often up to six months. The decision of how and where to bring charges is an important one, so the next section will briefly discuss the implications of bringing charges against suspected terrorists in military or federal court.

8.2 CONSIDERING MILITARY AND FEDERAL COURTS FOR TRYING TERRORISM SUSPECTS

Federal and military courts provide two options for trying terrorism suspects. Military courts are intended for trying aliens and federal courts for US citizens. There are exceptions and more complicated classifications, as discussed in the next section, but this section focuses on the advantages and disadvantages of trying suspects in these two venues. An important advantage in trying defendants in military courts is the ability to avoid the high costs of security in detaining a suspected terrorist in federal prison as opposed to a military base. Pretrial costs of detaining a suspected terrorist in proper isolation in accord with national security requirements can be cost prohibitive for many US jurisdictions. So, though controversial, detaining high-risk terrorism suspects in military bases (like Guantanamo) is the more practical option. However as discussed later, other considerations favor federal court.

8.2.1 *Federal Courts: High Prosecution Rates* *and Wide Variety of Crimes*

Federal courts are by far the preferred venue for prosecuting most US terrorism cases. There are over 4,000 federal crimes that may be used to charge suspected terrorists.[35] Perhaps in part because of this, federal courts have a very high success rate in trying terrorism cases; close to 100 percent conviction rates in high-profile cases.[36]

Despite the high success rate and multiple crimes available to charge, there are still arguments against prosecuting terrorism suspects in federal court. For example, some critics argued that Boston Bombing suspect Dzhokhar Tsarnaev should have been charged as an enemy combatant in a military court, despite his American citizenship.[37] Tsarnaev was eventually tried and convicted in a civilian federal court. The reason for this is that military commissions are unable to try US citizens.[38]

One reason to choose a military court over a federal jury trial is that there can often be a prohibitively high security cost in detaining high-profile defendants on US soil during and before trial, rather than at the Guantanamo military base.[39] For example, at the trial of the confessed operational mastermind of 9/11, Khalid Sheik Mohammed (KSM), New York Mayor Michael Bloomberg estimated that security for the trial could cost $200 million per year, which, for a five-year trial, could cost over $1 billion.[40] For this reason, it did not make sense to transfer KSM to federal court from military court.

In addition to potentially high security costs in detention, federal criminal courts have a high burden of proof, which, including strict evidentiary standards, gives rise to a very real fear of acquittal.[41] A jury acquitted Ahmed Khalfan Ghailani, the first Guantanamo detainee to be tried in federal court, of all but one of the 284 counts against him.[42] Ghailani was on trial for playing a major role in the Tanzania Al-Qaeda attack. His case represents the first time a jury has acquitted a terrorism defendant. Federal court standards prevented the testimony of a key witness against Ghailani because the government had learned of the witness through interrogation of Ghailani while he was in Central Intelligence Agency (CIA) custody. Despite the almost complete acquittal, Ghailani still received a life sentence in federal prison for the charge he was convicted of. Importantly, his years of detention did not violate his right to a speedy trial, so despite the federal trial, the court understood the uniqueness of this terrorism case. And his case set the stage for more federal trials of terrorism suspects.[43]

Overall, federal courts bring the advantage of the largest number of laws available to charge a defendant. In addition, federal courts come with a perfect rate of convictions for terrorism suspects in federal court. The disadvantages to trying terrorism suspects in federal court include the high costs of security and the strict evidentiary standards that leave a chance of acquittal.

8.2.2 *Military Courts: Lower Evidentiary Bar and Fewer Crimes*

As compared to federal courts, prosecutors use military courts much less frequently in trying terrorism suspects. The main purpose of military courts is to try enemies with the goal to aid the war effort by enforcing the law of war. Military courts only sit in a time of war and are limited to the prosecution of non-American citizens.[44] However, the use of military courts is controversial. President Obama favors federal courts for terrorism trials, but admitted that military courts "allow for the safety and security of participants and for the presentation of evidence gathered from the battlefield that cannot always be effectively presented in federals courts."[45] Military courts require fewer constitutional protections to those in federal court, allowing reduced evidentiary exclusions, permitting some forms of coerced confessions, and lacking *Miranda* rights.[46] Additionally, military courts allow for indefinite preventive detention of some terror suspects captured abroad and those brought to Guantanamo Bay.[47]

Military courts provide serious advantages in trying aliens. They lack the potential security risks of bringing terrorism suspects on US soil. Military courts also lack the rigorous evidentiary and constitutional protections provided by federal law. However, some serious disadvantages include the limited number of military laws (as compared to the 4,000 federal laws) available to charge terrorism suspects. For example, the US government held Ali Hamza al-Bahlul for seven years without bail until his trial and conviction before a military court. Al-Bahlul was a media consultant for Osama bin Laden prior to the 9/11 attacks. He made multiple propaganda videos, and even volunteered to be a 9/11 plane hijacker. Bin Laden refused his hijacking request because al-Bahlul was needed to run Al-Qaeda's propaganda campaign. In 2008, a military commission tried, and a military jury convicted, al-Bahlul of thirty-five counts of terrorism, including conspiracy, solicitation to commit murder, and providing material support for terrorism.[48] However, most of al-Bahlul's convictions were eventually overturned, on grounds that, in 2001, neither international law nor US law provided for soliciting murder or providing material support for war crimes.[49] A conspiracy charge remained, allowing the government to hold al-Bahlul for life in prison. Al-Bahlul's near-complete acquittal illustrates that military courts may lack some of the necessary laws to successfully try terrorism suspects when compared to federal courts.

Even so, because of the advantages provided in some cases – namely security and lower evidentiary requirements – there is certainly room for trying some suspected terrorists in military courts. Terrorism law has been shaped in large part by the international law of war, which has had a major influence, as will be discussed in the next section.

8.3 CLASSIFICATION OF TERRORISM SUSPECTS

There are several major (but overlapping) classifications of terrorism suspects that impact how a suspected terrorist is treated – and whether they have any chance for bail – when captured by the United States. The first two are terrorists and combatants. Combatants are those who under the law of war have authorization to fight for their country and do not target civilians. Terrorists are not combatants – but unlawful combatants because they target civilians, rather than military targets. The two other distinctions that are important in classification of terrorism suspects are citizens and aliens. Depending on the citizenship of a suspected terrorist, they may be subject to constitutional rights and eligible for trial in federal court. Generally, aliens are tried in military courts and lack constitutional rights. Those classified as unlawful combatants may be US citizens but lack the constitutional rights of US citizens, including the right to release before trial. An unlawful combatant who is an alien lacks any eligibility for constitutional rights or a trial in federal court. Therefore, classification of a terrorism suspect before trial is critical to determining what rights she is eligible for and where she is tried.

8.3.1 *Challenges in Classification by Government*

Justified by the War on Terror, terror suspects may be tried by the law of war, which separates individuals into combatants and civilians. Civilians are nonthreatening individuals. Combatants receive authorization to fight for their country, but must try to reduce the impact on civilians.[50] The international law of war protects combatants and civilians as prisoners of war, albeit with fewer rights than US citizens. For example, prisoners of war and enemy civilians may be detained without charges until the end of hostilities, which may drag on indefinitely.[51] Terrorists often employ tactics that endanger civilians, and therefore, under the law of war, are neither civilians or combatants.[52] This nonclassification creates ambiguity as to the proper treatment of terrorists, a problem with which the United States struggles.[53] The fate of a defendant is largely dependent upon his classification as civilian or combatant.

In 2002, President Bush categorized individuals detained as terrorists as enemy combatants, "notwithstanding their American citizenship."[54] Later that year, Jose Padilla, an American citizen, was arrested for allegedly participating in a plot to use a radioactive bomb in the United States.[55] After prosecutors failed to bring a charge, President Bush declared Padilla an enemy combatant.[56] Citing the international law of war as authority, the Bush Administration claimed the authority to detain indefinitely threats to national security, such as Padilla.[57] Adding insult to injury, because Padilla was not charged with a crime, the government denied him an attorney as well.[58] Padilla's case is not unique; other US citizens suspected to be terrorists have been indefinitely held with similar justifications.[59]

Disfavoring the title of enemy combatant, in 2009, President Obama began labeling suspected terrorists as unlawful combatants or other terms consistent with the Geneva Conventions. However, even Obama, despite promises never to indefinitely detain American citizens, signed a military spending bill that would allow terrorism suspects to be tried in military courts.[60] Obama did comment, "I have signed this bill despite having serious reservations with certain provisions that regulate the detention, interrogation, and prosecution of suspected terrorists."[61]

In US courts, the distinction between civilian, enemy combatant and unlawful combatant is important in the context of a defendant's citizenship. While the status and treatment of an unlawful combatant is unclear, US citizens suspected of terrorism should have more constitutional protections than aliens. In the next section, I will compare and contrast the actual treatment that US citizens and aliens receive at the hands of the US government. Though, these categories can blur when a citizen is deemed an unlawful combatant, allowing a US citizen to be treated as an alien under US federal or military law.

8.3.2 *Citizen Terrorists*

Courts may perform the same risk assessment for US citizen terrorism suspects, as for garden-variety criminal defendants, as discussed in Chapter 4. However, often terrorism defendants are treated differently. Considering the national security implications, courts may choose to focus on the dangerousness of the defendant, although as discussed in a previous section, flight risk and security are real concerns for terrorism defendants. In addition to the standard channel of a formal risk assessment, citizens who threaten national security may also be detained.

After 9/11, Congress authorized the President to detain US citizens who are a threat to national security with the Authorization for the Use of Military Force (AUMF).[62] Under the AUMF, and in pursuit of the originators of the 9/11 attacks, the military seized Yaser Esam Hamdi. Hamdi was born in the United States and moved to Saudi Arabia as a young child.[63] In 2001, the Northern Alliance arrested Hamdi, labeled him an unlawful combatant, and shipped him to the United States where, among other prisons, he spent time in Guantanamo Bay.[64] Hamdi contended that, as an American citizen, he deserved his constitutional protections, while the United States argued that as an enemy combatant they could hold Hamdi indefinitely, without charges or bail.[65] The Supreme Court decided that US citizens may be lawfully and indefinitely detained under the AUMF, but that Hamdi is entitled to an opportunity to rebut the factual basis of his classification.[66] Had Hamdi been labeled a civilian, the government would have had to grant him his constitutional rights, or at least invoked SAMs, or made another finding of flight risk or dangerousness.

Like Hamdi, American citizens captured overseas under terrorism charges may receive harsh treatment prior to their constitutional right to a fair trial. For example, John Walker Lindh, an American citizen, trained at an Al-Qaeda camp and fought alongside the Taliban in Afghanistan in 2001.[67] After his capture by the Northern Alliance in 2001, Lindh was detained at a nearby prison, where he was shot in the leg during a prison uprising.[68] For more than two weeks, the bullet remained in Lindh's leg while the FBI questioned him, sometimes using the enticement of medical treatment to coerce answers out of Lindh. After the interrogation, Lindh was prosecuted in US federal court.[69] A federal judge denied Lindh's request for bail, citing his "extreme flight risk."[70] Had Lindh been a civilian, the judge still could have denied him bail on dangerousness or flight risk grounds, but Lindh likely could have more successfully argued against his harsh treatment.

The American public appears to have their own sense of justice regarding bail for terrorists. After two bombs killed 3 people and injured over 170 at the 2013 Boston Marathon bombing, Dzhokhar Tsarnaev was arrested on terrorism charges for the bombing and held without bail.[71] The Onion – a satirical news service that prints fake news articles designed to catch people off guard, often by absurdly twisting the facts of trending current events – printed an article days after his arrest claiming that Tsarnaev was released after posting a $2,000 bail.[72] Some of Twitter's more gullible commentators were outraged that a murderer could receive bail.[73] While Twitter's credulous crowd may not provide as accurate a sample as a Gallup poll, the outrage associated with a fake release for a very public terrorism case shows that many Americans do not want suspected terrorists on the streets.

Hamdi, Lindh, and Tsarnaev are examples of American citizens suspected and/or convicted of terrorism. A common theme for each detention and denial of bail is national security, either through a fear of dangerousness or extreme flight risk. Certainly, we as the average American citizen want to feel safe from terrorism. On the other hand, we must be careful that we do not allow national security to create a new bogeyman: the citizen terrorist. While citizen terrorism suspects have been shown to have some abrogated rights, aliens suspected of terrorism have even fewer opportunities for pretrial release.

8.3.3 *Alien Terrorists*

Aliens suspected of terrorism are critically different from the suspected terrorists described in the previous section: they are not citizens of the United States. Unlawful combatants can be treated like aliens or US citizens, depending on the situation. There is precedent for US citizens being denied rights in the same way alien terrorism defendants are denied constitutional rights and rights to be tried in federal court.

Basic constitutional rights – rights that are so culturally embedded in the United States that most citizens do not regularly contemplate them – are not guaranteed to aliens. Some of these rights include the right against unreasonable searches and seizures (Fourth Amendment), the right to due process of law (Fifth Amendment), the right to a jury trial (Sixth Amendment), and the right against excessive bail (Eighth Amendment). One could argue that these rights should not be reserved to American citizens, but to all fellow humans. And indeed, Congress has specifically carved out rights for aliens, such as the mandatory criminal charges or deportation hearings in the Patriot Act, but they can fall significantly short of the constitutional guarantees.

As discussed earlier, the Patriot Act requires the detention of any alien who constitutes a threat to the United States.[74] The Attorney General makes this threat determination and may detain individuals in six-month increments without criminal charges, if necessary.[75] This is exactly what happened to KSM, who took personal responsibility for the planning of the 9/11 attacks.[76] In 2003, Northern Alliance forces captured KSM and held him in various overseas CIA prisons for three years before his eventual transfer to Guantanamo Bay.[77] Resting on the law of war, and partially justified by the Patriot Act, the government held KSM for many years without filing criminal charges. KSM's case is common for alien terrorists. With some limitations, they may be held indefinitely, ostensibly in the interest of national security.

Guantanamo Bay is an infamous US military prison where high-security threat prisoners are kept. Although President Obama ordered the facility closed in 2009, as of January 2017, at the end of Obama's presidency, there were still forty-one detainees held at Guantanamo.[78] Even after Obama's commitment, twenty-nine detainees were being held without charges.[79] These detainees are "too dangerous to transfer but not feasible for prosecution."[80]

Comparing the Guantanamo detainees with US citizen terrorists, it appears that US citizens are afforded a few more protections than aliens; at least US citizens will eventually go to trial. However, US citizens deemed unlawful combatants may be treated like aliens and detained indefinitely.

8.4 CONCLUSION

In the interest of national security, the United States may override the constitutional guarantees against excessive bail and the right to release before trial. Courts justify this decision in a few ways, despite Supreme Court precedent in *Stack*, by relying on the Patriot Act, IRITPA, and SAMs. The government often categorizes people as civilians and combatants, which helps define both the pretrial and trial rights of a person. Civilians are ordinary citizens who do not engage in terrorism, combatants are those who fight for an army against other military targets and are not terrorists. Also, people are categorized as aliens and citizens: citizens receiving the benefit of constitutional rights and a trial in federal court, unless they are labeled an unlawful or enemy combatant (which is a terrorist). If a suspected terrorist finally gets to trial, he may be tried in federal court or military court, with most terrorists being tried in federal courts. However, even in federal court, suspected terrorists are often detained without bail (or with excessively high bail set) and do not enjoy the right to release before trial. In military court, terrorism suspects (who are usually aliens) can be held indefinitely – some without charges – and lack the basic constitutional rights that accompany a federal trial. While some have criticized this current system of justice for terrorists, or the use of military courts and Guantanamo Bay as a detention facility at all, there are certain security risks in attempting to detain suspected terrorists on US soil that make it difficult to move all suspected terrorist trials to federal court. The number of aliens acting as terrorists also necessitates the use of military courts as aliens are eligible to be tried under the international laws of war or possibly under US law if they are suspected of terrorism inside US borders. Within these frameworks of law, the US government has choices. It could choose to limit the number of terrorism suspects detained indefinitely without charges and limit the number of US citizens ineligible for federal trial.

Unfortunately, the current legal landscape provides very few people the right to release before trial, as contemplated by the US Constitution.

However, given the threats to national security this may be justified in some instances, where terrorists target civilian groups in actions not contemplated by existing criminal regimes but by laws of war. However, in similar difficult times the United States in many ways upheld the constitutional right to release for communist suspects, providing a challenge to our current day acceptance of eliminating constitutional rights to preserve national security. Given this history, there should at least be a discussion of whether we are appropriately balancing the rights of defendants and the principles of American justice with the safety of the public.

9

International Bail

[R]ecognition of the inherent dignity and of the equal and inalienable rights of all members of the human family is the foundation of freedom, justice and peace in the world.

— International Covenant on Civil and Political Rights, Preamble

The right to release before trial is a critical human or constitutional right in most of the world. Commercial money bail is prohibited throughout the world and even constitutes a crime in Canada and England.[1] Despite these shared international values, in much of the world, defendants suffer excessively long detention, abuse, torture, and inhumane conditions after arrest and before trial. In some countries, defendants wait up to a year or more for trial, without any access to counsel. Pretrial detention is an epidemic in certain parts of the world. While one chapter certainly cannot provide a comprehensive understanding of how bail and detention function outside of the United States, it is important to consider and compare the rights to release inside and outside of the United States and get a pulse on the state of detention abroad. This chapter briefly considers the international state of pretrial detention, trends on how certain countries make pretrial decisions, and the effects of arbitrary detention.

Consider the following three scenarios of international pretrial detention conditions. For eleven days, Chinese officials arrest and detain Li Jianfeng in a cage approximately one meter square, with a strong spotlight shinning on him for 24 hours a day. They electrocute him on the ears and eyes and beat him until he is dizzy and suffers possible cerebral swelling.[2]

In Tunisia, officials arrest a woman for prostitution at her home on September 20, 2013. Officials take her into an office at Charles de Gaulle police station. One of the uniformed policemen leaves the office and comes back with an electric cable. He tells the woman that she must admit that she "work[s] as a prostitute with another guy from [her] neighborhood." He then beats her with a cable on her thighs, buttocks, and legs for 8 hours.[3]

In November 2009, European officials arrest and extradite Michael Turner and Jason McGoldrick to Hungary where they are locked in a former KGB prison for four months without any charges.[4] When first arriving in Hungary, officials hold Michael and Justin in a police-holding cell, which is a room without ventilation or even a toilet for three days.[5] They do not allow the suspects to call home and guards attempt to make them sign paperwork.[6] After the three days, Michaela and Jason are taken to court and denied bail.[7] Officials then drive them to a former KGB prison, with conditions so poor that it has a bucket for a toilet, and they remain in a small cell for three days.[8] In this jail, they endure constant noise, screaming, the sound of people being beaten, and the threat of a fictional guard that was "going to get" them, in an attempt to force them to confess.[9] After 150 days of being held without charge, Michael and Jason are finally released in February 2010.[10] In 2012, Michael and Jason finally face trial and are found guilty of fraud.[11] The punishment for this is a fine and a five-month suspended prison sentence.[12]

These three real-world examples demonstrate some of the conditions pretrial detainees face internationally. Abuse, lengthy detention without access to counsel, and forced confessions are not uncommon in certain parts of the world. The next section sets out international statistics on pretrial detention to provide perspective on the individual cases described earlier.

9.1 GENERAL STATE OF INTERNATIONAL PRETRIAL DETENTION

Pretrial detention is a major consideration in international criminal justice, affecting a large number of individuals. In the world generally, 32 percent of total prison populations are pretrial detainees who have not been convicted of a crime.[13] Roughly 50 out of every 100,000 people in the general population are pretrial detainees.[14] This translates to about 3 million people in pretrial detention throughout the world.[15] As these stories demonstrate, not only does pretrial detention effect a broad number of people, but pretrial detainees are at risk to suffer from severe and inhuman treatment, and poor prison conditions. Pretrial detainees can be subject to disease,[16] torture,[17] corruption,[18] and excessively long detention periods[19] before ever seeing a court. Pretrial prisoners also suffer from overcrowding,[20] filthy conditions,[21] and inadequate nutrition.[22]

As in the United States, reform of pretrial jail conditions is often not a priority internationally. When discussing prison reform and the justice system, pretrial detention tends to fall between the cracks. Many countries do not report pretrial detention statistics,[23] and some countries do not separate pretrial detainees from the general prison population.[24] Because of the comparatively high turnover rate of pretrial detainees, some countries fail to provide health-care, education, or training services to them, such that pretrial detention is much worse than prison.[25] This is analogous to the United States, where jail conditions pretrial are universally worse than prison conditions nationwide.

The presumption of innocence and the prohibition against arbitrary arrests are international standards, not just American principles.[26] United Nations standards dictate that "[n]o one shall be subjected to arbitrary arrest or deten-tion. No one shall be deprived of his liberty except on such grounds and in accordance with such procedure as are established by law."[27] In other words, under the International Covenant for Civil and Political Rights, no one should be deprived of his liberty unless the deprivation is consistent with established law. Like American standards, international standards dictate that pretrial detention can only be ordered if there is a reasonable belief the suspect was involved in the alleged crime and there is danger he or she might flee, or that there is a danger the course of justice will be impeded if he or she is released pending trial.[28] Further, pretrial detention is a means only to be used as a last resort, with regards to the investigation of the alleged crime, and for the protec-tion of society and the victim.[29] Finally, alternatives to pretrial detention, such as bail, conditional release, recognizance, or sureties, should be employed as early in the process as possible.[30] In addition to these international standards, many countries have individual state laws that apply to pretrial detention.

Most of the countries with high rates of pretrial detention are poor coun-tries. Of the top twenty countries with the highest rate of pretrial detainees compared to the prison population, eight are from sub-Saharan Africa, five are in Latin America, and three are in South Asia.[31] All but one of these twenty have been classified by the World Bank as developing, nine are "low income," seven are "lower-middle income," three are "upper-middle income," and only Uruguay is a "high income" economy.[32] Therefore, there seems to be a con-nection between a country's economy and the rate of pretrial detainees to the regular prison population.

9.2 DECIDING BAIL, DEPARTURES FROM JUSTICE

Despite ambitious international standards, countries vary widely in how they implement pretrial detention or release. In general, the closer countries adhere to the principles of international law and the three-prong factors – flight, danger to society or defendant, and whether justice would be served if defendant is released – the more fair the standards. However, some countries rely on considerations not related to these factors. Without consideration to objective standards, often the percentage of pretrial detainees increases. In some countries, pretrial detention is mandatory for very serious crimes or for crimes with strong evidence. In countries that adhere to this standard, the decision about pretrial detention or bail becomes essentially automatic, leading to arbitrary decisions that are not individualized. Many countries also adhere to pretrial detention proceedings that favor the prosecution. Others have no organized system to deal with those who are arrested, and defendants will wait in jail until a prosecutor is able to bring charges against them.

9.2.1 Mirroring International Standards

Countries that mirror international standards tend to have lower pretrial detention to general prison population rate than countries that do not. For example, both Germany[33] and England[34] closely mirror international law, and both have a lower percentage of pretrial detainees to the general prison population than the European average (about 25 percent).[35] These countries are also more likely to have other measures to promote justice, such as instruments to deter incorrect decisions[36] and restrictions on monetary bail.[37] When countries that mirror international standards add factors for bail consideration, those factors relate directly back to those international standards. For instance, in England, having a residence was a condition for 73 percent of people given bail in 1998;[38] this is reasonably related to assuring the accused does not flee. Further, considering the risk of reoffense is an objective factor that helps determine the possible danger imposed on society.[39]

Countries that mirror international standards also have adequate alternatives to pretrial detention. International standards require that detention before trial is only to be used as a last resort, if necessary to investigate the crime or to protect society and the victim.[40] Further, international standards dictate that the alternatives to pretrial detention, such as bail, conditional release, recognizance, or sureties, should be employed as early as possible.[41] The use of these alternatives is apparent in England. There are about 57,000 people that are currently released before trial in England,[42] while only 8,064 – about 12 percent of pretrial persons – are in pretrial detention.[43] As compared to the percentage detained in the United States – over 40–50 percent – this is a great improvement.

9.2.2 Considering Additional Factors

Often countries consider additional factors beyond the international standards for pretrial release in deciding whether to release pretrial suspects.

When relevant international factors for assuring a fair trial are adhered to, pretrial release appears to be administered more fairly and better exemplifies the presumption of innocence and the prohibition against arbitrary detention. Some countries consider other factors, causing pretrial detention rates to increase – often inadvertently. For example, in Canada the most common reason for pretrial detention is violation of conditions for release.[44] While this seems like a reasonable factor, it may prevent individuals from obtaining release without justification. Roughly 2/3 of detainees in Canada are charged with a nonviolent crime.[45] However, given that 70 percent of detainees in Ontario have substance abuse issues,[46] if one of the release conditions requires no substance abuse,[47] then many individuals will be detained due to a failure to comply with release conditions. Complying with these types of release conditions, while important, are not related to international standards that prioritize pretrial release unless there is an exception. Rather, it allows defendants to be detained before trial for substance abuse, which poses neither a direct danger to society,[48] nor a risk of flight, nor a concern with interfering with justice.

9.2.3 Emphasis on Severity of Crime

Many countries decide whether to release or detain an individual based on the severity of the punishment she is faced with or, the corollary, the seriousness of the crime alleged.[49] They range from mere factors to be considered, such as in Ireland,[50] to a basis for an automatic determination of some kind, such as in Belgium.[51] Some jurisdictions consider the severity of punishment as a factor relevant to flight risk because a greater prison sentence may cause a suspect to flee rather than face trial. Germany and England both consider the seriousness of the offense as a potential factor; however, Germany only allows this to be considered in conjunction with a possibility of reoffense.[52]

Countries with automatic, or near automatic, determinations seem to place a much higher emphasis on this factor. This strays from the international standards, though there is some historical basis for this under the common law as discussed in Chapter 1. While considering a defendant's past violent crime convictions is directly relevant to whether the defendant poses a risk of danger in release, the seriousness of the current charge should be less heavily considered. Even though it has some relevance to potential danger to society, it must first assume the defendant is guilty. In other words, a man accused of murder cannot be assumed to be at risk for murdering again, unless it is also assumed he committed the murder he is accused of. Since these decisions are automatic, or effectively automatic when the seriousness of the crime is weighed more heavily than others, they do not consider how likely the accused will be to refuse to surrender to custody or interfere with justice, or even whether the defendant is actually dangerous. When concerned about public safety, it is much less offensive to due process and more effective to focus on previous convictions than the severity of the crime charged.

9.2.4 *Proceedings That Favor the Prosecution*

Countries with low pretrial detention rates tend to have policies that favor the accused rather than the prosecution. These countries focus on providing fair trials rather than administrative efficiency as a priority. For example, if a prosecutor defaults on an affirmation for a decision, it is automatically decided in favor of the suspect.[53] These jurisdictions deliberately focus on making decisions on whether to detain or release a suspect in reasoned and fair manner, in accordance with international law. This prevents the arbitrary detention that occurs in a large part of the world and respects the presumption of innocence that defendants are given until they are proven guilty. In other jurisdictions, when defense counsel is not present to represent a defendant at a pretrial hearing, the prosecutor will be the only one presenting evidence on whether she should be released before trial. This practice – which is common throughout the world – clearly favors the prosecutor and causes judges to either rely too much on prosecutors' recommendations[54] or not rely on any legally valid factors at all.[55] Also, if pretrial release is denied based on evidence of guilt (which is a factor in many countries), juries can be biased by pretrial determinations. Denying bail on the basis of evidence of guilt effectually allows a judge to determine whether a suspect is guilty, without the benefit of a fair trial, and biases the jury against the suspect. This is also a violation of due process principles. Indeed, providing counsel, stopping arbitrary detention, and reserving any determinations about the defendant's guilt until trial are policies that avoid favoring the prosecution.

9.2.5 *Poorly Trained Judges*

It is required, under international law, that pretrial decisions are not arbitrary.[56] However, in many countries, including the United States, judges are not adequately trained on how to make pretrial decisions. Many judges rely on impermissible nonlegal factors,[57] their gut instinct, tradition, or prosecutorial recommendations.[58] And in many jurisdictions, judges do not have enough time to study the case files before making a decision.[59] As a result, pretrial release decisions become essentially automatic. In many jurisdictions, like in Greece, judges have been documented trying to satisfy a public desire for justice through detaining individuals before trial, which is unlawful.[60] Indeed, pretrial detention has become "perfunctory and formulaic" in many countries,[61] despite laws that require these decisions to be based on substantiated circumstances.[62] Many judges do not respect the fundamental right of release before trial since in practice many defendants are detained.

9.2.6 *Inadequate Defense*

Access to an attorney is necessary for effective representation in pretrial proceedings. Denying or limiting a suspect's access to legal counsel, or not allowing legal counsel to review files, can have severe implications. As discussed in Chapter 7, almost half of US jurisdictions fail to provide representation for pretrial hearings. Many international jurisdictions also fail to provide adequate counsel for hearings. Some countries limit the defendants' access to a defense attorney[63] or allow limited time to review the case files and prepare a defense.[64] In some countries, the presence of a defense attorney is more of a formality because the lawyers are drawn from a list without regard to their specialty.[65] As such, a lawyer without any background in criminal law may be assigned a criminal case.[66] Defendants can also be denied access to evidence.[67] Inadequate access to the tools necessary to prepare a defense is a common departure from justice in many countries.

Overall, many countries lack measures to ensure pretrial justice. Countries that mirror international standards and do not consider additional factors, particularly on the severity of the crime, often have lower pretrial detention rates. In addition, countries that create procedures that favor the accused, over the prosecution, also provide a more just pretrial environment. Another factor that matters more than almost anything else at the pretrial stage is providing defense counsel for a suspect's pretrial hearing. Training judges on the proper factors to consider in determining whether to release an individual is also helpful in ensuring pretrial justice. While it is clear that these important considerations will improve pretrial justice, the next section discusses the opposite: effects of arbitrary decisions in the pretrial context.

9.3 EFFECTS OF ARBITRARY INTERNATIONAL DETENTION

The more arbitrary pretrial decisions are, the higher the rates of detention in that country. When the rate of pretrial detention goes up, especially in poorer countries, then other problems tend to follow. Jails cannot accommodate the numbers of individuals entering each day. There are not appropriate numbers of lawyers to deal with the backlog of defendants. Pretrial defendants often suffer from poor prison conditions, diseases, and abuses. Corruption can often result where there is no appropriate system to provide defendants release before trial. Some countries rely heavily on confessions and obtain these using inhumane methods, including torture or other coercive methods of interrogation.[68] Underpaid workers in developing countries have been reported to use corruption to exact fees from defendants for the sole privilege of not subjecting them to torture, or to provide food and water.[69] Finally, pretrial detainees are at a high risk of catching diseases, which they can then pass on to their families or community.[70] This section will focus in greater detail on some of the problems that result when there are not systems in place to release defendants regularly before trial. It recounts some of the problems of overcrowding or abuses that occur in the pretrial context. Appendix 2 at the end of this book also provides additional examples and statistics on overcrowding, abuse, and other inhumane pretrial conditions faced by individuals in countries throughout the world.

9.3.1 *Poor Prison Conditions*

Many countries hold defendants in jail conditions that violate basic international standards. American jails are not immune to these problems with reports of health violations and inadequate medical care for inmates. The European Court of Human Rights holds that confinement to a prison cell for all but an hour of the day, without appropriate sanitary facilities, access to functioning showers and private toilet areas, is inhumane and degrading treatment in violation of Article 3.[71] However, there are many countries with at least one of these degrading conditions, and many with all of them.[72] Automatic and arbitrary decisions in favor of pretrial detention, coupled with long detention, lead to overcrowding.[73] International jails often have inadequate food, or little to no food at all. Some are unsanitary to the point of being unfit for human habitation. There are countries that give prisoners little, if any, time outside of their cell. Some of these problems result from a lack of money and resources.[74] Other times, government officials use horrific conditions to sway detainees into signing confessions in order to be transferred into more humane prisons.[75]

9.3.2 *Overcrowding in Jails*

Overcrowding is a problem in international jails and is exacerbated by increases in pretrial detainees. According to Article 3 of the European Convention on Human Rights,[76] it violates human dignity for an inmate to receive less than three square meters for a jail cell.[77] However, the world's prisons contain 1,577,800 people in excess of prison capacity.[78] Some countries have dire overcrowding, operating at double or triple their intended capacity.[79] Often, overcrowded cells contain a fraction of what is required for humane treatment, sometimes the equivalent of 1/4 of a twin-sized bed.[80] One prison in Haiti, which combines pretrial persons and convicted prisoners, only has 20 cells but 290 inmates.[81] Living in such small spaces and overcrowded cells has been equated to torture.[82] Overcrowding can also lead to unsanitary living conditions, discussed in more detail in the next section.

9.3.3 *Unsanitary Jail Conditions*

The conditions of jails in some countries are appalling. Some pretrial detention centers have been reported to contain rats that bite the detainees.[83] Some lack access to showers.[84] Some cells have no lighting, artificial or natural, no ventilation, and no running water, soap, bedding, seating, heat, or toilet paper.[85] There are even some cells coated in human excrement, and toilets that don't work,[86] or toilets that are little more than holes in the ground.[87] Even when it is cold and the floor is covered in human excrement, detainees in some countries have had to be barefoot.[88] Detainees have received foul smelling, filthy blankets to sleep on.[89] Some inmates are forced to drink from the same water that they use to "flush" the toilet.[90] Some jails provide inadequate water altogether or fail to provide any soap,[91] with which to wash after using the toilet.[92]

9.3.4 *Inadequate Access to Food*

Inadequate food is often provided to pretrial detainees in poor prisons.[93] Some countries won't provide inmates with any food.[94] For instance in Tunisia, the food provided is "fit for turtles" and is insufficient to prevent prisoners from going hungry.[95] Inadequate food can be blamed on resource constraints that may plague a country more broadly,[96] but still constitute violations of international law.[97] Inadequate food – and hunger – can force a defendant to plead guilty and affect their case in an unfair way.

9.3.5 *Insufficient Outdoor Time*

Time outside of a detention cell is required under international law; however, some countries provide little, if any, outdoor time. There are countries that permit only an hour outside a cell,[98] while some pretrial detainees are not permitted outside of their cells at all, except when they are escorted to interrogations.[99] Still others are kept in extreme isolation for all but a small fraction of the day.[100] Uruguay is an extreme example, where officials hold detainees in metal boxes and only allow them to leave the boxes for a maximum of 4 hours *per week*.[101] Detainees in these boxes have to drink water from the toilet and relieve themselves using bags or plastic bottles, which are then thrown into the courtyard.[102] Being confined to a cell for 23 hours or more a day essentially means that there is no reprieve from poor, overcrowded, and filthy prisons.

9.3.6 *Torture and Forced Interrogations of Suspects*

Torture is very common internationally for those held in pretrial detention.[103] Countries that torture use methods ranging from beatings with batons (Greece),[104] threats of rape (Tunisia),[105] and locking detainees in windowless and dark cells for nearly a full day (Hungary).[106] Torture can also be psychological, including exposure to constant noise, screaming, the sound of people being beaten, and threats of physical abuse.[107] Another form of psychological torture used is extended time in isolation. Some detainees in Zimbabwe, for instance, have spent nine months in complete solitary confinement, with no human contact and only 20 minutes a day for bathing, exercising, or laundry.[108] Torture can also extend to sexual humiliation. For example, there have been reports of women being arrested on minor charges and physically and sexually abused.[109] Additionally, in some prisons, women have been told to remove their underwear, were not given menstrual pads or toilet paper, and were told to clean themselves with their hands.[110]

Even in the countries that do not apply torture, or for which physical interrogation is less common, psychologically coercive methods are still implemented.[111] For instance, Japanese defendants have been "aggressively interrogated" between 8 and 12 hours at a time, while handcuffed to the chair for the entire period.[112] Further, suspects that have not been charged are frequently kept from being able to speak with anyone who isn't their attorney.[113] Even when suspects are allowed to meet with their family, it is often in the presence of a detention officer.[114]

9.3.7 *Corruption in Criminal Justice*

Many countries are steeped in corruption, particularly when it comes to criminal justice.[115] An activist, Stanislav Dmitrievsky, illustrated the problem of corruption in Russia by exclaiming that Russia runs "by making sure everyone is guilty of something."[116] Corruption occurs among judges deciding the fate of defendants,[117] and among the police officers charging for public services that should normally be provided for free.[118] In some countries, such as Sierra Leone, paying a bribe is cheaper than paying for bail.[119] In other countries, like Russia, bribes that used to be voluntary became mandatory, with a refusal to pay landing some in jail.[120]

Corruption also appears as a political measure in some countries like Mexico, Thailand, and Russia. For example, some countries engage in corruption in order to appear as though they are succeeding in the fight against crime.[121] Because of corruption, certain marginalized people – like poor, unpopular minorities or even business owners – are targeted for pretrial detention.[122] For example, a member of the Russian prison monitoring community remarked that jail is a tool for taking away business from an entrepreneur that is "destroying the middle class of Russia." As a result of corruption, some people are even arrested for crimes that there is no evidence that they committed.[123]

9.3.8 *Excessively Long Pretrial Detention*

There are two types of excessively long detention that violate the rights of suspects. The first is precharge detention, where a prisoner is held for several days or longer before even being charged.[124] The second is pretrial detention, where a detainee might be held for several years after being charged but before seeing the inside of a courtroom.[125] Both severely infringe on prisoner rights. Precharge detention is generally used for coercion purposes or torture,[126] and is the period where defendants are more likely to be denied access to a defense attorney.[127] Pretrial detention, as discussed previously, is essentially punishment without the benefit of a fair trial.[128] A defendant might be arrested and placed in pretrial detention even when the judge knows he or she will not be convicted, just because the pretrial detention will be lengthy and will therefore serve as "punishment" in the public eye.[129]

Further, there are international reports from investigators that the beginning of pretrial detention is often falsified.[130] Instead of being immediately taken to a police station, detainees are held either in the back of the police car for several hours or in clandestine "safe" houses for several days.[131] They are illegally interrogated and often abused in these situations.[132] The falsifying of the time a detention begins is a way to get around laws, which impose 72- or 48-hour limits on detention before being charged or shown to a magistrate.[133]

9.3.9 *Disease in Jail*

Jails are breeding grounds for disease.[134] Disease spreads faster in pretrial detention facilities than in prisons.[135] Disease is able to spread quickly because pretrial detention facilities, with few exceptions, do not screen for disease or provide health care, methadone therapy, or condom distribution.[136] Many of these things are provided for in prisons.[137] However, because pretrial detention centers have a high turnover rate and are more transitory and less organized than prisons, healthcare isn't provided.[138] This isn't a problem just for detainees. Detainees can get sick and spread their illness to their family and their community.[139] Prison guards are also at a high risk for contracting a disease.[140]

There is also inadequate medical care such that prisoners suffer from strokes,[141] heart attacks,[142] kidney failure,[143] and pancreatitis complications.[144] For instance, Russian officials held Natalia Gulevich in pretrial detention for eleven months, allegedly for an unpaid bank loan. Gulevich and her lawyer claimed that she was innocent and raiders wanted the office buildings she owned.[145] She went into kidney failure and did not receive medical attention.[146] The court responded by granting bail, but it was in the amount of $3.5 million.[147] She was unable to come up with the money, despite significant help from her husband and family members.[148] Investigators offered her freedom if she was willing to plead guilty. Gulevich refused.[149] It was only after the European Court of Human Rights in Strasbourg intervened that she received medical attention.[150]

9.3.10 *Death of Inmates*

It is not uncommon for suspects to die in pretrial detention abroad. Sometimes the cause of death is inadequate medical care,[151] heart attack,[152] or suicide.[153] It is difficult to say how many deaths are the cause of torture since the countries that torture people to death do not tend to be the most transparent countries. Some deaths in China are reported to be "suspicious,"[154] but the details of inmate deaths are difficult to uncover.[155]

9.4 CONCLUSION

Internationally, individuals lack access to release before trial, much like in the United States. About one-third of inmates internationally are held in pretrial detention and are not convicted criminals. While each country maintains individual pretrial release standards or practices, international law requires that people receive release before trial unless there is a danger the individual might flee or if they will disrupt the justice system such that a fair trial will not be possible. The international norm should be release before trial and the exception, detention. Individuals must only be detained in the first place if there is a reasonable belief that they committed the alleged crime.

Countries that mirror international standards often release individuals in a short amount of time. Those countries that lack adequate standards for judges or processes for pretrial detention allow defendants to suffer from excessive periods of detention. Many countries lack appropriate lack of counsel before trial, allow forced confessions, corrupt practices, and other abuses and poor conditions for inmates. Internationally, there are reports of inmate illness and death, lack of access to healthcare, food, water and time out of a jail cell, and other inhumane treatment. If release before trial became the international standard, many of these pretrial abuses would be mitigated. The best practice is for all countries to commit to complying with international standards on pretrial detention to avoid the abuses and injustice that plague the accused – who, after all, should be entitled to the presumption of innocence.

Money Bail

What has been demonstrated here is that usually only one factor determines whether a defendant stays in jail before he comes to trial. That factor is not guilt or innocence. It is not the nature of the crime. It is not the character of the defendant. That factor is, simply, money.

—Robert F. Kennedy, Former US Attorney General[1]

Money bail is a controversial and truly American phenomenon as the United States is one of only two countries in the world that allows commercial bail.[2] Money bail is an encompassing term that includes several types of financial bail as discussed in Chapter 3. It includes both commercial bail and other surety bonds and deposit bonds. The most commonly used type is commercial bail, where a defendant contracts with a bail bond company and pays a nonrefundable fee (usually 10 percent of total bail amount) in exchange for the bail company promising the court to return the defendant for trial. Other money bail options are unsecured surety bonds (where family or friends post money with a court and the court returns this money to the individual when the defendant appears) and deposit or percentage bail (where the defendant or family put up money or a deposit to the court and the court returns this when the defendant appears for trial). While this chapter refers to all of these financial options as money bail, the most offensive for constitutional and policy reasons is commercial money bail. While the other financial release options are disfavored because they unfairly punish the indigent, the defendant does receive their deposit or bail money back, and so it constitutes less of a financial strain. It also is less of a violation to the constitutional right to release because the defendant – who is still presumed innocent at this time – is not actually having to pay a price in order to obtain release from jail. However, even deposit bail (where a person is refunded their deposit) can be a constitutional violation if an individual is unable to obtain release because they cannot pay a deposit. No other country operates a commercial bail industry, and if they require defendants to pay money to obtain release on bail, the defendant receives the money back.[3] America is the only country (besides the Philippines) where money bail is regularly paid to a commercial bail company in order to allow a defendant to obtain release from jail before trial. In fact, in Canada, Australia, and England, offering money bail is a crime.[4] If release is truly a constitutional right, a defendant should not have to pay money to receive this right to freedom. Money bail discriminates against poor people who cannot obtain release simply because they cannot afford to pay less than $500 for bail.

This chapter reviews the problems caused by money bail and its history and growth – especially in the last twenty years due to the powerful bail industry lobby. It also reviews the recent constitutional challenges against money bail, some that have led to bans on money bail in certain counties. It also discusses the various proposed federal, state, and community reforms that have increased the use of pretrial services and increased the number of individuals obtaining release without reliance on money bail.

10.1 GENERAL PROBLEMS WITH MONEY BAIL

The statistics regarding money bail can be particularly shocking. At any given point, 60 percent of the US jail population is composed of people who have been arrested but are waiting for some resolution to their charges, including a majority of defendants not charged with a violent crime.[5] Many of these individuals are simply in jail because they could not afford to pay money bail. These financial implications burden defendants and their families, while also placing significant hardship on society as a whole. The Federal Reserve Bank of Boston estimates that 61 percent of people in jail are there awaiting trial at the cost of $9 billion annually to the nation.[6] On average, defendants are detained pending trial for a month when unable to post bail, and roughly 20 percent of these defendants eventually have their case dismissed and are acquitted. This means 100,000 people may spend roughly a month behind bars just to have their case dismissed. The personal impact from lost jobs, failure to pay rent, and inability to pay other basic necessities due to detention can cause untold harms that are difficult, if not impossible, to recover from.[7]

Some of the general problems with money bail include that it punishes those who are poor, causing those who cannot afford what is usually a small payment to remain incarcerated. Money bail also allows some very high-risk individuals to obtain release. Requiring money bail results in more pretrial incarceration, which actually increases recidivism rates, according to recent studies. Because individuals who cannot afford money bail remain incarcerated, they are more likely to engage in plea bargaining even if they are innocent as that may be the quickest route to release. Money bail does not only impact a defendant pretrial, it also increases the likelihood of conviction and receiving a sentence of incarceration. Even with all of these problems, the use of money bail has continued to grow and the amount of bail a defendant must pay has also increased. Each of these problems will be explored more in depth in the next section.

10.1.1 Punished for Being Poor

Several studies have concluded that poor defendants, who are considered to be low risk for flight and recidivism by a pretrial risk assessment analysis, are frequently detained in jails because they cannot afford bail while similarly situated wealthy defendants obtain release. Many defendants in pretrial detention might reasonably qualify for a release on recognizance, but instead these defendants are detained because they have been assigned money bail they cannot afford. There is no good reason for this, but it simply occurs since court systems have increasingly made money bail the default. Essentially, defendants are being incarcerated solely because they cannot make a payment. This detention, a result of presumptive bail practices, has been found to violate defendants' due process rights.[8] Indeed, the Fourteenth Amendment of the Constitution has been interpreted to prohibit "punishing a person for his poverty[.]"[9] Thus, people in detention before trial, simply because they are poor and cannot afford bail, are being punished unconstitutionally.

Quantitative evidence suggests that this violation is pervasive. In one study of New Jersey Jails, 38 percent of all inmates were only detained because they could not meet their financial bail. Another study performed by the Bureau of Justice Statistics over a period of fourteen years found that, among defendants detained until case disposition, only one in six had been denied bail, while five in six had bail set with financial conditions that were not possible for the defendant to meet. Roughly 30 percent of those awaiting trial in state prisons have bonds less than $5,000.[10] A higher bail amount is therefore correlated with a lower probability of release.[11]

The stories of Perchelle Richardson and Crystal Patterson highlighted here demonstrate the difficulties of money bail, particularly for the poor. Poor and wealthy defendants receive fundamentally different treatment in the criminal justice system simply because wealthy defendants have a few hundred dollars to pay bail and property to leverage in a case. Perchelle Richardson, a teenager, decided to take her neighbor's cell phone from an unlocked car. Shortly after she stole the neighbor's cellphone, Richardson felt guilty and knew what she had done was wrong. Before she could return the cell phone to her neighbor, police officers arrived and arrested her. When the police officers and Richardson were leaving the house, they told Richardson and her older sister that she would be able to go home that night. However, when Richardson's sister arrived at the police station, the police officers wouldn't let Richardson go because her sister couldn't pay the $200 surety bond for her $5,000 bail. As a result, Richardson remained in jail for fifty-one days, forced to miss school the entire time. Richardson's family didn't even have enough money to pay for a phone card to call her while she was in jail. Because Richardson was the only one able to watch her siblings at home, her family suffered financially to make up for her absence. If Richardson was not indigent, this cell phone incident may have been an unfortunate misunderstanding that would not involve any jail time.

In 2015, a nonprofit Washington, DC, legal clinic filed a class action lawsuit on behalf of Crystal Patterson, a California resident who lawyers say suffered an equal protection violation by the city of San Francisco after she was arrested for assault. In order to obtain pretrial release, Patterson was forced to pay a private bail bond company $15,000 plus interest to put up $150,000 bail to secure her release and allow her to care for her invalid grandmother. The day after her release the district attorney decided not to pursue charges, but Patterson still owed the bail bonds company a massive debt.[12] If Patterson was wealthy, she would not be facing this exorbitant cost, simply to exercise her constitutional right to obtain pretrial release.

10.1.2 *Allows High-Risk Individuals To Be Released*

Commercial bail bondsmen often allow high-risk individuals to be released, increasing danger to society. The money bail system releases 50 percent of people who would be judged as "high risk" in a risk-based system. Commercial bail agents have no duty to ensure public safety and prevent their clients from being rearrested. In fact, if their clients are rearrested, this in no way impacts their bail contract and in fact often provides these agents with a repeat customer. By the commercial bail bondsmen's own admission, the people that they do not provide sureties for are those who are at high risk for not appearing for their court dates, not those who are at high risk for rearrest, even for violent crimes. Those who are rearrested are loyal customers who will often return to the same bonds company to bail them out again. Others left in the jail by the bondsmen are those who cannot afford the money bail payment or have no collateral to receive a bail bond.

There are many accounts of high-risk defendants who paid money bail and commit crimes while on release. A recent burglary ring in California that collects about $10,000 per day has a practice of pooling their crime proceeds to bail each other out.[13] Those who are released continue to commit burglaries. Similarly, an Ohio man who attempted to kill his wife was able to finish the job after obtaining financial release before trial.[14] In Texas, a hitman for a Mexican drug cartel also was able to use money bail to be released.[15] After being charged with kidnapping and murder, the judge set bail at $250,000. The hitman, who makes up to $50,000 per murder, had no problem coming up with $25,000 to pay the bail bondsman. After release on money bail, he committed two more murders. The next time, bail was set at $400,000, and he bailed out again, committing more murders. When last arrested, he faced five murder charges and other felony charges. With money bail – which has no consideration for public safety – high-risk individuals will continue to be released before trial, posing a danger to society. It is impossible to mitigate all risks of crime when releasing defendants, but at least with a risk assessment judges can make an effort not to release those who are most likely to be violent and harm victims and witnesses on release.

10.1.3 Increases Recidivism

Even short periods of pretrial detention increase the risk of recidivism. Most jail inmates have been accused of low-level or nonviolent crimes and incarcerating them for even short periods leaves many more detainees hard, bitter, and, importantly, more likely to recidivate once released.[16] Individuals who are detained prior to trial are more likely to commit new crimes. In a recent study, the Arnold Foundation found that even two to three days in pretrial detention will increase an individual's likelihood of committing new crime.[17] Low-risk defendants are 40 percent more likely to commit a new crime if held for two to three days before their trial when compared to defendants held less than a day.[18] Those who are held for eight to fourteen days are 51 percent more likely to commit new crime.[19] A study done in Philadelphia and Pittsburgh found that assigning money bail increases the likelihood of conviction by 12 percent and increases recidivism by 4 percent.[20] Indeed, the impact of just a few days in detention is significant on recidivism.

10.1.4 Encourages Plea Bargaining, Even for Innocent

The money bail system also harms those who cannot afford bail by virtually forcing them to plea bargain. The longer a defendant spends in detention awaiting trial, the more likely they are to accept a plea deal. Often defendants choose to forgo their day in court because if they refuse to plead guilty they end up having to stay in jail a longer period than their potential sentence, creating a huge incentive to strike a quick plea deal regardless of guilt or innocence. One empirical study found that of the federal pretrial detainees in 1987 and 1988 about 85 percent received criminal convictions, the majority of which involved plea bargaining.[21] A recent study by researchers at Columbia University found that "the assessment of money bail" in itself, "rather than bail size appears to be causing convictions."[22] By contrast, released defendants have the ability to actively be involved in their defense, take steps to reduce the severity of a sentence by getting or keeping a job, maintain or reestablish family ties, and develop a record of compliance with release conditions.[23] Thus, the time defendants spend incarcerated awaiting trial has far-reaching effects, beyond simply detention.[24]

10.1.5 *Increases Conviction and Sentence*

The costs of pretrial detention reach beyond simple monetary costs. The time defendants spend in detention has a significant impact on their employment, family relations, and ultimate sentence length. For instance, consider the case of Lavette Mayes. In 2015, Lavette, who had no criminal record, got into an intense argument with a family member while in the middle of a heated divorce.[25] Chicago police arrested her for aggravated battery. At the time, she was renting a nice home that she lived in with her children and she had a business operating a school van service. After the arrest, the judge demanded a $250,000 bail, which Lavette could not afford. She spent fourteen months in Cook County Jail until a community bail fund helped her make bail after the judge reduced the amount. In that time, however, her business had collapsed and she lost her home. "I lost everything," Mayes, forty-six, said.[26]

Research shows that if a defendant comes to a sentencing hearing from jail they are more likely to receive a sentence of incarceration than a person who has been out on pretrial release. Not only is this a deprivation of their liberty, but it also significantly impedes their ability to develop a defense to the charges alleged against them. Detention also leads to a higher likelihood of conviction, regardless of what the crime was or if they had ever been charged or convicted of a crime before.[27] Indeed, in a recent University of Pennsylvania study, Megan Stevenson found that people arrested for crimes and detained due to their inability to pay money bail face up to a 30 percent increase in convictions – driven by increased guilty pleas – and an additional eighteen months of incarceration compared to those who are able to afford bail.[28]

And numerous other empirical studies show that the longer the period of pretrial detention, the higher the likelihood of conviction, even controlling for other factors.[29]

10.1.6 The Growing Problem of Money Bail

The most immediate impact of money bail is on the people who are stuck in jail awaiting trial because of it. The United States leads the world in pretrial detainees with over 500,000 people in jail every day simply because they cannot make bail.[30] Despite the inefficiencies in it, and the growing literature discussing the serious consequences of it, its popularity has continued to grow throughout the past decades.

In 1990, roughly one half of all defendants had financial conditions required for release. By 2004, this percentage rose to roughly two-thirds of all defendants having financial conditions required for release.[31] Release on recognizance (no money required) was the most common type of pretrial release in 1992, but by 2006, this had declined by 33 percent.[32] Overall, 70 percent of people charged with a felony were assigned money bail in 2006.[33] And by 2009, only 23 percent of all felony defendants were released pretrial on their own recognizance.[34] In other words, in 2009 felony cases, commercial bail bonds were used in four out of five releases that involved money and close to half of all jail releases.[35] In addition to requiring money bail more often, over the last twenty years, judges also increased bail amounts. Between 1992 and 2009, the average bail amount in felony cases increased 43 percent from $38,800 to $55,400.[36] Higher bail amounts and larger numbers of defendants being required to pay bail means simply that more and more defendants remain in jail since they are unable to afford release.

Another exacerbating problem is that the likelihood that an arrest will lead to jail booking has increased over the years. In 1984, when crime rates overall were higher, there were 51 jail bookings for every 100 arrests.[37] By 2012, there were 95 jail bookings for every 100 arrests.[38] A closer look at this demonstrates that many of these bookings are for misdemeanor crimes, a good number for minor drug offenses, which are the only category of crime that continued to increase through the 1990s.[39]

These increases are especially troubling as the ones who are significantly more likely to be detained are simply poor, not necessarily dangerous or likely to flee. It is often misdemeanor cases that produce many of today's pretrial detainees, despite low bails. In New York City, only 21 percent of arrestees could make their bail at arraignment for amounts less than $500, while in Virginia, only 8 percent of arrestees with bail set less than $5,000 could make bail.[40]

Just as money bail poses problems for indigent defendants who cannot pay small bail amounts, it also provides an opportunity for wealthier – and perhaps riskier – defendants to avoid detention. According to some scholars, these wealthier defendants who are released are frequently more dangerous than those that are detained.[41] So not only does releasing defendants based on financial means discriminate against defendants, it actually makes society less safe. And while money bail is not the preferred approach of any criminal justice expert or even most lawyers, it remains the default method of pretrial release used by judges.

10.2 HISTORY OF MONEY BAIL IN THE UNITED STATES

The roots of the US bail system predate America to England's medieval justice system.[42] In England, the use of bail went through various changes and developments, but generally relied on the presumption of innocence and protected against excessive bail.[43] In 1275, the Statute of Westminster limited the authority of sheriffs to grant bail to suspected criminals, who had previously been given complete control over releasing suspects. The king could still dictate that certain individuals should be held without bail.[44] The 1628 Petition of Right also emphasized the ability of both sheriffs and the king's judges to impose reasonable bail on a suspect.[45] And the 1689 English Bill of Rights declared that "excessive bail" should not be required, which later became an important principle in the US Constitution.[46] These standards of reasonable bail adopted from England were adopted by the colonies and incorporated in both the federal and state constitutions of the United States. The Judiciary Act of 1789 established a statutory right to bail at the federal level that provided an absolute right to bail in all noncapital cases and bail at the discretion of the judge in capital cases.[47] The Eighth Amendment of the Bill of Rights in 1791 further solidified that the accused should not be subject to excessive bail. The bail practiced in early America was not commercial, but was a third-party surety bail system where a family member would post bail for a defendant and receive their money back when the defendant appeared for his trial. The Supreme Court later indicated that "excessive bail" is any fine that is exponentially higher than what would be expected for the crime the defendant is accused of.[48] Thus early on in America, bail was practiced and was not to be excessive.

Commercial money bail did not exist until the late nineteenth century, and it was a creature of the West. Before that point, family or a friend provided a pledge guaranteeing an accused would appear in court. The friend would obtain their bail money back from the court when the accused appeared for his court date. Only when America expanded and there was an absence of extended family and friends did the accused have difficulty finding people to put up bail money. This occurred first in the West, where many left their families and friends for business opportunities. In 1896, two bartender brothers in San Francisco, Peter and Thomas McDonough, began posting bail money as a favor to lawyers who drank at their father's bar.[49] When the lawyers' clients appeared in court, the brothers got their money back. Seeing how necessary their service was, the McDonoughs then decided to charge a fee for their service for strangers. It was so successful that they formed the first bail bonding business, which eventually replaced the bar.[50] While there was some public stigma at first to this new American business, by the 1940s, bail bonds nationwide were high enough that many defendants had no choice but to either pay a bondsman or wait in jail until trial. What had started as a chance entrepreneurial success had expanded throughout the United States and transformed the criminal justice system. While commercial bail served a purpose in allowing defendants without any friends or family to obtain release from jail, it also led to defendants paying money in order to be released – and never receiving this money back. It also led to disparities between defendants based on wealth – those who could afford commercial bail and those who could not. These disparities have just worsened over time with increasing numbers of crimes on the books and higher proportions of those being arrested serving jail time.

Despite constitutional law that maintained that bail should not be excessive and that individuals should have access to release before trial, judges started to set high bail amounts in order to keep the accused behind bars. Sometimes defendants simply could not afford to pay small bail amounts, but the result was the same. Due to advocacy and public sentiment against the large numbers of individuals detained pretrial and some reaction against the burgeoning commercial bail industry, Congress took action and passed the Bail Reform Act of 1966. This provided US defendants a statutory right to obtain release on bail. The act's provisions changed federal bail law and outlined how it would be used for criminal defendants, including (1) the presumption favoring the release of defendants of noncapital cases; (2) pretrial release with conditions to incentivize future court appearances; (3) restriction on money bail bonds, allowing their use only if nonfinancial release options were unavailable; (4) the option of providing a 10 percent deposit of the entire bond's sum directly to the court in place of having a bondsmen pay the full sum; and (5) the review of bail bonds after a defendant was held for 24 hours or more.[51] After its passage, the majority of states passed similar laws mirroring the federal statute in their own bail system, including the emphasis on pretrial release when reasonable.[52]

The new federal law laid a foundation for changes in how bail would be used in pretrial proceedings, reflecting the intent of Congress at the time of the act's passage. The purpose of the statute was clearly expressed by Congress, going as far as including in its legislative history the proclamation that the "existing bail procedures in the courts of the United States ... in order to assure that all persons, regardless of their financial status, shall not needlessly be detained pending their appearance to answer charges, to testify, or pending appeal, when detention serves neither the ends of justice nor the public interest."[53] In contrast to later revisions to federal money bail, the purpose of the act did not include taking into consideration the potential of a defendant committing further crimes.[54] Congress went as far to state that pretrial bail is not to be used as a means of protecting society against the "possible commission of additional crimes from the accused."[55] This view towards pretrial money bail, however, would not last long.

The 1970s saw the rise of crime rates and a renewed focus on being "tough on crime" that continued through the 1980s.[56] During this time, many states began to consider the future dangerousness of a defendant as a factor in setting bail amounts after their arrest.[57] Reflecting these new attitudes toward bail and emboldened by recent judicial decisions supporting the use of money bail, Congress passed the Bail Reform Act of 1984.[58]

The Bail Reform Act of 1984 expanded the list of factors a judicial officer could consider in determining whether bail should be set in a particular case to include "the nature and seriousness of the danger to any person or the community that would be posed by the person's release."[59] In passing the act, the Senate was determined that the bill address "the alarming problem of crimes committed by persons on release."[60] The act included language allowing a court to determine if release on bail on a person's own personal recognizance is not enough to prevent the harm or danger to the community.[61] By allowing the court to take into consideration the defendant's potential for dangerousness, the act also added a rebuttable presumption for confinement if a defendant has committed certain offenses, such as a violent crime or serious drug crimes.[62] One of the lasting effects of the Bail Reform Act of 1984 is its increased use in keeping defendants incarcerated pretrial.

Another lasting effect is its contribution – or coincidental overlap with – the growth in use of money bail. The Bail Reform Act of 1984 resulted in judges setting bail based on a defendant's potential for "future dangerousness" instead of based on an individualized determination. The use of dangerousness as a factor for release has changed the way money bail has been used by judges to prevent release by some poor defendants, allowing more wealthy but high-risk defendants obtain release. In 1990, only 53 percent of felony defendants were assigned money bail in large counties, but by 2009, that number rose to 72 percent.[63] During this same time period, average bail amounts increased to nearly $61,000, almost a 46 percent increase from 1990.[64] These statistics provide a glimpse into how the widespread use of money bail is being applied to a defendant, both for serious and nonserious crimes.

Typically, when judges perceive (based on their intuition) that a person presents a high risk, we see those judges setting very high amounts of money bail as a means to try to keep that person in jail. This use of money bail is flawed in several ways. First, the judges are not being guided by validated risk assessments, so they make risk determinations based on "common sense," which is often not empirically sound. Second, not knowing a person's financial capacity, they have no way of knowing whether a certain dollar amount of bail will keep a person in jail or not. What often happens is that even low dollar amounts can be prohibitive to the very poor, but high dollar amounts are often insufficient to hold arrestees with means. In fact, one study found that 50 percent of high-risk people make bail under a money-based system. Finally, using money bail in this way is a perversion of the system. Indeed, at bail hearings judges should aim to set conditions under which a person may be safely released, *not* conditions that will prevent a person's release.

Money bail has a long history in the United States; however, its purpose has largely shifted. The historical purpose of money bail was to ensure the defendant arrived at his day in court. And importantly, the defendant or her family paid money to the court and always received their money back. However, starting in the late 1800s, money bail became a commercial industry, where defendants did not receive money back. It also became a proxy for how risky a defendant is, based on the intuition of a judge. With its growth and expansion throughout the United States, commercial money bail has become the preferred method of pretrial release and as discussed later serves as an impediment to defendants receiving their constitutional right to release before trial.

10.3 CHALLENGES TO MONEY BAIL

There are a growing number of questions regarding the constitutionality of money bail, particularly commercial bail, in its current form. The Eighth Amendment prohibits excessive bail, and sometimes high bails set simply to prevent a defendant from obtaining release have been found unconstitutional. The Fourteenth Amendment Equal Protection Clause has been found to prohibit money bail where poor defendants are disadvantaged and are not able to obtain the same right to release as wealthy defendants charged with the same crime. Similarly, the Due Process Clause has been used to strike down money bail assignments that are done without an individualized assessment, which takes the particular situation of the defendant into account. For this same reason, the Due Process Clause has invalidated bail schedules that set uniform bail based only on the crime charged. This section discusses these various challenges to money bail.

10.3.1 *Eighth Amendment Challenges to Money Bail*

Litigants have challenged the constitutionality of money bail with the Eighth Amendment, Excessive Bail Clause. As its name implies, this clause requires that "[e]xcessive bail shall not be required" and it has been used to stop judges from abusing money bail to prevent release before trial.[65] A few instances are discussed in Chapter 3, and others are discussed later. The Bail Reform Acts of 1966 and 1984 make clear that the presumption for defendants pretrial is release, unless there are special circumstances. The acts were passed partly because there were many judges who set high bail amounts simply to detain defendants, despite constitutional and Supreme Court prohibitions against this practice. On paper, as stated by Lauryn Gouldin, "[money bail p]roperly calculated, . . . is set at the precise amount that will induce a released defendant to return to court . . . and [while] there are real debates about how well bail serves this purpose, there is not much to debate about the purpose of bail."[66] But in reality, as one New York judge stated openly, "[B]ail is really being set to keep the person in custody. You have to kind of concede that."[67] Many jurisdictions state clearly that bail is set simply to ensure appearance at trial and for no other purpose.[68] And indeed, it is a clear violation of the Eighth Amendment to set bail at a high amount simply to prevent a defendant from obtaining release. Despite the clear purpose of bail, judges still set high bails to keep defendants locked up.[69]

However, some courts have used the Excessive Bail Clause to stop this. In *State* v. *Brown*, the New Mexico Supreme Court recently used the excessive bail clause to prohibit a high bail set to detain an individual.[70] In *Brown*, the defendant was accused of first-degree murder after stabbing the victim once with a pocket knife in the heart. However, the accused was found to have an IQ of seventy and severe intellectual disabilities. Despite these disabilities, and evidence in support of defendant from pretrial services and other experts demonstrating that he would be able to meet the terms of the pretrial release, the defendant was in detention for over two years awaiting trial on bail of $250,000. Being held on money bail implies the defendant could have been released, and the judge did not articulate any potential danger to the community in setting his bail. On appeal, the New Mexico Supreme Court held that the bail was set at a figure higher than an amount reasonably calculated to fulfill the purpose of adequately assuring the presence of the accused and was "excessive" under the Eighth Amendment.[71] The Supreme Court pointedly stated that the bail set was likely excessive due to a judicial fear of "election difficulties" and "media attacks" if they "faithfully honor the rule of law when it dictates an action that is not politically popular."[72] The court further encouraged judges not to set excessive bail due to these fears because "there is no way to absolutely guarantee that any defendant released on pretrial conditions will not commit another offense."[73] Indeed, the court made clear that judges should not preventatively detain defendants with high bail amounts, and that if they do, it violates the Eighth Amendment. The recognition by judges and courts that high bails are set to prevent defendants from obtaining release makes clear that violations of the Eighth Amendment are still common practice today.

However, the Eighth Amendment is seldom used to strike down unfair bail assignments. As one court in the Southern District of New York put it, although the Excessive Bail Clause contains no "absolute 'least restrictive conditions' requirement . . . it must preclude bail conditions that are more onerous than necessary" and those that deprive liberty.[74] Despite these protections, Eighth Amendment arguments are still exceedingly difficult to win. This is because the standard of review courts use when reviewing bail is typically the very low standard of abuse of discretion, under which very few bail requirements are found to be excessive.[75]

The Eighth Amendment is the only portion of the Constitution that deals directly with bail. However, the court's interpretation of this clause has severely limited the range and scope of cases that are brought under it and it has not been very successful at stopping money bail violations. Other constitutional provisions, including the Fourteenth Amendment discussed next, have been used with more success.

10.3.2 Fourteenth Amendment Challenges to Money Bail

The Fourteenth Amendment has been used to challenge bail determinations where the bail set disproportionately harms indigent individuals in violation of the Equal Protection Clause or when an individualized bail determination has not been made violating the Due Process Clause. The landmark 1978 case of *Pugh* v. *Rainwater*[76] found that without "meaningful consideration of other possible alternatives,"[77] jailing people because they cannot afford bail violates their due process and equal protection rights. *Pugh* set the stage for today's constitutional challenges to money bail. Using the Fourteenth Amendment to attack money bail has recently garnered additional momentum with the vocal support of the U.S. Department of Justice. In a 2015 case challenging the Clanton Alabama bail scheme,[78] the Department of Justice made clear that "[i]t is the position of the United States that [financial bond, set] without any regard for indigence, not only violates the 14th Amendment's equal protection clause but also constitutes bad public policy."[79] Due process concerns in money bail have also grown increasingly prevalent as courts find that a lack of individualized determination, with consideration of the particular defendant's financial situation, prior to setting bail violates individual rights.[80]

As demonstrated throughout this book, through the years, many defendants have been unfairly detained pretrial without access to due process or equal protection of the law. This is arguably one of the most serious issues in criminal justice today as indigent individuals are significantly more likely to be detained pending trial because of their inability to post bond. Further, too often judges adhere to strict bail schedules that offer little flexibility but are facially constitutional and thus very difficult to challenge as a whole. Despite this difficulty, the following sections explore the cases and arguments discussing when money bail statutes or judicial determinations violate either the Due Process or the Equal Protection Clauses of the Fourteenth Amendment.

10.3.2.1 Equal Protection Challenges

Many challenges to money bail statutes rely on the Equal Protection Clause and disparate impacts faced by indigent defendants. The standard of review in these cases is unfortunately very low. When reviewing a bail statute, the courts must simply find that the classification system is "rationally related to a legitimate governmental objective."[81] This is despite the alarming statistics, discussed in depth in Chapter 6, indicating that there is actually significant racial disparity caused by many bail schemes that should call for strict scrutiny instead. There is clear evidence that money bail practices disproportionately impact minority defendants as recent numbers show that blacks, Latinos, and Native Americans are twice as likely to remain in jail because they cannot afford money bail than their white counterparts.[82]

Equal Justice Under Law (EJUL) is a nonprofit civil rights organization that provides *pro bono* legal services.[83] This organization has taken on several cities and counties nationally to challenge the constitutionality of the practice of commercial money bail.[84] EJUL has filed ten class action money bail challenges across the United States, fighting to end the detention of individuals based on their poverty.[85] The group has succeeded in at least seven jurisdictions where money bail was done away with altogether, including cities in Alabama, Kansas, Mississippi, and Louisiana.[86] Additionally, they have filed suit and forced cities in Missouri and Louisiana to alter their bail systems and end the use of secured money bail for new detainees.[87] Before EJUL began their work, however, the necessary elements to prove that a bail scheme was a violation of the equal protection clause were exceedingly difficult to prove and only occurred in rare cases.

Equal Protection Under Law brought a successful suit in Missouri under the Equal Protection Clause. In June 2015, the Missouri district court ordered an injunction preventing the city from using secured money bail in any case (thereby outlawing commercial bail in the city) and issued a declaratory judgment stating that the Equal Protection Clause is violated when an individual is detained after an arrest because that person cannot afford to pay money bail.[88] The group relied on the Equal Protection Clause again in November 2015 to obtain a declaratory judgment in the Southern District of Mississippi. The federal court declared it unconstitutional for an individual to "be held in custody after an arrest because the person is too poor to post monetary bond."[89] Similarly in Tennessee, in an action brought by misdemeanor probationers challenging a detention scheme, the court granted a preliminary injunction holding that jailing probationers for failing to pay preset money bonds without an inquiry into their ability to pay violates the Fourteenth Amendment.[90]

In *Walker* v. *City of Calhoun*, a case out of Georgia, a federal district court granted a preliminary injunction against the City of Calhoun to prevent the city from detaining arrestees charged with misdemeanors until their policies conform to the Constitution.[91] The case involved an indigent arrestee who was held in jail for a week after being charged with a misdemeanor because of his inability to post the $160 money bail needed to be released.[92] The court based its reasoning on the Equal Protection Clause's protection against setting bail for an arrestee without taking into consideration an individual's indigent status.[93] The injunction decision primarily relied on cases supporting the notion that an individual should not be held in jail because of their inability to pay a fine, fee, or cash bond.[94] The government appealed this injunction to the Eleventh Circuit Court of Appeals and it was reversed on procedural grounds and sent back to the district court.[95] The appeal is important because this will be the first time that the issue of whether money bail violating the Equal Protection Clause was heard by a federal appellate court.[96]

In another recent suit, *Welchen* v. *Harris*, EJUL brought suit against the city and county of San Francisco, alleging their bail schedule is in reality a "wealth-based detention scheme" in violation of the Fourteenth Amendment's Equal Protection Clause.[97] County Sheriff Ross Mirkarimi has come out in support of this complaintant, stating that "the use of monetary conditions to detain pretrial defendants penalizes indigent arrestees solely based on their wealth status. The notion that someone's freedom depends on the amount of money they have is anathema to equality and justice."[98] The City of San Francisco District Attorney has also claimed that he will not defend the city's "unconstitutional" money bail system that unfairly harms the poor.[99] The first individual in the class action complaint brought by EJUL against San Francisco was arrested for shoplifting and conspiring with a department store employee in a series of thefts.[100] This individual's bail was set at $30,000, which she was unable to pay, so she remained in jail until her case was dismissed when the district attorney's office declined to file charges.[101] This case is still pending in California and may have significant impacts on money bail if there is a successful result.

In recent years, the Equal Protection Clause of the Fourteenth Amendment has successfully chipped away at the stronghold of commercial bail in the United States. While EJUL aims to end money bail, it is certainly still the default in almost all US jurisdictions. But more than ever, these recent constitutional challenges to money bail have gained traction in the courts.

10.3.2.2 Due Process Challenges

The story of Robert Blake provides an example of a successful Due Process Challenge to money bail. Robert Blake rented a movie, *Born on the Fourth of July*, and failed to return the videotape.[102] On July 5, 1993, Blake was arrested and charged with theft by fraudulent leasing. The court set Blake's bail at $300, but Blake only had $24 in savings. Blake was employed at the time of his arrest but owned no real estate. A bonding company would only post Blake's bond if he could raise $50 and have someone with a job sign for him. Blake was unable to satisfy these requirements. Alabama's bail law, which was new at the time, required an accused person to post bail, per the bail schedule, or for the accused to provide 72 hours of notice for the district attorney prior to the judicial bail hearing. Essentially, this law required defendants to be detained for 72 hours if they could not post bail, regardless of the crime. This law unfairly targets indigent defendants, while having very little impact on wealthy detainees.

A court analyzed constitutionality of this Alabama law in Blake's case. At the outset, the Alabama court recognized that the Fourteenth Amendment forbids any state from depriving "any person of life, liberty, or property, without due process of law." And indeed recognized that release is a constitutional right by stating that "liberty is the norm, and detention prior to trial . . . is the carefully limited exception."[103] The court then recognized the inherent Due

Process Clause violation in the Alabama scheme: "The pretrial detention of this defendant accused of a misdemeanor for possibly five or six days because of defendant's lack of resources interferes with the right of liberty, the premise of innocent until proven guilty, and shocks the conscience of this court."[104] The court went on to explain that detaining a defendant for 72 hours because they lack property or money is "[p]utting liberty on a cash basis," which was "never intended by the founding fathers as the basis for release pending trial."[105] Finally, after determining that this statute would allow a potentially dangerous criminal back on the streets quickly with no questions asked, while detaining a defendant who, say, forgot to return a movie to Blockbuster, the court found that "[t]he 72-hour delay has no reasonable basis for the protection of the public in any case where a non-violent defendant is held, merely because he has no money or anyone to pledge property for his release."[106] Accordingly, the court struck down the Alabama scheme as a violation of the Due Process Clause.

Similarly, Equal Protection Under Law has used Due Process arguments to challenge money bail practices. In Harris County Texas, the nonprofit won a case challenging bail practices because 80 percent of the county jail population is incarcerated simply because they cannot afford to make bail. These determinations without an individualized hearing for a particular defendant are violations of the Due Process Clause.[107] These cases provide hope as the Alabama and Texas schemes are very similar to other city and county bail schemes nationwide and provide important precedent to bring future constitutional challenges. Another Fourteenth Amendment challenge is to bail schedules that assign bail automatically based on the crime charged. These bail schedule challenges are discussed in the next section.

10.3.2.3 Bail Schedule Challenges

To further expedite pretrial hearings and respond to increasing numbers of arrests, some jurisdictions have created bail schedules.[108] Bail schedules are uniform tools that indicate what the bail amount or range should be for the crime charged. It is like a sentencing guideline, except designed for the pretrial context. For instance, in Harris County, Texas, the bail schedule starts with a proposal of $500 for first time low-level misdemeanor defendants with no prior record and increases from that starting point.[109]

A majority of counties surveyed in 2009 used money bail schedules, affixing a set bail amount to certain crimes.[110] Bail has a discriminatory effect on defendants who cannot afford bail because they are subject to release officials' discretion much more often than wealthy defendants, who quickly post the bail and are released.[111] Because bail is simple for courts, it has become the default release system for many jurisdictions over the past several decades.

There is heavy criticism of using money bail schedules for several reasons.[112] Most obviously, it neglects the fundamental constitutional right that a defendant has to release before trial as a default rule. In addition, money schedules ignore any observable presence or absence of risk and provide no information on whether the defendant may pose a danger to society, in case there is an exception.[113] Another problem is that judges may rely on the bail schedule and learn nothing about the defendant, or ignore information that may be presented about the individual circumstances of the defendant.[114] It certainly discourages a judge from seeking anything apart from the suggested bail on the schedule as this provides the quickest determination.[115]

Another problem with bail schedules is the discrepancy between them. A 2014 study conducted in New Mexico demonstrated that discrepancies in bond schedules can lead to disparities between defendants.[116] The study revealed that in Bernalillo County the majority of sexual offenses carry a "no bond hold," which means that all defendants accused of any of the listed sexual offenses are to be automatically detained pretrial. However, in Valencia County, there was an assigned bond amount at $100,000 for the exact same sexual offense.[117] Thus, in one county a defendant is detained and in another is allowed release for the same crime, thus demonstrating the lack of uniformity in bail schedules – even within a single state.[118]

Both the Due Process Clause and Equal Protection have been used to challenge bail schedules. The Due Process Clause argument against bail schedules is that they do not take into account individual circumstances in setting bail. The Equal Protection argument is that bail schedules do not consider the individual case of a defendant in setting bail, and disadvantage the poor vis-à-vis the wealthy in obtaining the constitutional right to release. A recent case that has raised these arguments is *Jones* v. *City of Clanton*.[119]

In *City of Clanton*, the plaintiff was jailed because she could not pay the money bail she was required to pay under the City of Clanton bail schedule. This case was brought on behalf of Christy Dawn Varden, a defendant who died before having the opportunity to even bring her claims. Ms. Varden was arrested and jailed for shoplifting, resisting arrest, failing to obey a police officer, and possession of drug paraphernalia – all misdemeanor offenses.[120] At the time Ms. Varden was arrested, a generic bail schedule was utilized, which meant that Ms. Varden was mandated $500 per misdemeanor charge. If able to pay the bond, defendants were granted immediate release. If unable to pay, they had to wait until the next court date, typically a Tuesday afternoon. The bail schedule required payment upfront and did not allow for secured release on recognizance or on an unsecured bond. In other words, a commercial bail bondsman was the only hope for a defendant to obtain release. This also meant indigent defendants (such as Varden) who could not afford bail could be held in detention for up to a week without any meaningful consideration of whether they posed a flight risk or a danger to the community and actually needed to be detained.

However, when the city discovered her lawsuit, Ms. Varden was immediately released and the city's bail policies changed. Specifically, the city now allows any person arrested on a misdemeanor violation to be released on an unsecured appearance bond as long as they don't have an outstanding warrant for failure to appear.[121] Under this updated policy, the city is still able to deny bail to anyone who poses a danger to themselves/others or whose release is precluded by statute. For anyone who does not obtain immediate release, the court will hold a hearing within 48 hours of the arrest to determine whether the person may be released and under what conditions. This settlement and the new bail schedule was deemed constitutional, and the issues regarding the past one were left undecided (although it was strongly implied the court would have found these unconstitutional). Though, the court in Varden's case found that the use of bail schedules to detain defendants without an individualized hearing violates the Due Process Clause of the Fourteenth Amendment.[122] The court also commented more broadly on the underlying problem with money based bail, "[C]riminal defendants, presumed innocent, must not be confined in jail merely because they are poor. Justice that is blind to poverty and indiscriminately forces defendants to pay for their physical liberty is no justice at all." [123]

The legality of nondiscretionary bail schedules has also been questioned in at least two other state Supreme Court decisions. In *Pelekai v. White*,[124] the Supreme Court of Hawaii found that a trial judge who rigidly followed the bail schedule without considering other characteristics of the defendant had abused their discretion. The defendant in question was unable to meet the bail required by the bail schedule and had moved for it to be reduced. In support of his argument, he provided evidence that he was a low flight risk and would appear in court. The judge, however, denied his requests because he had been assigned "the regular bail" provided by the schedule. In overturning the trial judge, the Hawaii Supreme Court held that the legislature had granted wide discretion to judges when setting bail, and that referencing the bail schedule as the standard when denying a defendant's request for reduction of that bail was an abuse of that discretion.[125]

Like Hawaii, the highest court in Oklahoma struck down a bail schedule as a violation of due process protections. The Oklahoma Court of Criminal

Appeals in 2002 also held that a bail schedule mandating a $15,000 bail for soliciting a prostitute violated the due process protections of the Oklahoma Constitution.[126] In determining this, the court held that the obvious intent of the section was pretrial punishment.[127] The court further found that the bail schedule at issue "unintentionally fosters the unnecessary detention of misdemeanants, indigents, and nondangerous defendants because they are unable to afford the sum mandated."[128]

More recently, EJUL challenged a bail schedule in Missouri with success. The plaintiff sought declaratory relief and class certification claiming that detention of arrestees for at least three days unless they pay a "generically set bond amount" violated the equal protection and Due Process Clauses of the Fourteenth Amendment.[129] The parties settled the suit after the court entered a declaratory judgment that holding an arrestee in custody because the person is too poor to post bail is a violation of the Fourteenth Amendment.[130] Following this, the court then ordered that the City of Velda stop utilizing secured money bail and further ordered the city to begin offering every arrestee release from custody on recognizance or an unsecured bond. However, persons brought before a court within 24 hours of arrest can still be detained if it is determined that they pose a danger to the community. The Eastern District of Missouri federal court held that "[n]o person may, consistent with the Equal Protection Clause of the Fourteenth Amendment to the United States Constitution, be held in custody after an arrest because the person is too poor to post a monetary bond."[131] Similarly, in the Southern District of Mississippi, in *Thompson v. Moss Point*, the federal court held that "[i]f the government generally offers prompt release from custody after arrest upon posting a bond pursuant to a schedule, it cannot deny prompt release from custody to a person because the person is financially incapable of posting such bond."

Money bail schedules continue to exist in most US jurisdictions, causing the greatest harm to indigent defendants who are severely disadvantaged in obtaining release from jail. The harm is not only to poor individuals, often accused of minor crimes, but these costs affect our broader society. Indeed, because pretrial detention leads to an increase in recidivism and an increased likelihood that a defendant will serve more jail time, the harm is not only to the defendant but to society. On top of these practical concerns, constitutional problems are rife as bail schedules do not provide an individualized determination of whether the defendant is safe to release, but instead release individuals based on a generic schedule. These schedules also fail to take into account the risks posed by the defendant, such that a poor nondangerous defendant is detained while a wealthy and potentially dangerous arrestee easily obtains release. This does not even consider the other potential constitutional violations of the Eighth Amendment as bail is set too high for a defendant to afford and is "excessive," or violates the presumption of innocence and due process because a defendant's right to release before trial is infringed.

10.4 BIG MONEY BAIL INDUSTRY

With all of the problems with commercial bail for both a defendant and the broader public, there may be a question of why it has grown so much in popularity or how it is even legal in the United States at all. There are three main reasons for this growth. First, commercial bail companies have argued (with some accuracy) that they are generally efficient and quick at releasing individuals and having them appear in court. They boast low failure to appear numbers for their clients. The most credible evidence to support this argument is a study by economists Alex Tabarrock and Eric Helland. Their results demonstrate that those released on bail bond are 28 percent less likely to fail to appear for their court date as compared to similarly situated individuals and 53 percent less likely to remain at large for an extended period of time.[132] However, those released on cash bonds had similarly low fugitive rates as those who obtained commercial bonds. And the study – significantly – didn't compare pretrial release supervision with these other release options. The District of Columbia, which avoids money bail and relies almost exclusively on pretrial supervision, has 91 percent release on recognizance with 90 percent appearing at every court date.[133] Given these numbers, it appears that some alternatives may provide even better results than commercial bail.

Second, commercial bail agents make the argument that they provide a private service to the public that is free to taxpayers. Because they privately contract with defendants to ensure that they appear in court, they do not represent a burden on public funds in the way government pretrial release options do. However, on the other hand, it is important to consider that commercial bail agents do not attempt to avoid rearrests of their clients and are focused solely on preventing failures to appear. In fact, the commercial bail agent is incentivized to have his client rearrested while released pretrial since they will likely get another call and another bail fee from the same person if they are taken to jail again. Accordingly, there are substantial numbers of individuals who are not "good" clients for commercial bail and in most jurisdictions without a public pretrial release option are unable to obtain release and remain in jail, which is much more costly to the public than pretrial release. Thus, reliance on a private option does not necessarily save the taxpayer money since there may be more individuals who are detained or not released on recognizance since commercial bail has become the norm in many jurisdictions.

Third, and probably the most significant cause of the growth in popularity of commercial bail as the most common release method, is that bail is a multibillion-dollar industry backed by special interest groups and a large insurance business. The bail industry has used lobbying efforts with its wealth to promote friendly legislation nationwide and has stopped bail reform efforts nationwide.[134] The use of money bail has increased substantially because of the influence the industry holds, particularly in the last twenty years. For instance, from 1994 to 2004, the percent of people in Harris County, Texas, on pretrial supervision required to post a bond increased from less than 3 percent to more than 60 percent.[135] The massive growth of bail as a method of pretrial release has not been coincidental but part of a strategic campaign by the bail industry. The next section discusses in further detail the lobbying efforts that have led to the growth of the bail industry and the limited requirements for bail forfeiture.

10.4.1 *Bail Industry Lobbying*

Lobbying is in large part an explanation of the success and growth of the commercial bail industry. The lobbying efforts for the bail industry are spearheaded by the American Bail Coalition (ABC), which represents over thirty surety companies that underwrite bail – in other words bail insurance. The bail insurance industry is a successful one. In 2012, American surety companies underwrote $13.5 billion in money bail bonds.[136] Sixty percent of these bonds are controlled by members of ABC.

The bail surety business is unique in its virtually foolproof profit model and has protected its business by investing in lobbying nationwide. Because bail sureties only pay claims when a bail bondsman goes out of business, they rarely pay. The bail company (or bondsman) pays if a defendant does not appear in court – and because of forfeiture laws this is also rare. One bail surety business, AIA Bail Bond Surety, that insures $700 million worth of bail a year boasts that they have never written a check to pay a bail loss.[137] Just as a comparison, property and auto insurance companies typically pay 40–60 percent of their revenue for losses. In contrast, the bail industry in 2012 paid a cumulative 1 percent of their revenue in bail losses. And because of this hefty profit, the surety business can afford to invest in lobbying efforts.

To this end, a group of nervous surety executives met in 1992 because the growth of pretrial services agencies was hurting the industry. Until 1992, the commercial bail industry was declining and sureties banded together to stop the decline.[138] This is when coordinated national lobbying efforts began. ABC sent letters to every county in the United States that had a pretrial service agency, citing data that claimed that commercial bail was more effective than pretrial services programs in getting defendants to appear for court.[139] These letters relied on Bureau of Justice Statistics data though it is disputed whether this data supports their claim. They also lobbied police, courts, and judges, chambers of commerce, rotary clubs, and others on bail convincing them that this private option was better for their budgets. The bail lobby was well-funded and extremely successful with state courts and legislatures. This lobbying movement was effective in reversing the growth of pretrial services. Indeed, in 1990 (before lobbying efforts), commercial bail was responsible for the release of 23 percent of releases, while 40 percent of individuals were released on recognizance.[140] These trends have reversed completely as today 23 percent of those released pretrial are released on recognizance and 49 percent have to rely on commercial bail.[141] And since 1990, the average bail amounts have tripled for felony cases so the revenues of ABC companies have increased 21 percent between 2004 and 2012.[142]

Bail lobbying efforts in the 1990s led to legislation in several states that helped advantage the bail industry. For instance, in 1993, bail lobbyists successfully passed a bill in New Orleans that required defendants to pay an extra 2 percent on top of their bail fee to the bail bondsman. This additional fee would be paid to the Sheriff's department, the district attorney, public defender, and the courts. In an interview, the lobbyist explained this scheme saying: "What [we] did . . . is . . . gave every criminal-justice player a financial interest in commercial surety." So if it was ever proposed to reduce reliance on commercial bail, "then you have every judge, every DA, every sheriff, every public defender's office saying, 'Wait a minute, you're taking money out of my pocket,'" he said. "The bail lobby is very powerful both locally and nationally. [Bondsmen] go to their legislators and seek provisions which are advantageous to their business model."[143] Another result of bail lobbying is forfeiture laws that make it very difficult for courts to collect bail fees from bondsmen when defendants fail to appear in court.

10.4.2 Bail Forfeiture or Lack Thereof

Commercial bail companies often avoid paying bail forfeitures when their clients do not appear in court. In other words, when defendants do not appear in court, many bail companies do not actually end up paying the full amount of bail, as the law requires. The way bail should work is that a defendant pays 10 percent of the full bail amount to the commercial bail agent and loses this money. The bail agent then promises to return the defendant to court for his court date, and if he does not, he must "forfeit" the entire bail amount to the court. So when forfeitures do not happen, this removes the incentive for bail companies to deliver clients to court. And it also eliminates the benefit of surety bonds from the court and public's perspective, and eliminates the purported public service commercial bail provides.

Nationwide forfeiture rates for bail are extremely low. In 2013, the state of New Jersey's Commission of Investigation reported bail bond companies paying only 12.5 percent of the forfeiture they owed on average.[144] In Utah, based on one year of data, only 1.7 percent of all surety bond cases involving a failure to appear resulted in a forfeiture.[145] In Dallas County, Texas, bail bond companies reportedly owe $35 million in forfeitures. One Colorado bondsman boasted that he had saved his company $400,000 by not paying forfeitures over the previous two years: "It's a game not to pay the forfeiture and I'm very good at what I do. There are a thousand tricks to not paying the court and after a few years I have it down pat."[146] Some jurisdictions encourage forfeiture avoidance by legally forgiving forfeitures with little effort on the part of the bondsman. In many jurisdictions, lobbying efforts have made it incredibly difficult for courts to collect bond money from commercial bail companies when a defendant does not appear for trial.[147]

A few states have tried to respond to this forfeiture problem and streamline bail collection from money bail companies. A few have adopted various measures to improve the collection process where a surety bond presence exists. In Florida, for instance, interest accrues against bond companies as time passes without payment, and courts refuse to accept future bonds until the forfeiture is paid.[148] In Connecticut, bail agents receive rebates for returning a defendant more quickly, but the opportunity to seek this remission expires after a year. All rebates are determined according to a schedule that relies on the number of days the defendant has been at large, and this schedule is standardized throughout the state.[149]

Despite these concerns over forfeiture, some states continue to pass laws to help bondsmen make even more of a profit. In 2013, Tennessee passed a law allowing bondsmen to end their responsibility for a defendant before their sentencing hearing. This law allowed bondsmen the opportunity to conclude their responsibility to the defendant after either a conviction or guilty plea.[150] This required the defendant to either pay for another bondsman, pay a deposit to the court (which they may not have), or wait for their sentencing hearing in jail.[151] After immediate backlash from practically the entire criminal law community, this statute was changed back to ensure that bondsmen are liable for their defendants up until their sentencing hearing.[152] Overall, with heavy lobbying by the bail industry, it is difficult to force bail companies to forfeit bail. In most states, bail companies and their sureties reap huge profits with very little downside, even if their clients fail to appear for court. Realizing this problem, there is a growing national movement and some individual states and even local communities are working to reduce reliance on money bail.

10.5 ABANDONING MONEY BAIL

There is a growing national consensus against commercial bail, and a concomitant effort to eliminate money bail altogether. The American Bar Association, the National Association of Counties, the International Association of Chiefs of Police, the American Civil Liberties Union, the National District Attorneys Association, and others have denounced commercial bail for unfairly discriminating against the poor and inappropriately relying on the private sector to protect important constitutional rights. In 2017, Senators Kamala Harris and Rand Paul proposed the "Pretrial Integrity and Safety Act" that aims to allow states to reform or replace their bail systems through federal funding.[153] Congressman Ted Lieu, Representative Bonnie Coleman, and others have proposed the "No Money Bail Act of 2016" that aims to eliminate all federal money bail and remove funding from states that allow money bail.[154] Former Attorney Generals Eric Holder and Loretta Lynch have condemned commercial bail as a major obstacle in cutting US incarceration rates,[155] and recently the Department of Justice declared money bail systems that detain defendants because they cannot afford bail unconstitutional.[156] This statement was historic in that this was the first time that the U.S. Department of Justice published any sort of opinion on the unconstitutionality of money bail. This statement drew national media attention and notably resulted in significant bail policy changes, ultimately setting the proper framework to change the course of bail reform.[157] In addition to these federal changes, several state courts and legislatures have proposed changes that aim to reduce reliance on money bail and community bail funds aim to help individuals pay high bails to avoid remaining behind bars.

10.5.1 *State Bail Reform Efforts*

There is active reform on the bail front in several US states.[158] Four states – Wisconsin, Illinois, Kentucky, and Oregon – have eliminated commercial bail and replaced it with pretrial services. Although some states do not directly regulate bondsman activity, currently twenty-one states have statutes favoring the release of defendants on a personal recognizance bond.[159] And in other states like New York, Connecticut, Maryland, Texas, Illinois, and Arizona, politicians and judges are demanding changes to money bail systems.[160]

Connecticut's governor recently announced a proposal for bail reform, which included a prohibition on setting money bail for anyone charged with a misdemeanor.[161] A 2016 constitutional amendment was passed in New Mexico authorizing only limited preventive detention and permitting those held on cash bond to petition the court for relief when they cannot afford bail.[162] As of April, the Arizona Supreme Court created a rule requiring all judges to first consider releasing a defendant without money bail – and if they set bail, to consider the accused's financial circumstances and set the least onerous bail amount.[163] In Maryland, the State's highest court recently adopted a landmark rule aimed at ending pretrial detention when a defendant cannot afford bail.[164] The Court of Appeals unanimously agreed on a compromise that instructs judges and commissions to first look to other ways to ensure a defendant appears for trial.[165] Under the new rule, judges and commissioners can and should use methods such as requiring drug counseling or Alcoholics Anonymous if that will ensure the defendant will appear for court. However, if the defendant presents a flight risk or poses a risk to the community that cannot be addressed through alternatives, the judge can still use money bail.[166]

Recent efforts are also under way in Texas, where Sandy Thompson, professor at University of Houston, has worked with the judiciary to create a resolution considering practical alternatives to money bail, including unsecured financial options and pretrial services. Texas has a bill currently pending that assures all defendants of a right to release and a bail determination based on a risk assessment.[167] In 2013, Kentucky passed a law that creates a presumption of release for low- and moderate-risk defendants and requires judges to justify in writing any decision to set financial bond on such a defendant. An assessment of Kentucky after reforms showed that 70 percent of defendants, half of them high risk, were released while their cases were pending, without any decrease in public safety (i.e., increased crime). Of those who were released, 90 percent of defendants made all their court appearances, demonstrating that without commercial bail Kentucky was successful in keeping crime rates low while releasing more people before trial.

Colorado and New Jersey recently instituted legislative bail reforms. In 2014, New Jersey passed legislation that moved it toward a risk-based system from a money-based system.[168] Under the New Jersey legislation, individuals are evaluated within 48 hours of arrest to determine the likelihood they will commit another offense, intimidate a witness, or flee.[169] Under the new system, defendants are assigned scores between 1 and 6, 1 being least risky.[170] Low-risk, nonviolent offenders are released on recognizance; high-risk offenders are released subject to conditions, and only defendants who pose the greatest risk will be detained without bail.[171] While bail is technically still an option, in reality judges have nearly done away with it. In fact, in the 3,382 cases that were processed in the first four weeks of implementation of the new system, judges set bail only three times.[172] Stuart Rabner, the state's chief justice, said that before the new system "a defendant who appeared in court would have been forced to post bail in a majority of cases."[173] There are certainly hiccups with any statewide reform, including some that complain that there are not enough resources to deal with the pretrial population, but overall the criminal justice community is grateful to no longer depend on money bail.[174]

Similarly, in 2013, Colorado enacted HB 13-1236, its first major overhaul of the pretrial bail statute since 1972.[175] This encouraged the use of risk assessment tools when determining which defendants should be released subject to supervision by a pretrial services agency. The first notable change is found in 16 C.R.S. § 1-104, the definition of bail is altered from an amount of money to simply a security – which allows for nonmonetary conditions.[176] The key overhaul, 16 C.R.S. § 4-103, focuses on determining the amount and type of bail, and requires courts to (1) determine the type of bond and conditions of release; (2) review the bond and conditions fixed upon return of an indictment or filing of an information or complaint; (3) give a presumption of release under least-restrictive conditions unless the defendant is unbailable pursuant to the constitutional preventive detention provisions; (4) individualize the conditions of release and express mandatory consideration of a defendant's financial condition or situation; (5) tailor all "reasonable" financial conditions and nonstatutory conditions of the bail to address any specific concerns; and (6) consider ways to avoid unnecessary pretrial detention.[177] For making these individualized bail determinations, the courts are encouraged to use an empirically developed risk assessment instrument – rather than common sense.[178] Other changes to Colorado law included eliminating provisions that presumptively set a monetary bail and ensuring that if a secured bond is ordered the defendant may make a motion for relief, which can only be denied within fourteen days of the motion and only after the judge has considered a risk assessment.[179] All of these changes combine to avoid the use of commercial bail where possible. Though commercial bail remains an option, at the discretion of a judge. In addition to state judicial and legislative changes and proposals, in many communities, individuals have started bail funds to help mitigate the harsh effects of money bail on the poor.

10.5.2 Community Bail Funds

In recent years, community groups across the United States have increasingly begun to use community bail funds to post bail on behalf of strangers, using a revolving pool of money.[180] These community bail funds have become a powerful presence in local criminal courthouses by providing bail for defendants who would otherwise be detained pending trial.[181] What distinguishes community bail funds from other sources of bail – such as family and friends, and crowdsourced individual bail funds – is that they are connected to bottom-up movements for change, posting bail for multiple defendants over time, using a rotating pool of money.[182] A community bail fund's interest in a defendant's case does not stem from a personal connection to each defendant. Rather the interest stems from broader beliefs regarding the overuse of pretrial detention among particular disadvantaged groups.[183]

Jocelyn Simonson, who has studied these funds, argues that when the "community" posts bail from a community bail fund, "an outsider organization can nullify an insider [court] decision by independently determining whether someone merits release pending trial."[184] Several bail funds have reported success in that over 90 percent of the defendants that they post bail for return to court.[185] There is also some important symbolism in that these funds "demonstrate through action that the community whose safety the court seeks to ensure may actually benefit from a defendant's release rather than from the setting of bail."[186] When the community posts bail through a fund, it recasts the place of the community in setting bail and emphasizes the role of the judge in both protecting the rights of the defendant and the community.[187] It also may encourage judges not to set high bail amounts to punish individual defendants for alleged crimes because the community is the body paying the price and demanding pretrial release.

But as these state and grassroots bail reform changes are happening nationwide, the bail industry is fighting these efforts. ABC has been present in each and every state that has considered (or is currently considering) reforms in bail. Not only are they working hard to stop the reduction in money bail but they continue to lobby for expansions in bail bonding. One that has received some traction in Michigan and Mississippi expands bail bondsman's role as a probation officer.[188] A person who is convicted of a crime can choose either to hire a bondsman to supervise them (like a probation officer would) or go to jail. If they have the money, they can pay the refundable fee to the court and have it returned. This expands bail – which has had negative consequences pretrial – into the postconviction setting and increases the possibilities for poor defendants to face detention simply because they lack the money to obtain release.[189] The fight against the money bail industry will continue nationwide as citizens and public advocacy groups are tired of a criminal justice system that disadvantages the poor and the bail industry works hard to protect its bottom line.

10.6 CONCLUSION

Overall, money bail has adverse consequences on defendants who are subjected to pretrial detention as a result of their indigent status. The history of
money bail shows how its use has changed over time. Money bail went from
a sum of money provided to the court that was returned, to a nonrefundable fee imposed on poor defendants that prevents many from receiving their
constitutional right to release before trial. There have been several successful constitutional challenges to money bail. Both the Eighth and Fourteenth
Amendments provide appropriate challenges to money bail. In recent years,
the Fourteenth Amendment Equal Protection and Due Process Clauses have
been helpful in challenging money bail – and even abolishing it in some cities
nationwide. Bail violates the Equal Protection Clause when one defendant
who is poor is unable to obtain release, while another who poses an equal
risk to society obtains release. Bail schedules are often seen as a due process
violation, as well as any schemes where judges set bail without an individualized determination of the circumstances of a particular defendant – not their
wealth. Despite these challenges, money bail has grown dramatically since
the 1990s to become the most popular pretrial release option. This is largely
because of successful lobbying of financial interests of the bail industry – both
bondsmen and their lucrative insurance backers. The growth has had a discriminatory affect against poor defendants and has cost states a lot of money
in increased incarceration costs. Not only do states often bear the costs of
increased detention before trial, but they often fail to pay courts when their
defendants do not appear – and get away with it due to their lobbying for prefer-
ential legislation that makes it nearly impossible for them to forfeit bail money.
The harms money bail imposes on defendants are significant and states are
beginning to take steps to mitigate the harmful effects. Some states and cities
have outright banned money bail and others have introduced legislation favoring other release options, like pretrial release using risk assessments.[190] This
fight between the money bail industry and the criminal justice community is
a live one as states constantly propose pretrial reforms while the industry fights
to retain its massive economic interest in criminal justice.

11

Optimal Bail: Using Constitutional and Empirical Tools to Reform America's Bail System

We don't have a system currently that does a decent job of separating who is dangerous and who isn't ... We only have a system that separates those who have cash and those who don't.

— Timothy Murry, former president of Pretrial Justice Institute[1]

Bail "reform" in America has typically resulted in locking more people up and reducing rights for defendants, but today's bloated and unjust US jail system begs for reform. The Bail Reform legislation of the 1960s and 1980s resulted in judges acquiring more legitimate reasons to keep someone behind bars pretrial. These periods brought legislation that allowed judges to legally detain more defendants for public safety reasons and "weigh the evidence" against defendants before trial, rather than simply detaining the defendants that were a flight risk. For this reason, this chapter discusses what "optimal bail," or bail reform in the modern age, should look like. Optimal bail, in contrast to the first and second generations of bail reform, focuses on both correct constitutional principles to govern bail and on releasing as many defendants safely while cutting incarceration costs. It identifies three principles that federal and state courts and legislatures should apply to ensure that all defendants have this right and that the public remains safe. All three of these principles are based on the history, constitutional analysis, and empirical analysis in the first ten chapters of this book. In each of the three sections, it also identifies tangible steps that can be taken to implement the three principles as well as state efforts – often backed with empirical data – that exemplify optimal bail and serve as a guide for the rest of the country.

The expansion of judges' rights to refuse pretrial release is evident in our ever-full jails. Just in the last ten years,[2] US jails have begun housing more pretrial detainees than convicts.[3] Before the Federal Bail Reform Act of 1984, pretrial release rates for defendants charged with felonies varied between

48 and 67 percent in different cities, and federally as many as 90 percent of defendants were released.[4] After the 1984 Act, the pretrial release rate dropped significantly. And just to see the comparison: in 1986, judges released 69 percent of federal defendants, and by 2004, judges only released 40 percent of federal defendants.[5] This increase of detention rates is evident at the state level as well. In the 1980s, pretrial detention rates were as low as 15 percent of all defendants prosecuted.[6] These rates have steadily risen; in 1990, 35 percent of defendants were being detained, and by 2009, 38 percent of defendants were being detained.[7]

So where most defendants were released before trial just a few decades ago, now most federal defendants are detained. And those who are released are released on less favorable terms. Where most defendants were released on their own recognizance (for free) in the 1990s, now most defendants have to pay to obtain release through commercial bail. And all other factors being equal, individuals detained pretrial are three times more likely to go to prison than someone charged who was released before trial.[8]

The three principles of optimal bail will help guide bail reform nationally. The first principle is that pretrial restraints of liberty should be limited to only where there is a proper legal basis.[9] The second principle is that there should be no pretrial determination of guilt without access to counsel. And the third principle is that a defendant's pretrial release should not be contingent on wealth. In line with these principles, there is national bail legislation proposed to reform bail at the federal and state level by reducing money bail, and many states are undertaking and succeeding at bail reform efforts with other initiatives. States where jails are overflowing with pretrial detainees have taken steps to increase pretrial release and reduce arrests. Increased incarceration raises costs to counties, which create an important local incentive to create sustainable long-term plans to deal with pretrial detention.[10] By utilizing a new model for predicting pretrial crime, creating alternatives to incarceration using technology, and expanding pretrial supervision and diversion programs and reducing money bail, states can dramatically save on detention costs. This chapter will discuss these practical reforms that help implement optimal bail principles.

11.1 THREE PRINCIPLES OF OPTIMAL BAIL

Three principles, rooted in the US Constitution and empirical data, help protect pretrial rights in a consistent and disciplined manner: defendants should be detained pretrial only with a proper legal basis; defendants are entitled to a presumption of innocence and counsel at bail hearings; and wealth should not interfere with an individual's constitutional right to release.

Current case law demonstrates that courts have neglected bail as a constitutional right. Instead, the focus on bail today is community safety and determining guilt. Clearer guidelines, preferably rooted in constitutional history and text, may be more effective to define the scope of pretrial bail reform and stop the slippery slope of reduced rights. The following sections lay out the three optimal bail principles – marshaled from the research presented in previous chapters in this book – to explain how pretrial detention can proceed in a constitutional manner. Each of the three principles provides the top reforms that effectuate the constitutionally backed right. By following these optimal bail rights, federal and state governments can improve incarceration rates (and criminal justice budgets), maintain public safety, all while releasing more individuals before trial. In each part, the principle is discussed, along with the practical reforms that help implement it. Many of these examples are backed by empirical data, and some take advantage of technology to release people safely before trial.

11.2 THE FIRST PRINCIPLE: DETAIN PRETRIAL ONLY IF PROPER LEGAL BASIS

First, pretrial restraints of liberty should be limited to only what is necessary and only where there is a proper legal basis. The pretrial default is the presumption of innocence and as few restraints of liberty as possible. The proper legal basis for restricting a person's liberty includes ensuring a person's attendance at trial and protecting the judicial process from interference by defendant. Though, if the defendant is detained (which should be a minority of cases), another proper basis is protecting the security of the facility while allowing the defendant full access to secure counsel communications, materials, and witnesses for trial preparation. Preventing judicial interference by a defendant may in some circumstances permit judges to consider the potential for future crimes on pretrial release where a defendant is a recidivist and has a serious record of prior convictions. If the court is permitted to consider a potential for future crimes (given a prior record), this determination should be done using sound empirical methods and a validated risk assessment.

To implement this first principle, the default for most defendants pretrial is release. Judges must release defendants pretrial unless there is a proper legal basis to detain them. To formulate a proper legal basis, the judge must rely on empirical data, not gut instinct. The empirical data detailed in Chapters 4–6 demonstrate how judges can decide which defendants are safe to release and which pose a high danger to the public. They can also help counties reduce racial bias in bail determinations and save money by releasing more individuals who are safe to release. This empirical information will help judges to make smarter bail decisions by relying on data rather than gut instinct alone. A defendant who poses a high risk of harming people while released from trial should be detained. Given the data, however, this is a very small number of defendants. The individuals with the highest risk to release – those with three or more convictions for a violent crime and charged with a violent crime – still only have a 6 percent risk of committing a violent crime while released. While it may make sense to detain these individuals, most felony defendants have less than a 3 percent chance of committing a violent crime while released.[11] Given this reality, we closely consider risk assessments next since they help judges determine which defendants pose a high risk of harm to others and which defendants are safe to release. To reiterate what has been said repeatedly throughout this book, a much larger percentage of defendants are safe to release (than are currently released), as the default should be release.

Respecting the liberty of defendants and not restraining them pretrial any more than is constitutionally permitted may involve the use of technology – including electronic monitoring. Many states have initiated reform programs that have increased release for defendants while reducing corrections costs. This section details various successful state efforts at bail reform that may serve as examples for other states and as a national model. By supervising defendants outside detention facilities, using ankle bracelets and other technology, a state can save money and may even improve pretrial behavior of defendants. Because many defendants do not present a significant risk to the community, the state can decrease costs and improve the pretrial detention system by measuring the defendant's risk and then assigning the least restrictive conditions of release, while still ensuring attendance in court.

11.2.1 *Proper Legal Basis to Detain*

The first principle asserts that a person's liberty should *only* be restricted when there is a proper legal basis. The reason for this is that the right to release is a constitutional right. Due process requires a defendant to be granted release pretrial, unless one of the exceptions applies. The exceptions include flight risk and, more recently, danger to the community. This historic right is traced from the Magna Carta through to the Bill of Rights and the founding of the US states. A defendant is deemed innocent until the judicial process is complete and it has been found otherwise.[12] In order to detain an individual properly before trial, there must be a hearing where defendant is represented and the government establishes with clear and convincing evidence that there are no conditions under which a defendant can be released safely.[13]

Accordingly, a proper legal basis to detain a defendant before trial is *not* a judge's feeling that the defendant is likely guilty. A proper legal basis is also not to prevent the defendant from committing additional crimes. A legal basis exists only where it is necessary to ensure the defendant's court appearance, protects the judicial process from interference, and secures the facility while granting the defendant full access to materials and witnesses for trial preparation when a defendant is detained. In order to determine whether there is a necessity to detain a defendant, a risk assessment should be conducted, as discussed later.

11.2.2 *Protecting Against Judicial Interference*

Protecting the judicial process from interference from defendants is a legitimate condition that would justify pretrial detention. Although due process requires that every defendant be granted a fair trial and guarantees release for most defendants, if a defendant substantially interferes with a fair trial, he should not be released before trial. It is important to prevent defendants from threatening witnesses or harming victims in any way while on release. If an individual poses a high risk of violent crime that cannot be mitigated with conditions, a judge should detain her. Given the risks posed however, this should be a small number of individuals. Also, courts should use other measures or conditions to prevent defendants from intervening before resorting to pretrial detention.

One of these other measures or conditions is called a "no-contact" bond. This is a condition that is imposed on a defendant to prevent her from intervening with individuals involved in the case. When this is imposed, it means the defendant cannot have any contact with whomever the judge orders. Contact includes anything from calls, letters, third-party contact, and direct physical contact. This condition is generally placed on a defendant charged with a violent crime, who has been released pretrial. Like all other release conditions, any violation could result in a revocation of the bond and the defendant being detained until the court date. "No-contact" conditions remain in effect for the entire duration of a criminal case or until there is a request that it be removed or lifted and the judge approves.[14] However, a defendant can be detained in an extreme case where the government can prove that there is a serious risk of the defendant threatening witnesses or interfering with them testifying at trial and that other conditions are not likely to be effective.[15] The government should carry the burden to prove this sort of threat of interference, and the presumption should always be of release before trial. Alternatively, the government can hold a defendant if there is a substantial risk due to the defendant's out-of-state or country connections that even with safety measures he will flee the jurisdiction. However, the flight risk issue is a much smaller one in the world of ankle bracelets, passport freezes, and tracking devices. Overall, unless there is a serious risk of interference by a defendant with witnesses or victims – with no conditions to mitigate the risk – a defendant should maintain her constitutional right to pretrial release. Again, to determine whether a defendant will inappropriately interfere with the judicial process upon release, judges should conduct a risk assessment.

11.2.3 *Securing Detention Facilities*

Securing a detention facility when a defendant is detained is another proper legal basis that allows a defendant's rights to be restricted. And if a defendant is detained for proper legal reasons, limits can be placed upon her while in detention. A defendant's liberty should be respected as much as possible while detained pretrial, so that due process principles are not violated. If all three of the optimal bail principles are respected, instances of detention will be rare.

However, even while detained, *all* defendants should be granted full access to materials and witnesses necessary for trial preparation. As discussed in Chapter 2, defendants maintain some rights to the presumption of innocence and due process while detained pretrial. While the Supreme Court in *Bell* v. *Wolfish* placed some limits on rights while a defendant is detained, these are only limits on rights to the extent they are necessary to maintain security at a detention facility. *Bell* dealt with a constitutional challenge to conditions at a temporary detention center that required pretrial detainees to share a room, prohibited them from receiving certain books or packages, and subjected them to mandatory body-cavity searches following outsider visits. The Supreme Court has made clear that some liberty restraints are permitted under due process principles. The key from *Bell* is that restrictions imposed to maintain security of the facility and to ensure the presence of defendant at trial are permissible.

For instance, strip searches that occur when a person is detained temporarily do not restrain a defendant's liberty. While they certainly infringe on a defendant's privacy rights, on the whole they do not violate the first optimal bail principle. Strip searches, while "embarrassing and distasteful when occurring for all defendants placed in a correctional facility, do not favor some defendants over others, deprive liberty, or allow judges to make trial-appropriate determinations about defendants before trial."[16]

Due process protects defendants from pretrial "punishment" and focuses on allowing them to prepare for trial – with minimal limits placed on defendants' liberty to secure the detention facility. Limits on a defendant pretrial that are likely to be unconstitutional are those that interfere with the defendant's ability to prepare an adequate defense. So limits on personal mail defendants can receive, invasive searches of defendants or other visitors of detention facilities, and defendants sharing a room are unlikely to be violations of constitutional rights. However, restrictions that would likely violate due process rights of pretrial detainees would be limits on the types and number of visitors they are able to receive while detained, restrictions in sharing documents that relate to witness preparation, special prohibitions on making calls, receiving confidential mail, and using library or computer facilities. These are particularly offensive to the presumption of innocence and due process principles that protect a defendant and require that a defendant maintains her innocence and unfettered access to materials used to defend herself at trial.

   In sum, this first principle accurately illustrates the limited times when a person's liberty should be restricted, and that is only when there is a proper legal basis. This legal basis exists to ensure that the defendant appears in court, the judicial process is protected from interference, and if a defendant is detained – the facility is secure while granting the defendant full access to materials and witnesses for trial preparation. To appropriately determine whether a proper legal basis to detain exists, the decision should be made using evidence and a pretrial risk instrument. Before discussing how to conduct a proper pretrial risk assessment, however, it is important to consider what the appropriate level of risk society should accept in releasing a defendant.

11.2.4 *Determining the Appropriate Level of Risk*

The first question a jurisdiction must address in creating a pretrial risk instrument is a theoretical one: what is the appropriate level of risk we should tolerate? Certainly, the answer from judges and policymakers would be as little as possible, as the thought of releasing an individual and having them commit a violent crime is a terrible one. It is one that weighs on the mind of many judges when they deny certain individuals the right to release. In Chapter 4, I've highlighted which defendants pose a high risk of committing violent crimes on release. Risk assessments – individualized to the needs of a particular jurisdiction – should be used to determine which defendants pose a low risk. My research with Frank McIntyre studying 100,000 defendants in seventy-five counties demonstrates pretty clearly that individuals charged with public order offenses, white-collar crime, drug offenses (both possession and trafficking), and older defendants (over forty) are very unlikely to commit a violent crime. Indeed, this study showed that if judges focused on releasing these groups of defendants and detained more individuals with a violent crime history (three or more convictions), judges could release up to 25 percent more defendants and reduce pretrial crime rates.[17] Indeed, in his recent book, *Locked In*, John Pfaff confirms that violent behavior is a "phase, not a state" and that prisoners "age out" and are unlikely to reoffend after a certain age.[18] Adam Gopnik further points out in a review of this book: "The fact is that if we let everyone convicted of a violent crime out of prison on his fortieth birthday there would be little risk for the rest of us. Like lifelong 'sex offenders,' violent recidivists are rarer than you might think."[19] Thus, age is an important consideration in determining which defendants to release pretrial – as those under forty pose a much greater risk than older defendants.

In my earlier work, I pointed out that the risk level posed by some average members of the public is actually higher than some of those released regularly pretrial.[20] In the general population, the probability that someone over the age of fifteen is arrested on a violent felony charge is 0.02 percent, which translates into about 1 in every 5,000 people.[21] Among teenage boys in the general population, the probability is 0.06 percent, so a little over 1 in every 2,000.[22] And the arrest rate for black teenage boys in inner city populations is likely to be higher than 0.2 percent, which is higher than some convicted felons.[23] These numbers are only interesting because clearly we would not arrest all black teenage boys because they pose a higher risk than white teenage boys – or even older individuals for that matter. Society simply has to be prepared to accept a higher amount of risk for certain groups in order to maintain constitutional rights for all. What these numbers do tell us is that, if we accept a certain level of risk from general members of the public, it probably does not make sense to incarcerate some equally safe felony defendants.

Sandra Mayson has fleshed out this argument in some interesting new research on pretrial release and risk.[24] She argues that as a society we need to determine the threshold risk at which we would allow restraint of a nonaccused person (or a member of the regular public). This obviously does not exist, therefore Mayson argues that because there are no "doctrinal, deontological, or instrumentalist arguments that justify otherwise impermissible restraint," we should not allow pretrial holding of defendants for dangerousness.[25] She argues that we must decide what degree and likelihood of risk is sufficient to warrant preventive interference with individual liberty, and once we determine that threshold, we should ensure that the methods of risk assessment and management are actually responsive to that threshold.[26] But in the meanwhile she suggests that we should specify that nothing less than a substantial likelihood of serious violent crime in the pretrial phase warrants restraint for dangerousness.[27] Second, she believes that pretrial risk assessment tools should measure and communicate the likelihood of serious violent crime.[28] And finally, she suggests we evaluate different types of potential interventions on the basis of their efficacy at reducing serious violent crime.[29] Mayson's focus pretrial is violent crime, and as my research points out, this is the most important factor for judges making pretrial decisions as well.

However, there is a strong argument for detention for those concerned about pretrial crime. Ronald Allen and Larry Laudan point out that while pretrial release benefits society by preventing detention of many innocent people, it costs society by releasing a greater number of felons on the streets for several more months.[30] Allen and Laudan's data rightly indicates that 15 percent of those released pretrial in a year – approximately 45,000 defendants – committed new crimes while on pretrial release, increasing the amount of pretrial crime considerably.[31] Much of this crime is not violent crime however; a very small number of pretrial defendants commit violent felonies while released on bail.[32] In my empirical study, Frank McIntyre and I found that several groups of federal defendants who are often detained are only about 1–2 percent likely to be arrested for a violent crime if released pretrial.[33]

These low violent crime rates are not exclusive to my study of large countries. For example, as recently as 2016, statistics show that only 3 percent of defendants released pretrial in Lucas County, Ohio, were arrested for violent crimes.[34] Similarly in New York, 3 percent of defendants released pretrial in 2001 were rearrested for violent crimes out of the 17 percent total that were rearrested.[35] This low pretrial violent crime rate should be directly proportionate to the number of defendants detained pretrial since the overall goal is to detain defendants who pose a substantial threat to the community. And as discussed in Chapter 4, with new empirical tools, violent crime risk can be predicted and those defendants that pose significant risk of violent crime can be singled out and detained to protect public safety. In addition, detaining or possibly placing restrictive conditions on individuals with an active criminal justice record when arrested may help reduce arrests before trial and should be considered in a risk assessment.

As I demonstrate in Chapter 5, the risk of violent crime for most pretrial defendants is relatively low, and this should be considered in determining the appropriate level of risk that society should be willing to tolerate. At the very least, what the bulk of research demonstrates is that too many defendants with extremely low violent crime risk are being detained before trial. If judges were more attuned to detaining only those who pose a serious violent crime risk pretrial, rather than simply allowing defendants who are more wealthy to be released based on their ability to receive money bail, we may be able to decrease the risk we are taking before trial and release more individuals.

A tool to help obtain this goal is a pretrial risk instrument, discussed in the next section.

11.2.5 *Using Pretrial Risk Instrument to Help Judges*

States should use pretrial risk assessment instruments to determine which defendants are likely to fail to appear in court or which pose a significant risk of committing a violent crime pretrial. This tool is typically a one-page summary of defendants' characteristics, which scores defendants on their likelihood of pretrial success (i.e., appearing in court) or the risk they pose of committing a violent crime.[36] This instrument usually consists of seven to ten questions concerning the defendant's alleged offense, criminal history, employment, residency, drug use, and mental health.[37] The defendant's responses are then tallied based on data that shows how each factor relates to pretrial failure. Once this is all gathered, the judge or other decision-maker uses this score to make a proper pretrial release decision. Pretrial instruments, based on empirical data, will improve the accuracy of these determinations.[38] To build further on the proficiency of pretrial risk assessment tools, early screening from an experienced prosecutor should be paired with it. Before a defendant's initial court appearance, an experienced prosecutor should screen all criminal cases then use the pretrial risk assessment tool to help aid them in their decision-making. This early screening allows for timely charges, dismissals, diversions, or other pretrial eligibility determinations.[39]

Jurisdictions vary in bail statutes, court rules, pretrial release options, and other factors. Because of this, ideally each jurisdiction should collect data to create and validate its own pretrial risk assessment instrument. These instruments should be reevaluated regularly to ensure their predictive accuracy. A chart comparing the various pretrial risk assessment tools appears in Appendix 1. In order to conduct these evaluations, jurisdictions should gather data about defendants' pretrial release, the quality and quantity of the supervision conditions imposed, pretrial behavior, and case outcome.[40] While these instruments cannot predict with 100 percent accuracy, research has shown that they provide higher accuracy in assessing the likelihood of defendants' pretrial failure than subjective assessments made by experienced judges and decision-makers.[41]

A new and potentially viable pretrial risk assessment option for many jurisdictions may be one created by the Laura and John Arnold Foundation (LJAF). LJAF created an assessment with the largest set of pretrial records ever assembled (1.5 million cases from 300 jurisdictions) and researchers analyzed the data and identified the nine factors that best predict whether a defendant will commit new crime, a new violent crime, or fail to appear if released.[42]

This risk assessment only considers factors related to the defendant's current charge, age, and criminal history (both failure to appear and prior violent crime). Though most risk assessments consider other factors – like employment, home-ownership, employment, and family status – these other factors are less predictive and more likely to discriminate on the basis of race. This relatively new tool is currently being tested in several jurisdictions by Jim Greiner and Christopher Griffin at Harvard's Access to Justice lab. While results have yet to be collected, many are hopeful that this tool that considers both violent crime risk and failure to appear will be validated nationwide.

Several states have experienced success with their own state pretrial risk assessments. Kentucky has implemented a pretrial instrument that has been so successful in assessing risk that the legislature mandated its use prior to *all* defendants' first appearances.[43] Mecklenburg County, North Carolina, followed Kentucky and also implemented their own pretrial risk assessment instrument in 2010. As a result, the average daily jail population was reduced by 33 percent.[44] A Virginia pretrial risk assessment was tested in a 2009 study. The study proved the accuracy of this assessment by showing that low-risk defendants had a 92.9 percent success rate, average-risk defendants had an 82.2 percent success rate, and high-risk defendants had a 68 percent success rate.[45] It is important to take note of the fact that even the highest risk defendants still had reasonable success rates with appropriate conditions of supervision.[46] Like Virginia, Washington DC relies on a highly successful risk assessment tool that includes release conditions for the highest risk defendants. This risk assessment considers thirty-eight factors, such as pretrial flight history, pending criminal justice actions, citizenship, substance abuse, and mental health. High-risk defendants assessed within this program have a wide variety of release conditions including frequent drug testing, stay away orders, substance abuse treatment, mental health treatment, and/or frequent contact requirements with pretrial officers.[47] Some of the defendants who are the highest risk may even be subject to home confinement, electronic tracking, or placement in halfway houses.[48] Statistics show that Washington DC pretrial assessments have been extremely successful: 89 percent of arrestees appear in all court proceedings, and 88 percent of arrestees have no rearrests.[49]

Pretrial risk instruments can help jurisdictions improve appearance at trial, reduce pretrial crime, and cut incarceration rates in their jurisdictions. A pretrial risk assessment is certainly an important tool in reforming bail in America. The next section provides more detail on how a jurisdiction can construct a pretrial risk assessment.

11.2.5.1 A Closer Look at Pretrial Risk Assessments

To construct a new prescreening tool, jurisdictions must adjust the tool and scoring system to match the characteristics of their respective populations.[50] This data should then be organized to determine cutoff scores at which offenders will be categorized as "higher" or "lower risk" or given a number of a scale of say, 1–10. The cutoff points will differ among jurisdictions, but can be chosen based on the percentage of the population the jurisdiction is able to supervise administratively or detain.[51]

Of all the states that have implemented a pretrial risk assessment, Colorado is one that custom tailored a tool after significant research and analysis. In order to design its pretrial assessment tool, the pretrial services program staff conducted interviews with 2,000 pretrial defendants and supervised them, collecting and analyzing their data.[52] Staff reviewed all defendants' charging documents, criminal history records, jail information systems, and pretrial case tracking systems. They also considered data on demographics, residence, employment, mental health, substance use/abuse, criminal history and past criminal involvement, and current charges. In the end, of all the defendants who participated in this study, Colorado released 66 percent of defendants on pretrial release, detained 33 percent, and purged approximately 1 percent of the cases for various reasons.[53]

The pretrial services program staff created a twelve-factor tool that assigned specific weight according to its individual contribution to a defendant's final risk score. The twelve factors, along with their maximum points allotted, are given in the following table.[54]

Pretrial risk factor	Maximum points
1) Having a home or cell phone	5
2) Owning or renting one's residence	4
3) Contributing to residential payments	9
4) Past or current problems with alcohol	4
5) Past or current mental health treatment	4
6) Age at first arrest	15
7) Past jail sentence	4
8) Past prison sentence	10
9) Having active warrants	5
10) Having other pending cases	13
11) Currently on supervision	5
12) History of revoked bond or supervision	4

The defendant's total risk score was then calculated by adding all of the points together, ranging on a scale of 0–82. Once a defendant received a score, he was placed into one of the following four categories.[55] Category 1 defendants have a 91 percent public safety rate, 95 percent court appearance rate, and 87 percent overall combined success rate. Category 4 defendants have a 58 percent public safety rate, 82 percent court appearance rate, and 68 percent overall combined success rate.[56]

Risk category	Risk score
1 (safest)	0–17
2	18–37
3	38–50
4 (highest risk)	51–82

Of the 2,000 defendants in the study, 20 percent of defendants were in category 1, 49 percent in category 2, 23 percent in category 3, and 8 percent in category 4.[57] Indeed only 8 percent of Colorado defendants were in the highest risk and posed a risk to the community of not appearing for their court date. With this low of a percentage of pretrial detainees at risk for pretrial failure, the rate of pretrial detention *should* be just as low. The importance of jurisdictions tracking the risk posed by pretrial defendants cannot be overemphasized. Without actual data that accurately accounts for defendant risk, judges tend to overestimate this risk and detain too many defendants before trial. Though, as discussed in the next section, Colorado's risk assessment tool may not be the best model for states, it demonstrates in detail how a risk assessment can help judges determine which defendants pose the highest risk.

11.2.5.2 Pretrial Risk Assessment Concerns

Pretrial risk assessments, while by comparison to money bail are wholly more fair for defendants and present a better bargain for counties, raise some concerns. These concerns can be carefully considered and addressed with the right risk instrument and careful data analysis and tracking after implementation.

An important consideration in a risk assessment is that there are two separate pretrial considerations – the risk of dangerousness (potential safety concerns of the community or witnesses) and the risk of flight. Often judges (and risk assessment instruments) merge the consideration of these risks inappropriately in assessing whether to release the defendant pretrial. Even the lauded LJAF risk assessment tool considers flight risk and dangerousness together.

Lauryn Gouldin demonstrates in her research that these two determinations should be considered separately.[58] For one, the burden of proof for detaining a defendant for dangerousness requires clear and convincing evidence, while the standard for flight risk is a preponderance of the evidence standard.[59] Additionally, considering these risks together may lead to overestimation of risk; instead, judges should conduct separate analyses for the two questions and impose separate conditions to mitigate the pretrial risks.[60]

Another concern is that risk factors may still rely too heavily on defendants' immutable characteristics, which include race, gender, age, socioeconomic status, and family background.[61] Indeed, if we are not careful, risk assessments could "worsen the intersectional racial, class, and gender disparities that already pervade our criminal justice system."[62] While none of the current risk assessment tests outright considers a person's race as a factor, "criminal record operates as a proxy for race."[63] And often socioeconomic, family, and neighborhood-related factors are highly race-correlated.[64] It is important to carefully assess the impact of race-correlated factors in a pretrial assessment to ensure that they are not cementing racial bias. Additionally, as discussed in Chapter 10, wealth is an important determinant of who is detained pending trial and minorities and those who are poor are more likely to feel the effects of pretrial detention.[65] For instance, even considering Colorado's careful and well-researched pretrial assessment tool, three of the factors explicitly consider wealth of the defendant: owning a house or phone, making residential payments, and paying rent. Many other state assessments are similar. Thus, even moving toward a risk-assessment model from a money bail schedule may not eliminate inequality completely. Risk assessments may still result in the disproportionate pretrial detention of poor and minority communities, if this is not carefully monitored and evaluated.[66] In sum, the best risk assessment considers flight risk and violence separately, and considers criminal history, criminal justice status, and the current charge to determine risk of release – without considering other factors that may unfairly bias minority and poor defendants. With a careful risk assessment and a policy that favors releasing the majority of defendants to respect the constitutional right to release before trial, we move closer to an optimal system of bail.

11.3 THE SECOND PRINCIPLE: NO PRETRIAL DETERMINATION OF GUILT AND NO BAIL HEARING WITHOUT COUNSEL

The second principle of optimal bail is that there should be no pretrial determination of guilt without access to counsel and no bail hearing without counsel. The pretrial decision should honor Due Process and the Sixth

Amendment and not consider the defendant's guilt. Since the bail reform of the 1980s, judges have "weighed" evidence of defendants' guilt before trial in considering whether they should be released. This involves an eyeball determination of guilt during a bail hearing, which, as Chapter 3 describes, is usually a 1–5-minute process without counsel present or evidence presented. This does not meet the demands of Due Process for determining guilt. Certainly, if the previous chapters of this book have established anything, it is the importance of the bail decision on the fate of the defendant. The bail determination is the difference between a defendant obtaining release and being able to adequately prepare for trial, obtaining a noncustodial and shorter sentence, maintaining employment and family responsibilities, and not being pressured to plead guilty. But not only is this decision harmful to a defendant but this pretrial determination of guilt also violates Due Process principles that require guilt to be determined exclusively at trial – and demand a presumption of innocence before that point. As discussed in Chapter 7, it also violates the principles of the Sixth Amendment that require a trial by a jury of one's peers as well as advice and representation of counsel at any important hearing. Further, the Sixth Amendment requires juries, not judges, to determine facts about a defendant's case, thus these facts cannot be determined before trial. And each defendant who cannot afford counsel must have an attorney to represent her at her bail hearing, as required by the Sixth Amendment and recent Supreme Court precedent.

The next section discusses the importance of prohibiting judges from "weighing" the evidence against defendants before trial.

11.3.1 No Weighing of Evidence Before Trial

In order to implement the second principle of optimal bail, there are several practical reforms discussed in greater detail in Chapters 2 and 7 that implement these important constitutional rights. First, statutes that allow "weighing" of any evidence of guilt before trial – and without a proper hearing – should be replaced, as they violate Due Process and the Sixth Amendment. There are twenty-seven state statutes and the federal standard that all allow weighing of evidence by judges before trial.[67] A judge determining that the weight of the evidence is against a defendant in a pretrial hearing without counsel is a clear violation of a defendant's constitutional rights.[68]

The second principle avoids the practice of judges determining prematurely whether individuals are guilty before they have had a fair trial. While the Due Process Clause requires a conviction of guilt by a jury in order to punish an individual, the Supreme Court has held that pretrial detention does not violate due process.[69] In 1987, *United States* v. *Salerno* addressed the constitutionality of the Bail Reform Act and authorized pretrial detention on the basis of "future dangerousness" and after considering the "nature of circumstances" of the defendant's alleged crime. The Supreme Court stated that pretrial detention – in and of itself – did not equate to "impermissible punishment before trial" because it is imposed as a regulatory measure to prevent danger in the community.[70] The court held that since the Bail Reform Act has a "legitimate and compelling regulatory purpose" and offers procedural protections, the act does not violate due process.[71] However, the court stated specifically that the defendant would be represented by counsel at this initial hearing, have the right to present witnesses and cross examine government witnesses, and have counsel represent her. And while the federal system does guarantee counsel at bail hearings, most states (over half) do not provide these procedural protections. Therefore, the "weighing of evidence" and other determinations made pretrial in most states and in some federal cases are likely to violate the due process clause.

Federal bail law, 18 U.S.C. § 3142(g), allows as a factor in determining detention a consideration of the "weight of the evidence" against a defendant. Typically, this "weight" is considered quickly and without respect to due process in the bail hearing (which can last thirty minutes or less). This is inappropriate in the federal context, where defendants continue to maintain the constitutional right to release in most cases. Especially after *Apprendi* and its progeny have established the importance of judges not making factual decisions, and reinvigorating the jury's right to make all determinations of fact.[72] This "weighing" language is also repeated in many state bail laws that also allow weight of the evidence to be considered in determining bail. Many states allow weight of the evidence as a consideration in a bail hearing and these statutes should be revised as a violation of Due Process. And in the federal system, where defendants are not allowed an opportunity to examine witnesses and present evidence at a bail hearing, these rights should be extended.

On top of violating Due Process, judges are infringing upon the Sixth Amendment right to trial by jury in determining facts at the bail hearing. The presumption of innocence guaranteed to criminal defendants is removed when judges are deciding matters of guilt or innocence at the pretrial phase. The only way to safeguard an accused's presumption of innocence is to leave all issues of guilt and innocence up to a jury. Judges are constitutionally barred from making such determinations because of the right to a trial by jury and thus should not be doing so. When judges decide facts before trial, they use an unacceptable and unconstitutional standard of proof; the only standard appropriate for criminal matters is beyond a reasonable doubt.

The importance of the jury as the finder of fact has only begun to be revisited pretrial – as it has been in the sentencing context with *Apprendi* and its progeny – and it is imperative that judicial actions pretrial are examined under a Sixth Amendment lens. Indeed, weighing facts about a defendant's guilt before trial is both a violation of Due Process and the Sixth Amendment.

11.3.2 *Counsel at Every Bail Decision*

All defendants should have counsel to represent them at a pretrial bail hearing. Only about half of jurisdictions in the United States provide counsel for a bail hearing even though Supreme Court precedent makes it clear that counsel should represent defendants at every critical hearing. The bail decision is the most important decision – besides arrest – that determines the fate of each defendant. Studies over the years have demonstrated that having an attorney advocate for defendants at bail hearings significantly improves the accused's probability of being released on her own recognizance, having their bail reduced (and by a larger amount), having bail set affordably, and spending less time in jail. In addition, not having counsel at a bail hearing results in possible self-incrimination, increased incarceration, inability to prepare an adequate defense, and additional pressure to plead guilty despite innocence. Because of this, the right to counsel must be extended to the pretrial phase for defendants nationally in order to combat the injustices of current bail practices.

In addition, a landmark Supreme Court case on bail, *Rothgery* v. *Gillespie County* holds that when there is potential substantial prejudice, there is a need for counsel to represent a defendant. If initial appearances are deemed as "critical stages," it would essentially guarantee an attorney to be present during initial hearings.[73] It is hard to imagine with all of the evidence mounted in this book and recent studies supporting this premise that the bail hearing would not be considered a "critical" stage of the criminal process for a defendant. The Sixth Amendment Right to Counsel should apply to bail as a "critical stage."[74] According to the Supreme Court in *Coleman*, a bail setting should be considered a critical stage because defense counsel could "expose fatal weaknesses in the State's case, learn about the allegations in order to prepare 'a proper defense,' and make 'effective arguments' for an early psychiatric examination or release."[75] However, earlier, in *Gerstein* v. *Pugh*, the court indicated that pretrial custody has a limited effect and therefore is not a critical stage.[76]

Certainly *Rothgery* has challenged this notion, in at least finding that Texas's pretrial hearing determining bail and access to counsel constituted a critical hearing.[77] Rothgery's Sixth Amendment rights were violated when he was unable to receive counsel at the initial hearing and he was actually told that the appointment of counsel would delay setting bail and his release from jail. He was placed in a difficult situation – as many pretrial defendants are – of "proceeding without counsel or remaining in custody."[78] Thus, Rothgery waived his right to counsel in order to have bail set. He could not afford bail and remained in jail anyway for six months without a lawyer. Six months later, Rothgery was finally assigned a lawyer who obtained a bail reduction, allowing Rothgery to get out of jail. While the holding in Rothgery was a narrow one, the Supreme Court affirmed that the Sixth Amendment right to counsel attaches at a "criminal defendant's initial appearance before a judicial officer, where he learns the charge against him and his liberty is subject to restriction."[79] Indeed, after *Rothgery*, defendants can make a strong argument that the initial bail hearing is a critical hearing where the Sixth Amendment requires a defendant to have access to counsel. In addition to the strong precedent supporting this right, there is a high likelihood of harm and increased likelihood of conviction resulting from detention before trial at this hearing. Further, as demonstrated in Chapter 5, there are substantial costs of pretrial detention that also critically impact a defendant's case. Overall, there is a compelling argument that not having counsel at a bail hearing is a violation of the Sixth Amendment.

11.3.3 *Defendant Access to Legal Materials*

Criminal defendants have a constitutional right to adequate, effective, and meaningful access to the courts.[80] The Sixth Amendment of the US Constitution guarantees defendants the right to representation and to their own defense in criminal proceedings.[81] In addition to the right to counsel, the Sixth Amendment should include the right to access legal materials – including law books, witnesses, and other tools required to prepare a defense.[82] The right "require[s] prison authorities to assist inmates in the preparation and filing of meaningful legal papers by providing prisoners with adequate law libraries or adequate assistance from persons trained in the law."[83] However, the law does *not* require states to enable a prisoner to litigate effectively. The Supreme Court stated that there is no clear law stating that a defendant has a constitutional right to law library access.[84] Some courts have concluded that states satisfy their obligations simply by offering defendants the right to counsel. And interpret this to not include providing access to legal research materials if a defendant chooses to proceed *pro se*.[85]

Unfortunately, the law remains unclear on how much access to and what types of materials defendants should have for trial preparation. In a recent case, James Calvert, accused of shooting his ex-wife, was being detained pretrial. Calvert fired his lawyers and decided to take on his own defense.

While preparing for trial, he argued that the prison law library was inadequate and requested that a laptop computer be provided to him. A Texas judge granted Calvert access to a laptop in his jail cell for two hours a day, five days a week, with limited access to the Internet. The judge ordered that no one else could access the machine. When officers searched Calvert's jail cell, they found that he had been using the laptop to help other jail inmates with their cases and because of this, Calvert's laptop was confiscated. He fought to get his computer privileges back but at Calvert's hearing, Matt Bingham, the county's district attorney, maintained that Calvert has no legal right to have computer access in his jail cell.[86]

In a 2006 case with a different outcome, Allan Case also decided to defend himself against a first-degree murder charge. While he was detained in King County Jail, he had limited access to law books, research materials, and copies of his case documents. In preparation, Case was allowed to use a single laptop that was shared by more than 1,000 inmates. However, the county jail began contracting with Westlaw, an online legal-research database, to provide additional legal services to the inmates. All *pro se* inmates were given up to four hours a week of computer time, where they had unlimited access to state and federal court cases, statutes, legal opinions, periodicals, and even free telephone support. At any given time, King County Jail has approximately twenty to twenty-five *pro se* inmates in custody. While this new program cost the county a significant amount of money, the administrators explained that the program was necessary "at a time *pro se* defense appears to be on the rise and recent court decisions and new rules have clarified and strengthened the rights of inmates to access legal resources."[87] Some jurisdictions have made accommodations for defendants to obtain the materials they need to prepare for trial, with respect to optimal bail principles.

The next section discusses the third principle of optimal bail, which demands that money bail is reduced or eliminated and an increasing number of defendants be released on recognizance and through pretrial release programs.

11.4 THE THIRD PRINCIPLE: RELEASE NOT BASED ON WEALTH AND INCREASED ALTERNATIVES TO INCARCERATION

The third principle of optimal bail is that a defendant's pretrial release should not be contingent on wealth or ability to pay a bail. As demonstrated in Chapters 2 and 3, release on bail is a constitutional right for most defendants. Constitutional rights cannot be parsed based on the wealth of a defendant and thus all defendants should have access to release based on objective legal factors rather than the money in their bank account. The Eighth Amendment protects against the setting of high bails simply to prevent a defendant from obtaining release before trial. Equal protection protects against discrimination against poor defendants who cannot obtain release when similarly situated wealthy defendants are able to obtain release. Due Process requires a consideration of a defendant's situation in order to determine release and prohibits a uniform setting of a money bail amount based simply on the crime charged. To effectuate this principle, money bail should be reduced substantially or eliminated. Bail schedules should be eliminated as unconstitutional. Alternative methods of release should be increased – and pretrial supervision and monitoring should replace money bail in most jurisdictions. Finally, citations should be issued in lieu of arrest and diversion should be increased to reduce the numbers of defendants entering the criminal justice system.

11.4.1 *Eliminate Money Bail*

To effectuate the third optimal bail principle, there are several tangible approaches suggested in Chapter 10, including eliminating reliance on commercial bail (money bail). First, and most importantly, the reliance on money bail as the primary (or even a viable) option for pretrial release should be eliminated in favor of public pretrial options or release on one's own recognizance. The United States is one of the only countries in the world that allows commercial involvement in criminal justice. Money bail is not in the constitutional interest of defendants or in the financial interests of the county or even in the public interest of society. Money bail has grown substantially since the 1990s – where about half of defendants relied on commercial bail – to 2009 where 70 percent or more of people released in the state system have to pay to be released. This system disproportionately harms poor and minority defendants who sometimes cannot obtain release over a few hundred dollars bail. It is also not safe for society. If people receive bail based on their wealth rather than the risk they pose, potentially more dangerous but wealthy defendants are released, requiring society to take on a greater risk of pretrial crime. Other low-risk individuals remain incarcerated, at high costs to states nationwide, simply because they do not have money to pay bail. Several states have eliminated money bail for policy reasons and as violations of the Equal Protection and Due Process Clauses, and others are working toward this end.

States have the option of legislating money bail away or litigants can challenge it on constitutional grounds. Both methods have been successful recently. New Jersey recently took legislative efforts to overhaul its bail system to replace money bail almost entirely with a pretrial risk assessment and supervision model. Other states like Colorado and Kentucky have made substantial changes to undermine the money bail industry and allow more people to obtain release without having to pay a private party. The challenge with broad statewide legislative change is that the bail industry (including bondsmen and insurance backers) is wealthy and invests a lot in fighting any efforts to reduce reliance on money bail, as it hurts their bottom line.

Another more piecemeal approach has been used successfully, however. In several cities nationwide, litigants (usually represented by EJUL) have challenged money bail on constitutional grounds using the Eighth Amendment and Fourteenth Amendment Equal Protection and Due Process Clauses. The Eighth Amendment prohibits excessive bail, and sometimes high bails set simply to prevent a defendant from obtaining release have been found unconstitutional. The Fourteenth Amendment Equal Protection Clause has been found to prohibit money bail where poor defendants are disadvantaged and are not able to obtain the same right to release as wealthy defendants charged with the same crime. Similarly, the Due Process Clause has been used to strike down money bail assignments that are done without an individualized assessment, which takes the particular situation of the defendant into account. For this same reason, the Due Process Clause has invalidated bail schedules that set uniform bail based on the crime charged. All of these constitutional arguments have been successful in several jurisdictions, providing hope that even where legislative change is difficult due to heavy lobbying, individual counties can eliminate money bail.

11.4.2 *Eliminate Bail Schedules*

Second, and part and parcel of the first step, uniform bail schedules should be eliminated as a violation of the Due Process Clause. Most jurisdictions rely on a bail schedule that assigns a dollar amount for different types of charges, but these schedules do not assess defendants' individual risks, and permit defendants to pay bail in order to be released without *ever* being screened.[88] Money bail schedules cause the greatest harm to indigent defendants, who are severely disadvantaged in obtaining release from jail. The harm is not only inflicted on poor individuals, often accused of minor crimes, but these costs are also imposed on society at large. Indeed, because pretrial detention leads to an increase in recidivism and an increased likelihood that a defendant will serve more jail time, the financial burden is not only on the defendant but on society.

Bail schedules also lead to high-risk defendants being released simply because they can afford money bail, while leaving countless low-risk defendants incarcerated. On top of these practical concerns, constitutional problems are rife, as bail schedules do not provide an individualized determination of whether the defendant is safe to release but release individuals based on a generic schedule. Both the Due Process Clause and Equal Protection have been used to challenge bail schedules. The Due Process Clause argument against bail schedules is that they do not take into account individual circumstances in setting bail. The Equal Protection argument is that bail schedules do not consider the individual case of a defendant in setting bail, and disadvantage the poor vis-à-vis the wealthy in obtaining the constitutional right to release. There is also a compelling argument that bail schedules are violations of the Eighth Amendment. The argument here is that if bail is set that is too high for a defendant to afford, it is constitutionally "excessive," thus a defendant's right to release before trial is infringed.

Several courts have found that bail schedules are a due process violation, and that they should be eliminated nationwide.[89] Recent successes in eliminating bail schedules have been seen in seven jurisdictions including Missouri and Mississippi. For instance, in *Thompson v. Moss Point*, the Mississippi federal court held that "[i]f the government generally offers prompt release from custody after arrest upon posting a bond pursuant to a schedule, it cannot deny prompt release from custody to a person because the person is financially incapable of posting such bond."[90] The court here recognized the inequity of keeping someone detained because they cannot pay an amount listed on a bail schedule. In Texas, where the county faces a lawsuit over money bail practices, the district attorney has expressed her support to eliminate bail. Indeed, the district attorney of Harris County expressed that bail reform was necessary and long overdue.[91] She states that prosecutors do not want to be "complicit in a system that incentivizes presumptively innocent people to plead guilty merely to expedite their release from custody."[92] Similarly, Kamala Harris, a former district attorney and current California Senator, has also expressed her distaste for money bail, calling it unconstitutional.[93] With all of the momentum against money bail, and pending legislation, a potentially effective approach in reducing money bail reliance is challenging bail schedules nationwide.

11.4.3 *Expand Pretrial Release and Electronic Monitoring*

Money bail should be replaced with a public pretrial release program, release on recognizance (depending on the crime), or electronic monitoring, available for all defendants. There are currently more than 300 pretrial release programs throughout the country and these should be expanded to every jurisdiction. This not only better protects the constitutional rights of defendants but also ultimately eliminates some of states' incarceration costs. For instance, placing defendants in pretrial release supervision programs rather than incarceration can reduce costs for each defendant from up to $45,000 per year in incarceration to $432 for pretrial release.[94] Some pretrial release programs have been shown to increase subsequent court appearances and decrease pretrial crime.[95] These efforts – in Kentucky, North Carolina, New York, and New Jersey – demonstrate emerging innovations that states have adopted in recent years that will serve as a model for other states and the federal bail system. A broader discussion of pretrial release programs can be found in Chapter 3.

11.4.3.1 Pretrial Supervision

Pretrial supervision and monitoring reminds defendants of their upcoming court dates and sometimes of conditions to follow while released. Pretrial release programs inform judges about the background of the defendant, including living arrangements, employment, community ties, and criminal history. Some jurisdictions use pretrial risk assessments, discussed earlier, to access the defendant's risk profile. Once defendants' risk levels are determined through these tools, results are then presented at the defendants' initial appearances, allowing judges and prosecutors to use this information to better determine what type of release would best assure community safety. When the defendants are released pretrial, the pretrial services program would then conduct all necessary supervision and monitoring.[96] This information ultimately leads to a better prediction of risk posed by each individual defendant and can lead to less unnecessary detention.[97] Common conditions used in pretrial release include routine check-ups with a pretrial case manager, court date reminders, drug/alcohol testing, GPS supervision, and/or treatment referrals. Research has shown that when low-risk defendants undergo heavy supervision it actually creates poor outcomes and wasted valuable resources. Indeed, a defendant who is low risk and supervised heavily may be more likely to recidivate according to some studies. Thus, heavy supervision should only be used for high-risk defendants or those who specifically need or request it.[98] For lower-risk defendants, release on recognizance without conditions or electronic monitoring is most appropriate.

A simple reminder to defendants by pretrial services is effective in reducing failure to appear rates. In some jurisdictions, failure to appear is as high as 25–30 percent, depending on the type of crime. And the consequences for defendants in failing to appear include receiving additional court dates, enhanced penalties, or other consequences, adding on even more costs to the defendants themselves. In a 2010 field study in Nebraska, researchers randomly placed 7,865 misdemeanor defendants who had committed nonwaivable, nontraffic offenses, from fourteen Nebraska county courts into four groups. Three groups received one of three different court date postcard reminders. The first group received a simple reminder of the time and place of their hearing. The second group received postcards with a reminder and a description of possible penalties that will be imposed for failing to appear at the court date. The third group of defendants received the simple reminder, possible sanctions, and a message that explained the defendants' ability to speak on their own behalf when appearing at court and described that they would be treated with respect by the judge.[99] The fourth group received no reminder. This study measured the effectiveness of each of the four different categories of reminders at reducing failure to appear rates.[100] Without any reminder, 12.6 percent of defendants failed to appear in court. However, with any postcard the failure to appear rate dropped from 12.6 percent to 9.7 percent. The most effective postcard was one that included the sanctions, with an 8.3 percent failure to appear rate.[101] This study shows that sending defendants a reminder actually does reduce the failure to appear rate among misdemeanor defendants.

The savings for jurisdictions using pretrial release can be substantial. In the Southern District of Iowa, for instance, the average cost of detaining a defendant pretrial is $19,253 and the average cost of releasing a defendant pretrial is $3,860. This figure includes the cost of supervision and the alternatives to detention. This means the average savings per defendant, released pretrial, is $15,393. When the Southern District of Iowa increased their release rate during 2008 and 2009, there was an actual cost savings of $1.7 million from the 110 additional defendants being released.[102] Indeed, in Iowa, creating a pretrial release program improved outcomes and created substantial savings.

11.4.3.2 Electronic Monitoring

A critical tool that is growing in popularity for many jurisdictions in pretrial supervision is electronic monitoring.[103] These monitoring devices can take many forms, one of them being radio transmitters. Radio transmitters can ensure that a defendant stays within certain boundaries within specific hours and can even ensure that a defendant stays away from certain areas – such as parks, schools, or even other individuals. GPS tracking devices are another tool that is able to continuously monitor a defendant either "through passive recordings that can later be reviewed or through active observations of real-time activities."[104] These are typically enforced with an ankle monitor.

Electronic monitoring devices not only allow defendants more freedom, but also reduce the large costs associated with pretrial detention. In the 1990s, it was found that federal electronic monitoring cost between $2.77 and $9.04 daily while pretrial detention costs ranged between $50 and $123 a day. And more recently in 2008, Miami-Dade County costs were cut "from approximately $20,000 per pretrial defendant to $400 annually for released, monitored defendants" due to the use of electronic monitoring. Southern Iowa also used this same technology and $1.7 million was saved over one fiscal year – from 2008 to 2009 – and 15 percent more defendants were being released.[105]

While electronic monitoring is better than detention, it does raise some concerns. Often the cost of ankle monitors is borne by defendants and can cost over $100 per week or more, or are based on a sliding scale.[106] These costs can discriminate against indigent defendants who cannot afford the hefty monitoring fees. Often the appearance of an ankle monitor makes it difficult for a defendant to maintain gainful employment. In addition, there is arguably a privacy argument under the Fourth Amendment that argues against the broad adoption of ankle monitoring. Still, electronic monitoring allows a defendant to remain at home and to keep their job and family intact. It also allows a defendant to better prepare for trial, justifying the demands of pretrial due process.

11.4.3.3 Collection and Analysis of Performance Measures

While these three optimal bail principles are all backed by empirical data and supported by long-held constitutional principles, it is still vital to track any bail reforms. To gauge the effectiveness of the bail reform measures introduced, jurisdictions must collect and analyze data regularly. Collecting and analyzing this data allows pretrial service agencies to assess more accurately their programs' effectiveness in meeting both agency and justice system goals. This data comes from jails, pretrial services, police departments, courts, and probation departments. Some of the most important areas to measure are appearance rate (percentage to make all court appearances), safety rate (arrests or new charges), success rate (appearance at court dates), and a pretrial detainee's length of stay.[107] It may also be helpful to measure risk assessment recommendations and how often they are followed, how long defendants have to wait to obtain pretrial supervision, what percentage are detained, and how long they remain on supervision.[108] All of these metrics will help track the effectiveness of pretrial release programs and help in considering improvements where success is lacking.

11.4.4 *Citations in Lieu of Arrest*

And finally, because pretrial restraints on liberty should be limited, arrests should be reduced to only where necessary to protect the public. Citations, diversions, or warnings should act as substitutes where appropriate as avoiding arrest is one way to better preserve the presumption of innocence.

Diversion programs also allow defendants to receive treatment rather than incarceration and help with the second principle of optimal bail. Several states and the American Bar Association – who has actively opposed money bail since 2002 – are investing and developing these sorts of alternatives to incarceration.[109] Some programs include giving citations and fines rather than arresting individuals for minor crimes. For instance, in Iowa, alternatives to incarceration saved the district $1.7 million in 2008–9.[110] In addition to saving money, the district was able to release 15 percent more defendants with an increased rate of court appearance and a decreased rate of arrests for new crimes.[111] Another alternative used in Germany is where charges are filed when a crime occurs but an individual is not arrested. While this has not been used in the United States, it also provides a possible way to not infer guilt on a defendant before trial. Finally, detaining pretrial individuals separately from convicted individuals is another method that could help avoid inferring guilt of pretrial detainees. This could also help reduce recidivism and pretrial crime, and is a best practice used by some countries internationally. Studies in the United States show that those detained pretrial – even for a few days – are more likely to commit crimes upon release. This could potentially be reduced if pretrial detainees – who were not safe to release – were detained separately from the convicted inmates.

There is precedent for using citations in lieu of arrest with traffic tickets. Rather than incarcerating every person who breaks a traffic law (which is often a misdemeanor), police officers usually give citations or fines in lieu of incarceration. When traffic violations first started becoming a common occurrence, police departments found it necessary to make physical arrests in every traffic violation. As the use of cars increased, traffic violations became more numerous and the arrest procedure proved to be too cumbersome for police departments to handle.[112] This same logic applies to bail reform today. The rate of incarceration has become extremely high for a large number of minor crimes and adopting a citation procedure can help relieve some overincarceration.[113] This idea of giving citations or fines in lieu of incarceration is a practice that has been successfully applied in the traffic context and could be applied with other minor crimes as well.

Citations in lieu of arrest have been implemented in many jurisdictions as a pretrial reform. In 2007, Texas passed a law giving police officers discretion to either arrest a suspect or instead write a citation for a low-level crime. Some of the minor crimes included were criminal mischief, graffiti, theft by check, theft of service, bringing contraband into a correctional facility, driving with an invalid license, and possession of less than four ounces of marijuana.[114] Police departments reported savings in incarceration costs and an increase in public safety because the limited resources and personnel spent less time booking defendants and more time patrolling cities.[115]

Following Texas' lead, Washington DC proposed legislation that broadens a police officer's authority to issue citations in lieu of arrest for misdemeanors. One tool used in DC is citation release. This allows individuals, who are arrested for a misdemeanor, to be released only on a promise to appear at their future court date. In DC, all offenses, other than violent offenses and armed felonies, have a scheduled bond or collateral amount. If an individual does not want to "post-and-forfeit," they may post the proscribed amount in order to be released. The individual will then be released and receive a notice for a future court appearance.[116] In DC, citation release is available to all individuals arrested unless a defendant does not meet certain enumerated conditions.[117] However, in all instances, it is important to note that citations are provided as an option for some low-level crimes, and officers may not choose it.[118] For instance, with speeding tickets, we see this in situations where officers arrest a speeding driver rather than give a citation if the speed is considered "a willful or wanton disregard for the safety of persons or property."[119] This idea of giving citations or fines in lieu of incarceration is a practice that has been successfully applied in the traffic context and could be applied with other minor crimes as well.

Another alternative to incarceration is diversion, as discussed in Chapter 3, where a defendant once arrested is not taken to jail but entered into a treatment program. For instance, in Kentucky, two diversion programs are Misdemeanor Diversion and Deferred Prosecution.[120] The Misdemeanor Diversion program provides defendants with an alternative to prosecution, with treatment that assists defendants in avoiding a criminal conviction, helps defendants make positive changes in their lives, and prevents them from committing future crimes.[121] Similarly, the Deferred Prosecution program allows defendants to choose to enter drug court to deal with an addiction or agree to pretrial supervision. However, eligibility for this program is narrower than other programs because only defendants who are charged with first or second offenses of possession of a controlled substance are eligible, and they are not required to plead guilty in order to be accepted.[122] Other diversion programs exist for juveniles and for those suffering from mental health issues. The goal of diversion programs is to help defendants to treat the root causes of their criminal behavior and help them remove themselves from the otherwise sure path of incarceration. Both diversion and citation programs provide meaningful alternatives to incarceration and help avoid a difficult road for many defendants. By avoiding incarceration, these programs also help preserve the optimal bail principle that protects the constitutional right to release without consideration of a defendant's wealth.

11.5 CONCLUSION

Bail "reform" in America has typically resulted in locking more people up and reducing rights for defendants; but due to the distended and expensive US jail system, it is necessary to reevaluate priorities in bail reform. The Bail Reform Acts of the 1960s and 1980s resulted in judges acquiring additional legitimate reasons to keep someone behind bars pretrial. These two acts allowed judges to legally detain more defendants and "weigh the evidence" against defendants before trial, rather than simply detaining the defendants who were a flight risk. Soon thereafter, incarceration before trial increased federally and in states due to changes in laws that focused on public safety and lobbying by the commercial bail industry, which increased reliance on money bail. An additional devastating result was a loss of bail as a foundational constitutional right for most defendants.

For this reason exactly, optimal bail is necessary. This chapter has explained what optimal bail – or bail reform in the modern age – should look like. Optimal bail, in contrast to "bail reform," focuses on the correct constitutional principles to govern bail and implements these principles with practical reforms focused on releasing as many defendants safely while cutting incarceration costs. There are three primary principles identified within this chapter – and supported by the research in the earlier chapters of this book – that federal courts, state courts, and legislatures should apply to ensure that all defendants maintain the constitutional right to release and that the public remains safe.

This concluding chapter brought together the various constitutional and empirical principles that run throughout the substantive chapters on bail and paired them with practical reforms that will improve bail in America. It started with three principles of optimal bail based on historic and constitutional themes in the book and the focus on bail as a constitutional right, with a particular focus on the Sixth Amendment and Due Process Clause. These optimal bail principles implement empirical findings in this book regarding violent crime, prediction, race, cost considerations, and judicial decision-making on bail.

These optimal bail principles are, first, pretrial restraints of liberty should be limited to only what is necessary and only where there is a proper legal basis. These exceptions include when a defendant poses a serious flight risk, will substantially interfere with the judicial process by intimidating witnesses and harming victims, or poses a serious danger to the community that no pretrial conditions can mitigate. If defendant is detained for any of these reasons, the only limits placed on defendant during detention should relate to securing the facility and defendant should have unfettered access to counsel, potential witnesses, and materials to help prepare for her trial. Under this first principle, detention should be a rare occurrence that the government should have to justify with substantial proof that defendant poses too high a risk to be safely released. Rather than relying on common sense, a judge must consult a risk assessment and appropriate prediction tools before detaining anyone before trial.

The second principle of optimal bail is that there should be no pretrial determination of guilt without access to counsel and no bail hearing without counsel. The Sixth Amendment requires that a defendant be entitled to a lawyer at her bail hearing and adequate legal materials if detained. It also requires judges to refrain from "weighing" any evidence before trial or making any judgments about the potential guilt of the defendant before a jury trial. Instead, release should be based on neutral principles like flight risk or substantial risk to the community.

The third principle of optimal bail is that a defendant's pretrial release should not be contingent on wealth or ability to pay bail. In accord with constitutional principles, reliance on money bail and bail schedules should be eliminated where it disadvantages poor and minority defendants. Rather than releasing defendants based on whether they can pay a bondsman, most defendants obtain the constitutional right to release, except those who pose too high a risk to society. And where possible, police should avoid arrests with citations, and judges should divert defendants into treatment programs to avoid incarceration in the first place. All of these efforts would help create an optimal bail system in America that would release a larger number of safe indigent defendants and reduce pretrial crime rates.

If there was an opportune time to implement optimal bail, it is now. Momentum is building to reform bail nationwide. There are two federal bills pending to improve pretrial practice by eliminating money bail and states are undertaking and succeeding at bail reform efforts. Many states, specifically ones where jails are overflowing with pretrial detainees, have taken steps to make changes in pretrial release policies. States including Kentucky, North Carolina, Colorado, and others have cut costs by reducing money bail, releasing more people pretrial, and reducing crime rates at the same time. In accord with constitutional protections, this book demonstrates that we can still respect a defendant's liberty while keeping the public safe from violent crime. By utilizing a new model for predicting pretrial crime, creating alternatives to incarceration through technology, and expanding pretrial supervision programs, states can dramatically save on detention costs. Indeed, the changes in bail recommended by this book can lead to dramatic improvements in the rights of defendants, help reduce jail overcrowding, and allow for a more efficient and just criminal justice system.

Selected pretrial risk assessment tools: risk factors*

	PSA	COMPAS	FL PRAI	VPRAI	CPAT	PTRA	ORAS-PAT	IRAS-PAT
Separate risk scores for FTA / rearrest?	Yes	Yes	No	No	No	No	No	no
Assess risk of rearrest for violent crime specifically?	Yes	Yes	No	No	No	No	No	No
Jurisdiction(s)	Many	FL	FL	VA	CO	Fed.	OH	IN
Requires interview	No	Yes	Yes	Yes	Yes	Yes	Yes	Yes
Static/dynamic/both	Static	Both	Both	Both	Both	Both	Both	Both
# Factors/scales	9	15	11	8	12	14	7	7
Risk factors: relate to								
Current charge	X	X	X	X		X		
Prior pending charge(s)	X	?		X	X	X		
Prior conviction(s)	X	X	X	X	X	X		
Prior violent conviction(s)	X	X		X				
Prior FTA(s)	X	X	X	X	X	X	X	X
Residence		X	X	X	X	X	X	X
Employment		X	X	X		X	X	X

(continued)

Selected pretrial risk assessment tools: risk factors* (Cont.)

	PSA	COMPAS	FL PRAI	VPRAI	CPAT	PTRA	ORAS-PAT	IRAS-PAT
Drug/alcohol abuse		X	X	X	X	X	X	X
Working phone		?	X		X			
Age	X	?	X		X	X	X	X
Active warrant(s)		?			X			
Mental health		?	X		X			
Under supervision		?			X			
Education		X				X		
Citizenship		?				X		
Marital status		?		X				
Prior custodial sentence	X	?				X	X	X

*This chart was created by Sandra G. Mayson, "Bail Reform and Restraint for Dangerousness: Are Defendants a Special Case?" (working paper, University of Pennsylvania Law School): 12 "This chart expands on a model created by the Pretrial Justice Institute, see "Pretrial Risk Assessment: Science Provides Guidance on Assessing Defendants," *Pretrial Justice Institute* (2015): 3–4, accessed March 30, 2017, www.pretrial.org/download/advocacy/Issue%20Brief-Pretrial%20Risk%20Assessment%20(May%202015).pdf. The chart also draws directly from the following sources: "The Public Safety Assessment (PSA)," *Laura and John Arnold Foundation*, accessed March 16, 2017, www.arnoldfoundation.org/wp-content/uploads/PSAInfographic .pdf; "Federal Pretrial Risk Assessment Instrument (PTRA)" (version 2.0, March 1, 2010): 1–4; Christopher T. Lownkamp and Jay Whetzel, "The Development of an Actuarial Risk Assessment Instrument for U.S. Pretrial Services," *Federal Probation Journal* 73 (2009): 33; Timothy P. Cadigan and Christopher T. Lownkamp, "Implementing Risk Assessment in the Federal Pretrial Services System," *Federal Probation Journal* 75 (2011): 32. Timothy P. Cadigan et al., "The Re-Validation of the Federal Pretrial Services Risk Assessment (PTRA)," *Federal Probation Journal* 76 (2012); "The Colorado Pretrial Assessment Tool (CPAT)," *Pretrial Justice Institute* (2012): 15–18; James Austen et al., "The Florida Pretrial Risk Assessment Instrument," *JFA Institute*, 13; Edward J. Latessa et al., "The Creation and Validation of the Ohio Risk Assessment System (ORAS)," *Federal Probation Journal* 74 (2010); Edward Latessa et al., "Creation and Validation of the Ohio Risk Assessment System: Final Report," (2009): 49–50; "Indiana Risk Assessment System," *University of Cincinnati* (2010): 1-1 - 1-2; Marie VanNostrand, "Assessing Risk Among Pretrial Defendants in Virginia: The Virginia Pretrial Risk Assessment Instrument," *Virginia Department of Criminal Justice Services* (2003): 6; Marie VanNostrand and Kenneth J. Rose, "Pretrial Risk Assessment in Virginia," *Luminosity* (2009): 2; Thomas Blomberg et al., "Validation of the COMPAS Risk Assessment Classification Instrument" (2010): 15–16; Julia Angwin et al., "Machine Bias," *ProPublica.com*, May 23, 2016; "Developing a National Model for Pretrial Risk Assessment," *Laura and John Arnold Foundation* (2013): 3–4; "Results from the First Six Months of the Public Safety Assessment – Court in Kentucky," *Laura and John Arnold Foundation* (2014): 3."

APPENDIX 2

This appendix provides some additional details on regional and specific country practices in pretrial detention. It is meant as a supplement to Chapter 9. While not a comprehensive survey, the data, stories, and information in this appendix should be helpful to the reader who wants to gain greater insight on the state of global pretrial detention.

REGIONAL DATA ON INTERNATIONAL BAIL PRACTICES

The following section provides data on the pretrial detention practices of the various regions of the world. It also provides some insight into whether over-crowding is a problem in the region discussed.

EUROPE

In Europe, 18.8% of total prison population are pretrial detainees.[1] Another way of expressing the number of pretrial detainees is per 100,000 of the general population. There are 38.6 pretrial detainees per 100,000 of the general population.[2] The average ratio of pretrial detainees to prisoners is about 25%.[3] Europe does not have an overcrowding problem as their prisons are 18,800 prisoners below the prison capacity.[4] The average length of pretrial detention in Europe is 167 days.[5]

European region	% of total prison population are pretrial detainees	Pretrial detainees per 100,000 of general population
Central Europe	11.9[a]	23.4[a]
Eastern Europe	17.9[a]	74.2[a]
Balkan countries	20.2[a]	31[a]
Western Europe	21.9[a]	24.4[a]
Nordic countries	26.2[a]	18.2[a]

[a]"Presumption of Guilt: The Global Overuse of Pretrial Detention," *Open Society Foundations, Justice Initiative* (2014): 18, last accessed December 21, 2016, www.opensocietyfoundations.org/sites/default/files/presumption-guilt-09032014.pdf.

ASIA

In Asia, 40.6% of total prison population are pretrial detainees.[6] Another way of expressing this is 33.7 pretrial detainees per 100,000 of the general population.[7] There are 43.1 pretrial detainees per 100,000 of the general population.[8] Asian prisons contain 1,099,000 prisoners in excess of the prison capacity.[9]

Asian region	% of total prison population are pretrial detainees	Pretrial detainees per 100,000 of general population
Central Asia	13.6[a]	25.7[a]
Middle East/West Asia	32.4[a]	75[a]
East Asia	37.9[a]	57.7[a]
South Asia	65.5[a]	23.1[a]

[a]"Presumption of Guilt: The Global Overuse of Pretrial Detention," *Open Society Foundations, Justice Initiative* (2014): 17, last accessed December 21, 2016, www.opensocietyfoundations.org/sites/default/files/presumption-guilt-09032014.pdf.

AFRICA

In Africa, 34.7% of total prison population are pretrial detainees.[10] Another way of expressing the number of pretrial detainees is per 100,000 of the general population. There are 33.7 pretrial detainees per 100,000 of the general population. African prisons contain 230,300 prisoners in excess of prison capacity.[11]

African region	% of total prison population are pretrial detainees	Pretrial detainees per 100,000 of general population
North Africa	26.2[a]	30.8[a]
Southern Africa	31.7[a]	48.4[a]
East Africa	32.8[a]	44.2[a]
West Africa	55.6[a]	20.8[a]
Central Africa	59[a]	53.5[a]

[a]"Presumption of Guilt: The Global Overuse of Pretrial Detention," *Open Society Foundations, Justice Initiative* (2014): 17, last accessed December 21, 2016, www.opensocietyfoundations.org/sites/default/files/presumption-guilt-09032014.pdf.

AMERICAS

In the Americas, 27.9% of total prison population are pretrial detainees.[12] Another way of expressing the number of pretrial detainees is per 100,000 of the general population. There are 107.4 pretrial detainees per 100,000 of the general population.[13] The Americas' prisons contain 560,200 prisoners in excess of prison capacity.[14]

American region	% of total prison population are pretrial detainees	Pretrial detainees per 100,000 of general population
North America	20.2[a]	130.9[a]
Central America	40.7[a]	87.3[a]
South America	41.1[a]	96[a]
Caribbean	44.9[a]	92.1[a]

[a]"Presumption of Guilt: The Global Overuse of Pretrial Detention," *Open Society Foundations, Justice Initiative* (2014): 17, last accessed December 21, 2016, www.opensocietyfoundations.org/sites/default/files/presumption-guilt-09032014.pdf.

OCEANIA

In Oceania, 22.3% of total prison population are pretrial detainees.[15] Another way of expressing this is 28 pretrial detainees per 100,000 of the general population.[16] Oceania's prisons contain 900 prisoners in excess of prison capacity.[17]

COUNTRY BAIL SPECIFICS

This section provides some specifics on how various countries handle pretrial detention decisions. It also details some instances of abuse and poor prison conditions faced by inmates pretrial. It is not intended to provide a systematic review of all of the countries and their pretrial detention practices, but provides a glimpse into pretrial detention in various countries in the world. It is ordered alphabetically.

BELGIUM

Of the 9,971 people incarcerated in Belgium, 2,543, or 25.5%, are pretrial detainees.[18]

Under Belgian law, bail is referred to as "preventative detention"[19] because it emphasizes the policy of avoiding unnecessary detention before trial.[20] This reflects Belgian policy that an accused is innocent until proven guilty, and therefore preventative detention is considered the exception, rather than the rule.[21] However, Belgian law must balance this presumption against "legitimate interests of the society that offenses be uncovered and the offenders be punished."[22] Preventative detention can continue to the final decision on appeal, not just trial.[23]

If an accused in Belgium faces imprisonment of less than three months, a judge cannot order detention, so a defendant is automatically released.[24] An accused may be detained after a hearing if he or she is caught in the act, if the punishment for the offense is more than three years, or a more serious penalty.[25] If an accused is a Belgian resident, he or she can be placed in pretrial detention only for "serious and exceptional reasons in the interest of public security," and those reasons must be stated.[26] These instances give judges discretion in the detention hearings. However, when the accused is facing a sentence of forced labor for 15 years or more, the judge cannot grant release, unless the prosecutor consents.[27] If a person is sentenced to only a fine or probation, they must be released immediately by the trial court.[28] Further, if the defendant's sentence equals the time he or she was in detention, he or she must be set free.[29]

Procedural matters are aligned in an accused's favor for bail proceedings. For example, an order for pretrial detention must be affirmed within five days.[30] If it is not affirmed within a month, the accused is set free.[31] Further, if a prosecutor is required to consent to a judge lifting the order for pretrial detention, and remains silent, consent is presumed and the accused goes free.[32]

Preventative detention can be revoked after it is granted if the accused fails to appear or breaks a condition of the preventative detention.[33] An accused may be given preventative detention either by paying a monetary bail or not.[34]

If he or she is required to pay bail, the money will be returned if the accused complies with the conditions.[35] Otherwise, the money goes to the state (not a private company, as in the United States, see Chapter 10).[36] As a general rule, however, most people are released without paying bail.[37]

BRAZIL

There are reports of appalling conditions in jails for inmates in Brazil. According to one report, in Brazil, bare cells without light are jammed tight with naked prisoners.[38] Cells can reek of vomit and feces.[39] Suspects can be thrown in pretrial detention unfairly for a "public order" offense.[40] One public defender, Patrick Cacicedo, reports that "[n]obody knows what 'public order' really means. It is a vague term. When the authorities do not have a concrete motive to send someone to pretrial detention – and they almost never do – the majority of the time they use that clause."[41]

CANADA

In Canada, the reasons for placing a suspect in pretrial detention are three-fold: to prevent flight, to protect the public from a likelihood of the suspect reoffending, and to maintain confidence in the judicial system.[42] Bail is set by the court, and the conditions of release can include curfews, anger management counseling, prohibition on possessing firearms, substance abuse treatment, and fines for failure to appear in court or comply with bail conditions.[43] Commercial (money) bail is prohibited.[44]

In Canada, there are 41,049 people in prison, 35.2% pretrial detainees or remanded (sent back to jail after a hearing or until trial) prisoners.[45] On an average day, another source estimates that 54.5% of those behind bars are in pretrial detention.[46] Of the pretrial detainees, 2/3 are charged with nonviolent offenses, and violation of a release condition is the most common reason for being placed in pretrial detention.[47] Bail also disproportionately impacts aboriginals, with 25% detained, which is just under 4% of the aboriginal population.[48] Blacks were also more likely to be detained than other races, and one-third of detainees are homeless.[49] Finally, there is a disproportionate amount of people with mental health or substance abuse issues in pretrial detention.[50]

CHILE

Because of the serious human rights abuses in Chile in the 1970s and 1980s, Chile initiated reforms to its criminal justice system.[51] One reform involves putting a two-year time limit on investigations which can limit the amount of time a person is held pretrial.[52]

CHINA

In 2009, seven people died under suspicious circumstances in Chinese police custody.[53] The Chinese government claims to have improved pretrial detention practices by providing legal aid, videorecorded interrogations, and improvements in treatment to pretrial detainees, due to a lack of transparency, it is difficult to ascertain whether conditions have improved.[54]

ENGLAND

There are about 57,000 people that are currently released on bail in England,[55] while only 8,064 are in pretrial detention.[56] So about 88% of people successfully get and remain released before trial. These 8,064 pretrial detainees are 10.34% of the total prison population of 77,983, which is less than half of the European average percentage.[57]

In England, an accused has a right to trial within 112 days, or about 4 months, and an absolute right to bail if he or she has been in pretrial detention for 182 days, which is about 6 months.[58] While some conditions can still be imposed, neither a surety nor security may be imposed as conditions.[59] However, before the 182 days has elapsed, the prosecution may submit an application for extension.[60] The delay may only be granted in the case of sufficient need, such as illness, and the Crown must have made all expedient efforts.[61]

If the time constraints are not violated, an accused has the general right to bail when he or she is brought before a magistrate or crown court in connection with a crime, or when he or she applies to the court for bail, or a variation of bail.[62] There are two standards for granting bail. The first is for those accused whose crimes are punishable with imprisonment.[63] The second is for those accused whose crimes are not punishable with imprisonment, such as a fine.[64]

With regard to imprisonable offenses, the right to bail has several statutory exceptions.[65] A court may deny bail if there is "substantial grounds for believing" that an accused will not surrender to custody, or that he will commit another crime while on bail, interfere with witnesses, or that he will obstruct the course of justice.[66] In deciding bail, courts are also able to consider, among "any others [factors] which appear to be relevant," such as the seriousness of the crime, the character of the accused (including community ties), the accused's record in abiding by previous bail obligations, and the "strength of the evidence of his having committed the offence [sic] or having defaulted."[67]

If granted bail, then conditions cannot be imposed on the accused, except to ascertain that the accused did not do any of the actions for which he would have been denied bail.[68] For example, having a residence was a condition for 73% of people given bail in 1998.[69] One of the least common conditions is sureties, being imposed in only 6% of cases.[70] While a surety helps prevent flight, it can also be used to prejudice lower income people who cannot afford a surety.[71]

With regard to nonimprisonable offenses, the refusal of bail is much simpler. An accused may be denied bail if he or she has previously failed to surrender to custody and will likely fail to surrender again,[72] if denying bail is in the interest of the accused's protection,[73] if the accused is already in custody as part of another criminal sentence,[74] or if the accused has been arrested pursuant to Section 7 (when a defendant's case is adjourned for injuries or a report and release is impractical while the report is being made).[75] Additionally, an accused may not be granted bail for an indictable, imprisonable or nonimprisonable, offense, if it appears that the accused was already on bail when he or she committed the offense.[76]

FRANCE

In France, 18,444[77] people are in a form of pretrial detention,[78] out of a total prison population of 57,876.[79] So around 31.9% of incarcerated people are pretrial detainees.[80]

The procedure for determining pretrial detention in France is skewed in favor of the prosecution.[81] The judge in charge of determining pretrial detention doesn't have time to study files in depth, which creates an incomplete judicial review.[82] Despite the law that requires decisions to be based on "precise and substantiated circumstances,"[83] pretrial release decisions are "perfunctory and formulaic."[84] An order might simply assert that a person must be detained to "prevent a suspect absconding," without reference to any facts that might have led to the conclusion.[85] Further, one of the factors for consideration, "public order" is poorly defined and too broad, and could therefore include a wide array of facts that permitted a decision of detention too easily.[86]

The alternative to pretrial detention is judicial supervision. Judicial supervision is harder to order than pretrial detention.[87] It's also more expensive than pretrial detention as it involves health and drug treatment.[88] Judicial supervision comes in two forms: reporting or socio-educational.[89] The latter has been delegated to the private sector, which is a problem because many of the sectors that manage socio-educational obligations, especially bail organizations, have closed down due to a lack of resources.[90] The closure of these organizations reduces options available to judges and further increases pretrial detention.[91]

GAMBIA

Gambia automatically denies bail only to those accused of financial corruption.[92] There are limited exceptions to this rule, only with special circumstances. Even then, the accused must pay one-third of the amount of money involved in the crime, and he or she must find at least two sureties who will put up another third of the money stolen in the crime.[93] This can easily be a substantial amount of money.[94] Gambia can also deny bail if a trial occurs within a reasonable time.[95] It must, however, add the exceptions for special circumstances warranting bail.[96]

GERMANY

Of the total German prison population, about 15.1% are pretrial detainees.[97] German officials detain suspects for three reasons: defendant poses a flight risk, suspicion that evidence may be tampered with, and, for serious crimes, the risk of reoffending.[98] Monetary bail is infrequently used,[99] and usually assigned to wealthy defendants who will be required to pay.[100] Sureties may also be used, but there is a prohibition on commercial bail.[101] Alternatives to pretrial detention include conditional release, which might include reporting duties, restraint on location, restraint on leaving the country, a monetary guarantee, house arrest, restraint of activities related to the alleged crime, or a hold on a suspect's bank account.[102]

In Germany, the maximum length of pretrial detention is six months, but it is possible to have that extended.[103] Indeed in some extreme cases, judges have detained suspects between three to five and a half years.[104] These excessive periods of pretrial detention are lawful with adequate cause, and when the case was dealt with expeditiously.[105] There have been some concerns that officials have used pretrial detention to leverage confessions.[106]

Overall, however, pretrial detention is on the decline in Germany.[107] This is possibly due to the increase in noncustodial sentences, such as community service or fines.[108] Another reason for the low number of pretrial detainees is likely because German prosecutors often conduct an investigation, and can even file charges, without arresting a defendant.[109] Indeed, another helpful practice is that if pretrial suspects are ultimately acquitted, or if charges are dropped against them, the government compensates them at about $12.00 per day.[110]

GREECE

In Greece, a suspect may be placed in pretrial detention if he or she is accused of a felony and at risk of flight, at risk of reoffending, or has been declared guilty for prison escape or violations of restrictions concerning residency.[111] The most problematic element in determining detention is the likelihood of reoffending because it relies on a vague consideration of a suspect's characteristics.[112] Some judges have also decided pretrial release based on the seriousness of the crime, though that is not an element that should be taken into consideration.[113] An alternative to pretrial detention in Greece is conditional release.[114] Under Article 282(1) of the Greek Criminal Procedure Code, appropriate conditions include restraints on residency and moving, a prohibition on leaving the country, restraints on communicating with certain people, and the payment of a surety.[115] In practice, these alternatives to detention are not regularly used.[116]

In Greece, 1/3 of inmates are pretrial detainees.[117] One class of people especially prone to pretrial detention are foreign nationals because they don't have a local address.[118] Foreign nationals make up 65% of the pretrial detention population.[119] Pretrial detention is meant to be used only in exceptional circumstances where a conditional release won't secure a suspects' attendance at trial or prevent him or her from reoffending.[120] Judges are able to extend pretrial detention from six months to twelve months without justification.[121] However, extending beyond twelve months requires detailed justifications as it is meant to be an exceptional circumstance.[122] While the eighteen-month limit of pretrial detention should be strict, one way to circumvent this limit is by fragmenting the cases.[123] Fragmentation is achieved when a suspect is accused of multiple crimes, but only prosecuted for one or two, and formally accused of the others later; even if all the charges rise from the same case.[124] These circumstances should be rare and only imposed in serious cases, however this is abused.[125]

One of the reasons for the high rate of pretrial detention in Greece is because pretrial detention is used as a crime-fighting measure, with a vigilante mentality.[126] This is especially true of white-collar crimes during the economic crisis.[127] Another reason is that the structure of judicial system predisposes judges to accept the prosecutor's recommendations.[128] When the judge disagrees with a prosecutor, there are further proceedings.[129] However, there is no automatic right to review for the suspect when the judge agrees with the prosecutor.[130] Further, the defense has limited access to case files and is frequently given no more than 5 minutes to analyze the file and prepare a defense.[131] When legal aid is involved for an indigent defendant, the presence of a defense attorney is more of a formality because the lawyers are drawn from a list without regard to their specialty.[132] As such, a lawyer without any background in criminal law may be assigned a criminal case.[133]

Pretrial detainees are not detained separately from convicted prisoners, except for lawyers, police officers, homosexuals, and certain classes of marginalized criminal defendants.[134] Prison conditions are difficult in Greece. In 2009, the European Committee for the Prevention of Torture and Inhuman or Degrading Treatment or Punishment (CPT) reported many allegations of beatings that amounted, in some cases, to torture.[135] Most of the beatings were "kicks, slaps, punches and blows, with batons and other objects, including on the soles of feet and on fingers, mainly during questioning by the security Police, but also upon apprehension."[136] Doctors, in many cases, found injures that were consistent with the reports of abuse, such as black eyes, bruises all over the body, a potentially fractured zygomatic arch (indicates getting punched in the face), and tramline bruising (indicates getting hit with a baton).[137] Many who suffered abuse feared retaliation so they did report the beatings to Greek authorities.[138] Despite reports, Greek authorities have refused to believe that ill-treatment of inmates is a problem.[139]

GUATEMALA

In Guatemala, pretrial detention is, according to the law, only permitted in cases with exceptional circumstances, and with specific conditions.[140] Pretrial decisions should be based on the presumption of innocence after reforms.[141] The maximum pretrial detention period is a year, or the possible sentence for the alleged crime.[142] Despite the reforms, pretrial detention is still a major problem because of corruption, inefficiency, a weak defense bar, and lack of respect for the rule of law.[143]

HAITI

Overcrowding is a challenge in Haiti. One prison in Haiti, which combines pretrial persons and prisoners, only has 20 cells but 290 inmates.[144] Haitian prisons allocate about 0.4 m² per person, about one-quarter of a twin-sized bed, where international standards recommend 5.4 m².[145] However, pretrial jails serve with two meals a day, maintain a recreation area, and good medical care.[146]

HUNGARY

In Hungary, pretrial detention is almost always requested by prosecutors, even without any risk of flight.[147] The official guidelines give two general criteria for ordering pretrial detention in Hungary. The first is that the crime is punishable by imprisonment, and the second is that there is "a well-founded suspicion" the suspect is guilty. In cases where the court considers flight risk, there is not a high bar. Often people with strong ties to Hungary, or who had voluntarily surrendered themselves into custody, are still considered at risk for flight.[148] The important factors for determining release appear to be a possibility of a lengthy sentence, or previous convictions – even when the previous conviction was for a minor offense or an offense that occurred a long time ago.[149] When these two conditions are met, the defendant is almost always detained.[150] Pretrial detention is even more routine because defense counsel is not granted access to the case during the pretrial stage.[151] Further, when judges make a decision on whether to grant a prosecutor's request for pretrial detention, the judge relies exclusively on information from the prosecutor.[152] These factors tend to slant the decision about pretrial detention in favor of the prosecution.[153]

Bail is either not available or too expensive for most of those accused, and judges fear public criticism too much to allow suspects release without bail, or on their own recognizance.[154] There are alternatives to bail in Hungary, such as house arrest, but they are rarely used.[155] One of the problems in implementing reform is the fear that citizens will perceive reforms as the police or judges going soft on criminals.[156] There is a limit of two years in pretrial detention.[157] However, for serious offenses, this can be extended to four years.[158]

In Hungary, the threat of pretrial detention has been used to obtain evidence for a guilty verdict.[159] Other forms of pressure are also used to get evidence, such as promises of release for a confession or testimony against codefendants, and poor prison conditions.[160]

ICELAND

Iceland is a country that mirrors international standards. Of the 119 people incarcerated in 2015, only 8 people were held in pretrial detention, or 15.1%.[161] Further, the constitutional prescription against arbitrary arrest and detention is generally followed.[162] Pretrial detention may only be ordered if the charge carries a punishment greater than a fine or punitive custody.[163] Further, pretrial detention can never be longer than necessary.[164]

ITALY

Italy has one of the highest percentages of pretrial detainees in Europe, at 40% of the prison population.[165] The slow-paced justice system contributes to serious overcrowding in Italian prisons.[166] Italy has the most crowded jails in the EU, "with close to 67,000 detainees held in jails built for 45,000."[167] A 2013 law is meant to solve the problem, limiting pretrial detention to those who face a sentence of five years or more.[168] However, there remains deep concern that this law will actually be implemented.[169]

Under Italy's current legal guidelines, pretrial detention is not to exceed eighteen months during the proceedings of the first instance.[170] Release can be granted unless there is strong evidence the crime was committed, or there is a high risk the suspect may reoffend, tamper with evidence, obstruct investigations, or flee.[171] Pretrial detention is mandatory when there is "serious circumstantial evidence of certain specific crimes."[172] The conditions for release may include restraints on residency, restraints on the suspect's ability to leave the territory of the state, reporting, house arrest (or order to be at the house during certain times of day), avoiding contact with people related to the alleged crime, or an obligation to stay in mental institution or drug rehabilitation.[173] Conditions can also include bans on the exercise of parental authority, public service, professional or business activities, and a ban on being the director of a company.[174] Access to an attorney is denied at the start of detention, and questioning also occurs without a lawyer.[175]

IRELAND

According to the 1997 Bail Act, in determining pretrial release, the courts in Ireland may consider the likely sentence, seriousness of the offense charged or apprehended, strength of evidence in support of the charge, previous convictions (including convictions pending on appeal), and any other crime for which the accused is charged and waiting for trial.[176] The courts in Ireland may also consider an accused's addiction to controlled substances.[177]

Pretrial release in Ireland is conditioned on the accused not committing another crime, and that the accused "shall otherwise be of good behavior [sic]." Courts may impose other conditions including restricting the accused to a certain location, limiting capacity to travel, and periodic reporting to police.[178] The most common condition is requiring the suspect to surrender his or her passport.[179]

In Ireland, the total number of people incarcerated, including pretrial and immigration warrants, is 3,135.[180] Of these, 543, or 17.3%, are pretrial detainees.[181] Ireland does not impose a legal limit to the length of pretrial detention, though a review is needed after thirty days.[182] In practice, suspects remanded into custody can spend twelve months in pretrial detention without legal review for the detention.[183]

JAPAN

While accused people in Japan have a legal right both to be informed of the charges against them and to a judicial determination about the legality of the detention within 72 hours, according to reports, some can be detained up to twenty-three days without either.[184] Pretrial release is not available during these twenty-three days.[185] And accused persons in pretrial detention are subject to forced interrogation without an attorney present.[186] Though the accused do have the right to a consultation with an attorney.[187] Guidelines are in place to prevent interrogations from going longer than 8 hours, but these guidelines are not always followed.[188] Many detainees are "aggressively interrogated" between 8 to 12 hours at a time, while handcuffed to a chair for the entire period.[189] While physical abuse during interrogation has become less common, psychologically coercive methods are still implemented.[190] Further, people that are within the twenty-three-day period before being charged are frequently kept from being able to speak with anyone who isn't their attorney.[191] When suspects are allowed to meet with their family, it is in the presence of a detention officer.[192]

After indictment, detainees, or their families or other representatives may request pretrial release.[193] Bail is sometimes granted in exchange for a confession, even though that practice is illegal.[194] Confessions may also be only partially recorded, which can cause them to be misleading.[195] The most common form of a misleading confession is the "read aloud, or yomi-kikase."[196] A police officer is recorded reading or summarizing a suspect's confession, and the footage is selectively recorded.[197] This method of confession recording also limits the evidence of any psychologically coercive tactics that might have been used.[198] The majority of pretrial detainees confess, though the Japanese government insists the interrogation guidelines prevent compulsory confessions.[199] There were 540 complaints about interrogations in Japan, and 38 confirmed violations of interrogation guidelines in 2012.[200] This manner of interrogation can lead to abuse, corruption, and the perversion of justice.

LUXEMBOURG

Luxembourg has a low prison population, with just 300 pretrial detainees,[201] 85% of which are foreign nationals.[202] However, this 300 constitutes about 47% of the total prison population.[203]

In Luxembourg, pretrial detention can only be imposed when the crime alleged carries a sentence of two years or more and when there are "serious indications of the defendant's guilt."[204] In addition, it must be found that there is a risk of flight, or a risk the suspect will suppress evidence, or there is reason to believe the suspect will reoffend.[205] For the risk of flight, the risk is presumed when the possible sentence is at least five years in prison.[206] A defense lawyer's presence is mandatory at pretrial detention hearings, though the presence may be waived.[207] In practice, pretrial detention ends when the length of the detention equals the possible sentence for the alleged crime.

If a judge releases a defendant, she may impose conditions including restraints on location or leaving the home, reporting requirements, cooperation with identification, restraints on driving, restraints on communicating with certain people, a monetary security, prohibition on carrying weapons, complying with control measures (such as drugs), and complying with familial financial obligations.[208]

MEXICO

In Mexico, the cost of pretrial detention is high. The median cost to the detainee is 2,004,873 pesos, which includes labor cost, risk of death or illness, employer payments to social security, and corruption payments (extra-legal charges).[209] Extra-legal charges are because things like food, water, bedding, and clothing are not commonly given to pretrial detainees.[210] As such, the detainees must provide for these necessities themselves.[211] Detainees occasionally must also pay to avoid beatings, make phone calls, and secure sleeping arrangements.[212] The median cost to the state is 5,794,839 pesos.[213] This includes detainee's support, the criminal process, health care provided to relatives, and employer contributions to social security.[214] The median cost to the family of the detainees is 1,907,053 pesos.[215] This includes more extra-legal payments, attorney fees, time spent visiting detainees, and assisting or supporting the detainees.[216] Finally, the median cost to society is 1,403,546 pesos.[217] This includes lost productivity and services by social organizations.[218]

In Mexico, in an effort to look like they are winning "the drug war," accused drug lords are caught, paraded in front of the media, and then three-quarters are released.[219] Further, officials can hold precharge detainees in jail for forty days.[220] Being detained increases the likelihood of torture, and 70 of 130 detainees at one detention center showed signs of violence.[221] For the ones that are charged, statements are induced by torture, and there is often little evidence – either before or after the detention – that establishes reasonable suspicion.[222]

POLAND

In Poland, many suspects are held in pretrial detention because of inadequate representation and failure to thoroughly review pretrial motions.[223] Despite laws that comply with international standards, pretrial detention is a general rule in practice.[224] This is because available alternatives to pretrial detention are not considered, judges are poorly trained and unfamiliar with EU standards, prosecutor recommendations about detentions are usually adopted by judges, courts are overwhelmed and don't have time to review pretrial detention motions, and suspects do not receive either adequate representation or access to evidence.[225]

RUSSIA

Russia has the second highest rate of incarceration in the world, after the United States.[226] Russia has 871,609 people incarcerated, 40,840 of these are in pretrial detention.[227] While this is a low percentage, around 4.7% which is close to the lowest percentage of pretrial detainees in Europe (3.1% for FYRO Macedonia), it is striking that the amount of people in pretrial detention alone exceeds the total number of people incarcerated, including pretrial, for forty-one other countries in Europe,[228] such as Belgium, Denmark, Czech Republic, Ireland, Norway, Romania, Scotland, Sweden, and Portugal.[229] It's also important to note that the number of pretrial detainees does not include those serving less than six months and consensually kept in SIZOs, or pretrial detention centers.[230] Pretrial detention in Russia can last two to three years.[231]

Russia is steeped in corruption, and payoffs and bribes are common.[232] Some report that judges that pretend they are independent do not keep their jobs.[233] A victim of the abuse of pretrial detention is Andrei Kudoyarov, a principal at a very successful school.[234] After requesting money that would be used to improve school conditions, such as new microscopes and fresh paint, he was accused of bribery.[235] The only evidence against him was a videotape of a man pretending to be a parent and offering him $8,000 for the school.[236] Even though Kudoyarov planned to use this money for school improvements, he should not have allowed the pretend parent to hand over the money.[237] A judge refused to release him for five months as he waited for the trial he never had.[238] Kudoyarov died of a heart attack in pretrial detention, at age forty-seven.[239] His attorney says that his punishment, if he was convicted, would have probably been a fine.[240] His attorney also said the investigators "did their best to see that he would not live until his trial."[241] Two weeks after Kudoyarov died, the prosecutors returned the case, strongly implying there hadn't been enough evidence against him.[242] Even while Kudoyarov was in jail, he would tell stories, give history lectures, and organize exercises for the other inmates.[243]

Death, beatings, and serious illness are extremely common in Russian pretrial detention.[244] In 2010, fifty-nine people died in Moscow's pretrial detention centers.[245] Part of the problem is that bribes that used to be voluntary have now become mandatory to conduct business in Russia.[246] Refusing to pay will often land business people in jail.[247] In other instances, individuals in political opposition to the Russian government have been held for long periods in detention, up to a year.[248]

SIERRA LEONE

Corruption and lengthy detention periods are common in Sierra Leone. In recent years, the average time spent detained between arrest and the first court appearance was twenty days.[249] The average bail amounts, further, were about twenty-five times greater than the average weekly earnings.[250] Bribes were cheaper, at only four times as much as the average weekly earnings. About 13% of detainees reported being asked for bribes in order to obtain release.[251]

TANZANIA

Tanzania, unlike many countries, allows statutorily denials of bail. Tanzania automatically denies bail to those accused of murder or treason, those sentenced previously for three or more years,[252] those who previously violated bail, those on bail at the time of alleged offense, those who have been accused of a property crime worth more than 10 million shillings, and to those who need incarceration for protection.[253] These, unlike in many countries, are not factors to be considered by a judge, but are mandatory refusals of bail created by the legislature. The general presumption is that these factors demonstrate a danger to society or a likelihood of flight.[254]

The constitution of Tanzania requires a hearing before any form of detention,[255] and an automatic determination removed that hearing. However, in 1990, one of these mandatory refusals of bail where the offense involved a violent robbery was struck down as unconstitutional by its highest court.[256] After this ruling, automatic detention could only be justified if it was in the interests of the defense or public safety or order.[257] As it was drafted, the mandatory bail refusal could be triggered by a generally nonviolent suspect, such as in self-defense, not just the violent robber.[258] Since this case, some have argued that all of the mandatory denial of bail sections of the Criminal Procedure Act are suspect to the same overbroad nature as the violent robbery provision.[259] However, the Court of Appeals declined to rule on the other sections, and they are currently still valid.[260]

THAILAND

In 2014, political pressures to solve crime quickly might have led the police in Thailand to beat suspects in order to obtain confessions.[261] Two murder suspects reportedly confessed to killing Hanna Witheridge and David Miller, British tourists. One of the suspects alleges that "police beat and threatened him with electrocution."[262] The tourism industry is suffering in Thailand, after an army coup in May 2014, so there was a lot of pressure to solve the tourists' murder.[263]

TUNISIA

In Tunisia, police can hold suspects for six days before either filing charges, releasing them, or transferring them to jail.[264] These six days can be extended to twelve days with an ongoing investigation.[265] During this time, detainees are denied access to lawyers or their families, which already limits the suspect in preparing for her trial, as the first moments after arrest are most important in gathering evidence and witnesses to mount a defense.[266]

The Tunisia code of criminal procedure only guarantees a right to an attorney after an appearance before the investigative judge.[267] By that time, however, nearly half of the suspects have signed a police statement, usually a confession, without reading it.[268] This statement is used against a suspect during trial.[269] One detainee signed fifty statements.[270] The detainees don't read the statements because they were either prevented from reading them by the police or they were too scared to ask to read them.[271] Some that sign confessions allege that police coerced them with physical violence.[272]

Despite the fact that Tunisia is one of the first countries in the Middle East and North Africa to institute an independent mechanism to prevent torture,[273] about 57% of pretrial detainees are mistreated during arrest and interrogation.[274] This includes being insulted, humiliated, threatened with rape, shoved, slapped, punched, kicked, and beaten with sticks and batons.[275] There are reports of suspects being forced to confess through severe beatings.[276] The abuse allegations are often not included in medical records so there is often no proof of this abuse.[277] Some detainees get electrocuted, though the use of electric devises is only allowed when the use of force is lawful.[278]

URUGUAY

Jail conditions for pretrial detainees are reportedly difficult. Some pretrial detention centers in Uruguay hold detainees in metal boxes and only allow detainees to leave these boxes for a maximum of four hours a week.[279] Detainees in these boxes had to drink water from the toilet and relieve themselves using bags or plastic bottles, which were then thrown into the courtyard.[280] In summer, these boxes become extremely hot.[281]

VENEZUELA

Venezuela's new criminal procedure code is the Codigo Organico Processal Penal (COPP).[282] COPP dictates that a person may not be denied pretrial release unless he or she is caught red handed, or if there is a danger he or she will obstruct the investigation.[283] No pretrial detention may be longer than an accused's possible minimum sentence, and it cannot exceed two years.[284]

ZIMBABWE

Zimbabwe pretrial detentions are reportedly inhumane. There are some cells coated in human excrement and toilets that don't work.[285] Two women spent nine months in complete solitary confinement, with no human contact and only 20 minutes a day for bathing, exercising, or laundry.[286] Some cells have no light, artificial or natural, no ventilation, no running water, soap, bedding, seating, heating, or toilet paper.[287] Detainees at times are not given any food, medical treatment, or blankets. Further, despite the cold and human excrement on the floor, detainees are not given shoes.[288] Some detainees report torture.[289] Women have been told to remove their underwear and were not given menstrual pads or toilet paper, and were told to clean themselves with their hands.[290] Women are arrested on flimsy charges and physically and sexually abused.[291]

Endnotes

DEDICATION

1. Shawn Carter, Jay Z: For Father's Day, I'm Taking On the Exploitative Bail Industry, *Time* (June 16, 2017), http://time.com/4821547/jay-z-racism-bail-bonds/, last accessed July 31, 2017.
2. Kamala Harris and Rand Paul, To Shrink Jails: Lets Reform Bail, *NY Times* (Op-Ed July 20, 2017), www.nytimes.com/2017/07/20/opinion/kamala-harris-and-rand-paul-lets-reform-bail.html, last accessed July 31, 2017.

INTRODUCTION

1. Shana Conklin, "Juveniles Locked in Limbo: Why Pretrial Detention Implicates A Fundamental Right," *Minnesota Law Review* 96 (2012): 2151.
2. Laura Sullivan, "Bail Burden Keeps U.S. Jails Stuffed with Inmates," *NPR*, last modified January 21, 2010, www.npr.org/2010/01/21/122725771/Bail-Burden-Keeps-U-S-Jails-Stuffed-With-Inmates, last accessed July 31, 2017.
3. Laura Appleman, "Justice in the Shadowlands," *Washington & Lee Law Review* 69 (2012): 1300.
4. Shana Conklin, "Juveniles Locked in Limbo: Why Pretrial Detention Implicates A Fundamental Right," *Minnesota Law Review* 96 (2012): 2151.
5. Robert Lewis, "No Bail Money Keeps Poor People Behind Bars," *WNYC News*, last modified September 19, 2013, www.wnyc.org/story/bail-keeps-poor-people-behind-bars, last accessed July 31, 2017. Twenty-eight percent will make it at some later point after time in jail, 13 percent will be released on their own recognizance after a period of time in jail, and 40 percent of New York City defendants will stay in jail until their case has been decided.
6. Thomas E. Scott, "Pretrial Detention Under the Bail Reform Act of 1984: An Empirical Analysis," *American Criminal Law Review* 27 (1989): 3.
7. *Stack* v. *Boyle*, 342 U.S. 1 (1951).
8. Thomas E. Scott, "Pretrial Detention Under the Bail Reform Act of 1984: An Empirical Analysis," *American Criminal Law Review* 27 (1989): 9.
9. *United States* v. *Salerno*, 481 U.S. 739 (1986).

10. *Release and Detention Pending Judicial Proceedings*, U.S. *Code* 18 (2011), §§ 3142 (a)(1) et seq.

11. *United States* v. *Cisneros*, 328 F.3d 610 (10th Cir. 2003).

12. "The Price of Freedom: Bail and Pretrial Detention of Low Income Nonfelony Defendants in New York City," *Human Rights Watch* (2010): 20–5.

13. Shana Conklin, "Juveniles Locked in Limbo: Why Pretrial Detention Implicates A Fundamental Right," *Minnesota Law Review* 96 (2012): 2171.

14. Sandra Guerra Thompson, "Do Prosecutors Really Matter?: A Proposal to Ban One-Sided Bail Hearings," *Hofstra Law Review* 44 (2016): 1168; "Jail Inmates at Midyear 2014," *U.S. Department of Justice* (2015): 4, www.bjs.gov/content/pub/pdf/jim14.pdf, last accessed July 31, 2017.

15. Sandra Guerra Thompson, "Do Prosecutors Really Matter?: A Proposal to Ban One-Sided Bail Hearings," *Hofstra Law Review* 44 (2016): 1168; "Jail Inmates at Midyear 2014," *U.S. Department of Justice* (2015): 4, www.bjs.gov/content/pub/pdf/jim14.pdf, last accessed July 31, 2017. This is from 1996 to 2014.

16. Todd D. Minton & Zhen Zeng, U.S. Dep't of Justice, *Jail Inmates in 2015*, at 2 (2016).

17. U.S. Department of Justice, Bureau of Justice Statistics, *Prisoners in 2013*, by E. Ann Carson (2015): 3 (see Table 2), accessed March 2, 2017, www.bjs.gov/content/pub/pdf/p13.pdf.

18. U.S. Department of Justice, Bureau of Justice Statistics, *Prisoners in 2014*, by E. Ann Carson, (2015): 3 (see Table 2), accessed March 2, 2017, www.bjs.gov/content/pub/pdf/p14.pdf.

19. U.S. Department of Justice, Bureau of Justice Statistics, *Prisoners in 2015*, by E. Ann Carson and Elizabeth Anderson, (2016): 5 (see Table 2), accessed March 2, 2017, www.bjs.gov/content/pub/pdf/p15.pdf.

20. Sandra Guerra Thompson, "Do Prosecutors Really Matter?: A Proposal to Ban One-Sided Bail Hearings," *Hofstra Law Review* 44 (2016): 1168; "Jail Inmates at Midyear 2014," *U.S. Department of Justice* (2015): 4, www.bjs.gov/content/pub/pdf/jim14.pdf, last accessed July 31, 2017.

21. Cynthia E. Jones, "'Give Us Free': Addressing Racial Disparities in Bail Determinations," *New York University Journal of Legislative and Public Policy* 16 (2013): 934–5.

22. "Annual Survey of Jails: Jurisdiction-Level Data," *U.S. Department of Justice, Bureau of Justice Statistics*, www.icpsr.umich.edu/icpsrweb/ICPSR/studies?sortBy=7&q=annual+survey+of+jail, last accessed July 31, 2017.

23. "Jail Inmates at Midyear 2014," *U.S. Department of Justice* (2015): www.bjs.gov/content/pub/pdf/jim14_sum.pdf, last accessed July 31, 2017.

24. Sandra Guerra Thompson, "Do Prosecutors Really Matter?: A Proposal to Ban One-Sided Bail Hearings," *Hofstra Law Review* 44 (2016): 1170; Christopher T. Lowenkamp et al., "Investigating the Impact of Pretrial Detention on Sentencing Outcomes," *Arnold Foundation* (November 2013): 3, www.arnoldfoundation.org/wp-content/uploads/2014/02/LJAF_Report_state-sentencing_FNL.pdf, last accessed July 31, 2017.

25. Sandra Guerra Thompson, "Do Prosecutors Really Matter?: A Proposal to Ban One-Sided Bail Hearings," *Hofstra Law Review* 44 (2016): 1170; Christopher T. Lowenkamp et al., "Investigating the Impact of Pretrial Detention on Sentencing

Outcomes," *Arnold Foundation* (November 2013): 3, www.arnoldfoundation .org/wp-content/uploads/2014/02/LJAF_Report_state-sentencing_FNL.pdf, last accessed July 31, 2017.

26. Laura Sullivan, "Inmates Who Can't Make Bail Face Stark Options," *NPR*, January 22, 2010, www.npr.org/templates/story/story.php?storyId=122725819, last accessed July 31, 2017.

27. Laura Appleman, "Justice in the Shadowlands," *Washington & Lee Law Review* 69 (2012): 1301.

28. Amanda Petteruti and Nastassia Walsh, "Jailing Communities: The Impact of Jail Expansion and Effective Public Safety Strategies," *The Justice Policy Institute* (April 2008): 15, available at www.justicepolicy.org/images/upload/08-04_rep_jailing communities_ac.pdf, last accessed August 15, 2017.

29. Laura Sullivan, "Inmates Who Can't Make Bail Face Stark Options," *NPR*, January 22, 2010, www.npr.org/templates/story/story.php?storyId=122725819, last accessed July 31, 2017.

30. William S. Laufer, "The Rhetoric of Innocence," *Washington Law Review* 70 (1995): 357.

31. Stephanie Clifford, "Prosecutors Are Reading Emails from Inmates to Lawyers," *N.Y. Times* (July 22, 2014).

32. Sandra Guerra Thompson, "Do Prosecutors Really Matter?: A Proposal to Ban One-Sided Bail Hearings," *Hofstra Law Review* 44 (2016): 1164; Douglas L. Colbert, "Prosecution Without Representation," *Buffalo Law Review* 59 (2011): 384–6.

33. Sandra Guerra Thompson, "Do Prosecutors Really Matter?: A Proposal to Ban One-Sided Bail Hearings," *Hofstra Law Review* 44 (2016): 1175; Douglas L. Colbert, "Prosecution Without Representation," *Buffalo Law Review* 59 (2011): 384–6. Reporting on a national survey of pretrial practices inquiring about the appointment of counsel at bail hearings.

34. State and Local Expenditures on Corrections and Education: A Brief from the U.S. Department of Education, Policy and Program Studies Service (July 2016), last accessed February 2017, www2.ed.gov/rschstat/eval/other/expenditures-corrections-education/brief.pdf. See also "State Spending for Corrections: Long Term Trends and Recent Criminal Justice Policy Reforms," *The National Association of State Budget Officers* (September 11, 2013): 4.

35. "The Socioeconomic Impact of Pretrial Detention, *Open Society Justice Initiative* (February 2011), www.opensocietyfoundations.org/reports/socioeconomic-impact-pretrial-detention, last accessed July 31, 2017; Laura I. Appleman, "Justice in the Shadowlands: Pretrial Detention, Punishment & The Sixth Amendment," *Washington & Lee Law Review* 69 (2012): 1310. One Oregon county estimates the cost per inmate is $234 per day. "Inside the Wild, Shadowy, and Highly Lucrative Bail Industry," *Mother Jones*, May/June, 2014, www.motherjones .com/politics/2014/06/bail-bond-prison-industry, last accessed July 31, 2017. In New York it is $460 per day. "NYC's Jail Population: Who's There and Why?," *NYC Independent Budget Office*, August 22, 2013, www.ibo.nyc.ny.us/cgi-park2/2013/08/ nycs-jail-population-whos-there-and-why, last accessed July 31, 2017.

36. "Soaring Costs for California's Failing Prison System," *KPBS*, www.kpbs.org/ news/2010/jan/08/overcrowded-and-expensive-governor-addresses-calif, last accessed July 31, 2017; David Brodwin, "How High Prison Costs Slash Education and Hurt

the Economy," *U.S. News*, May 24, 2012, www.usnews.com/opinion/blogs/economic-intelligence/2012/05/24/how-high-prison-costs-slash-education-and-hurt-the-economy, last accessed July 31, 2017.

37. "California's Annual Cost to Incarcerate an Inmate in Prison," *Legislative Analyst's Office*, last modified December 2016, www.lao.ca.gov/PolicyAreas/CJ/6_cj_inmatecost, last accessed July 31, 2017.

38. "State Spending Per Student at CSU and UC Remains Near the Lowest Point in More Than 30 Years," California Budget & Policy Center, http://calbudgetcenter.org/wp-content/uploads/Higher-Education-Historical-CSU-and-UC-GF-Spending-GF-Spending-per-Student-Chart.pdf last accessed July 31, 2017. This includes state funding for University of California and California State University higher education institutions.

39. State and Local Expenditures on Corrections and Education: A Brief from the U.S. Department of Education, Policy and Program Studies Service (July 2016), last accessed February 2017, www2.ed.gov/rschstat/eval/other/expenditures-corrections-education/brief.pdf.

40. Katy Reckdahl, "Behind Bars for Lack of Money," *Texas Jail Project* (December 16, 2012), www.texasjailproject.org/2013/11/behind-bars-for-lack-of-money.

41. Shima Baradaran and Frank McIntyre, "Predicting Violence," *Texas Law Review* 90 (2012): 552.

42. Cynthia E. Jones, "'Give Us Free': Addressing Racial Disparities in Bail Determinations," *New York University Journal of Legislative and Public Policy* 16 (2013): 934–5.

43. *United States* v. *Scott*, 450 F.3d 863 (9th Cir. 2006).

44. "Report of the Sentencing Project to the United Nations Human Rights Committee," *The Sentencing Project* (2013): 1.

1 HISTORY OF BAIL IN AMERICA

1. 4 William Blackstone, Commentaries on the Laws of England *300 (1765–1769).

2. Though there is some limited evidence that in capital cases defendants were denied bail for public safety reasons, not just flight. Anthony Highmore, A Digest of the Doctrine of Bail: In Civil and Criminal cases vii, 194 (1783).

3. *Hunt* v. *Roth*, 648 F.2d 1148 (8th Cir. 1981), *vacated as moot*, 455 U.S. 478 (1982); the history of bail from medieval England to the American colonies is similarly recounted in *Hunt* v. *Roth*.

4. Ibid.

5. An Act to Establish the Judicial Courts of the United States, Pub. L. No. 1–20, 1 Stat. 91–92 (1789).

6. Ibid.

7. *Ex parte* Milburn, 34 U.S. 704 (1835).

8. *Hudson* v. *Parker*, 156 U.S. 277, 285 (1895) ("The statutes of the United States have been framed upon the theory that a person accused of crime shall not, until he has been finally adjudged guilty in the court of last resort, be absolutely compelled to undergo imprisonment or punishment, but may be admitted to bail, not only after arrest and before trial, but after conviction, and pending a writ of error." Noting that the "only 'proper security,' then, in a criminal case, is security for the appearance of a prisoner admitted to bail.").

9. Ibid.
10. Fed. R. Crim. P. 46(c) (1951).
11. Regulation and Restriction of Immigration in General, 8 U.S.C. § 156 (1946) ("Pending the final disposal of the case of any alien so taken into custody, he *may* be released under a bond . . . .").
12. U.S. *ex rel. Potash* v. *Dist. Dir. of Immigration & Naturalization at Port of New York,* 169 F.2d 747 (1948) (emphasis added).
13. U.S. *ex. rel. Heikkinen* v. *Gordon,* 190 F.2d 16 (8th Cir. 1951).
14. *Stack et al.* v. *Boyle,* 342 U.S. 1 (1951).
15. *Carlson et al.* v. *Landon,* 342 U.S. 524 (1952).
16. An Act to Revise Existing Bail Practices in Courts of the United States, and for Other Purposes, Pub. L. No. 89–465, 80 Stat. 214–17 (1966).
17. *Gavino* v. *McMahon,* 499 F.2d 1191 (2d Cir. 1974) (emphasis added).
18. *Gerstein* v. *Pugh,* 420 U.S. 103 (1975).
19. Ibid.
20. *Bell* v. *Wolfish,* 441 U.S. 520 (1979).
21. *Schall* v. *Martin,* 467 U.S. 253 (1984).
22. Ibid.
23. Joint Resolution Making Continuing Appropriations for the Fiscal Year 1985, and for Other Purposes, Pub. L. No. 98-473, 98 Stat. 1837-2199 (1984).
24. Ibid. § 3142(e)(2), (f)(1).
25. Release and Detention Pending Judicial Proceedings, 18 U.S.C. § 3142(f) (2011).
26. Ibid. § 3142(e)(3).
27. Release and Detention Pending Judicial Proceedings, 18 U.S.C. §§ 3142(g) et seq (2011).
28. Ibid. § 3142(a), (c).
29. Thomas H. Cohen, Pretrial Detention and Misconduct in Federal District Courts, 1995–2010 (February 2013 Bureau of Justice) ("The number of defendants with cases disposed in federal district courts more than doubled from 45,635 in 1995 to 100,622 in 2010. The number of defendants with cases disposed who were detained pretrial increased by 184 percent, from 27,004 in 1995 to 76,589 in 2010. Growth in the number of pretrial detentions was driven primarily by immigration caseloads, which increased by 664 percent, from 5,103 cases in 1995 to 39,001 in 2010. The percentage of drug defendants detained pretrial increased from 76 percent in 1995 to 84 percent in 2010. Weapons caseloads nearly tripled between 1995 and 2010, and the percentage of weapons defendants detained pretrial increased from 66 percent to 86 percent during the same period.").
30. Release and Detention Pending Judicial Proceedings, 18 U.S.C. § 3142(i) (2011).
31. *United States* v. *King,* 849 F.2d 485 (11th Cir. 1988).
32. *United States* v. *Jessup,* 757 F.2d 378 (1st Cir. 1985).
33. Ibid.

2 BAIL AS A CONSTITUTIONAL RIGHT

1. *United States* v. *Barber,* 140 U.S. 164, 167 (1891).
2. Pretrial Justice Institute, "Guidelines for Analyzing State and Local Pretrial Laws" (Pretrial Justice Institute, 2017), 11, https://university.pretrial.org/HigherLogic/System/DownloadDocumentFile.ashx?DocumentFileKey=f47afcf3-8bb9-7423-f23d-10ea7702f84c, last accessed July 28, 2017.

3. The nine states are Georgia, Hawaii, Maryland, Massachusetts, New Hampshire, New York, North Carolina, Virginia, and West Virginia. Ibid.

4. The nineteen states, along with their respective constitutional provisions, are Alabama (Ala. Const., art. I, § 16), Alaska (Alaska Const., art. I, § 11), Arkansas (Ark. Const., art. 2, § 8), Connecticut (Conn. Const., art. 1, § 8), Delaware (Del. Const., art. I, § 12), Idaho (Idaho Const., art. I, § 6), Indiana (Ind. Const., art. I, § 17), Iowa (Iowa Const., art. I, § 12), Kansas (Kan. Const., Bill of Rights, § 1), Kentucky (Ky. Const., Bill of Rights, § 16), Maine (Me. Const., art. I, § 10), Minnesota (Minn. Const., art. I, § 7), Montana (Mont. Const., art. II, § 21), Nebraska (Neb. Const., art. I, § 9), Nevada (Nev. Const., art. I, § 7), North Dakota (N.D. Const., art. I, § 11), South Dakota (S.D. Const., art. VI, §8), Tennessee (Tenn. Const. art. I, § 15), and Wyoming (Wyo. Const., art. I, § 14). Ibid.

5. Ala. Const., art. I, § 16.

6. The twenty-two states, along with their respective constitutional provisions, are Arizona (Ariz. Const., art. II, § 22), California (Cal. Const., art. I, § 12), Colorado (Colo. Const., art. II, § 19), Florida (Fla. Const., art. I, § 14), Illinois (Ill. Const., art. I, § 9), Louisiana (La. Const., art. I, § 18), Michigan (Mich. Const., art. I, § 15), Mississippi (Miss. Const., art. III, § 29), Missouri (Mo. Const., art. I, § 20), New Jersey (N.J. Const., art. I, § 11), New Mexico (N.M. Const., art. II, § 13), Ohio (Ohio Const., art. I, § 9), Oklahoma (Okla. Const., art. II, § 8), Oregon (Or. Const., art. I, § 14), Pennsylvania (Pa. Const., art. I, § 14), Rhode Island (R.I. Const., art. I, § 9), South Carolina (S.C. Const., art. I, § 15), Texas (Tex. Const., art. I, § 11b), Utah (Utah Const., art. I, § 8), Vermont (Vt. Const., art. II, § 40), Washington (Wash. Const., art. 20), and Wisconsin (Wis. Const., art. I, § 8). Schnacke, "Guidelines for Analyzing State and Local Pretrial Laws," 12.

7. Cal. Const. art. I, § 12.

8. Specifically, the first two exceptions to the right to bail are in cases where defendants are (1) "charged with a capital offense when there is substantial evidence to support the charge;" and (2) "charged with a felony while on probation or parole, or while free on bail awaiting trial on a previous felony charge, when there is substantial evidence to support the new felony charge." Utah Const., art. I, § 8(1) (a)–(b).

9. Ibid. at 8(1)(c).

10. Utah Code § 77-20-1(2)(c). Pretrial Justice Institute, "Guidelines for Analyzing State and Local Pretrial Laws," 13.

11. Jennifer Gonnerman, "Before the Law," *The New Yorker*, October 6, 2014, www.newyorker.com/magazine/2014/10/06/before-the-law, last accessed July 17, 2017.

12. Avianne Tan, "Kaleif Browder: The Life and Death of the Man Who Spent 3 Years Without Trial on Rikers Island," *World News*, June 9, 2015, www.abcnews.go.com/US/kalief-browder-life-death-man-spent-years-trial/story?id=31643296, last accessed July 27, 2017.

13. James Ridgeway and Jean Casella, "America's 10 Worst Prisons: Rikers Island," *Mother Jones*, May 14, 2013, www.motherjones.com/politics/2013/05/america-10-worst-prisons-rikers-island-new-york-city, last accessed July 27, 2017.

14. Tan, "Kaleif Browder."

15. Ibid.

16. U.S. Const. amend. XIV, § 2.

17. Heidi Joy Herman, "United States v. Salerno: The Bail Reform Act Is Here to Stay," *DePaul Law Review* 38 (1988): 174–5.
18. *Coffin v. United States*, 156 U.S. 432 (1895).
19. *In re* Winship, 397 U.S. 358 (1970) (Harlan, J., concurring).
20. Matthew J. Hegreness, "America's Fundamental and Vanishing Right to Bail," *Arizona Law Review* 55 (2013): 932; *Duncan v. Louisiana*, 391 U.S. 145 (1968); *Washington v. Glucksberg*, 521 U.S. 702 (1997).
21. Hegreness, "Right to Bail," 909.
22. Fed. R. Crim. P. 46 (a)(1).
23. *See Hudson v. Parker*, 156 U.S. 277 (1895).
24. *Stack v. Boyle*, 342 U.S. 1 (1951).
25. Hegreness, "Right to Bail," 932.
26. Hegreness, "Right to Bail," 932 (*citing Schilb v. Kuebel*, 404 U.S. 357, 365 (1971)).
27. *United States v. Salerno*, 481 U.S. 739 (1987) (holding that "the restrictions on liberty imposed by the pretrial detention provisions of the Bail Reform Act of 1984 constitute permissible regulation rather than impermissible punishment").
28. Heidi Joy Herman, "United States v. Salerno," 175 (*citing United States v. Salerno*, 794 F.2d 64, 77 (2d Cir.1986)) (Feinberg, C.J., dissenting) (government has concrete basis for predicting accused will commit additional crimes).
29. The Associated Press, "Former Fairfax Officer, of Culpeper, Denied Bail on Murder Charge, Collapses in Courtroom," *The Daily Progress*, August 19, 2015, www.dailyprogress.com/news/crime/ex-cop-of-culpeper-denied-bail-on-fairfax-murder-charge/article_f70e28ea-4687-11e5-9369-f3c4cf107614.html, last accessed July 27, 2017; Tom Jackman, "Ex-Fairfax Officer Adam Torres Pleads Guilty to Manslaughter in Shooting Death of John Geer," *The Washington Post*, April 18, 2016, www.washingtonpost.com/news/true-crime/wp/2016/04/18/ex-fairfax-officer-adam-torres-pleads-guilty-to-manslaughter-in-shooting-death-of-john-geer/?utm_term=.f79863ffc6a9, last accessed July 28, 2017.
30. David Ferrara, "Judge 'Shocked' Vegas Man has been Locked Up 6 Years Without Conviction," *Las Vegas Review-Journal*, July 7, 2015, www.reviewjournal.com/local/local-las-vegas/judge-shocked-vegas-man-has-been-locked-up-6-years-without-conviction/, last accessed July 28, 2017.
31. U.S. Const. amend. VIII.
32. *Galen v. County of Los Angeles*, 477 F.3d 652 (9th Cir. 2007); *United States v. Polouizzi*, 697 F. Supp. 2d 381 (E.D. N.Y. 2010) (stating that "[e]xcessive bail" under the Eighth Amendment is bail set at a figure higher than an amount reasonably calculated to fulfill its purpose).
33. *United States v. Polouizzi*, 697 F. Supp. 2d 381 (E.D. N.Y. 2010).
34. *United States v. Scott*, 450 F.3d 863 (9th Cir. 2006).
35. "Factors in Fixing Amount of Bail in Criminal Cases," *American Law Reports* 72 (1931).
36. *Stack v. Boyle*, 342 U.S. 1 (1951).
37. *United States v. Salerno*, 481 U.S. 739 (1987).
38. Ibid.
39. *Narducci v. State*, 952 So. 2d 622 (Fla. Dist. Ct. App. 2007); *Alexander v. Broward Cty. Sheriff's Office*, 6 So. 3d 707 (Fla. Dist. Ct. App. 2009) (holding that excessive bond is tantamount to no bond).

40. Samuel Wiseman, "Pretrial Detention and the Right to be Monitored," *Yale Law Journal* 123 (2014): 1349.
41. Ibid.
42. Samuel Wiseman, "Discrimination, Coercion, and the Bail Reform Act of 1984: The Loss of the Core Constitutional Protections of the Excessive Bail Clause," *Fordham Urban Law Journal* 36 (2009): 148.
43. Debra Cassens Weiss, "Judge Censured for Excessive Bail, Severe Attitude," *ABA Journal*, February 8, 2008, www.abajournal.com/news/article/judge_censured_for_excessive_bail_severe_attitude/, last accessed July 27, 2017.
44. Nicholas C. Krieger and Davidde A. Stella, "Professional Responsibility," *Wayne Law Review* 55 (2009): 571–73.
45. Ibid.
46. Ibid.
47. Ibid.
48. Ibid.
49. Ibid.
50. Ibid.
51. Ibid.
52. U.S. Const. amend. XIII, § 1.
53. *McGarry v. Pallito*, 687 F.3d 505 (2d Cir. 2012).
54. Ibid.
55. Tan, "Kaleif Browder."
56. Ibid.
57. *Stack v. Boyle*, 342 U.S. 1 (1951).

3 THE BAIL PROCESS: HOW PRETRIAL RELEASE OPERATES AND THE TYPES OF RELEASE BEFORE TRIAL

1. 42 Ohio St. 401, 404.
2. 648 F.2d 1148, 1163 (8th Cir. 1981).
3. John Jay College of Criminal Justice, "Pretrial Practice: Building a National Research Agenda for the Front End of the Criminal Justice System," (October 26–27, 2015), available at http://johnjaypri.org/wp-content/uploads/2016/05/ArnoldReport2_webversion.pdf, last accessed August 15, 2017.
4. Ibid., 7.
5. Thomas H. Cohen, Ph.D., Pretrial Release and Misconduct in Federal District Courts, 2008–2010, November 2012, available at www.bjs.gov/content/pub/pdf/prmfdc0810.pdf, last accessed July 27, 2017.
6. Thomas H. Cohen and Brian A. Reaves, Pretrial Release of Felony Defendants in State Courts (2007), available at www.bjs.gov/content/pub/pdf/prfdsc.pdf, last accessed July 27, 2017.
7. Thomas H. Cohen and Brian A. Reaves, Pretrial Release of Felony Defendants in State Courts State Court Processing Statistics 1990–2004 (2007), available at www.bjs.gov/content/pub/pdf/prfdsc.pdf, last accessed July 27, 2017.
8. Ibid., A small amount were emergency releases.
9. Cohen, Pretrial Release and Misconduct in Federal District Courts, 2008–2010.
10. Cynthia Jones, *"Give Us Free": Addressing Racial Disparities in Bail Determinations*, 16 Legis. & Pub. Pol'y 919, 922 (2013).

11. Ibid., 921.

12. Malizia, Kathryn. "Assembly Line Justice." *The New Journal*. September 1, 2002. www.thenewjournalatyale.com/2002/09/assembly-line-justice/, last accessed July 27, 2017.

13. Paul Heaton, Sandra Mayson and Megan Stevenson, "The Downstream Consequences of Misdemeanor Pretrial Detention," *Stanford Law Review* 69 (2017): 720, 730 (describing Harris County Texas bail hearings as lasting an average of one minute and many others taking two minutes or three minutes); Megan Stevenson, "Distortion of Justice: How the Inability to Pay Bail Affects Case Outcomes," *University of Pennsylvania Law School* (2016): 5, January 8, 2017 (describing Philadelphia bail hearings lasting one minute or less).

14. "Bail Fail: Why the U.S. Should End the Practice of Using Money for Bail." Justice Policy Institute. September 2012. www.justicepolicy.org/uploads/justicepolicy/documents/bailfail_executive_summary.pdf, archived at http://perma.cc/V7PS-GAKM, last accessed July 27, 2017.

15. Ridgeway, James, and Jean Casella. "America's 10 Worst Prisons." May 14, 2013. www.motherjones.com/politics/2013/05/america-10-worst-prisons-rikers-island-new-york-city, last accessed July 27, 2017.

16. "Pretrial Injustice." Pretrial Justice Institute. www.pretrial.org/the-problem/pretrial-injustice/, archived at http://perma.cc/R6UA-MCPY, last accessed July 27, 2017.

17. Ibid.

18. Ibid.

19. Ibid.

20. Ibid.

21. Lindsey Devers, *Bail Decision making: Research summary*, Bureau of Justice Assistance U.S. Dep't of Justice 1, January 24, 2011, www.bja.gov/Publications/BailDecisionmakingResearchSummary.pdf, archived at http://perma.cc/UBG5-9R6L, last accessed July 28, 2017.

22. "Bail Fail: Why the U.S. Should End the Practice of Using Money Bail."

23. Although judges do make bail and pretrial detention decisions during bail hearings, judges are not the only decision makers. In some jurisdictions, administrative employees like bail commissioners and magistrate judges are permitted to decide what kind of bail prisoners receive and how much bail prisoners receive. See *infra*.

24. Jones, "Give Us Free": Addressing Racial Disparities in Bail Determinations, 923.

25. Ibid., 959.

26. Ibid., 933.

27. Ibid., 923.

28. *Powell v. Alabama*, 287 U.S. 45, 57 (1932).

29. Jones, *"Give Us Free": Addressing Racial Disparities in Bail Determinations*, 931.

30. Pretrial Services Agency for the District of Columbia, accessed October 2, 2014, www.psa.gov/?q=programs/court_support#assessing, archived http://.perma.cc/6YP4-GZWZ, last accessed July 27, 2017.

31. *Congressional Budget Justification and Performance Report Fiscal Year 2013 Pretrial Services Agency for the District of Columbia*, Pretrial Services Agency 6, February 2012, www.csosa.gov/about/financial/budget/2013/FY13-PSA-Budget-Submission.pdf, archived at http://perma.cc/3TF5-M54G, last accessed July 27, 2017.

32. Jones, *"Give Us Free": Addressing Racial Disparities in Bail Determinations*, 923.
33. Ibid..
34. Malizia, *Assembly Line Justice*.
35. How Long Is Too Long? When Pretrial Detention Violates Due Process, 60 Tenn. L. Rev. 1.
36. Ibid.
37. *United States v. Accetturo*, 783 F.2d 382, 388 (3d Cir. 1986).
38. *United States v. Ojeda Rios*, 846 F.2d 167 (2d Cir. 1988).
39. Ibid., 169.
40. Jesselyn McCurdy, "The 1980s Called. They Want Their Mandatory Minimums Back," *American Civil Liberties Union* (blog), September 18, 2013 (2:27 p.m.), www.aclu.org/blog/criminal-law-reform/1980s-called-they-want-their-mandatory-minimums-back. Though, numbers are starting to drop with recent policy shifts in reducing enforcement of federal drug laws, which has helped decrease prison numbers 14 percent from 2013 to 2017. See www.bop.gov/about/statistics/population_statistics.jsp, last accessed July 27, 2017 and www.uscourts.gov/news/2017/04/25/policy-shifts-reduce-federal-prison-population, last accessed July 27, 2017.
41. Arpit Gupta, Christopher Hansman and Ethan Frenchman, "The Heavy Costs of High Bail: Evidence from Judge Randomization," *The Journal of Legal Studies* 45 2 (2016): 471–505.
42. An Act Relating to the Criminal Justice System, Making an Appropriation Therefore, and Declaring an Emergency, H.B. 463, 11 Reg. Sess (2011):69.
43. "Updates on National Pretrial Reforms," *American Bar Association* (2015): 1–12.
44. *Release and Detention Pending Judicial Proceedings*, U.S. Code 18 (2011), § 3142(f); Under the act, to determine if a defendant should be detained pretrial, a judge must first determine if there is any basis to hold a detention hearing by considering §3142 factors. Second, the government must show "no condition or combination of conditions" "will reasonably assure the [defendant's] appearance . . . and the safety of . . . the community[.]"
45. Amber Widgery, "Guidance for Setting Release Conditions," *National Conference of State Legislature*, May 5, 2015, www.ncsl.org/research/civil-and-criminal-justice/guidance-for-setting-release-conditions.aspx last accessed July 27, 2017.
46. Michael R. Jones, "Unsecured Bonds: The as Effective and Most Efficient Pretrial Release Option," *Pretrial Justice Institute* (2013): 3, available at www.pretrial.org/download/research/Unsecured+Bonds,+The+As+Effective+and+Most+Efficient+Pretrial+Release+Option+-+Jones+2013.pdf last accessed August 15, 2017.
47. Widgery, "Guidance for Setting Release Conditions."
48. "ACLU-NJ Hails Passage of NJ Bail Reform as Historic Day for Civil Rights", *American Civil Liberties Union*, August 4, 2014, www.aclu.org/news/aclu-nj-hails-passage-nj-bail-reform-historic-day-civil-rights, last accessed July 27, 2017.
49. *An Act Concerning Court Administration, Supplementing Titles 2A and 2B of the New Jersey Statutes, and amending P.L. 1995, c. 325*, Public Law 2014, *New Jersey 2014 Session Law Service* 31 (2014): 2A:162-15 et. seq.
50. Ibid.
51. New Jersey (State). Legislature. Senate. *A Concurrent Resolution Proposing an Amendment to Article I, Paragraph 11 of the Constitution of the State of New Jersey*, S.C.R. 128 (July 10, 2014).

52. John Clark and D. Alan Henry, "Pretrial Services Programming at the Start of the 21st Century: A Survey of Pretrial Services Programs," *U.S. Department of Justice* (2003): 46.

53. Marie VanNostrand, Virginia Dep't of Criminal Justice Services, *Assessing Risk among Pretrial Defendants in Virginia: The Virginia Pretrial Risk Assessment Instrument* (2003). Since then, other states have conducted pretrial risk-assessment studies to develop tools that can be used in all communities within those states. See, e.g., Pretrial Justice Inst., *The Colorado Pretrial Assessment Tool (CPAT)* (2012). And the Laura and John Arnold Foundation has developed and tested a tool normed for all jurisdictions across the country. Laura and John Arnold Foundation, *Developing a National Model for Pretrial Risk Assessment* (2013).

54. "Updates on National Pretrial Reforms," 1–12.

55. Delaware (State). Legislature. Senate. *An Act to Amend Title 16 of the Delaware Code Relating to Health Planning and Resources Management*, S.B. 226 (June 8, 2016).

56. "Delaware Access to Justice Commission's Committee on Fairness in the Criminal Justice System: A Report on Bail & Pretrial Detention," *Equal Justice Initiative* (October 2015): 2.

57. Gupta, Hansman and Frenchman, "The Heavy Costs of High Bail," 1–40; this study found that defendants are 62 percent more likely to be assessed cash bail than other kinds of bail.

58. Cohen and Reaves, Pretrial Release of Felony Defendants in State Courts.

59. Pretrial Justice Institute, "Rational and Transparent Bail Decision Making: Moving from a Cash-Based to a Risk-Based Process," (March 2012): 3, available at www.safetyandjusticechallenge.org/wp-content/uploads/2015/05/Rational-and-Transparent-Bail-Decision-Making.pdf, last accessed August 15, 2017.

60. Ky. Rev. Stat. Ann. § 431.525(1)(a)–(e) (West 2012).

61. 2011 Ky. Acts. 12.

62. Robert Veldman, "Pretrial Detention in Kentucky: An Analysis of the Impact of House Bill 463 During the First Two Years of Its Implementation," *Kentucky Law Journal* 102 (2014): 789–90.

63. Ibid.

64. Cohen and Reaves, Pretrial Release of Felony Defendants in State Courts, 1.

65. Gupta, Hansman and Frenchman, "The Heavy Costs of High Bail," 1–40.

66. Stevenson, "Distortion of Justice: How the Inability to Pay Bail Affects Case Outcomes," 1–40.

67. Bernadette Rabuy and Daniel Kopf, "Detaining the Poor: How Money Bail Perpetuates an Endless Cycle of Poverty and Jail Time," *Prison Policy Initiative*, May 10, 2016, www.prisonpolicy.org/reports/incomejails.html, last accessed July 27, 2017.

68. Adam Liptak, "Illegal Globally, Bail for Profit Remains in U.S.," *N.Y. Times*, January 29, 2008, www.nytimes.com/2008/01/29/us/29bail.html?_r=0, last accessed July 27, 2017.

69. "Updates on National Pretrial Reforms," 1–12.

70. Katie Bo Williams, "Does the Bounty-Hunting Industry Need Reform?" *The Atlantic* (July 23, 2015) ("Bounty hunters usually grab national attention only when somebody gets shot, but in many states, they're an active part of the criminal-justice system. The modern bail-recovery industry, mostly identified with Wild-West-like

Hollywood depictions like Dog the Bounty Hunter or the novels by Janet Evanovich, is largely invisible to the public eye. This kind of incident usually drives two separate criticisms: that America's archaic bail system disproportionately impacts the poor, and that bounty hunters are acting as wildly unregulated quasi-police.")

71. Robert G. Morris, "Pretrial Release Mechanisms in Dallas County, Texas: Differences in Failure to Appear (FTA), Recidivism/Pretrial Misconduct, and Associated Costs of FTA," *University of Texas at Dallas* (2013): 7.

72. Kan. Stat. Ann. § 22-2802 (5) (West 2007).

73. Kan. Stat. Ann. § 22-2802 (5)(a)–(f) (West 2007).

74. The Supreme Court has not yet ruled on the constitutionality of denying property bail.

75. The Supreme Court of Missouri follows this precedent in *State* v. *Jackson*, 384 S.W.3d 208, 217 (Mo. 2012).

76. *Ward v. Rock Against Racism*, 491 U.S. 782 (1989).

77. Evan Horowitz, "If Crime is Falling, Why Aren't Prisons Shrinking," *The Boston Globe*, January 15, 2015, https://www.bostonglobe.com/metro/2015/01/15/crime-falling-why-aren-prisons-shrinking/sAjkk7opj9hQufs4WwrKKM/story.html last accessed September 18, 2017; Michael G. Maxfield & Terry L. Baumer, "Home Detention with Electronic Monitoring: Comparing Pretrial and Postconviction Programs," *Crime & Delinq.* 36 (1990): 532.

78. Samuel R. Wiseman, "Pretrial Detention and the Right to be Monitored," *Yale Law Journal* 123 (2014): 1118–625; *Electronic Monitoring Program*, Mesa, Ariz., www.mesaaz.gov/city-hall/court/electronic-monitoring, last visited January 17, 2017.

79. Ibid. See also "Criminal Justice Reform," New Jersey Judiciary Pretrial Services Program (May 2017) available at www.judiciary.state.nj.us/forms/12088_cjr_pretrial_svcs_brochure.pdf last accessed September 14, 2017.

80. Wiseman, "Pretrial Detention and the Right to be Monitored"; *United States* v. *O'Brien*, 895 F.2d 810, 814-16 (1st Cir. 1990) (one electronic monitoring program reduced the rate of flight but involved monitoring as well and explained that "evidence concerning the effectiveness of the bracelet alone only arguably rebuts the presumption of flight"); see also Timothy P. Cadigan, *Electronic Monitoring in Federal Pretrial Release*, Fed. Probation, March 1991, at 26, 29–30 (electronically monitored defendants had higher failure to appear rates in one study but they were used for only high-risk defendants, so conclusions were difficult to make); see also William Bales et al., U.S. Dep't of Justice, A Quantitative and Qualitative Assessment of Electronic Monitoring 6 (2010) (explaining that Cadigan's study lacked statistical controls).

81. "2009 Survey of Pretrial Services Programs," *Pretrial Justice Institute* (August 11, 2009): 7.

82. "Pretrial Services & Supervision," *Pretrial Justice Center for Courts*, www.ncsc.org/Microsites/PJCC/Home/Topics/Pretrial-Services.aspx; "The most recent survey of pretrial services agencies in 2009 identified over 300 jurisdictions with pretrial services programs, but that number has grown along with the movement for pretrial justice reform. From 2012 to 2014, six states enacted legislation to authorize or establish statewide pretrial services programs (Colorado, Hawaii, Nevada, New Jersey,

Vermont and West Virginia). There are over 3000 counties in the United States, however."

83. Cohen and Reaves, "Pretrial Release of Felony Defendants in State Courts," 3.

84. Cynthia A. Mamalian, "State of the Science of Pretrial Risk Assessment," *Pretrial Justice Institute* (October 2011): 7, available at www.bja.gov/publications/pji_pretrialriskassessment.pdf, last accessed August 15, 2017; Marie VanNostrand, "Legal and Evidence Based Practices: Applications of Legal Principles, Laws, and Research to the Field of Pretrial Services," *U.S. Department of Justice* (2007): 13–14.

85. Restrictions are imposed according to needs, location, and access to outside resources; restrictions may include curfew, court notification, drug testing, or electronic monitoring.

86. *State v. Jorgenson*, 312 P.3d 960 (Wash. 2013).

87. "Evidence-Based Practices in Pretrial Screening and Supervision," *Vera Institute of Justice* (2010): 5–6.

88. Marie VanNostrand et al., "State of the Science of Pretrial Release Recommendations and Supervision," *Pretrial Justice Institute* (June 2011): 16–21, available at www.pretrial.org/download/research/PJI%20State%20of%20the%20Science%20Pretrial%20Recommendations%20and%20Supervision%20(2011).pdf, last accessed August 15, 2017.

89. "Updates on National Pretrial Reforms," 1–12. In 2012, 4,000 misdemeanor defendants in Kentucky went through diversion programs, with 87 percent of participants successfully completing the program. Participants performed almost 25,000 hours of community service and paid victims over $56,700 in restitution.

90. The same study found that employment and education conditions were rarely given, while contact restrictions were the most common condition imposed. William Bales et al., "A Quantitative and Qualitative Assessment of Electronic Monitoring," *National Criminal Justice Reference Service* (2010): xii–20.

91. Cohen and Reaves, Pretrial Release of Felony Defendants in State Courts, 5.

92. "Updates on National Pretrial Reforms," 1–12; By contrast, 72 percent of unsuccessful participants were sentenced to imprisonment when convicted.

93. "The Development of Guidelines for Financial Bond Recommendations," *Central Connecticut State University* (2009): 10; jurisdictions that implemented the *Decision Aid* program (a program designed to assist in making recommendations regarding conditional release) found that 18 percent fewer clients were held in pretrial detention.

94. Barry Mahoney, Bruce D. Beaudin, John A. Carver III, Daniel B. Ryan, Richard B. Hoffman, "Pretrial Services Programs: Responsibilities and Potential," *National Institute of Justice* (March 2001): 4–5, available at www.ncjrs.gov/pdffiles1/nij/181939.pdf, last accessed August 15, 2017.

95. *United States v. Brown*, No. CR–08–489–PHX–PGR (MHB), 2008 WL 2757322, at *2 (D. Ariz. July 14, 2008); conditions need only be "reasonably calculated to fulfill" a government interest and "assure the appearance of the person" or "Assure the safety of any other person and the community[.]"

96. Florida operates twenty-nine pretrial release programs that provide supervision for defendants charged with a wide range of criminal charges once they are released. The programs do not consider indigency as a factor for eligibility, but

most of the defendants they serve are indigent. Most of Florida's programs conduct investigations of detainees, have representatives at defendants' initial court appearance, and make release recommendations to the court. Most also provide regular drug and alcohol testing so that they may bring problems to the court's attention. "Pretrial Release Programs Vary Across the State; New Reporting Requirements Pose Challenges," *Office of Program Policy Analysis & Government Accountability* (December 2008): 2, www.oppaga.state.fl.us/Reports/pdf/0875rpt .pdf, last accessed July 27, 2017. These programs are all publicly funded and end up costing less than incarceration. Most of the programs are funded and administered locally at the county level. Because of this, there are dramatic differences in the size and budget of the programs. Ibid.

97. "Frequently Asked Questions About Pretrial Release Decision Making," *American Bar Association*: 6.

98. "Evidence-Based Practices in Pretrial Screening and Supervision," 6–7.

99. "Pretrial Reform in Kentucky," *Pretrial Services Administrative Office of the Courts* (2013): 7.

100. Mark S. Waller, Shannon M. Carey, Erin Farley and Michael Rempel, "Testing the Cost Savings of Judicial Diversion," *Center for Court Innovation* (March 2013): 35, available at www.courtinnovation.org/sites/default/files/documents/NY_Judicial%20Diversion_Cost%20Study.pdf, last accessed August 15, 2017.

101. Ibid.

102. Ibid., V.

103. John Jay College of Criminal Justice, "Pretrial Practice: Rethinking the Front End of the Criminal Justice System," (March 2015): 5, available at http://johnjaypri.org/wp-content/uploads/2016/04/RoundtableReport_web1.pdf, last accessed August 17, 2017.

104. Doug McVay et al., "Treatment or Incarceration?," *Justice Policy Institute* (2004): 5, www.justicepolicy.org/uploads/justicepolicy/documents/04-01_rep_mdtreatmentorincarceration_ac-dp.pdf, last accessed July 27, 2017.

105. Ibid.

106. Ibid.

107. Jillian Rose Lim, "Treatment vs. Punishment: Poll Finds Americans Prefer Rehab Over Jail for Drug Offenders," *Medical Daily*, April 4, 2014, www.medicaldaily .com/treatment-vs-punishment-poll-finds-americans-prefer-rehab-over-jail-drug-offenders-274660, last accessed July 27, 2017. In addition, from 2001 to 2014, the percentage of people who believed the government should get rid of the minimum mandatory sentences for drug crimes increased from 47 percent to 63 percent.

108. See *Hudson v. Parker*, 156 U.S. 277 (1895).

4 BAIL AND PREDICTION OF CRIME

1. *United States* v. *Melendez-Carrion*, 790 F.2d 984, 988, 1003 (2d Cir. 1986).

2. Manny Fernandez, "Manslaughter Charge for Tulsa Officer Who Killed Black Driver," *N.Y. Times*, September 22, 2016, www.nytimes.com/2016/09/23/us/tulsa-officer-charged-in-fatal-shooting-of-black-driver.html, last accessed July 27, 2017.

3. Ibid.
4. Ibid.
5. "Oklahoma Officer Betty Shelby Surrenders to Authorities, is Released on Bail," *NBC 26*, September 23, 2016, www.nbc26.com/news/national/oklahoma-officer-betty-shelby-surrenders-to-authorities-is-released-on-bail, last accessed July 27, 2017.
6. For example, a Texas man who killed his wife in public and essentially admitted to the killing was released on a $200,000 bond. Christian McPhate, "Deadly Flower Mound Love Triangle Leave Wreckage in Its Wake," *Dallas Observer*, August 16, 2016, www.dallasobserver.com/news/deadly-flower-mound-love-triangle-leaves-wreckage-in-its-wake-8585149, last accessed July 27, 2017. Dave Lieber and Marina Trahan Martinez, "Why a Man Accused of Killing Estranged Wife on a Southlake Street Was Freed on Low Bail," *Dallas News*, November 11, 2016, www.dallasnews.com/news/watchdog/2016/11/11/man-accused-killing-estranged-wife-southlake-street-freed-low-bail, last accessed July 27, 2017.
7. Evie Lotze, John Clark, D. Alan Henry, & Jolanta Juszkiewicz, *The Pretrial Services Reference Book*, Pretrial Servs. Res. Ctr. (December 1999).
8. Shima Baradaran and Frank McIntyre, "Predicting Violence," *Texas Law Review* 90 (2012): 552.
9. Brian A Reaves, "Felony Defendants in Large Urban Counties, 2009 Statistical Tables," *Bureau of Justice Statistics* (2013): 15, accessed July 27, 2017, www.bjs.gov/content/pub/pdf/fdluc09.pdf.
10. Baradaran and McIntyre "Predicting Violence," 541.
11. Ibid., 553.
12. Ibid.
13. Ibid.
14. Ibid., 557.
15. Except for murder, rape and robbery.
16. Reaves, "Felony Defendants," 21 (see table 19).
17. Ibid.
18. Ibid.
19. Ibid.
20. Ibid.
21. Shima Baradaran, "Drugs and Violence," *Southern California Law Review* 88 (2014): 267.
22. "2009 Survey of Pretrial Services Programs," *Pretrial Justice Institute* (2009): 66, accessed January 25, 2017, www.pretrial.org/download/pji-reports/new-PJI%20 2009%20Survey%20of%20Pretrial%20Services%20Programs.pdf, last accessed July 27, 2017. Also, only 37 percent of pretrial programs surveyed calculate rearrest rates within the program, so the data is not comprehensive. Thomas H. Cohen and Brian Reaves, Pretrial Release of Felony Defendants in State Courts, State Court Processing Statistics 1990–2004 (2007), available at www.bjs.gov/content/pub/pdf/prfdsc.pdf, last accessed July 27, 2017; Baradaran and McIntyre, "Predicting Violence," 522.
23. Ibid.
24. Cohen and Reaves, "Pretrial Release," 9.

25. Ibid.
26. Marie VanNostrand and Christopher T. Lowenkamp, "Assessing Pretrial Risk Without a Defendant Interview," Laura and John Arnold Foundation (2013): 10, accessed July 27, 2017, www.arnoldfoundation.org/wp-content/uploads/2014/02/LJAF_Report_no-interview_FNL.pdf.
27. Reaves, "Felony Defendants," 21 (see table 19).
28. Ibid.
29. Jonathon Lloyd and Andrew Blankstein, "Singer Chris Brown Released on $250 Bail After Being Booked on Charges of Assault With a Deadly Weapon," *NBC Los Angeles*, August 31, 2016, www.nbclosangeles.com/news/local/Investigation-LAPD-Tarzana-Chris-Brown-391749091.html, last accessed July 27, 2017.
30. Ibid.
31. Ibid.
32. Baradaran and McIntyre, "Predicting Violence," 504.
33. Ibid., 505–6.
34. Ibid., 507–8.
35. Ibid., 506–7.
36. Ibid., 523.
37. Ibid., 515–16.
38. Ibid., 505.
39. The characteristics were (1) the nature and circumstances of the offense charged; (2) the weight of the evidence against the defendant; (3) the defendant's family ties; (4) the defendant's employment; (5) the defendant's financial resources; (6) the defendant's character and mental conditions; (7) the defendant's past conduct; (8) the length of the defendant's residence in the community; (9) the defendant's record of convictions; and (10) any record of the defendant's appearances at court proceedings, flight to avoid prosecution, or failure to appear at court proceedings. Ibid., 516.
40. Ibid.
41. The first factor, the initial charge and surrounding circumstances, was, "little better than a random indicator of recidivism." Equally poor predictors included factors three (defendant's family ties), four (the defendant's occupational status), and five (economic situation). Factors six (character and mental health) and seven (past conduct) were of little help because so many of the defendants shared them. Ibid., 517–18.
42. Ibid., 520.
43. Ibid., 521.
44. Ibid., 523.
45. "Data Collection: State Court Processing Statistics," *Bureau of Justice Statistics* (2009), accessed July 27, 2017, www.bjs.gov/index.cfm?ty=pbdetail&iid=4845.
46. Nancy Ritter, "Predicting Recidivism Risk: New Tool in Philadelphia Shows Great Promise," *NIJ Journal* 271 (2013): 9.
47. Ibid. The 2007 study of felony defendants in state courts used logistic regression to assess the impact of certain characteristics independent of others. Generally, this study correlated high rearrest rates with drug charges, young defendants, male defendants, and multiple previous arrests. Low rearrest rates were associated with murder and rape charges, older defendants, female defendants, and first arrests.

When predicting violent crimes specifically, the initial offense and past criminal history is a strong predictor. For violent crime risk, an initial violent crime charge predicted the highest chances of a rearrest for violence. The most dangerous group in terms of violent rearrests are teenage men charged with murder, with four or more prior arrests, a currently active criminal justice status, and a prior violent felony conviction.

48. Ibid., 2.
49. Ibid., 3.
50. "Public Safety Assessment: Risk Factors and Formula," *Laura and John Arnold Foundation* (2016): 4, accessed January 24, 2017, www.arnoldfoundation.org/wp-content/uploads/PSA-Risk-Factors-and-Formula.pdf.
51. "Public Safety Assessment," *Laura and John Arnold Foundation*, accessed December 15, 2016, www.arnoldfoundation.org/initiative/criminal-justice/crime-prevention/public-safety-assessment/.
52. Edward J. Latessa et al., "The Creation and Validation of the Ohio Risk Assessment System," *Federal Justice* 74 (2010): 16. Other states sponsor a pretrial risk assessment. All Virginia pretrial service agencies use the Virginia Pretrial Risk Assessment Instrument (VPRAI). Marie VanNostrand and Gena Keebler, "Pretrial Risk Assessment in the Federal Court," *U.S. Department of Justice* (2009), accessed January 22, 2017, www.pretrial.org/download/risk-assessment/Pretrial%20Risk%20Assessment%20in%20the%20Federal%20Court%20Final%20Report%20%282009%29.pdf. Colorado developed the Colorado Pretrial Assessment Tool (CPAT) to use across jurisdictions. "The Colorado Pretrial Assessment Tool (CPAT)," *Colorado Association of Pretrial Services* (2015): 1, accessed January 20, 2017, www.capscolorado.org/yahoo_site_admin/assets/docs/CPAT_Manual_V21_06-29-2015.179175025.pdf. Florida has developed the Florida Pretrial Risk Assessment Instrument. James Austin et al., "Florida Pretrial Risk Assessment Instrument," *The JFA Institute* (2012): 1, accessed January 24, 2017, www.pretrial.org/download/risk-assessment/FL%20Pretrial%20Risk%20Assessment%20Report%20(2012).pdf.
53. VanNostrand and Lowenkamp, "Assessing Pretrial Risk," 5.
54. Ritter, "Predicting Recidivism Risk"; Geoffrey C. Barnes and Jordan M. Hyatt, "Classifying Adult Probationers by Forecasting Future Offending," (2012), accessed January 25, 2017, www.ncjrs.gov/pdffiles1/nij/grants/238082.pdf.
55. Cynthia A. Mamalian, "State of the Science of Pretrial Risk Assessment," *Pretrial Justice Institute* (October 2011): 7, available at www.bja.gov/publications/pji_pretrialriskassessment.pdf, last accessed August 15, 2017.
56. For example, Allegheny County, PA, is the only county-level program to be recognized as a model program by the American Bar Association. Bruce Barron, "Pretrial Decision Making: How a Model Pretrial Services Program Changed Allegheny County's Criminal Justice System," *The Allegheny Department of Human Services* (July 2014): 3, available at www.pretrial.org/download/infostop/Pretrial%20Decision-Making-%20How%20a%20Model%20Pretrial%20Services%20Program%20Changed%20Allegheny%20County%E2%80%99s%20Criminal%20Justice%20System%20-%20Allegheny%20County%202014.pdf, last accessed August 15, 2017.

57. Anna Maria Barry-Jester, Ben Casselman, and Dana Goldstein, "The New Science of Sentencing," *The Marshall Project* (2015), accessed January 25, 2017, www.themarshallproject.org/2015/08/04/the-new-science-of-sentencing.

58. Ritter, "Predicting Recidivism Risk," 15.

59. Los Angeles uses PredPol ("Predictive Policing"), which forecasts where and when crime will occur, or who might be a perpetrator or victim, using software that relies on algorithms. Justin Jouvenal, "Police Are Using Software to Predict Crime. Is It a 'Holy Grail' or Biased Against Minorities?" *The Washington Post*, accessed November 17, 2016, www.washingtonpost.com/local/public-safety/police-are-using-software-to-predict-crime-is-it-a-holy-grail-or-biased-against-minoritics/2016/11/17/525a6649-0472-440a-aae1-b283aa8e5de8_story.html?wpisrc=nl_draw2&wpmm=1.

60. Ritter, "Predicting Recidivism Risk," 5.

61. Ibid., 9.

62. Ibid.

63. Ibid.

64. Ibid.

65. Ibid.

66. Barnes and Hyatt, "Classifying Adult Probationers," 41.

67. Ritter, "Predicting Recidivism Risk," 9.

68. Barnes and Hyatt, "Classifying Adult Probationers," 40–1.

69. Ritter, "Predicting Recidivism Risk," 8.

70. Ibid.

71. Baradaran and McIntyre, "Predicting Violence," 549–50.

72. Ibid., 508.

73. Ibid., 512–13.

74. Barnes and Hyatt, "Classifying Adult Probationers," 37–41.

75. "2009 Survey," 36.

76. Baradaran and McIntyre, "Predicting Violence," 509. Yet, some argue that the weight this factor carries should be limited as some studies indicate the correlation between present offense charged and future crimes is weaker than originally believed. Ibid., 522. Moreover, studies show that more seriously charged defendants have lower than average rearrest rates. Reaves, "Felony Defendants," 21 (see table 19).

77. Baradaran and McIntyre, "Predicting Violence," 510–11.

78. Ibid., 541; Barry-Jester, Casselman, and Goldstein, "The New Science of Sentencing."

79. Barnes and Hyatt, "Classifying Adult Probationers," 27–8; "2009 Survey," 38 (see figure 4); VanNostrand and Lowenkamp, "Assessing Pretrial Risk," 5.

80. Baradaran and McIntyre, "Predicting Violence," 512.

81. "2009 Survey," 38 (see table 26).

82. William M. Grove et al., "Clinical Versus Mechanical Predictions: A Meta-Analysis," *Psychological Assessment* 2000 12 (2000): 19–30, accessed January 24, 2017, www.psych.umn.edu/faculty/grove/096clinicalversusmechanicalprediction.pdf.

83. Mamalian, "Science of Pretrial Risk," 24.

84. "2009 Survey," 36.

85. Michael S. Woodruff, The Excessive Bail Clause: Achieving Pretrial Justice Reform Through Incorporation, 66 *Rutgers L. Rev.* 241, 293–94 (2013).

86. VanNostrand and Lowenkamp, "Assessing Pretrial Risk," 3.

87. KY Rev. Stat. Ann. § 431.066(3)–(4) (2012).

88. "2009 Survey," 36.

89. "Results from the First Six Months of the Public Safety Assessment – Court in Kentucky," *Laura and John Arnold Foundation* (2014): 1, accessed January 25, 2017, www.arnoldfoundation.org/wp-content/uploads/2014/02/PSA-Court-Kentucky-6-Month-Report.

90. Amber Widgery, "Providing Pretrial Services," *National Conference of State Legislatures* (2015): 2, accessed January 25, 2017, www.ncsl.org/documents/cj/crimebrieffinal.pdf.

91. Brief for the ACLU as Amicus Curiae, *Brooks v. Com.*, Not Reported in S.E.2d., 2004 WL 136090 (2004), accessed January 25, 2017, acluva.org/wp-content/uploads/2003/10/150604-Amicus-Curiae-on-sex-offender-risk-guidelines-2003-case.pdf. The case in question dealt with the risk assessment's application to post-conviction sentencing, but pretrial detention raises the same concerns.

92. Ibid., 6–16.

93. Ibid., 12–13.

94. Ibid., 13–14.

95. *Brooks v. Commonwealth*, Not Reported in S.E.2d., 2004 WL 136090, 1 (2004).

96. Ibid.

97. *U.S. v. Salerno*, 481 U.S. 739 (1987).

98. Baradaran and McIntyre, "Predicting Violence," 520.

99. Cohen and Reaves, "Pretrial Release," 8.

100. "The War on Marijuana at Black and White," *American Civil Liberties Union* (2013): 17–19, accessed January 25, 2017, www.aclu.org/files/assets/aclu-thewaronmarijuana-rel2.pdf.

101. Shima Baradaran and Frank McIntyre, "Race, Prediction and Pretrial Detention," *Journal of Empirical Legal Studies* 10 (2013).

102. Baradaran and McIntyre, "Predicting Violence," 523.

103. Mamalian, "Science of Pretrial Risk," 14.

104. Lindsay C. Ahlman and Ellen M. Kurtz, "The APPD Randomized Controlled Trial in Law Risk Supervision: The Effect of Law Risk Supervision on Rearrest" (2008), accessed January 25, 2017, www.courts.phila.gov/pdf/report/APPD-Low_Risk_Internal_Evaluation.pdf.

105. Mamalian, "Science of Pretrial Risk," 19.

106. Morris L. Thigpen et al., "Measuring What Matters—Outcome and Performance Measures for the Pretrial Services Field," *Nationals Institute of Corrections* (2011), accessed January 25, 2017, www.pretrial.org/download/performance-measures/Measuring%20What%20Matters.pdf.

107. Mamalian, "Science of Pretrial Risk," 23–4.

108. Ibid.

109. Ibid.

110. VanNostrand and Lowenkamp, "Assessing Pretrial Risk," 10.

111. For example, Access to Justice Lab at Harvard Law School is conducting a multisite study of a new pretrial risk scoring mechanism developed by the

Arnold Foundation called the Public Safety Assessment. "Pre-Trial Release," *Harvard Law School*, accessed July 27, 2017, http://access2justice.wpengine.com/current-projects/signature-studies/pre-trial-release/.

112. "2009 Survey," 36 (see Figure 4).

113. Barnes and Hyatt, "Classifying Adult Probationers," 39; VanNostrand and Lowenkamp, "Assessing Pretrial Risk"; VanNostrand and Keebler, "Pretrial Risk Assessment in the Federal Court"; Reaves, "Felony Defendants"; "2009 Survey"; Mamalian, "Science of Pretrial Risk," 14; Baradaran and McIntyre, "Predicting Violence"; Kristen Bechtel et al., "Identifying the Predictors of Pretrial Failure: A Meta Analysis," (2011), accessed January 24, 2017, www.pretrial.org/download/risk-assessment/Identifying%20the%20Predictors%20of%20Pretrial%20Failure%20-%20A%20Meta%20Analysis%20(June%202011).pdf; Audrey O. Hickert et al., "Pretrial Release Risk Study, Validation, & Scoring: Final Report," *Utah Criminal Justice Center* (2011), accessed January 24, 2017, www.ucjc.utah.edu/wp-content/uploads/PretrialRisk_UpdatedFinalReport_v052013.pdf; Cohen and Reaves, "Pretrial Release"; Charles Summers and Tim Willis, "Pretrial Risk Assessment Research Summary," *Bureau of Justice Statistics* (2010), accessed January 24, 2017, www.bja.gov/Publications/PretrialRiskAssessmentResearchSummary.pdf.

114. Baradaran and McIntyre, "Predicting Violence."

115. Ibid.

116. Barnes and Hyatt, "Classifying Adult Probationers," 18. "The history of actuarially-developed forecasts demonstrates that they can out-perform subjective human judgments in most, if not all, situations" Stephen Gottfredson and Laura Moriarty, "Statistical Risk Assessment: Old Problems and New Applications," *Crime and Delinquency* 52 (2006): 180.

117. The three exceptions are murder, rape, and robbery.

5 INDIVIDUAL AND SOCIETAL COSTS OF PRETRIAL DETENTION

1. Steve Schmadeke, Cash bail under fire as discriminatory while poor inmates languish in jail, *Chicago Tribune*, November 15, 2016, www.chicagotribune.com/news/local/breaking/ct-cook-county-cash-bail-met-20161114-story.html, last accessed July 25, 201.

2. "United States Crime Rates 1960–2015," *Disaster Center*, last accessed July 25, 2017, www.disastercenter.com/crime/uscrime.htm.

3. "State Spending for Corrections: Long Term Trends and Recent Criminal Justice Policy Reforms," *The National Association of State Budget Officers*, September 11, 2013.

4. "The Socioeconomic Impact of Pretrial Detention," *Open Society Justice Initiative*, February 2011, www.opensocietyfoundations.org/reports/socioeconomic-impact-pretrial-detention, last accessed July 25, 2017.

5. James J. Stephan, "State Prison Expenditures, 2001," *Bureau of Justice Statistics Special Report* (June 2004): 2, www.bjs.gov/content/pub/pdf/spe01.pdf, last accessed July 25, 2017.

6. The Legislative Analyst's Office reported that in 2016 it cost $70,836 to incarcerate an inmate in prison in California. "California's Annual Cost

to Incarcerate an Inmate in Prison," *Legislative Analyst's Office*, last modified December 2016, www.lao.ca.gov/PolicyAreas/CJ/6_cj_inmatecost; Brian Resnick, "Chart: One Year of Prison Costs More Than One Year at Princeton," *The Atlantic*, November 1, 2011, www.theatlantic.com/national/archive/2011/11/chart-one-year-of-prison-costs-more-than-one-year-at-princeton/247629.

7. Douglas L. Colbert, Raymond Paternoster, and Shawn Bushway., "Do Attorneys Really Matter? The Empirical and Legal Case for the Right of Counsel at Bail," *Cardozo Law Review* 23 (2002): 1757; Albert W. Alschuler, "Preventative Pretrial Detention and the Failure of Interest-Balancing Approaches to Due Process," *Michigan Law Review* 85 (1986): 517.

8. On average, incarceration results in $4,960 and $1,205 in lost federal and state tax revenues, respectively. Loren A.N. Buddress, "Federal Probation and Pretrial Services – A Cost-Effective and Successful Community Corrections System," *Federal Probation* 61 (1997): 10.

9. William A. Brockett, Jr., "Presumed Guilty: The Pre-Trial Detainee," *Yale Review of Law & Social Action* 1 (1970): 21.

10. Jeffrey Mann, "Liberty Takings: A Framework for Compensating Pretrial Detainees," *Cardozo Law Review* 26 (2005): 1974.

11. Mark Pogrebin et al., "The Collateral Costs of Short-Term Jail Incarceration: The Long-Term Social and Economic Disruptions," *Corrections Management Quarterly* 66 (2001): 66; John Hagan and Ronit Dinovitzer, "Collateral Consequences of Imprisonment for Children, Communities, and Prisoners," *Crime & Justice: A Review of Research* 26 (1999): 121–9; Jeremy Travis et al., "Families Left Behind: The Hidden Costs of Incarceration and Reentry," *Urban Institute: Justice Policy Center* (2005): 2–4.

12. "The High Cost of High School Dropouts: What the Nation Pays for Inadequate High Schools," *Alliance for Excellent Education*, Issue Brief (2009): 4.

13. Pogrebin et al., "The Collateral Costs of Short-Term Jail Incarceration: The Long-Term Social and Economic Disruptions"; Mann, "Liberty Takings: A Framework for Compensating Pretrial Detainees," 1974.

14. Ralph B. Taylor, "The Impact of Crime on Communities," *Annals of the American Academy of Political and Social Science* 539 (1995): 37.

15. Wesley Skogan, "Fear of Crime and Neighborhood Change," *Crime and Justice: A Review of Research* 8 (1986): 207; Robert T. Greenbaum and George E. Tita, "The Impact of Violence Surges on Neighborhood Business Activity," *Urban Studies* 41 (2004): 2510.

16. William J. Stuntz, "The Political Constitution of Criminal Justice," *Harvard Law Review* 50 (2006): 784.

17. Gloria Penner and Joanne Faryon, "Soaring Costs for California's Failing Prison System," *KPBS*, Jan. 8, 2010,www.kpbs.org/news/2010/jan/08/overcrowded-and-expensive-governor-addresses-calif; David Brodwin, "How High Prison Costs Slash Education and Hurt the Economy," *U.S. News*, May 24, 2012, www.usnews.com/opinion/blogs/economic-intelligence/2012/05/24/how-high-prison-costs-slash-education-and-hurt-the-economy.

18. "California's Annual Cost to Incarcerate an Inmate in Prison."

19. This number includes state funding for University of California and California State University higher education institutions. "State Spending Per Student at

CSU and UC Remains Near the Lowest Point in More Than 30 Years," *California Budget & Policy Center*, last accessed January 22, 2016, http://calbudgetcenter .org/resources/state-spending-per-student-at-csu-and-uc-remains-near-the-lowest-point-in-more-than-30-years.

20. Marc Santora, City's Annual Cost Per Inmate is $168,000, Study Finds, N.Y. *Times* (August 23, 2013), www.nytimes.com/2013/08/24/nyregion/citys-annual-cost-per-inmate-is-nearly-168000-study-says.html, last accessed August 7, 2017.

21. Shima Baradaran and Frank L. McIntyre, "Predicting Violence," *Texas Law Review* 90 (2012): 502.

22. Ibid. at 540.

23. Mann, "Liberty Takings: A Framework for Compensating Pretrial Detainees," 1968; Thomas Bak, "Pretrial Release Behavior of Defendants Whom the U.S. Attorney Wished to Detain," *American Journal of Criminal Law* 30 (2002): 63–4.

24. Mann, "Liberty Takings: A Framework for Compensating Pretrial Detainees," 1968; Thomas H. Cohen and Brian A. Reaves, "Pretrial Release of Felony Defendants in State Courts," 8 (2008): 1–11; Benjamin Landis, "Jury Trials and the Delay of Justice," *American Bar Association Journal* 56 (1970): 951–2; Andrew W. Bogue and Thomas G. Fritz, "The Six-Man Jury," *South Dakota Law Review* 17 (1972): 288–9; Julie Berry Cullen and Steven D. Levitt, "Crime, Urban Flight, and the Consequences for Cities," *The Review of Economics and Statistics* 81, no. 2 (1999): 159.

25. "Pretrial Criminal Justice Research," *Laura and John Arnold Foundation*, November 2013, www.arnoldfoundation.org/wp-content/uploads/2014/02/LJAF-Pretrial-CJ-Research-brief_FNL.pdf.

26. Keith L. Alexander, "11 Defendants on GPS Monitoring Charged with Violent Crimes in Past Year in D.C.," *Washington Post*, February 9, 2013, www.washington post.com/local/11-defendants-on-gps-monitoring-charged-with-violent-crimes-in-past-year-in-dc/2013/02/09/9237be1e-6c8b-11e2-adao-5ca5fa7ebe79_story.html, last accessed July 25, 2017.

27. Ibid.

28. Low-risk people detained for just 2–3 days after their arrest were found to have 39 percent higher odds of being arrested for a new crime while on pretrial release, while those held 4–7 days were 50 percent more likely to be arrested during this pretrial period. Christopher T. Lowenkamp, Marie VanNostrand, and Alexander Holsinger, *The Hidden Costs of Pretrial Detention* 11, 17–18 (November 2013), available at www.arnoldfoundation.org/wp-content/uploads/2014/02/LJAF_Report_hidden-costs_FNL.pdf, last accessed August 15, 2017. The same patterns existed for moderate-risk defendants. Ibid. And this connection between pretrial incarceration and increased recidivism was still in place after the criminal case was disposed. For example, low-risk individuals who were incarcerated pretrial for 2–3 days were 1.17 times more likely to recidivate during a 24-month post-disposition period. Ibid., 28.

29. Samuel R. Wiseman, "Pretrial Detention and the Right to be Monitored," *Yale Law Journal* 123, no. 5 (2014): 1354.

30. "Pretrial Criminal Justice Research," 2, www.arnoldfoundation.org/wp-content/uploads/2014/02/LJAF-Pretrial-CJ-Research-brief_FNL.pdf, last accessed July 25, 2017.

31. *Powell* v. *Alabama*, 287 US 45 (1932).
32. *Stack* v. *Boyle*, 342 US 1 (1951).
33. Cynthia Jones, "'Give Us Free': Addressing Racial Disparities in Bail Determinations," *Legislature and Public Policy* 919 (2013): 936.
34. Esmond Harmsworth, "Bail and Detention: An Assessment and Critique of the Federal and Massachusetts Systems," *New England Journal on Criminal & Civil Confinement* 22 (1996): 220.
35. Ibid.
36. Ibid.
37. "Pretrial Criminal Justice Research," 2, www.arnoldfoundation.org/wp-content/uploads/2014/02/LJAF-Pretrial-CJ-Research-brief_FNL.pdf.
38. Thomas H. Cohen and Brian Reaves, Pretrial Release of Felony Defendants in State Courts, State Court Processing Statistics 1990-2004 (2007), available at www.bjs.gov/content/pub/pdf/prfdsc.pdf, last accessed July 27, 2017.
39. Christopher T. Lowenkamp et al., "Investigating the Impact of Pretrial Detention on Sentencing Outcomes," *Arnold Foundation* (November 2013): 10–11. www.arnoldfoundation.org/wp-content/uploads/2014/02/LJAF_Report_state-sentencing_FNL.pdf, last accessed July 25, 2017.
40. Ibid.
41. Ibid.
42. Ibid.
43. Gail Kellough and Scot Wortley, "Remand for Plea: Bail Decisions and Plea Bargaining as Commensurable Decisions," *The British Journal of Criminology* 42 (2002): 201.
44. Ibid.
45. "Pretrial Injustice," *Pretrial Justice Institute*, www.pretrial.org/the-problem/pretrial-injustice, last accessed July 25, 2017.
46. Robert Lewis, "No Bail Money Keeps Poor People Behind Bars," *WNYC News*, September 19, 2013, www.wnyc.org/story/bail-keeps-poor-people-behind-bars.
47. "The Price of Freedom: Bail and Pretrial Detention of Low Income Nonfelony Defendants in New York City," *Human Rights Watch* (December 2010): 29, www.hrw.org/sites/default/files/reports/us1210webwcover_0.pdf.
48. Ibid., at 71.
49. This defendant had multiple convictions for drug and larceny offenses at the time of his arrest. Lewis, "No Bail Money Keeps Poor People Behind Bars".
50. "The Price of Freedom: Bail and Pretrial Detention of Low Income Nonfelony Defendants in New York City," 20.
51. *City of Billings* v. *Layzell*, 789 P.2d 221 (Mont. 1990).
52. Ibid.
53. Bak, "Pretrial Release Behavior of Defendants Whom the U.S. Attorney Wished to Detain," 64–5; Doris J. James, "Profile of Jail Inmates, 2002," *Bureau of Justice Statistics* (July 2004), www.bjs.gov/content/pub/pdf/pji02.pdf last accessed July 25, 2017.
54. "Collateral Costs: Incarceration's Effect on Economic Mobility," *The Pew Charitable Trusts* (2010): 11–12, www.pretrial.org/download/research/Collateral%20Costs%20of%20Incarceration%20(Pew%202010).pdf, last accessed July 25, 2017.

55. Ian O'Donnell, "Book Review: Prisons and Penal Purpose: Measuring 'Performance' in English Jails," *Criminal Law Forum* 8 (1997): 111.
56. Ted R. Miller, Mark A. Cohen, and Brian Wiersema, "Victim Costs and Consequences: A New Look," *National Institute of Justice* (1996): 9, available at www.ncjrs.gov/pdffiles/victcost.pdf, last accessed August 15, 2017.
57. Pogrebin et al., "The Collateral Costs of Short-Term Jail Incarceration: The Long-Term Social and Economic Disruptions," 64–65.
58. "Incarceration and Family Relationships: A Fact Sheet," *National Healthy Marriage Resource Center*, 2010, http://healthymarriageinfo.org/docs/Incarceration Family.pdf.
59. Allen J. Beck, "Sexual Victimization in Prisons and Jails Reported by Inmates, 2011–12," *Bureau of Justice Statistics* (May 2013): 8–9, www.bjs.gov/content/pub/pdf/svpjri1112.pdf.
60. Unfortunately, suicide was the leading cause of death for jail inmates since 2000, claiming 918 lives in 2010. Margaret E. Noonan, "Mortality in Local Jails and State Prisons, 2000–2010 – Statistical Stables," *U.S. Department of Justice* (December 2012): 2, www.bjs.gov/content/pub/pdf/mljsp0010st.pdf; and Margaret Noonan et al., U.S. Dep't of Justice, Mortality in Local Jails and State Prisons, 2000–2013 – Statistical Tables 1, 3 (2015), with jail inmates taking their own lives about three times the rate of the general population. Lindsay M. Hayes, U.S. Dep't of Justice, National Study of Jail Suicide: 20 Years Later, 45 (2010). Pretrial detainees committed a majority of these suicides. Noonan, *supra*, at 12. This was particularly during the first seven days of incarceration when the inmates feel the initial shock. *Id.* at 10.
61. Pogrebin et al., "The Collateral Costs of Short-Term Jail Incarceration: The Long-Term Social and Economic Disruptions," 69; Katherine Nesbitt, "Preventative Detention of Terrorist Suspects in Australia and the United States: A Comparative Constitutional Analysis," *Boston University Public Interest Law Journal* 17 (2007): 67.
62. Kathryn Malizia, "Assembly Line Justice," *The New Journal*, September 1, 2002, www.thenewjournalatyale.com/2002/09/assembly-line-justice.
63. Harmsworth, "Bail and Detention: An Assessment and Critique of the Federal and Massachusetts Systems."
64. For more detail see my research in Shima Baradaran Baughman, "The Costs of Pretrial Detention," *Boston University Law Review* 97 (2017): 1, www.bu.edu/bulawreview/files/2017/03/BAUGHMAN.pdf, last accessed July 25, 2017.
65. Laura Sullivan, "Inmates Who Can't Make Bail Face Stark Options," *National Public Radio*, last modified January 22, 2010, www.npr.org/templates/story/story.php?storyId=122725819.
66. "Collateral Costs: Incarceration's Effect on Economic Mobility," 12.
67. "When a Parent is Incarcerated, A Primer for Social Workers," *The Annie E. Casey Foundation* (2011): 3, www.aecf.org/m/resourcedoc/aecf-WhenAParentIs IncarceratedPrimer-2011.pdf.
68. Ibid.
69. Ibid.
70. Kristin Turney, "Stress Proliferation Across Generations? Examining the Relationship Between Parental Incarceration and Childhood Health," *Sage Journals* 55 (2014): 312, doi: 10.1177/0022146514544173.

71. "Clemency Recepients," *U.S. Department of Justice*, last modified January 26, 2015, www.justice.gov/pardon/clinton-commutations; Nancy Goldstein, "All Alone in the World, Children of the Incarcerated," *The Raw Story*, www.rawstory.com/exclusives/goldstein/all_alone_110905.htm.

72. Ibid.

73. Ibid.

74. Ibid.

75. Baughman, "Costs of Pretrial Detention," www.bu.edu/bulawreview/files/2017/03/BAUGHMAN.pdf.

76. Baughman, "Costs of Pretrial Detention," 9, Table 1.

77. Ibid.

78. Ibid.

79. Ibid. It would also save \$1,341 relative to universal release (i.e., releasing all defendants).

80. Baughman, "Costs of Pretrial Detention."

81. Ibid.

6 RACE AND BAIL IN THE CRIMINAL JUSTICE SYSTEM

1. *Pena-Rodriguez* v. *Colorado*, – S. Ct. –, 2017 WL 855760, *12 (March 6, 2017).

2. The Sentencing Project, *Report of the Sentencing Project to the United Nations Human Rights Committee: Regarding Racial Disparities in the United States Criminal Justice System* (2013).

3. Cynthia Jones, "'Give Us Free': Addressing Racial Disparities in Bail Determinations," *New York University Journal of Legislation & Public Policy* 16 (2013): 938.

4. Marvin D. Free, Jr., "Race and Presentencing Decisions in the United States: A Summary and Critique of the Research," *Criminal Justice Review* 27 (2002): 206.

5. Jones, "'Give Us Free,'" 942.

6. Traci Schlesinger, "Racial and Ethnic Disparity in Pretrial Criminal Processing," *Justice Quarterly* 22 (2005): 171–72.

7. E. Ann Carson, *Prisoners in 2014* (U.S. Department of Justice 2015), 5, www.bjs.gov/content/pub/pdf/p14.pdf.

8. "Criminal Justice Fact Sheet," NAACP.org, accessed January 4, 2017, www.naacp.org/criminal-justice-fact-sheet/.

9. Ibid.

10. Ibid.

11. Adam Gopnik, "The Caging of America: Why Do We Lock Up So Many People?," *The New Yorker*, January 30, 2012; Michelle Alexander, *The New Jim Crow: Mass Incarceration in the Age of Colorblindness* (New York: The New Press 2012) (Alexander advances the argument that the disproportionate rate of incarceration of African-Americans allows discrimination against minorities – employment discrimination, housing discrimination, etc. – that would ordinarily be illegal.)

12. Topos Partnership and Marc Kerschhagel, *Public Opinion, Media Depictions, and Media Consumption* (New York: The Opportunity Agenda 2011).

13. Michael A. Fuoco, "Media Urged to Change Portrayal of Blacks," *Pittsburgh Post-Gazette*, November 12, 2011, www.post-gazette.com/local/city/2011/11/02/Media-urged-to-change-portrayal-of-blacks/stories/201111020233.

14. Partnership and Kerschhagel, *Public Opinion, Media Depictions, and Media Consumption.*
15. Craig Reinarman and Harry Levine, eds., "The Crack Attack: Politics and Media in the Crack Scare," in *Crack in America: Demon, Drugs, and Social Justice* (Los Angeles: University of California Press 1997), 18–51.
16. Ibid.
17. Shima Baradaran, "Drugs and Violence," *Southern California Law Review* 88 (2015): 298–300.
18. 132 CONG. REC. S13752 (daily ed. September 11, 1986) (quoting Senator Evans); Baradaran, "Drugs and Violence," 251.
19. 132 CONG. REC. S13752 (daily ed. September 11, 1986) (quoting Senator Evans).
20. Katherine Beckett, "Setting the Public Agenda: 'Street Crime' and Drug Use in American Politics," *Social Problems* 41, no. 3 (1994): 425; Baradaran, "Drugs and Violence," 249.
21. Barbara A. Schwabauer, "The Emmett Till Unsolved Civil Rights Crime Act: The Cold Case of Racism in the Criminal Justice System," *Ohio State Law Journal*, 71 (2010): 658.
22. Scott Ehlers, Vincent Schiraldi, and Eric Lotke, An Examination of the Impact of California's Three Strikes Law on African-Americans and Latinos (October 2004 Justice Policy Institute).

    An analysis of California Department of Corrections' data reveals that African Americans and Latinos are imprisoned under Three Strikes at far higher rates than their white counterparts. African Americans are overrepresented in California's prison population in general, and that overrepresentation is heightened in the state's application of the Three Strikes law. African Americans make up 6.5 percent of the population, but they make up nearly 30 percent of the prison population, 36 percent of second strikers, and 45 percent of third strikers. The proportion of Latinos in California's population is fairly similar to the proportion of Latinos in the prison and striker populations, though both are higher than whites. Although just over 32.6 percent of the overall population is Latino, almost 36 percent of the prison population is Latino and 32.6 percent of strikers are Latino.

23. Hilary E. LaBar, "The Fair Sentencing Act Isn't All It's 'Cracked' Up to Be: How Recent Congressional Action on Federal Crack Cocaine Sentencing Schemes Failed to End the Disparity Between Crack and Powder Cocaine Offenses," *Syracuse Law Review* 64 (2014): 317.
24. David Cole, *No Equal Justice: Race and Class in the American Criminal Justice System* (New York: The New York Press 1999), 8.
25. Ibid., 141–42.
26. The Fair Sentencing Act of 2010 reduced the sentencing disparity between offenses for crack and powder cocaine from 100:1 to 18:1. Public Law 111–220.
27. Human Right Watch, "Targeting Blacks: Drug Law Enforcement and Race in the United States" (May 2008), 3, 45, available at www.hrw.org/reports/2008/us0508/us0508webwcover.pdf, last accessed August 15, 2017.
28. Nico Savidge, "Analysis: Blacks in Madison Arrested at More than 10 Times Rate of Whites," *Wisconsin State Journal*, August 31, 2015, www.host.madison.com/wsj/news/local/crime-and-courts/analysis-blacks-in-madison-arrested-at-more-than-times-rate/article_fd52f630-9647-5541-8114-a2541b8a8924.html.

29. "Compare Arrest Rates," USA Today, accessed January 31, 2017, www.gannett-cdn .com/experiments/usatoday/2014/11/arrests-interactive/.

30. Charles J. Ogletree, Jr., *The Presumption of Guilt: The Arrest of Henry Louis Gates, Jr. and Race, Class, and Crime in America* (New York: St. Martin's Press 2012), 136–8.

31. *Floyd v. City of New York*, 959 F. Supp. 2d 540 (August 12, 2013) (holding the city of New York liable for direct and indirect racial profiling in deciding who to stop while on patrol).

32. Shima Baradaran, "Rebalancing the Fourth Amendment," *The Georgetown Law Journal* 102 (2014): 54–55. Matthew R. Durose et al., U.S. Dep't Justice, Contacts Between Police and the Public, 2005, at 1 (2007), available at www.bjs.ojp.usdoj .gov/content/pub/pdf/cppo5.pdf. (In 2005, the total number of white drivers stopped by the police was higher than the rate of black drivers, but black drivers were much more likely to be searched once they had been stopped.)

33. Rich Morin, Kim Parker, and Andrew Mercer, *Behind the Badge* (Pew Research Center 2017) (noting that there are serious concerns within the police community that there is a lack of accountability when officers conduct their jobs poorly), www.pewsocialtrends.org/2017/01/11/behind-the-badge/#fn-22351-1.

34. Charles R. Lawrence, III, "The Id, the Ego, and Equal Protection: Reckoning with Unconscious Racism," *Stanford Law Review* 39 (1987): 380.

35. Melissa Neal, *Bail Fail: Why the U.S. Should End the Practice of Using Money for Bail* (Justice Policy Institute 2012), 28, www.justicepolicy.org/uploads/ justicepolicy/documents/bailfail.pdf.

36. David Arnold, Will Dobbie, Crystal S. Yang, *Racial Bias in Bail Decisions* (May 2017) available at www.princeton.edu/~wdobbie/files/racialbias.pdf, last accessed July 25, 2017.

37. Ethan Bronner, "Complaint Accuses U.S. Judge in Texas of Racial Bias," *New York Times*, June 5, 2013.

38. Matt Volz, "Former U.S. District Judge Richard Cebull Sent Hundreds of Bigoted Emails Throughout Tenure," *Associated Press*, January 25, 2014.

39. "Criminal Justice Fact Sheet," www.naacp.org/criminal-justice-fact-sheet/, last accessed August 7, 2017.

40. "Criminal Justice Fact Sheet".

41. Mario L. Barnes, "Black Women's Stories and the Criminal Law: Restating the Power of Narrative," *UC Davis Law Review* 39 (2006): 963–64.

42. Shima Baughman, "Subconstitutional Checks," *Notre Dame Law Review* 92 (2017): 1071.

43. Sonja B. Starr and M. Marit Rehati, "Racial Disparity in Federal Criminal Charging and Its Sentencing Consequences" (working paper, University of Michigan Law School, 2012), 1, www.ssrn.com/abstract=1985377; and Sonja B. Starr and M. Marit Rehati, "Mandatory Sentencing and Racial Disparity: Assessing the Role of Prosecutors and the Effects of Booker," *Yale Law Journal* 213 (2013): 1.

44. Starr, "Racial Disparity" 24.

45. Ibid.

46. *Calhoun v. United States*, 133 S. Ct. 1136 (2013).

47. Lincoln Caplan, "'You've Got African-Americans, You've Got Hispanics'", *New York Times*, February 26, 2013, www.takingnote.blogs.nytimes.com/2013/02/26/youve-got-african-americans-youve-got-hispanics/.
48. Ibid.
49. *Calhoun v. United States*, 133 S. Ct. 1136 (2013).
50. Ibid. at 1136, 1137–38.
51. Baughman, "Subconstitutional Checks."
52. Schlesinger, "Racial and Ethnic Disparity," 181.
53. Ibid.
54. Jones, "'Give Us Free,'" 922.
55. Schlesinger, "Racial and Ethnic Disparity," 181.
56. David Kairys, "Unconscious Racism," *Temple Law Review* 83 (2011): 858.
57. Ibid.
58. Ibid.
59. Ibid.
60. Ibid.
61. Ibid.
62. Ibid., 859.
63. Ibid.
64. Schlesinger, "Racial and Ethnic Disparity," 183.
65. Ibid., 181–83.
66. "Pretrial Injustice: No Wisdom in the System – Kalief Browder," Pretrial Justice Institute, accessed January 31, 2017, www.pretrial.org/the-problem/pretrial-injustice/.
67. Schlesinger, "Racial and Ethnic Disparity," 172.
68. Ibid., 181–4.
69. Ibid., 184.
70. Ibid.
71. Laura I. Appleman, "Justice in the Shadowlands: Pretrial Detention, Punishment, & the Sixth Amendment," *Washington and Lee Law Review* 69 (2012): 1360.
72. "Pretrial Injustice: Getting on the Judge's Bad Side – Juan Delgado Perez," Pretrial Justice Institute, accessed January 31, 2017, www.pretrial.org/the-problem/pretrial-injustice/.
73. Ibid.
74. Maire VanNostrand, *New Jersey Jail Population Analysis: Identifying Opportunities to Safely and Responsibly Reduce the Jail Population* (Luminosity 2013), 13, www.drugpolicy.org/sites/default/files/New_Jersey_Jail_Population_Analysis_March_2013.pdf.
75. Ibid., 14.
76. Neal, *Bail Fail*, 10–14, www.justicepolicy.org/uploads/justicepolicy/documents/bailfail.pdf. Also, in 1998, 25 percent of prisoners had bail amounts over $25,000. Just six years later, in 2004, that number had increased to 37 percent.
77. Richard Williams, "Bail or Jail," National Conference of State Legislatures, accessed January 31, 2017, www.ncsl.org/research/civil-and-criminal-justice/bail-or-jail.aspx.
78. Neal, *Bail Fail*, 10–14, (September 2012).

79. Shawn D. Bushway and Jonah B. Gelbach, "Testing for Racial Discrimination in Bail Setting Using Nonparametric Estimation of a Parametric Model" (working paper, 2011), 37, papers.ssrn.com/sol3/papers.cfm?abstract_id=1990324.

80. Ibid.

81. Ibid.

82. Jones, "'Give Us Free,'" 922.

83. Black defendants are 5.8 percentage points more likely to be detained than they would be if they had posted bail at the same rate as nonblack defendants. Megan Stevenson, "Distortion of Justice: How the Inability to Pay Bail Affects Case Outcomes" (working paper, University of Pennsylvania Law School 2017), 25. If black defendants and those from low-income neighborhoods posted bail at the same rate as nonblacks or those from wealthier neighborhoods, Stevenson argues, about half of the gap in detention rates would disappear. Ibid., 26.

84. Shima Baradaran, "Race, Prediction, and Discretion," *George Washington Law Review* 81 (2013): 211.

85. Ibid., 212

86. Ibid., 211.

87. Ibid.

88. For a fuller empirical analysis of this issue, see Frank McIntyre and Shima Baradaran, "Race, Prediction, and Pretrial Detention," *Journal of Empirical Legal Studies* 10 (2013): 741–70.

7 BAIL AND THE SIXTH AMENDMENT RIGHTS TO COUNSEL AND JURY TRIAL

1. Karen Houppert, "Bail System Creates Another Hurdle for Poor Defendants, Including Recent Protestors," *Baltimore City Paper*, May 19, 2015, www.citypaper.com/news/mobtownbeat/bcpnews-bail-system-creates-another-hurdle-for-poor-defendants-including-recent-protestors-20150519-story.html#page=1, last accessed July 25, 2017.

2. Shaila Dewan, "When Bail Is Out of Defendant's Reach, Other Costs Mount," *The New York Times*, June 10, 2015, www.nytimes.com/2015/06/11/us/when-bail-is-out-of-defendants-reach-other-costs-mount.html, last accessed July 25, 2017.

3. Ibid.

4. Douglas L. Colbert, Raymond Paternoster, and Shawn Bushway, "Do Attorneys Really Matter? The Empirical and Legal Case for the Right of Counsel at Bail," *Cardozo Law Review* 23 (2002): 1753.

5. Ibid.

6. *Gideon v. Wainwright*, 372 U.S. 335, 344 (1963).

7. *Miranda v. Arizona*, 384 U.S. 436, 473, (1966).

8. Colbert, Paternoster, and Bushway, "Do Attorneys Really Matter? The Empirical and Legal Case for the Right of Counsel at Bail," 1723–4; Douglas L. Colbert, "Prosecution Without Representation," *Buffalo Law Review* 59 (2011): 428.

9. Bernard Botein, "The Manhattan Bail Project: Its Impact on Criminology and the Criminal Law Processes," *Texas Law Review* 43 (1965): 326.

10. Joseph L. Lester, "Presumed Innocent, Feared Dangerous: The Eighth Amendment's Right to Bail," *N. Kentucky Law Review* 32 (2005): 6. See, *Stack* v.

Boyle, 342 U.S. 1, 4, (1951) ("Unless this right to bail before trial is preserved, the presumption of innocence, secured only after centuries of struggle, would lose its meaning").

11. See Shima Baradaran, "The Presumption of Punishment," *Criminal Law & Philosophy Journal* 8 (2014): 391.

12. Due Process of Law Act 1354 28 Edw 3 c 3.

13. See Matthew J. Hegreness, "America's Fundamental and Vanishing Right to Bail," *Arizona Law Review* 55 (2013): 938.

14. See Shima Baradaran and Frank L. McIntyre, "Predicting Violence," *Texas Law Review* 90 (2012): n. 1 (*citing* Judiciary Act of 1789, chapter 20, §33, 1 Stat. 73, 91 (requiring bail to be admitted in all criminal cases "except where the punishment may be death," in which case admission would be only at the judge's or court's discretion)).

15. Proffatt, J. "A treatise on trial by jury" (Cambridge, MA: Riverside Press, 1876); See also Baradaran, "The Presumption of Punishment."

16. See Ibid.

17. The Bail Reform Act, 98 Stat. 1976 (1984).

18. *United States* v. *Salerno,* 481 U.S. 739, 746–7 (1987).

19. Laura Appleman, "Justice in the Shadowlands: Pretrial Detention, Punishment, & the Sixth Amendment," *Washington and Lee Law Review* 69 (2012): 1304.

20. Ibid., 1351.

21. See ibid.

22. U.S. Const. amend. VI.

23. *Apprendi* v. *New Jersey,* 530 U.S. 466, 499 (Scalia concurring).

24. See *Blakely* v. *Washington,* 542 U.S. 296, 306–7 (2004).

25. See ibid., 303–4.

26. See *S. Union Co.* v. *United States,* 567 U.S. 343 (2012).

27. See ibid. (Holding that *Apprendi* applies to the imposition of criminal fines).

28. Baradaran, "The Presumption of Punishment," 391–406; see also Appleman, "Justice in the Shadowlands: Pretrial Detention, Punishment, & the Sixth Amendment," 1353.

29. *In re* Winship, 397 U.S. 358, 363, (1970) (*quoting Coffin* v. *United States* 156 U.S. 432, 453 (1895)).

30. 18 U.S.C. § 3142(e).

31. See *United States* v. *Salerno,* 481 U.S. 739, 747 (1987).

32. See William Blackstone, *Commentaries on the laws of England* (Chicago: Blackstone Institute, 1915); See also Baradaran, "The Presumption of Punishment," 404.

33. See *Cnty. of Riverside* v. *McLaughlin,* 500 U.S. 1661 (1991).

34. "Don't I Need a Lawyer?: Pretrial Justice and Right to Counsel at First Judicial Hearing," *The Constitution Project National Right to Counsel Committee,* www .pretrial.org/download/infostop/Don%27t%20I%20Need%20a%20Lawyer%20-%20 Constitution%20Project%202015.pdf, last accessed August 15, 2017.

35. Melissa Neal, "Bail Fail: Why the U.S. Should End the Practice of Using Money for Bail," *Justice Policy Institute* (September 2012): 36, www.justice policy.org/uploads/justicepolicy/documents/bailfail.pdf, archived at www .//perma.cc/7PLF-GR42, last accessed July 25, 2017.

36. Ibid.

37. Botein, "The Manhattan Bail Project: Its Impact on Criminology and the Criminal Law Processes."
38. Scott Kohler, "Vera Institute of Justice: Manhattan Bail Project," *Ford Foundation*, 1962, https://cspcs.sanford.duke.edu/sites/default/files/descriptive/manhattan_bail _project.pdf, last accessed July 25, 2017.
39. Ibid.; see *generally* Sam Roberts, *A Kind of Genius Herb Sturz and Society's Toughest Problems* (Canada: Public Affairs 2009).
40. Kohler, "Vera Institute of Justice: Manhattan Bail Project," 1962.
41. Ibid.
42. Botein, "The Manhattan Bail Project: Its Impact on Criminology and the Criminal Law Processes."
43. Kohler, "Vera Institute of Justice: Manhattan Bail Project," 1962.
44. Botein, "The Manhattan Bail Project: Its Impact on Criminology and the Criminal Law Processes."
45. Ibid., 327.
46. Ibid.
47. Kohler, "Vera Institute of Justice: Manhattan Bail Project," 1962.
48. Botein, "The Manhattan Bail Project: Its Impact on Criminology and the Criminal Law Processes," 327.
49. Ibid., 327–8.
50. Ibid., 328.
51. Ibid.
52. Ibid.
53. Colbert, Paternoster and Bushway, "Do Attorneys Really Matter? The Empirical and Legal Case for the Right of Counsel at Bail," 1728.
54. Ibid., 1719, at n.72.
55. Ibid., 1736.
56. Ibid., 1728.
57. Ibid.
58. Ibid., 1721.
59. Ibid., 1728–9.
60. Ibid., 1729–30.
61. Ibid., 1738–9.
62. Ibid., 1752.
63. Ibid., 1753.
64. Ibid., 1736.
65. Ibid., 1753.
66. Ibid., 1753–4.
67. Ibid., 1758. Students met with seventy-eight defendants who had attorneys and sixty-two who did not and discussed with them their perception of fair treatment at their pretrial hearings. When questioned on a scale of 1 to 10, ranging from very unsatisfied to very satisfied, about the satisfaction level of the bail review hearing, the LAB defendants average was 7.14 and the non-LAB defendants average was 5.44. Moreover, when probed about satisfaction in treatment from the judge, LAB clients had an average of 7.0 and non-LAB clients averaged 5.78.
68. Ibid., 1762.
69. U.S. Const. amend. VI.

70. See Charlie Gerstein, "Plea Bargaining and the Right to Counsel at Bail Hearings," *Michigan Law Review* 111 (2013): 1514 (citing *Rothgery* v. *Gillespie Cnty.*, 554 U.S. 191, 194–5 (2008); *United States* v. *Gouveia*, 467 U.S. 180, 188 (1984) ("[The right attaches] at or after the initiation of adversary judicial criminal proceedings – whether by way of formal charge, preliminary hearing, indictment, information, or arraignment." (citation omitted) (internal quotation marks omitted)); *Brewer* v. *Williams*, 430 U.S. 387, 398–9 (1977)).

71. See *Rothgery* v. *Gillespie Cnty., Tex.*, 554 U.S. 191, 212 (2008).

72. See ibid., n.16.

73. "Don't I Need a Lawyer?: Pretrial Justice and Right to Counsel at First Judicial Hearing," 17 (2015).

74. Colbert, "Prosecution Without Representation," 351.

75. Ibid., 350.

76. See ibid.

77. Ibid., 350–1.

78. *Rothgery* v. *Gillespie Cnty., Tex.*, 554 U.S. 191, 194–7 (2008).

79. Ibid., at 212–13.

80. *Rothgery*, 554 U.S. 191, 212 (2008); See also "Sixth Amendment – Attachment of Right to Counsel," *Harvard Law Review* 122 (2008): 309.

81. *Rothgery*, 554 U.S. 191, 218 (2008) (Alito concurring). Justice Alito also deliberately highlighted the fact that the issue of "whether there was any critical stage prior to indictment that warranted appointment of counsel in Rothgery's case" was left unanswered. "Sixth Amendment – Attachment of Right to Counsel."

82. See *United States* v. *Wade*, 388 U.S. 218 (1967).

83. *Bell* v. *Cone*, 535 U.S. 685 (2002).

84. See *Rothgery*, 554 U.S. 191 (2008).

85. Colbert, "Prosecution Without Representation," 382–3.

86. Ibid., 384–6.

87. Ibid., 389.

88. Ibid.

89. Ibid., 396.

90. Ibid., 400–4.

91. Ibid., 405–9.

92. See *Fenner* v. *State*, 381 Md. 1, 846 A.2d 1020 (2004).

93. Douglas L. Colbert, "Coming Soon to A Court Near You – Convicting the Unrepresented at the Bail Stage: An Autopsy of A State High Court's Sua Sponte Rejection of Indigent Defendants' Right to Counsel," *Seton Hall Law Review* 36 (2006): 664.

94. Ibid., 654.

95. U.S. Const. amend. VI.

96. Shima Baradaran, "Restoring the Presumption of Innocence," *Ohio State Law Journal* 72 (2011): 769.

97. Clara Kalhous and John Meringolo, "Bail Pending Trial: Changing Interpretations of the Bail Reform Act and the Importance of Bail from Defense Attorneys' Perspectives," *Pace Law Review* 32 (2012): 848.

98. Stephanie Clifford, "Prosecutors Are Reading Emails from Inmates to Lawyers," *The New York Times*, July 22, 2014, www.nytimes.com/2014/07/23/nyregion/us-is-reading-inmates-email-sent-to-lawyers.html.

99. Derek Gilna, "Courts Divided on Confidentiality of Attorney-Prisoner Email," *Prison Legal News*, July 6, 2016, www.prisonlegalnews.org/news/2016/jul/6/courts-divided-confidentiality-attorney-prisoner-email.

100. Nick Pinto, "The Bail Trap," *The New York Times*, August 13, 2015, www.nytimes.com/2015/08/16/magazine/the-bail-trap.html?_r=0.

101. Shaila Dewan, "When Bail is Out of Defendant's Reach, Other Costs Mount," *The New York Times*, June 10, 2015, www.nytimes.com/2015/06/11/us/when-bail-is-out-of-defendants-reach-other-costs-mount.html.

102. Ibid.

103. See *supra* part 7.2.2.

104. Mary T. Phillips, "A Decade of Bail Research in New York City," *New York City Criminal Justice Agency* (2012): 116.

105. Pinto, "The Bail Trap," 2015.

8 PRETRIAL DETENTION AND TERRORISM IN POST-9/11 AMERICA

1. Antony R. Duff, "Notes on Punishment and Terrorism." *American Behavioral Scientist* 48, no. 6 (2005): 761.

2. Karen J. Greenberg, "Guilty Until Proven Guilty: Threatening the Presumption of Innocence," *The Huffington Post*, November 18, 2010, www.huffingtonpost.com/karen-j-greenberg/guilty-until-proven-guilt_b_785728.html, last accessed July 26, 2017

3. See Uniting and Strengthening America by Providing Appropriate Tools Required to Intercept and Obstruct Terrorism (USA PATRIOT ACT), Pub. L. No. 107-56, 115 Stat. 272 (2001); Greenberg, "Guilty Until Proven Guilty: Threatening the Presumption of Innocence."

4. *Stack v. Boyle*, 342 U.S. 1, 4 (1951).

5. Ibid., 6.

6. Ibid., 4.

7. *U.S. v. Mohamud*, No 2:15-cr-00095-JLG (OH, U.S. District Court for the Southern District of Ohio Eastern Division, April 16, 2015).

8. Ibid.

9. Ibid.

10. Kathy Lynn Gray, "Columbus man indicted on terrorism charges by federal grand jury," *The Columbus Dispatch*, April 17, 2015, www.dispatch.com/content/stories/local/2015/04/16/columbus-man-terrorism-indictment.html, last accessed July 27, 2017.

11. See John Futty, "$2.5 Million Bail Sought for Columbus Terrorism Suspect; Court Appearance Today," *The Columbus Dispatch*, February 25, 2015; see also Gray, "Columbus man indicted on terrorism charges by federal grand jury."

12. Larry D. Thomason, "Intelligence Collection and Information Sharing within the United States," *Brookings*, December 8, 2003, www.brookings.edu/testimonies/intelligence-collection-and-information-sharing-within-the-united-states, last accessed July 27, 2017.

13. *U.S. v. Abdurahman*, 107 F.Supp.3d 992, 994 (D.Minn. 2015).
14. Laura Yuen, "Minnesotan Charged with Trying to Aid ISIS Released to Halfway House," *MPR News,* January 27, 2015, www.mprnews.org/story/2015/01/27/yusuf-released-to-halfway-house, last accessed July 27, 2017.
15. 18 U.S.C.S. § 3142 (e)(3)(C) (2008).
16. § 2332b(g)(5).
17. National Intelligence Act of 2004, § 10197, § 10230.
18. 28 C.F.R. § 501.2(a) (2007).
19. Ibid.
20. Jeanne Theoharis, "My Student, The Terrorist," *The Chronicle Review,* April 3, 2011, www.chronicle.com/article/My-Student-the-Terrorist/126937.
21. See Laura Rovner and Jeanne Theoharis, "Preferring Order to Justice," *American University Law Review* 61 (2012): 1363–86.
22. Ibid.
23. 28 C.F.R. § 541.21 (2011).
24. 8 U.S.C.S. § 1226a(a)(1) (2001).
25. § 1226a (a)(3).
26. § 1226a (a)(5).
27. § 1226a (a)(7).
28. *Hedges v. Obama*, 724 F.3d 170, 185 n.83 (2d Cir. 2013) (listing statements of senators regarding Section 1031 of the Authorization for Use of Military Force and its authorization of indefinite detention).
29. Lindsey Graham and John McCain, "How to Handle the Guantanamo Detainees," *Wall Street Journal,* May 6, 2009, www.wsj.com/articles/SB124157680630090517, last accessed July 27, 2017.
30. 18 U.S.C. § 3142(d).
31. *Id.* § 3142(d); *U.S. v. Santos-Flores*, 794 F.3d 1088, 1091 (9th Cir. 2015).
32. 8 U.S.C. § 1226(e).
33. 8 U.S.C. § 1226(c); *Demore v. Kim*, 538 U.S. 510, 531 (2003).
34. *Rodriguez v. Robbins*, 804 F.3d 1060, 1081, 1084 (9th Cir. 2015) certiorari granted by *Jennings v. Rodriguez*, 136 S.Ct. 2489 (June 20, 2016).
35. John S. Baker, Jr. and Dale E. Bennett, "Measuring the Explosive Growth of Federal Crime Legislation," *The Federalist Society for Law and Public Policy Studies,* fedsoc.server326.com/Publications/practicegroupnewsletters/criminallaw/crimreportfinal.pdf, last accessed July 27, 2017.
36. Greenberg, "Guilty Until Proven Guilty: Threatening the Presumption of Innocence."
37. Melanie Getreuer, "Why Civilian Courts are best for Terror Trials, Especially Boston Bombing Suspect," *The Christian Science Monitor,* April 30, 2013, www.csmonitor.com/Commentary/Opinion/2013/0430/Why-civilian-courts-are-best-for-terror-trials-especially-Boston-bombing-suspect, last accessed July 27, 2017.
38. 10 USCA § 948c (2009).
39. Greenberg, "Guilty Until Proven Guilty: Threatening the Presumption of Innocence."
40. Robin Simcox, "The Presumption of Innocence: Difficulties in Bringing Suspected Terrorists to Trial," (2013): 32, henryjacksonsociety.org/wp-content/uploads/2013/12/The-Presumption-of-Innocence.pdf, last accessed July 27, 2017.

41. See Federal Rules of Evidence, 28 U.S.C.A., (2016); *see also Sullivan* v. *Louisiana*, 508 U.S. 275, 277–8 (1993) (holding "[w]hat the factfinder must determine to return a verdict of guilty is prescribed by the Due Process Clause. The prosecution bears the burden of proving all elements of the offense charged, and must persuade the factfinder beyond a reasonable doubt of the facts necessary to establish each of those elements") (internal citations and quotations omitted).

42. *United States* v. *Ghailani*, 761 F. Supp. 2d 167, 170 (S.D.N.Y. 2011), aff'd, 733 F.3d 29 (2d Cir. 2013), cert. denied, 2014 WL 272119 (U.S. March 10, 2014).

43. See *Hamdan* v. *United States*, 696 F.3d 1238, 1250 n. 10 (D.C. Cir. 2012); *Al-Nashiri* v. *MacDonald*, 2012 WL 1642306 (W.D. Wash. May 10, 2012) (not reported in F. Supp. 2d).

44. 10 USCA § 948c (2009).

45. President Barack Obama, "Remarks by the President on National Security," *The White House* May 21, 2009, www.obamawhitehouse.archives.gov/the-press-office/remarks-president-national-security-5-21-09, last accessed February 9, 2017.

46. Bob Egelko, "Military Tribunals Not the Same as U.S. Courts," *SF Gate*, May 23, 2009, www.sfgate.com/news/article/Military-tribunals-not-the-same-as-U-S-courts-3232033.php, last accessed July 27, 2017.

47. Robert Chesney and Jack Goldsmith, "Terrorism and the Convergence of Criminal and Military Detention Models," *Stanford Law Review* 60 (2008): 1100.

48. Jenny Percival, "Guantanamo Jury Jails Bin Laden Media Chief for Life," *The Guardian*, November 4, 2008, www.theguardian.com/world/2008/nov/04/guantanamo-bin-laden-bahlul, last accessed July 27, 2017.

49. *Al Bahlul* v. *United States*, 767 F.3d 1, 31 (D.C. Cir. 2014).

50. Additional Protocol I of 1977, Art. 51. (1994).

51. Jennifer K. Elsea, "Detention of American Citizens as Enemy Combatants," *CRS Report for Congress* (March 15, 2004): 7, www.fas.org/irp/crs/RL31724.pdf, last accessed July 27, 2017.

52. Ibid.

53. Ibid.

54. Ibid., 2.

55. Padilla ex rel. *Newman* v. *Bush*, 233 F. Supp. 2d 564, 572–3 (S.D.N.Y. 2002), opinion adhered to on reconsideration sub nom. Padilla ex rel. *Newman* v. *Rumsfeld*, 243 F. Supp. 2d 42 (S.D.N.Y. 2003).

56. Ibid., 582.

57. Elsea, "Detention of American Citizens as Enemy Combatants", 2.

58. Ibid.

59. Ibid., 3.

60. National Defense Authorization Act for Fiscal Year 2012 § 1021.

61. "Press Release, Statement by the President on H.R. 1540," *Office of the Press Secretary*, December 31, 2011, https://obamawhitehouse.archives.gov/the-press-office/2011/12/31/statement-president-hr-1540, last accessed July 27, 2017.

62. *Hamdi* v. *Rumsfeld*, 542 U.S. 507, 518 (2004).

63. Ibid., 510.

64. Ibid.

65. Ibid.

66. Ibid., 533.

67. *United States* v. *Lindh*, 227 F. Supp. 2d 565, 567 (E.D. Va. 2002).
68. Ibid., 569.
69. See *United States* v. *Lindh*, 212 F. Supp. 2d 541 (E.D. Va. 2002).
70. Jessica Reaves, "John Walker. Bail Denied," *Time*, February 6, 2002, http:// content.time.com/time/nation/article/0,8599,199677,00.html, last accessed July 27, 2017.
71. Milton J. Valencia, "Tsarnaev Defense Seeks More Time," *Boston Globe*, September 27, 2013, www.bostonglobe.com/2013/09/27/tsarnaev/OWd5DpoKbP 8F6AZBvsC7EL/story.html, last accessed July 27, 2017.
72. "Dzhokhar Tsarnaev Posts Bail," *The Onion*, April 24, 2013, www.theonion.com/ article/dzhokar-tsarnaev-posts-bail-32184.
73. Connor Adams Sheets, "Did Dzhokhar Tsarnaev Post Bail? Twitter Reacts Hilariously to 'Onion' Article," *International Business Times*, April 24, 2013, www .ibtimes.com/did-dzhokhar-tsarnaev-post-bail-twitter-reacts-hilariously-onion-article-1215571, last accessed July 27, 2017.
74. 8 U.S.C.S. § 1226a(a)(1) (2001).
75. § 1226a (a)(7).
76. "Verbatim Transcript of Combatant Status Review Tribunal Hearing for ISN 10024," *CNN*, www.i.a.cnn.net/cnn/2007/images/03/14/transcript_ISN10024.pdf, last accessed February 12, 2017.
77. Barney Henderson, "Khalid Sheikh Mohammed, the 9/11 Mastermind, 'Was Allowed to Redesign Vacuum in Prison'," *The Telegraph*, July 11, 2003, www .telegraph.co.uk/news/worldnews/september-11-attacks/10173359/Khalid-Sheikh-Mohammed-the-911-mastermind-was-allowed-to-redesign-vacuum-in-prison .html, last accessed July 27, 2017.
78. "Guantanamo by the Numbers," *Human Rights First*, January 20, 2017, www .humanrightsfirst.org/sites/default/files/gtmo-by-the-numbers.pdf, last accessed July 27, 2017.
79. "Guantanamo by the Numbers," *American Civil Liberties Union*, December 2016.
80. Jennifer K. Elsea, "Comparison of Rights in Military Commission Trials and Trials in Federal Criminal Court," *Congressional Research Service* (March 21, 2014): 3, www.fas.org/sgp/crs/natsec/R40932.pdf, last accessed July 27, 2017.

9 INTERNATIONAL BAIL

1. Specifically, the work of a commercial bondsman is a crime synonymous with witness tampering or bribing a juror – i.e., obstruction of justice. Adam Liptak, "Illegal Globally, Bail for Profit Remains in U.S.," *New York Times*, January 29, 2008, www.nytimes.com/2008/01/29/us/29bail.html, last accessed July 27, 2017.
2. Moritz Birk et al., *Pretrial Detention and Torture: Why Pretrial Detainees Face the Greatest Risk* (New York: Open Society Foundations, 2011), www .opensocietyfoundations.org/sites/default/files/pretrial-detention-and-torture-06222011.pdf, last accessed July 27, 2017.
3. Amna Guellali, *Cracks in the System Conditions of Pre-Charge Detainees in Tunisia* (Human Rights Watch, 2013), 37, www.hrw.org/sites/default/files/reports/ tunisia1113_ForUpload_1.pdf, last accessed July 27, 2017.

4. *BBC Inside Out South Report: Michael Turner and Fair Trials International*, video, run time 10:46, March 11, 2013, www.youtube.com/watch?v=frgeJmrbMZU, last accessed July 27, 2017.
5. Ibid.
6. Ibid.
7. Ibid.
8. Ibid.
9. Ibid.
10. Ibid.
11. "Michael Turner – Hungary," *Fair Trials*, last modified March 9, 2016, www .fairtrials.org/cases/michael-turner/, last accessed July 27, 2017. They are found guilty of defrauding Hungary of about £12,000.
12. Ibid.
13. Martin Schonteich, *Presumption of Guilt: The Global Overuse of Pretrial Detention*, (New York: Open Society Foundations, 2014), 17, last accessed December 21, 2016, www.opensocietyfoundations.org/sites/default/files/presumption-guilt-09032014.pdf, last accessed July 27, 2017.
14. Ibid.
15. Roy Walmsley, *World Pre-trial/Remand Imprisonment List (second edition)* (International Centre for Prison Studies, 2015), www.prisonstudies.org/sites/default/ files/resources/downloads/world_pre-trial_imprisonment_list_2nd_edition_1 .pdf, last accessed July 27, 2017.
16. Notable is the significantly high rate of TB in Russia, which is almost 70 times higher in pretrial than in the general public, and outbreaks of hepatitis C in Californian prisons and HIV/AIDS in South African prisons. David Berry, *Socioeconomic Impact of Pretrial Detention* (New York: Open Society Foundations, 2011), 15, www.opensocietyfoundations.org/sites/default/files/socioeconomic-impact-pretrial-detention-02012011.pdf, last accessed July 27, 2017.
17. For example, Human Rights Watch interviewed a Tunisian woman who relayed her story of being arrested, beaten by police officers, and later denied medical care for her injuries. Guellali, *Cracks in the System*, 37–8.
18. Detainees in Mexico pay an estimated 42.3 million U.S. dollars annually for "extra-legal" expenses charged for basic privileges such as "making a phone call, securing a place to sleep, and avoiding or lessening beatings." Berry, *Socioeconomic Impact*, 30.
19. Nigeria, for example, has an average pretrial detention duration of 3.7 years. Ibid., 15.
20. The world's prisons contain 1,577,800 people in excess of prison capacity. Schonteich, *Presumption of Guilt*, 30. Further, of 204 countries listed by the ICPS, 113 are at 100 percent or over. "Highest to Lowest – Occupancy Level (based on official capacity)," *World Prison Brief*, 2017, www.prisonstudies.org/highest-to-lowest/occupancy-level?field_region_taxonomy_tid=14, last accessed July 27, 2017.
21. For example, a report examining the conditions of pretrial detention facilities in Zimbabwe reported excrement on floor of cells. *Pretrial Detention in Zimbabwe* (ZLHR, Law Society of Zimbabwe, 2013), 30, www.osisa.org/sites/default/files/ pre-trial_detention_in_zimbabwe.pdf, last accessed July 27, 2017.
22. For example, some reports indicate that no food is given in Zimbabwe. Ibid.; and very poor food is given in Tunisia. Human Rights Watch, *Tunisia: Perils of*

Pre-charge Detention, video, 7:48, December 5, 2013, www.hrw.org/news/2013/12/05/
tunisia-perils-pre-charge-detention, last accessed July 27, 2017.

23. A recent report on pretrial detention statistics indicated that there was no available information for China. Walmsley, *World Pre-trial/Remand*.

24. Pretrial detainees in Greece are usually kept in the same facilities as convicted prisoners. *Pre-Trial Detention in Greece* (Fair Trials International, 2013), 7, www .fairtrials.org/wp-content/uploads/Greek-communique-EN.pdf,   last   accessed December 27, 2016.

25. Berry, *Socioeconomic Impact*, 20.

26. United Nations General Assembly, Resolution 217A, "Universal Declaration of Human Rights," December 10, 1948, Article 11(1), http://un.org/en/universal-declaration-human-rights/, last accessed July 27, 2017. See also European Court of Human Rights, "European Convention on Human Rights," 1950, Article 5 & 5(i)(c); "African Charter on Human and Peoples' Rights," June 27, 1981, Articles 7(1) & (7)(1)(d), www.1.umn.edu/humanrts/instree/z1afchar.htm; Inter-American Commission on Human Rights, Resolution 1/08, "Principles and Best Practices on the Protection of Persons Deprived of Liberty in the Americas," March 13, 2008, Principle   III(1)–(2),   www.oas.org/en/iachr/mandate/Basics/principlesdeprived .asp, last accessed July 27, 2017.

27. United Nations General Assembly, "International Covenant on Civil and Political Rights," December 19, 1966, Article 9, http://treaties.un.org/doc/publication/unts/ volume%20999/volume-999-i-14668-english.pdf, last accessed July 27, 2017.

28. "Eighth United Nations Congress on the Prevention of Crime and the Treatment of Offenders," December 14, 1990, www.un.org/documents/ga/res/45/a45r121.htm, last accessed July 27, 2017.

29. United Nations General Assembly, Resolution 45/110, "United Nations Standard Minimum Rules for Non-custodial Measures (The Tokyo Rules)," December 14, 1990, Rule 6, www.un.org/documents/ga/res/45/a45r110.htm, last accessed July 27, 2017.

30. Ibid.

31. Schonteich, *Presumption of Guilt* 18.

32. Ibid.

33. Amanda Petteruti, *Finding Direction: Expanding Criminal Justice Options by Considering Policies of Other Nations* (Washington, DC: Justice Policy Institute, 2011), 3, www.justicepolicy.org/uploads/justicepolicy/documents/pretrial_deten-tion_and_remand_to_custody.pdf, last accessed July 27, 2017.

34. Bail Act, 1976, c. 63, § 4(2).

35. England and Wales is at 13.8 percent, Germany is at 18 percent. Walmsley, *World Pre-trial/Remand*.

36. In Germany, suspects that are ultimately acquitted, or against whom the charges are dropped, can be compensated for their time in pretrial detention at about $12.00 per day. Richard S. Frase, "German Criminal Justice as a Guide to American Law Reform: Similar Problems, Better Solutions?," *Boston College International and Comparative Law Review* 18 (1995): 328.

37. In Germany, one study says monetary bail was used 12 percent of the time. Ibid., 329. Further, monetary bail is usually given to wealthy defendants who will be required to pay. Petteruti, *Finding Direction*, 3. England also recognizes the danger

of sureties, realizing it can also be used to prejudice lower income people who cannot afford a surety. A.M. van Kalmthout, M.M. Knapen, and C. Morgenstern, "Pretrial Detention in the European Union, An Analysis of Minimum Standards in Pre-trial Detention and the Grounds for Regular Review in the Member States of the EU" (WLP 2009), 953, http://citeseerx.ist.psu.edu/viewdoc/download?doi= 10.1.1.194.618&rep=rep1&type=pdf, last accessed July 27, 2017.

38. A.M. van Kalmthout, M.M. Knapen, and C. Morgenstern, "Pretrial Detention," 953.

39. Example is from Germany. Petteruti, *Finding Direction*, 3.

40. United Nations General Assembly, Resolution 45/110, "United Nations Standard Minimum Rules for Non-custodial Measures (The Tokyo Rules)."

41. Ibid.

42. Laura Harmes, "Law Society Calls for 28-day Limit on Police Bail," *BBC Radio 5 Live*, May 28, 2013, www.bbc.com/news/uk-22624648, last accessed July 27, 2017.

43. Data includes Wales. Marcelo F. Aebi and Natalia Delgrande, *Council of Europe Annual Penal Statistics: Space 1* (Strasbourg: Council of Europe, 2008), www .ristretti.it/commenti/2007/novembre/pdf/detenzione_europa_2006.pdf, last accessed July 27, 2017.

44. *By the Numbers: Crime, Bail and Pre-trial Detention in Canada* (Toronto: Canadian Civil Liberties Association, 2014), 1, ccla.org/cclanewsite/wp-content/ uploads/2015/02/2014-07-23-By-the-numbers1.pdf, last accessed July 27, 2017.

45. Ibid.

46. Ibid.

47. Which is common, as well as curfews, anger management counseling, prohibition on possessing firearms, and fines for failure to appear in court or comply with bail conditions. Petteruti, *Finding Direction*, 3.

48. Statistically, drug defendants are the least likely to be violent when released pretrial. Shima Baradaran, "Drugs and Violence," *Southern California Law Review* 88 (2015): 234.

49. For example, suspects accused of financial corruption in Gambia are automatically denied bail, with few exceptions. John Quigley, "The Tanzania Constitution and the Right to a Bail Hearing," *African Journal of International and Comparative Law* 4 (1992): 178 (quoting Special Criminal Court Act 1979, 696).

50. Bail Act 1997 (Act No. 16/1997) § 2(2)(a)–(f), www.irishstatutebook.ie/eli/1997/ act/16/enacted/en/html, last accessed July 27, 2017.

51. Automatic release if less than three months, and automatic detention if the punishment is greater than fifteen years of forced labor, unless the prosecutor consents. George E. Glos, "Bail, Probation and Parole in Belgian Law," *International Journal of Legal Information* 14 (1986): 102.

52. That is, the possibility of reoffense could only be considered for serious crimes. Petteruti, *Finding Direction*, 3.

53. Such is the case in Belgium. Glos, "Bail, Probation and Parole."

54. For example, in Hungary, the majority of judges have been found to almost always grant the prosecutor's motion to order detention pre-trial. *Pre-trial Detention in Hungary* (Fair Trials International, 2013), 1–2, www.fairtrials.org/wp-content/ uploads/Hungary-PTD-communique.pdf, last accessed December 23, 2016.

55. For example, judges in Greece rely on the severity of the crime, which is impermissible under Greek law. *Pre-Trial Detention in Greece*, 2.
56. United Nations General Assembly, "International Covenant on Civil and Political Rights."
57. For example, Greek judges continue to overuse pretrial detention, using factors that have been outlawed by the legislature, such as avoiding similar future offenses in their reasoning, *Pre-Trial Detention in Greece*, 2.
58. For example, most Hungarian judges have been found to agree to prosecutors' requests "almost automatically." *Pre-trial Detention in Hungary*, 1–2.
59. For example, reports have highlighted concerns with French judges making detention decisions in haste, without taking the time to look at the files in depth. *Pre-Trial Detention in France* (Fair Trials International, 2013), 2, www.fairtrials.org/communique-pre-trial-detention-in-france/, last accessed July 27, 2017.
60. *Pre-Trial Detention in Greece*, 2, 27.
61. In France, detention orders often cite general reasons for detaining an individual, without addressing how these reasons apply to the detainee specifically. *Pre-Trial Detention in France*, 4.
62. French law allows pretrial detention to be ordered only where the detention will preserve evidence or material clues; prevent witness or victim coercion; protect suspects or ensure their availability; end an offense or public disturbance; or prevent unlawful collusion between a suspect and his or her associate. Code de procédure pénale [C. pr. pén.] [Criminal Procedure Code] 144.
63. Local expert groups in Poland have noted that Defendants generally do not have adequate representation. "Communique Following Meeting in Poland to Discuss Pre-Trial Detention," *Fair Trials International*, February 13, 2013, www.fairtrials.org/publications/communique-following-meeting-in-poland-to-discuss-pre-trial-detention/, last accessed July 27, 2017. There have been reported concerns in Italy that detainees are often denied access to lawyers before being questioned. "Appendix 2 Pre-trial Detention Comparative Research" (Fair Trials International), 22, www.ec.europa.eu/justice/newsroom/criminal/opinion/files/110510/appendix_2_-_comparative_research_en.pdf, last accessed December 28, 2016; And detainees in Tunisia have no right or access to an attorney in the initial period after arrest. Human Rights Watch, *Tunisia: Perils of Pre-charge Detention*.
64. In Greece, defense attorneys are frequently given only five minutes with the case file to prepare a defense. *Pre-Trial Detention in Greece*, 4.
65. As is the case in Greece, where defendants are often appointed attorneys that have no criminal law background. Ibid., 4, 27.
66. Ibid.
67. For example, Poland. "Communique Following Meeting in Poland," *Fair Trials International*.
68. Birk et al., *Pretrial Detention and Torture*, 36.
69. As is the case in Mexico. Berry, *Socioeconomic Impact*, 45.
70. Most notable is the significantly high rate of TB in Russia, which is almost 70 times higher in pretrial than in the general public, and outbreaks of hepatitis C in Californian prisons, and HIV/AIDS in South Africa. Berry, *Socioeconomic Impact*, 15.

71. Ananyev and Others v. Russia, App. Nos. 42525/07 & 60800/08 (Eur. Ct. H.R. Jan. 10, 2012); Ingrid Burke, "Russia Scrambles to Improve Detainee Rights Record Under ECHR Guidance," *RAPSI*, September 1, 2013, www.rapsinews.com/judicial_analyst/20130109/265853623.html, last accessed July 27, 2017.

72. Overlap because the inability to leave the cell in some cases amounts to torture, as does the filthy conditions, and overcrowding. Also, overcrowding can cause filthy conditions, which in turn can cause disease to spread.

73. *Report on International Prison Conditions* (United States Department of State, Bureau of Democracy, Human Rights and Labor), 2, www.state.gov/documents/organization/210160.pdf, last accessed December 28, 2016.

74. Birk et al., *Pretrial Detention and Torture*, 37.

75. For example, in Greece pretrial detention is sometimes used to convince detainees to confess or to testify against a co-defendant. *Pre-Trial Detention in Greece*, 6–7. Also, in Hungary, reports have found that some investigating officials will use the mere threat of pretrial detention to obtain evidence. "Hungarian Experts' Concern Over Pre-Trial Detention," *Fair Trials International* (2013), www.fairtrials.org/publications/hungarian-experts-concern-over-pre-trial-detention-2, last accessed December 28, 2016.

76. *Ananyev and Others* v. *Russia*, App. Nos. 42525/07 & 60800/08 (Eur. Ct. H.R. Jan. 10, 2012).

77. Burke, "Russia Scrambles to Improve Detainee Rights Record."

78. Schonteich, *Presumption of Guilt* 30. Further, of 204 countries listed by the ICPS, 113 are at 100 percent or over. "Highest to Lowest," *International Centre for Prison Studies*.

79. One example is Nigeria, where one prison reported holding 2,420 detainees despite only having the capacity to hold 800. Birk et al., *Pretrial Detention and Torture*, 37.

80. Haitian prisons, for example, have about 0.4 square meters – which is about one quarter of a twin sized bed – while international standards recommend 5.4 square meters. This figure references prisoners, not pretrial detainees, but Haiti is a country that does not always separate the prisoners from detainees; so prison conditions reflect the reality of pretrial conditions for many detainees. "Extreme Prison Overcrowding and Lengthy Pre-Trial Detention Continue in Haiti Despite International Court Order," *Institute for Justice and Democracy in Haiti*, July 3, 2013, www.ijdh.org/2013/07/topics/law-justice/extreme-prison-overcrowding-and-lengthy-pre-trial-detention-continue-in-haiti-despite-international-court-order/, last accessed July 27, 2017.

81. This gives 0.7 square meters per person. Further, only forty-four of the inmates are sentenced prisoners; the rest are pretrial detainees. Frédéric Gouin, "Prolonged Pretrial Detention Creates Overcrowding in Haitian Prisons," *MINUSTAH/Office of the High Commissioner for Human Rights*, accessed May 6, 2015, https://minustah.unmissions.org/prolonged-pretrial-detention-creates-overcrowding-haitian-prisonsla-d%C3%A9tention-provisoire-prolong%C3%A9e, last accessed July 27, 2017.

82. Ibid.

83. In a detention center in Tunisia, for example, Human Rights Watch discovered that several detainees reported the presence of rats in their cells and showed evidence of rat bites on their skin. Ibid., 32.

84. Human Rights Watch reported that every facility in Tunisia they visited for a recent study gave detainees no access to showers. Ibid., 4.
85. As has been observed in detention facilities in Zimbabwe. *Pretrial Detention in Zimbabwe*, 30.
86. Ibid.
87. One detention facility in Tunisia provides only a "toilet hole" for bathroom relief. Guellali, *Cracks in the System*, 29.
88. In Zimbabwe, these types of conditions were found to be prevalent in detention facilities throughout the country. *Pretrial Detention in Zimbabwe*, 30.
89. The Bouchoucha Detention Center in Tunisia keeps detainee cells at cold temperatures, while providing them only dirty blankets with which to keep warm. Ibid., 27.
90. In Tunisia's Kairouan Detention Center, detainees are provided a faucet – which the prison guards control – to use for both cleaning the toilet and drinking water. Ibid., 29.
91. In Tunisia, the justification for not providing soap is that inmates might do something "immoral" with it, or swallow pieces in an effort to hurt themselves. Ibid., 31.
92. A letter from Human Rights Watch to the Prime Minister of Tunisia indicates that one of the main issues reported by detainees is the ability to keep clean due to lack of access to basic cleaning agents like soap. Ibid., 56.
93. Human Rights Watch has reported that, in Tunisia, the most prevalent problem is lack of adequate nutrition and that prisoners report receiving as little as bread, lettuce, and sauce twice a day. Ibid., 56.
94. For example, some detainees in Zimbabwe were held for days without food. *Pretrial Detention in Zimbabwe*, 30.
95. Guellali, *Cracks in the System*, 30.
96. Human Rights Watch has recognized that resource constraints in third-world countries like Zambia are a serious consideration in implementing national detention standards. Katherine Wiltenburg Todrys, *Unjust and Unhealthy: HIV, TB, and Abuse in Zambian Prisons* (New York: Human Rights Watch, 2010), 8, www.hrw.org/sites/default/files/reports/zambia0410webwcover.pdf, last accessed July 27, 2017.
97. "Every prisoner shall be provided by the administration at the usual hours with food of nutritional value adequate for health and strength, of wholesome quality and well prepared and served." United Nations General Assembly, Resolution 70/175, "United Nations Standard Minimum Rules for the Treatment of Prisoners (the Nelson Mandela Rules)," December 17, 2015, Rule 22, www.un.org/en/ga/search/view_doc.asp?symbol=A/RES/70/175, last accessed July 27, 2017.
98. For example, this has been reported in both Hungary and Russia. *BBC Inside Out South Report: Michael Turner*; Burke, "Russia Scrambles to Improve Detainee Rights Record."
99. Guellali, *Cracks in the System*, 29.
100. In Zimbabwe, two pretrial detainees were held in complete isolation – save 20 minutes a day for laundry, bathing, and exercise – for months. *Pretrial Detention in Zimbabwe*, 32.
101. In summer, these boxes become extremely hot. Birk et al., *Pretrial Detention and Torture*, 37.

102. Ibid.
103. In fact, the majority of torture that occurs worldwide occurs in pretrial detention. Ibid., 17.
104. As has been reported in Greece. *Report to the Government of Greece.*
105. Human Rights Watch interviewed seventy Tunisian detainees, forty of which said they had been mistreated by guards in such ways as being threatened with rape. Human Rights Watch, *Tunisia: Perils of Pre-charge Detention.*
106. *BBC Inside Out South Report: Michael Turner.*
107. Ibid.
108. *Pretrial Detention in Zimbabwe*, 32.
109. Ibid., 35.
110. Ibid., 33.
111. For example, physical interrogations have become less common in Japan, but have been replaced with psychologically coercive tactics. Further, some prosecutors have been shown to edit interrogation recordings at-will to hide these questionable tactics. *Japan 2013 Human Rights Report* (United States Department of State, Bureau of Democracy, Human Rights and Labor, 2013), 6–7, www.state .gov/documents/organization/220409.pdf, last accessed December 28, 2016.
112. Ibid., 6.
113. This is especially problematic in countries like Japan, where there is a twenty-three-day long period before defendants are tried. Ibid., 7.
114. Ibid., 6.
115. For example, "extra-legal" charges in Mexico. Berry, *Socioeconomic Impact*, 30. Another example is the problem faced in Russia, where businesspeople are sometimes jailed in return for bribes from competitors. Kathy Lally, "Laws to Rein in Russia's Pretrial Detention System are Ignored," *The Washington Post*, November 25, 2011, www.washingtonpost.com/world/europe/laws-to-rein-in-russias-pre-trial-detention-system-are-ignored/2011/11/04/gIQAeNvmnN_story.html, last accessed July 27, 2017.
116. Lally, "Laws to Rein in Russia's Pretrial Detention System."
117. Ibid.
118. Things like food, water, bedding, and to avoid being beaten. Berry, *Socioeconomic Impact*, 30.
119. "The Socioeconomic Impact of Pretrial Detention in Sierra Leon," *Open Society Justice Initiative* (2013): 42, last accessed April 14, 2015, www.issuu.com/undp/docs/ the_socioeconomic_impact_of_pretria_a7486b030e4a06, last accessed July 27, 2017.
120. Lally, "Laws to Rein in Russia's Pretrial Detention System."
121. In Mexico, in an effort to look like they are winning "the drug war," accused drug lords are caught, paraded in front of the media, and then three quarters are released. Schonteich, *Presumption of Guilt* 119. Also, in Thailand, police have been accused of torturing suspects in an effort to solve crimes quickly in the face of international pressure. "Thailand: Tactics of Police Questioned in Investigations of Tourist Murders," *The Associated Press*, October 8, 2014, www.nytimes.com/2014/10/09/world/asia/thailand-tactics-of-police-questioned-in-investigation-of-tourists-murders.html?ref=topics, last accessed July 27, 2017.

122. Business owners are targeted in Russia. Lally, "Laws to Rein in Russia's Pretrial Detention System." Poor and marginalized groups are targeted in South Africa, Egypt, Cote D'Ivoire, Cape Verde, Senegal, and Gambia, though a part of this is because poor and marginalized people cannot afford bail. Berry, *Socioeconomic Impact*, 23.

123. A Mexican detainee, who was tortured, was accused of kidnapping a person who wasn't even in Mexico at the time of the alleged kidnapping. Schonteich, *Presumption of Guilt* 119.

124. For example, detainees are held for forty days in Mexico, six days in Tunisia, and up to twenty-three days in Japan. Ibid.; Human Rights Watch, *Tunisia: Perils of Pre-charge Detention*; *Japan 2013 Human Rights Report*, 6.

125. Nigeria, for example, has an average pretrial detention duration of 3.7 years. Berry, *Socioeconomic Impact*, 15. Further, two years is common in Chile. Jonathan L. Hafetz, "Pretrial Detention, Human Rights, and Judicial Reform in Latin America," *Fordham International Law Journal* 26 (2002–2003): 1762.

126. Schonteich, *Presumption of Guilt* 120.

127. In Tunisia, detainees are also denied access to their families. Human Rights Watch, *Tunisia: Perils of Pre-charge Detention*.

128. Some countries, such as those in Lain America, do not intentionally punish pretrial defendants in this manner. Their system is traditionally inquisitorial, rather than adversarial, which is much slower because it investigates extensively before ever going to court. Hafetz, "Pretrial Detention, Human Rights, and Judicial Reform in Latin America," 1758.

129. For example, white collar criminal defendants in Greece have been subject to this type of "punishment" because of public perception in the face of an economic crisis; this is also discussed in section D(i), *supra. Pre-Trial Detention in Greece*, 3, 27.

130. Schonteich, *Presumption of Guilt* 124.

131. Ibid.

132. Ibid.

133. Ibid.

134. Most notable is the significantly high rate of TB in Russia, which is almost seventy times higher in pretrial than in the general public, there are also outbreaks of hepatitis C in Californian prisons, and HIV/AIDS in South Africa. Berry, *Socioeconomic Impact*, 15.

135. Ibid., 21.

136. Ibid.

137. Ibid.

138. Ibid., 20.

139. Ibid.

140. Ibid., 21.

141. For example, in Russia, Stanislav Kankia, who was accused of fraud, suffered four strokes that left him brain damaged, barely able to speak, and partly blind, but the court ruled his health was fine. Lally, "Laws to Rein in Russia's Pretrial Detention System."

142. For example, in Russia, Andrei Kudoyarov, who died. Will Englund, "Bribery Charge Perplexes Moscow School," *The Washington Post*, October 26, 2011,

www.washingtonpost.com/world/europe/bribery-charge-perplexes-moscow-school/2011/10/21/gIQA33vnGM_story.html, last accessed July 27, 2017.

143. For example, in Russia Natalia Gulevich, who was in prison for eleven months. Lally, "Laws to Rein in Russia's Pretrial Detention System."
144. For example, in Russia, Sergei L. Magnitsky, who died in pretrial detention at age 38. Ibid.
145. Ibid.
146. Ibid.
147. Ibid.
148. Ibid.
149. Ibid.
150. Ibid.
151. In Russia, Sergei L. Magnitsky was beaten, denied treatment for pancreatitis, and died. He was not alone. In 2010, fifty-nine people died in Moscow's pretrial detentions alone. Ibid.
152. For example, Russian Andrei Kudoyarov, a principal at a very successful school, was held before trial for months before he died of a heart attack. Englund, "Bribery Charge Perplexes Moscow School."
153. For example, in Latvia, the stress of waiting for trial for two years, while barred from speaking with either his family or a lawyer, caused a fifteen-year-old pretrial detainee to hang himself. Agence France-Presse, "Pretrial Detentions Worrying Eastern Europe," *New York Times*, November 19, 2000, www.nytimes.com/2000/11/19/world/pretrial-detentions-worrying-eastern-europe.html, last accessed July 27, 2017.
154. In 2009, seven people died under suspicious circumstances in Chinese police custody. Michael Wines, "China Daily Assails Prisoner Abuses," *New York Times*, March 24, 2009, www.nytimes.com/2009/03/25/world/asia/25china.html?r=0, last accessed July 27, 2017. Further, there are some that say Russian detainee Sergei L. Magnitsky did not die from pancreatitis, but died as a result of torture. "Sergei Magnitsky's Torture and Murder in Pre-Trial Detention," *Stop the Untouchables*, www.russian-untouchables.com/eng/torture-and-death/, last accessed July 27, 2017.
155. The Chinese police claimed that two of those seven died due to illness, which the family members deny. Wines, "China Daily Assails Prisoner Abuses."

10 MONEY BAIL

1. Robert F. Kennedy, "Address by Attorney General Robert F. Kennedy to the American Bar Association House of Delegates" (speech, San Francisco, CA, August 6, 1962), Department of Justice, www.justice.gov/sites/default/files/ag/legacy/2011/01/20/08-06-1962%20Pro.pdf, last accessed August 1, 2017.
2. Adam Liptak, "Illegal Globally, Bail for Profit Remains in U.S.," *N.Y. Times*, January 29, 2008, www.nytimes.com/2008/01/29/us/29bail.html, last accessed August 1, 2017.
3. Ibid. The Philippines is the other country. Other countries rely on money in their bail systems, but the defendant receives their money back when they appear for

their court date. There is no commercial bail allowed, and this is illegal in almost all of the world.

4. Criminal Code, R.S.C., ch. C-46, s. 139 (1985) (Can.) laws-lois.justice.gc.ca/eng/acts/C-46/section-139.html, last accessed August 1, 2017. Law Reform Commission of Western Australia, "Review of Bail Procedures," *Law Reform Commission* (1977). Bail Act, 1976, c. 63 (Eng.) www.legislation.gov.uk/ukpga/1976/63, last accessed August 1, 2017.

5. *Jones v. The City of Clanton*, No. 215CV34-MHT, 2015 WL 5387219 at *3 (M.D. Ala. September 14, 2015).

6. Francesca Forrest, "Guilty Until Proven Innocent: The Problem with Money Bail." *Federal Reserve Bank of Boston*, May 27, 2015, www.bostonfed.org/commdev/c&b/2015/summer/Francesca-Forrest-the-problem-with-money-bail.htm, last accessed August 1, 2017.

7. Laura Sullivan, "Inmates Who Can't Make Bail Face Stark Options," *National Public Radio*, January 22, 2010, www.npr.org/templates/story/story.php?storyId=122725819, last accessed August 1, 2017.

8. Sharon Aungst, "Pretrial Detention & Community Supervision," *CAFWD* (2012): 8, caforward.3cdn.net/7a60c47c7329a4abd7_2am6iyh9s.pdf, last accessed February 27, 2017.

9. *Bearden v. Georgia*, 461 U.S. 660, 671 (1983).

10. Samuel R. Wiseman, "Pretrial Detention and the Right to be Monitored," *Yale Law Journal* 123 (2014): 1346.

11. Thomas H. Cohen and Brian A. Reaves, "Pretrial Release of Felony Defendants in State Courts," *Bureau of Justice Statistics* (2007): 3, www.bjs.gov/content/pub/pdf/prfdsc.pdf, last accessed March 3, 2017.

12. "A California Lawsuit over the Cash Bail System Could Prompt Changes across the U.S.," *L.A. Times*, December 26, 2015, www.latimes.com/local/california/la-me-bail-bond-lawsuit-20151226-story.html, last accessed August 1, 2017. See also Alex Emslie, "Lawsuit to Reform S.F. Bail System Hits Snag – But Will Continue," *California Report*, January 27, 2016, www2.kqed.org/news/2016/01/27/federal-judge-sends-bail-reform-effort-back-to-the-drawing-board/, last accessed August 1, 2017.

13. Micheal Balsamo, "Burglars of a Feather 'Flock' Together in Los Angeles," *U.S. News* March 30, 2017, www.usnews.com/news/best-states/california/articles/2017-03-30/burglars-of-a-feather-flock-together-in-los-angeles, last accessed August 1, 2017.

14. Michael E. Miller, "An Ohio Man Allegedly Tried to Kill his Ex-wife. When he got out on Bail, Police say he Finished His Crime," *The Washington Post*, December 10, 2015, available atwww.washingtonpost.com/news/morning-mix/wp/2015/12/10/an-ohio-man-allegedly-tried-to-kill-his-ex-wife-when-he-got-out-on-bail-police-say-he-finished-his-crime, last accessed August 1, 2017.

15. Susan Carroll, "Drug cartel hires Texas teens as border hitmen," *The Chronicle*, April 15, 2007, www.chron.com/news/houston-texas/article/Drug-cartel-hires-Texas-teens-as-border-hitmen-1825635.php, last accessed August 1, 2017.

16. Arthur R. Angel, Eric D. Green, Henry R. Kaufman, and Eric E. Van Loon, "Preventive Detention: An Empirical Analysis," *Harvard Civil Rights-Civil Liberties Law Review* 6 (1971): 352.

17. Christopher T. Lowenkamp, Marie VanNostrand, and Alexander Holsinger, "The Hidden Costs of Pretrial Detention," *Laura and John Arnold Foundation* (2013): 4, www.arnoldfoundation.org/wp-content/uploads/2014/02/LJAF_Report_hidden-costs_FNL.pdf, last accessed March 3, 2017.
18. Ibid.
19. Ibid.
20. Arpit Gupta, Christopher Hansman, and Ethan Frenchman, "The Heavy Costs of High Bail: Evidence from Judge Randomization," *The Journal of Legal Studies* 45, no. 2 (June 2016): 471–505.
21. Wiseman, "Pretrial Detention" 1356.
22. Gupta, Hansman, and Frenchman, "The Heavy Costs of High Bail: Evidence from Judge Randomization."
23. Barry Mahoney, "Pretrial Services Programs: Responsibilities and Potential," *National Institute of Justice* (2001): 4–5, www.ncjrs.gov/pdffiles1/nij/181939.pdf, last accessed February 27, 2017.
24. "Public Defense Advocate: Cash-bail System 'a Mechanism for Incarceration.'" The Fault Lines Digital Team. October 9, 2015. The Fault Lines Digital Team, "Public Defense Advocate: Cash-bail System 'a Mechanism for Incarceration,'" *Al Jazeera America*, October 9, 2015, http://america.aljazeera.com/watch/shows/fault-lines/articles/2015/10/9/public-defense-advocate-cash-bail-system-now-a-mechanism-for-incarceration.html, last accessed August 2, 2017.
25. Teresa Wiltz, Locked Up: Is Cash Bail on the Way Out? (March 1, 2017), available at www.pewtrusts.org/en/research-and-analysis/blogs/stateline/2017/03/01/locked-up-is-cash-bail-on-the-way-out last accessed August 2, 2017.
26. Ibid.
27. Anne Rankin, "The Effect of Pretrial Detention," *New York University Law Review* 39 (1964): 641.
28. Megan T. Stevenson, Distortion of Justice: How the Inability to Pay Bail Affects Case Outcomes (January 12, 2017), available at SSRN: https://ssrn.com/abstract=2777615 or http://dx.doi.org/10.2139/ssrn.2777615, last accessed August 2, 2017.
29. Douglas J. Klein, "The Pretrial Detention 'Crisis': The Causes and the Cure," *Journal of Urban and Contemporary Law* 52 (1997): 293.
30. Wiseman, "Pretrial Detention."
31. Cohen and Reaves, "Pretrial Release," 2–3.
32. "Bail Fail: Why the U.S. Should End the Practice of Using Money for Bail," *Justice Policy Institute* (2012): 2.
33. Ibid.
34. Ram Subramanian et al., "Incarceration's Front Door: The Misuse of Jails in America," *Vera Institute of Justice* (2015): 29.
35. Ibid.
36. Ibid. This is in constant dollar values.
37. Ibid., 22.
38. Ibid., 22. Note that "While not all admissions come from arrests—warrants for people suspected of parole and probation violations, for example, provide another route to jail—the growth in admissions even as arrest rates have declined reflects changing policies rather than growth in more serious crimes by high-risk individuals."

39. Ibid. 22–3.
40. Ibid.
41. The Fault Lines Digital Team, "Public Defense Advocate."
42. *State v. Brown*, 338 P.3d 1276, 1283 (N.M. 2014).
43. Ibid., 1284; For a further examination into the history of money bail and pretrial detention in the United States, see generally Shima Baradaran, "Restoring the Presumption of Innocence," *Ohio State Law Journal* 72 (2011), which analyzed the history of pretrial detention and the presumption of innocence at the time of arrest.
44. Statute of Westminster, 1275, 3 Edw. 1 (Eng.).
45. Petition of Right, 1628, 3 Car. 1 (Eng.).
46. Bill of Rights, 1689, 1 W. & M. Sess 2 (Eng.).
47. See Judiciary Act of 1789, 1 Stat. 73 (1789).
48. *Stack v. Boyle*, 342 U.S. 1 (1951).
49. Shane Bauer, "Inside the Wild, Shadowy, and Highly Lucrative Bail Industry," *Mother Jones*, May/June 2014, www.motherjones.com/politics/2014/06/bail-bond-prison-industry, last accessed August 2, 2017.
50. The company was so successful that it earned the nickname of "Old Lady of Kearny Street" who "furnished bail by the gross to bookmakers and prostitutes, kept a taxi waiting at the door to whisk them out of jail and back to work." "The Old Lady Moves On," *Time Magazine*, August 18, 1941, content.time.com/time/magazine/article/0,9171,802159,00.html, last accessed August 2, 2017.
51. See generally 18 U.S.C. §§ 3141–51.
52. Timothy R. Schnacke, Michael R. Jones, and Claire M. B. Booker, "The History of Bail and Pretrial Justice," *Pretrial Justice Institute* (2010), www.pretrial.org/download/pji-reports/PJI-History%20of%20Bail%20Revised.pdf, accessed August 2, 2017.
53. H.R. REP. NO. 89-1541(1966), *reprinted in* 1966 U.S.C.C.A.N. 2293, 2295.
54. Ibid., 2296.
55. Ibid.
56. Ibid.
57. "Bail Fail."
58. See *Schall v. Martin*, 467 U.S. 253, 269–71 (1984). This case provided for the pretrial detention of juveniles due to public safety considerations that the defendant posed and the nature of confinement before trial satisfy the regulatory purpose of the Due Process Clause. *Bell v. Wolfish*, 441 U.S. 520, 560–1 (1979). The Supreme Court found that pretrial detention did not violate the Due Process Clause because it fulfilled a legitimate governmental purpose and was not punishment in itself.
59. Floralynn Einesman, "How Long Is Too Long? When Pretrial Detention Violates Due Process," *Tennessee Law Review* 60 (1992): 11.
60. S. REP. 98-225, 3, 1984 U.S.C.C.A.N. 3182, 3185.
61. 18 U.S.C. § 3142(b).
62. Ibid.
63. "Fines, Fees, and Bail," *Council of Economic Advisers Issue Brief* (2015): 6, accessed March 9, 2017, obamawhitehouse.archives.gov/sites/default/files/page/files/1215_cea_fine_fee_bail_issue_brief.pdf.

64. Ibid.
65. U.S. Const. amend. XII.
66. Lauryn P. Gouldin, "Disentangling Flight Risk from Dangerousness," *Brigham Young University Law Review*, no. 3, 2016 (2016): 864.
67. Shaila Dewan, "When Bail Is Out of Defendant's Reach, Other Costs Mount," N.Y. *Times*, June 10, 2015, www.nytimes.com/2015/06/11/us/when-bail-is-out-of-defendants-reach-other-costs-mount.html, last accessed August 2, 2017.
68. Shima Baradaran and Frank McIntyre, "Predicting Violence," *Texas Law Review* 90 (2012): 510. Timothy R. Schnacke, "Fundamentals of Bail: A Resource Guide for Pretrial Practitioners and a Framework for American Pretrial Reform" *National Institute of Corrections* (2014): 90, www.clebp.org/images/2014-09-04_Fundamentals_of_Bail.pdf, last accessed March 1, 2017.
69. Gouldin, "Disentangling Flight Risk from Dangerousness," 862. Wiseman, "Pretrial Detention," 1346 n.2. Jocelyn Simonson, "Bail Nullification," *Michigan Law Review* 115 (2017): 603–4.
70. *Brown*, 338 P.3d 1276.
71. Ibid., 1278 (Citing *Stack* v. *Boyle*, 342 U.S. 1 (1951)).
72. Ibid., 1293
73. Ibid.
74. Wiseman, "Pretrial Detention," 1383.
75. See *United States* v. *McConnell*, 842 F.2d 105 (5th Cir. 1988). *State* v. *Anderson*, 319 Conn. 288, 331 (2015).
76. *Pugh* v. *Rainwater*, 572 F.2d 1053 (5th Cir. 1978).
77. Ibid.
78. *Jones*, 2015 WL 5387219.
79. Statement of Interest of the United States, *Jones* v. *City of Clanton*, No. 2:15-cv-34-MHT-WC (M.D. Ala. Feb. 13, 2015). Lorelei Lair, "Court Systems Rethink the Use of Financial Bail, Which Some Say Penalizes the Poor," *American Bar Association Journal*, April 1, 2016, www.abajournal.com/magazine/article/courts_are_rethinking_bail, last accessed August 2, 2017.
80. *Jones*, 2015 WL 5387219.
81. *State* v. *Blake*, 642 So. 2d 959, 961 (Ala. 1994).
82. Cherise Burdeen, "The Dangerous Domino Effect of Not Making Bail," *The Atlantic*, April 12, 2016, www.theatlantic.com/politics/archive/2016/04/the-dangerous-domino-effect-of-not-making-bail/477906/ last accessed August 2, 2017.
83. "Ending the American Money Bail System." *Equal Justice Under Law*, www.equaljusticeunderlaw.org/wp/current-cases/ending-the-american-money-bail-system/, last accessed March 9, 2017.
84. See *Pierce* v. *City of Velda City*, No. 4-15-cv-570-HEA (Doc. 16) (E.D. Mo . June 3, 2015) (issuing Declaratory Judgment); *Cooper* v. *City of Dothan*, No. 1:15-cv-425-WKW (M.D. Ala. June 18, 2015) (Doc. 7) (granting Temporary Restraining Order).
85. Ibid.
86. Evan Sernoffsky, "Group Files Class-action Complaint to Scrap S.F.'s Cash-bail System." SFGate, October 29, 2015, www.sfgate.com/news/article/Group-files-suit-to-scrap-S-F-s-unfair-6599294.php, last accessed August 2, 2017. *Jones*, 2015 WL 5387219. *Pierce*, No. 4-15-cv-570-HEA. *Cooper*, No. 1:15-cv-425-WKW. *Powell* v. *The City of St. Ann*, No. 4:15-cv-00840 (E.D. Mo. 2015). *Thompson* v. *Moss*

Point, Mississippi, No. 1:2015cv00182, Doc. 19 (S.D. Miss. 2015). *Snow* v. *Lambert*, Civil No. 15-567-SDD-RLB (M.D. La. 2015). *Martinez* v. *City of Dodge City*, No. 2:15-cv-09344 (D. Kan. 2016).

87. Ibid.
88. *Pierce*, No. 4-15-cv-570-HEA at 1.
89. See *Thompson*, No. 1:15cv182LG-RHW.
90. *Rodriguez* v. *Providence Community Corrections, Inc.*, No. 315CV01048, 191 F. Supp. 3d 758, 775–6, 779 (M.D. Tenn. June 9, 2016).
91. *Walker* v. *City of Calhoun, Georgia*, No. 4:15-CV-0170-HLM, 2016 WL 361612, at *14 (N.D. Ga. January 28, 2016).
92. Ibid., *1.
93. Ibid., *10.
94. Ibid., *10–11; see *Bearden*, 461 U.S. at 671. The Court held that the Equal Protection Clause of the Fourteenth Amendment generally prohibits "punishing a person for his poverty."
95. *Brief of Petitioner-Appellant, Walker* v. *City of Calhoun Georgia*, No. 4:15-CV-0170-HLM, No. 16-10521 (11th Cir. June 14 2016), available at http://pdfserver.amlaw .com/dailyreport/Editorial/WalkerAppellantBrief.pdf, last accessed August 2, 2017. *United States* v. *Al-Marri*, No. 03-3674 (7th Cir. Nov. 12, 2003).
96. *Walker*, 4:15-cv-00170-HLM; Case No. 16-10521 (11th Cir. 2017).
97. *Welchen* v. *Harris, et al.* 2:16-at-0090 (E.D. Cal. Jan 2, 2016). See the Complaint at www.equaljusticeunderlaw.org/wp/wp-content/uploads/2015/10/1-S.F.-Complaint .pdf, last accessed August 2, 2017.
98. Tamara Aparton, "Federal Lawsuit Seeks to End Money Bail in SF," *San Francisco Public Defender*, October 29, 2015, www.sfpublicdefender.org/news/2015/10/ federal-lawsuit-seeks-to-end-money-bail-in-sf/, last accessed August 2, 2017.
99. Jonah Lamb, "SF Won't Defend 'Unconstitutional' Bail System in Lawsuit," *San Francisco Examiner*, November 1, 2016, www.sfexaminer.com/sf-wont-defend-unconstitutional-bail-system-lawsuit/, last accessed August 2, 2017.
100. Sernoffsky "Group Files Class-action Complaint."
101. Ibid.
102. *Blake*, 642 So. 2d 959.
103. Ibid., 961
104. Ibid., 966
105. Ibid.
106. Ibid.
107. Complaint, *O'Donnell* v. *Harris County*, No. 4:16-cv-01414 (S.D. Tex. May 19, 2016). Eesha Pandit, "Criminal Injustice in Texas: Thousands Stay Jailed in Just One County Because They Can't Pay Bail—and It's Happening All Over the U.S.," *Salon*, June 5, 2016, www.salon.com/2016/06/05/criminal_injustice_in_ texas_thousands_stay_jailed_in_just_one_county_because_they_cant_pay_bail_ and_its_happening_all_over_the_u_s/, last accessed August 2, 2017.
108. Lindsey Carlson, "Bail Schedules: A Violation of Judicial Discretion?" *Criminal Justice* 26 (2011): 13–14.
109. Paul Heaton, Sandra Mayson and Megan Stevenson, "The Downstream Consequences of Misdemeanor Pretrial Detention," *Stanford Law Review* 69: 711, (2017).

110. "Pretrial Justice in America: A Survey of County Pretrial Release Policies, Practices and Outcomes," *Pretrial Justice Institute* (2009): 5–7.
111. Ibid., 7.
112. See Cynthia A. Mamalian, "State of the Science of Pretrial Risk Assessment," *Pretrial Justice Institute* (2011): 21–3. See also American Bar Association, Pretrial Release Standard 10-5.3 (e).
113. "Pretrial Justice in America," 7.
114. Ibid., 6.
115. Curtis E.A. Karnow, "Setting Bail for Public Safety," *Berkeley Journal of Criminal Law* 13:1, 13–14 (2008).
116. Dan Cathey and Isaac Vallejos, "New Mexico Bail Bond Schedules: A Comparison of Bernalillo County's Bond Schedule to 21 New Mexico Jurisdictions," *University of New Mexico Institute for Social Research* (2014).
117. Ibid., 2.
118. Ibid., 2–3.
119. *Jones*, 2015 WL 5387219.
120. *Jones*, 2015 WL 5387219, at *1.
121. Ibid. "Thus, an arrestee can be released without any upfront payment, but will be required to pay the bond if she does not appear for her scheduled court date."
122. Ibid., *2 and *7.
123. Ibid., *3.
124. *Pelekai v. White*, 75 Haw. 357, 861 P.2d 1205 (1993).
125. Ibid., 1211.
126. *Clark v. Hall*, 2002 OK CR 29, 53 P.3d 416 (2002).
127. Carlson, "Bail Schedules" 4.
128. Ibid.
129. *Pierce*, No. 15-cv-00570.
130. Ibid.
131. Ibid.
132. Eric Helland and Alexander Tabarrok, "The Fugitive: Evidence on Public Versus Private Law Enforcement from Bail Jumping," *Journal of Law and Economics* 93 (2004). Those released on bail bonds were 21 percent likely to have not appeared in court after having missed the original trial, whereas those released on their own recognizance were 32 percent likely to have still not appeared in court.
133. Pretrial Services Agency for the District of Columbia, available at www.psa.gov/?q=data/performance_measures, last accessed August 2, 2017.
134. Spike Bradford, "For Better or for Profit: How the Bail Bonding Industry Stands in the Way of Fair and Effective Pretrial Justice." *Justice Policy Institute*, September 18, 2012, www.justicepolicy.org/research/4388, last accessed August 2, 2017.
135. Ibid.
136. American Bail Coalition Newsletter, October 2010, www.asc-usi.com/userfiles/BailResources/ABC_Newsletter%20V1.pdf, last accessed August 2, 2017.
137. Ibid.
138. Ibid.
139. Bauer, "Inside the . . . Bail Industry."

140. Pheny Z. Smith, "Felony Defendants in Large Urban Counties, 1990," *Bureau of Justice Statistics* (May 1993): 9 (see Table 10), available at www.bjs.gov/content/pub/pdf/fdluc90.pdf, last accessed August 15, 2017.

141. Brian A. Reaves, "Felony Defendants in Large Urban Counties, 2009 – Statistical Tables," *Bureau of Justice Statistics* (2013): 20 (see Figure 14), available at www.bjs.gov/content/pub/pdf/fdluc09.pdf, last accessed August 15, 2017.

142. Bauer, "Inside the . . . Bail Industry." See also Smith, "Felony Defendants," 9 (see Table 11). Reaves, "Felony Defendants," 19 (see Table 16).

143. Bauer, "Inside the . . . Bail Industry."

144. "Inside Out: Questionable and Abusive Practices in New Jersey's Bail-Bond Industry," *State of New Jersey Commission of Investigation,* (2013): 52.

145. Report to the Utah Legislature, "A Performance Audit of Utah's Monetary Bail System," Report No. 2017-01 (2017): iii. There is a statewide 26 percent failure to appear rate for all cases involving a commercial surety.

146. Robert G. Morris, "Pretrial Release Mechanisms in Dallas County, Texas: Differences in Failure to Appeal (FTA), Recidivism/Pretrial Misconduct, and Associated Costs of FTA." *Dallas County (Texas) Criminal Justice Advisory Board* (January 2013), available at www.utdallas.edu/epps/ccjs/dl/Dallas%20 Pretrial%20Release%20Report%20-FINAL%20Jan%202013c.pdf, last accessed August 15, 2017.

147. For example, in Utah, "Forfeitures are rare because of the opportunities for automatic bond exonerations permitted in statute coupled with long forfeiture grace periods, which increase the likelihood that a bond will be exonerated." Report to the Utah Legislature, "A Performance Audit," iii.

148. "Florida Registration Memo to Bail Bond Agents." January 2015.

149. "Inside Out: Questionable and Abusive Practices in New Jersey's Bail-Bond Industry."

150. Tennessee S.B. 736, 108th General Assembly (2013).

151. Ibid.

152. Tenn. Code § 40-11-138.

153. "Congressman Ted W. Lieu Introduces the 'No Money Bail Act of 2016,'" Press Release, February 24, 2016, www.lieu.house.gov/media-center/press-releases/congressman-ted-w-lieu-introduces-no-money-bail-act-2016-0, last accessed August 2, 2017.

154. Eric Holder, "Attorney General Eric Holder Speaks at the National Symposium on Pretrial Justice" (speech, National Symposium on Pretrial Justice, Washington, DC, June 1, 2011), www.justice.gov/opa/speech/attorney-general-eric-holder-speaks-national-symposium-pretrial-justice last accessed August 2, 2017. "Under former U.S. Attorney General Loretta Lynch, the Department of Justice was critical of the cash bail system, arguing that it contributes to inequities and rewards the wealthy with their freedom while penalizing the poor. When bail is set unreasonably high, people are behind bars only because they are poor. Not because they're a danger or a flight risk — only because they are poor," Lynch said in 2015 at a White House conference on the issue." Wiltz, Locked Up: Is Cash Bail on the Way Out?.

155. Statement of Interest of the United States, *Jones* v. *City of Clanton.*

156. Kamala Harris and Rand Paul, "To Shrink Jails: Lets Reform Bail," *New York Times* (Op ed July 20, 2017), www.nytimes.com/2017/07/20/opinion/kamala-harris-and-rand-paul-lets-reform-bail.html, last accessed July 31, 2017.

157. "Ending the American Money Bail System," accessed August 2, 2017, www.equaljusticeunderlaw.org/wp/our-mission/.

158. These states include Utah, California, Kentucky, Colorado, New Jersey, Delaware, Maryland, New Mexico, New York, Nevada, Utah, Louisiana, and Ohio. California: Alexei Koseff, "California considers an end to bail: 'We're punishing people simply for being poor,'" The Sacramento Bee (February 4, 2017), HYPERLINK "http://www.sacbee.com/news/politics-government/capitol-alert/article130682914.html" www.sacbee.com/news/politics-government/capitol-alert/article130682914.html, last accessed August 2, 2017; see also L.J. Williamson, "Legislators introduce bills to overhaul state bail system," San Francisco Daily Journal (December 6, 2016); Kentucky: Public Safety and Offender Accountability Act, H.B. 463 (Ky. 2011); Admin. Office of the Courts, Pretrial Reform in Kentucky 5-8 (Ky. Courts of Just., 2013); Colorado: Timothy R. Schnacke, Best Practices in Bond Setting: Colorado's New Pretrial Bail Law 4 n.12 (2013); New Jersey Matt Arco, Christie Signs Bail Reform Measure, Lauds Lawmakers for Bi-partisanship, NJ.Com (August 11, 2014). Other states reportedly considering bail reform include Alaska, Connecticut, Delaware, Maryland, New Mexico, New York, Nevada, and Ohio. Press Release, [Alaska] Governor Signs Justice Reinvestment Law with Sweeping Changes to Pretrial Policy (Pretrial Justice Inst., July 11, 2016); Connecticut Moves to Reform Cash Bail System for Low-level Defendants, Between the Lines, Btonline.org (February 3, 2016); Public Welfare Foundation, Smart Pretrial Reform in Delaware, Publicwelfare.org (April 22, 2015); Governor's Commission to Reform Maryland's Pretrial System: Final Report (December 19, 2014); James C. McKinley, Jr., State's Chief Judge, Citing 'Injustice,' Lays Out Plans to Alter Bail System, N.Y. Times (October 1, 2015); Thomas Cole, Lawmakers Give Final OK to Bail Reform Measure, Albuquerque Journal (February 17, 2016); Geoff Dornan, Feds Agree to Help Study and Pay for Nevada Bail Reform Project, Nevada Appeal (February 11, 2016); Ben Winslow, Big Changes Could be Coming to Utah Criminal Justice System, Fox 13 (January 25, 2016) HYPERLINK "http://www.fox13now.com/2016/01/25/" www.fox13now.com/2016/01/25/big-changes-could-be-coming-to-utahs-criminal-justice-system/, last accessed August 2, 2017; Sara Dorn, Developing 'Fair' Bail System Goal of Ohio Panel, Cleveland.com (May 17, 2016).

159. Amber Widgery, "Guidance for Setting Release Conditions," *National Conference of State Legislatures*, May 5, 2015, www.ncsl.org/research/civil-and-criminal-justice/guidance-for-setting-release-conditions.aspx, last accessed August 2, 2017.

160. Dewan, "When Bail Is Out of Defendant's Reach, Other Costs Mount,". "In Illinois, lawmakers last month introduced proposals that could eliminate bail for first-time, nonviolent offenders or abolish cash bail. In Maryland, the Supreme Court last month chose to change the state's cash bail system significantly. In January, New Jersey began a new system of pretrial detention, in which judges can only set bail as a last resort. Lawmakers in California, Connecticut, Maryland and New York also have legislation pending that would remake their states' cash bail systems." Wiltz, "Locked Up: Is Cash Bail on the Way Out?".

161. Christine Stuart, "Malloy Pitches Bail Reform as Part of Connecticut's Second Chance Society 2.0," *New Haven Register*, January 28, 2016, www.nhregister.com/article/NH/20160128/NEWS/160129552, last accessed August 2, 2017.

162. New Mexico S.J.R 1, ch. CA 1, 52nd Legislature, 2nd Session (2016). See also Nick Wing, "New Mexico Votes to Reform Bail System That Jails People Just Because They're Poor," *Huffington Post*, January 4, 2017, www.huffingtonpost.com/entry/new-mexico-amendment-1_us_5817a3cfe4b0990edc32ed05, last accessed August 2, 2017.

163. Wiltz, Locked Up: Is Cash Bail on the Way Out?. "Last month, the Arizona Supreme Court also struck down a voter-approved provision in the state constitution that had eliminated the right for people accused of sex crimes to be considered for bail."

164. Michael Dresser, "Maryland's Bail System Gets a Major Overhaul," *Governing*, February 8, 2017, www.governing.com/topics/public-justice-safety/tns-maryland-bail-court.html, last accessed August 2, 2017.

165. Ibid.

166. Ibid.

167. Texas H.B. 3011, § 1, Art. 1.07, 85th Legislature (2017). Texas S.B. 1338, § 1, Art. 1.07, 85th Legislature (2017).

168. New Jersey, P.L 2014, Ch. 31, §1–20. See also, "ACLU-NJ Hails Passage of NJ Bail Reform as Historic Day for Civil Rights," *American Civil Liberties Union*, August 4, 2014, www.aclu.org/news/aclu-nj-hails-passage-nj-bail-reform-historic-day-civil-rights?redirect=criminal-law-reform/aclu-nj-hails-passage-nj-bail-reform-historic-day-civil-rights, last accessed August 2, 2017.

169. Ibid.

170. Lisa W. Foderaro, "New Jersey Alters Its Bail System and Upends Legal Landscape," *N.Y. Times*, February 6, 2017, www.nytimes.com/2017/02/06/nyregion/new-jersey-bail-system.html, last accessed August 2, 2017.

171. Ibid.

172. Ibid.

173. Ibid.

174. Craig McCarthy, "Bail Reform Has Been a 'Challenge' for Law Enforcement, Prosecutors Say," *nj.com*, January 29, 2017, www.nj.com/middlesex/index.ssf/2017/01/nj_bail_reform_has_been_a_challenge_for_law_enforc.html, last accessed August 2, 2017.

175. Timothy R. Schnacke, "Best Practices in Bond Setting: Colorado's New Pretrial Bail Law," *Center For Legal and Evidence Based Practice* (July 2013): 1, available at www.pretrial.org/download/law-policy/Best%20Practices%20in%20Bond%20Setting%20-%20Colorado.pdf, last accessed August 15, 2017.

176. Colo. Rev. Stat. § 16-1-104 (2013).

177. Colo. Rev. Stat. § 16-4-103 (2013).

178. Colo. Rev. Stat. § 4-103 (3) (b) (2013).

179. Colo. Rev. Stat. § 16-4-104 (2013); Colo. Rev. Stat. § 16-4-105 (2013); Colo. Rev. Stat. § 16-4-107 (2013).

180. Simonson, "Bail Nullification," 585.

181. Ibid., 597.

182. Ibid., 598.
183. Ibid., 599. See, e.g., "Bail: A Costly Injustice," *Brooklyn Community Bail Fund*, accessed August 2, 2017, www.brooklynbailfund.org [https://perma.cc/V5YZ-JDY2]. "Ninety percent of people in our jails because they can't pay bail are Black or Hispanic. Their poverty alone imprisons them. The result is two systems of criminal justice: one for those who have and one for those who do not."
184. Simonson, "Bail Nullification," 604–5.
185. Ibid., 606. (citing "Second Annual Report 2015" *Bronx Freedom Fund*, http://static1.squarespace.com/static/54e106e1e4b05fac69f108cf/t/5681561eb204d52319b86854/1451316766890/2015+Annual+Report.pdf, last accessed August 2, 2017; "2015–2016 Annual Report" *Brooklyn Community Bail Fund*, www.brooklynbailfund.org/2015-annual-report; "Massachusetts Bail Fund: Campaign Details" *Classy.org*, www.classy.org/events/Massachusetts-bail-fund/e75475).
186. Simonson, "Bail Nullification," 618.
187. Ibid., 638. "When community bail funds intervene at [the moment when a judge decides whether or not money bail will be so high that it will lead to a defendant's pretrial detention], they shift the meaning of bail—and ultimately, justice—back into the hands of the people most affected by the practice."
188. Shadd Maruna, Dean Dabney, and Volkan Topalli, "Putting a Price on Prisoner Release: The History of Bail and a Possible Future of Parole," *Sage Journals, Punishment and Society*, July 20, 2012, http://journals.sagepub.com/doi/abs/10.1177/1462474512442311.
189. Max Ehrenfreund, "What's Wrong with Making People Post Bail After Trial," *Washington Post*, March 16, 2015, www.washingtonpost.com/news/wonk/wp/2015/03/16/whats-wrong-with-making-people-post-bail-after-trial/?utm_term=.9a0632d65373, last accessed August 2, 2017. See, Miss. Code Ann. §99-5-39. Michigan H.B. 4437, § 614, 95th Legislature (2009).
190. See, for example Harris and Paul, "To Shrink Jails, Let's Reform Bail," www.nytimes.com/2017/07/20/opinion/kamala-harris-and-rand-paul-lets-reform-bail.html, last accessed August 1, 2017.

11 OPTIMAL BAIL: USING CONSTITUTIONAL AND EMPIRICAL TOOLS TO REFORM AMERICA'S BAIL SYSTEM

1. Shane Bauer, "Inside the Wild, Shadowy, and Highly Lucrative Bail Industry," *Mother Jones*, May 2014, www.motherjones.com/politics/2014/06/bail-bond-prison-industry, last accessed August 2, 2017.
2. From 1990 to 2007, the population of pretrial detainees housed in jails has increased from about 50–62 percent. Nat'l Ass'n of Counties, Jail Population Management: Elected County Officials' Guide to Pretrial Services 4 (2009); Bureau of Justice Statistics, Prison and Jail Inmates at Midyear 7 (2000); Bureau of Justice Statistics, Prison and Jail Inmates at Midyear 5 (2007).
3. U.S. Dept. of Justice, Bureau of Justice Statistics, Annual Survey of Jails: Jurisdiction-Level Data, 1985–7, 1989–92, 1995–7, 2000–4, 6, www.icpsr.umich.edu/icpsrweb/ICPSR/studies?sortBy=7&q=annual+survey+of+jails), last accessed August 2, 2017.

4. Shima Baradaran and Frank L. McIntyre, "Predicting Violence," *Texas Law Review* 90 (2012): 497.
5. Dep't of Justice, Bureau of Justice Statistics, Compendium of Federal Justice Statistics 47, 49 (2004).
6. A BJS report states that a study of eight urban jurisdictions reported a 15 percent pretrial detention rate by the 1980s. Steven R. Schlesinger, "Pretrial Release and Misconduct" (Bureau of Justice Statistics, 1985), 1, www.bjs.gov/content/pub/pdf/prm-foo.pdf, last accessed August 2, 2017.
7. Pheny Z. Smith, "Felony Defendants in Large Urban Counties, 1990" (Bureau of Justice Statistics, 1993), 8, www.bjs.gov/content/pub/pdf/fdluc90.pdf, last accessed August 2, 2017; Brian A. Reaves, "Felony Defendants in Large Urban Counties, 2009 – Statistical Tables" (Bureau of Justice Statistics, 2013), 15, www.bjs.gov/content/pub/pdf/fdluc09.pdf, last accessed August 2, 2017.
8. Christopher R. Lowenkamp, Marie VanNostrand, and Alexander Holsinger, "Investigating the Impact of Pretrial Detention on Sentencing Outcomes" (Laura and John Arnold Foundation, 2013), 3; www.arnoldfoundation.org/wp-content/uploads/2014/02/LJAF_Report_state-sentencing_FNL.pdf, last accessed August 2, 2017.
9. Some of these principles were first discussed in Shima Baradaran, "Restoring the Presumption of Innocence," *Ohio State Law Journal* 72 (2011): 723–76.
10. Baradaran and McIntyre, "Predicting Violence."
11. Baradaran and McIntyre, "Predicting Violence" tables (considering state data from the seventy-five largest counties in the United States).
12. Baradaran, "Restoring the Presumption of Innocence," 772–6; *United States v. Doyle*, 130 F.3d 523, 539 (2d Cir. 1997) ("Unless and until the Government meets its burden of proof beyond a reasonable doubt, the presumption of innocence remains with the accused . . . throughout all stages of the trial and deliberations.").
13. The court should be allowed to detain an individual before trial when (1) it finds by clear and convincing evidence, after a due-process hearing, that the person poses such a high level of risk that no condition or combination of conditions could provide a reasonable assurance that the public's safety will be protected, that the defendant will appear in court if released pretrial, or that the judicial system's integrity will not be imperiled; and (2) all other requirements for pretrial detention set forth in the ABA's *Standards for Criminal Justice: Pretrial Release* (3d ed., 2007) and the law has been met.
14. See, e.g., "Personal Protection Orders," Kalamazoo County Government, www.kalcounty.com/opa/dv/ppo.html, last accessed August 2, 2017 (defining "no-contact" bond conditions in Kalamazoo County, Michigan).
15. Baradaran, "Restoring the Presumption of Innocence," 768; *United States v. Salerno*, 481 U.S. 739, 748 (1987) (holding that there is a legitimate public interest in detaining a defendant if he presents a danger to a witness).
16. Baradaran, "Restoring the Presumption of Innocence" (Compare *Stanley v. Henson* 337 F.3d 961, 967–8 (7th Cir. 2003) (allowing pretrial strip search with battery misdemeanor charges), with *Masters v. Crouch*, 872 F.2d 1248, 1255 (6th Cir. 1989) (denying a pretrial strip search for a minor offense)).

17. Ibid., 46.
18. John Pfaff, Locked In (Basic 2017)
19. Adam Gopnik, "How We Understand Mass Incarceration," *New Yorker* (April 10, 2017), www.newyorker.com/magazine/2017/04/10/how-we-misunderstand-mass-incarceration, last accessed August 2, 2017.
20. Baradaran and McIntyre, "Predicting Violence," 544.
21. Ibid.
22. Ibid.
23. The arrest rate for an average black teenager is higher than the arrest rate for a middle-age female convicted felon according to my research with Frank McIntyre.
24. Sandra G. Mayson, "Bail Reform and Restraint for Dangerousness: Are Defendants a Special Case?" (working paper, University of Pennsylvania Law School).
25. Ibid.
26. Ibid., 42.
27. Ibid., 43.
28. Ibid.
29. Ibid., 44.
30. Ronald Allen and Larry Laudan, "Deadly Dilemmas II: Bail and Crime" (working paper, Northwestern University School of Law, 2008), 8, https://papers.ssrn.com/sol3/papers.cfm?abstract_id=1314085, last accessed August 2, 2017.
31. Ibid.
32. Baradaran and McIntyre, "Predicting Violence," 527.
33. Ibid., 531.
34. "New Data: Pretrial Risk Assessment Tool Works to Reduce Crime, Increase Court Appearances," Laura and John Arnold Foundation, last modified August 8, 2016, www.arnoldfoundation.org/new-data-pretrial-risk-assessment-tool-works-reduce-crime-increase-court-appearances/, last accessed August 2, 2017.
35. Qudsia Siddiqi, *Predicting the Likelihood of Pretrial Failure to Appear and/or Re-Arrest for a Violent Offense Among New York City Defendants* (New York: New York City Criminal Justice Agency, 2009), 13.
36. Pretrial Justice Institute, "Pretrial Risk Assessment 101: Science Provides Guidance on Managing Defendants," 2, www.bja.gov/publications/pji_pretrialrisk assessment101.pdf, last accessed August 2, 2017.
37. Ibid. (citing Cynthia A. Mamalian, *State of the Science of Pretrial Risk Assessment* (Washington, DC: Pretrial Justice Institute, 2011)).
38. Ibid., 1.
39. Association of Prosecuting Attorneys, *Policy Statement on Pretrial Justice*, www.pretrial.org/download/policy-statements/APA%20Pretrial%20Policy%20 Statement.pdf, last accessed August 2, 2017.
40. Pretrial Justice Institute, "Pretrial Risk Assessment 101," 4.
41. Ibid.
42. The nine factors and how they are considered in the assessment are outlined in the graph below. Boxes where an "X" occurs indicate that the presence of this risk factor increases the likelihood of that outcome – FA, NCA, or NVCA – for any given defendant.

Relationship between risk factors and pretrial outcomes*

Risk factor	Failure to appear (FA)	New criminal activity (NCA)	New violent criminal activity (NVCA)
1. Age at current arrest		X	
2. Current violent offense			X
Current violent offense and twenty years old or younger			X
3. Pending charge at the time of the offense	X	X	X
4. Prior misdemeanor conviction		X	
5. Prior felony conviction		X	
Prior conviction (misdemeanor or felony)	X		X
6. Prior violent conviction		X	X
7. Prior failure to appear in the past two years	X	X	
8. Prior failure to appear older than two years	X		
9. Prior sentence to incarceration		X	

*In determining the risk of a potential outcome, each factor is assigned a weighted point value according to the strength of the relationship between that factor and the outcome. For example, in determining a defendant's risk of Failure to Appear, one of the factors the court would look at is whether the defendant has any prior failures to appear older than two years. If they have zero, add zero points; if they have one, add two points; and if they have two or more, add four points. The higher the final weighted score, the more likely the defendant is to Fail to Appear.

43. Pretrial Justice Institute, "Pretrial Risk Assessment 101," 5.
44. Ibid.
45. Ibid., 3 (citing Marie VanNostrand and Ken Rose, *Pretrial Risk Assessment in Virginia* (Virginia Department of Criminal Justice Services, 2009), available at www.pretrial.org/download/risk-assessment/VA%20Risk%20Report%202009.pdf, last accessed August 15, 2017).
46. Ibid.
47. "Defendant Supervision," Pretrial Services Agency for the District of Columbia, accessed March 1, 2017, www.psa.gov/?q=programs/defendent_supervision.
48. Ibid.
49. KiDeuk Kim and Megan Denver, *A Case Study of the Practice of Pretrial Services and Risk Assessment in Three Cities* (District of Columbia Crime Policy Institute, 2011), 8, www.docplayer.net/7545576-A-case-study-on-the-practice-of-pretrial-services-and-risk-assessment-in-three-cities.html, last accessed August 2, 2017.
50. Hawaii uses a proxy tool made up of three questions and a scoring process that the state has validated. The proxy score helps categorize offenders, separating the higher-risk offenders who will receive a full assessment, from the lower-risk offenders who may be placed under minimal supervision with no pretrial detention.

First, jurisdictions should select a random sample of at least 300 cases of active probationers, and gather data regarding their current age, age at first arrest, and number of prior adult arrests. Each of the categories should then be scored. For an individual's current age, in relation to the remainder of the population, a value of 2, 1, or 0 is assigned. The youngest will be given the highest score of 2 while the oldest receive the lowest of 0. For age at first arrest, a value of 3, 2, or 1 is assigned. Similar to the scoring of an individual's current age, the youngest will receive the highest score and the oldest receive the lowest. For the defendant's number of prior adult arrests, a value of 3, 2, or 1 will also be assigned. Those with the highest number of priors will be assigned a score of 3, the middle third of the population a score of 2, and those with the least number of priors a score of 1. Brad Bogue, William Woodward, and Lore Joplin, "Using a Proxy Score to Pre-Screen Offenders for Risk to Reoffend" (2006), 1, www.pretrial.org/download/risk-assessment/Using%20 a%20Proxy%20Score%20to%20Pre-screen%20Offenders%20(Bogue,%20 Woodward,%20Joplin%202006).pdf, last accessed August 2, 2017.

51. Ibid. This proxy tool provides correction agencies with a cost-effective tool to pre-screen offenders for their potential risk and is an extremely efficient way to categorize offenders based off of their first contact with law enforcement.

52. "The Colorado Pretrial Assessment Tool (CPAT)" (Pretrial Justice Institute, October 19, 2012), 3, www.pretrial.org/download/risk-assessment/CO%20 Pretrial%20Assessment%20Tool%20Report%20Rev%20-%20PJI%202012.pdf, last accessed August 3, 2017.

53. Ibid., 10.

54. Ibid., 13.

55. Ibid., 18.

56. Ibid., 18.

57. Ibid., 19.

58. Lauryn Gouldin, "Disentangling Flight Risk from Dangerousness," *Brigham Young University Law Review* 3 (2016): 871.

59. Ibid., 873.

60. Ibid., 886.

61. Melissa Hamilton, "Back to the Future: The Influence of Criminal History on Risk Assessments," *Berkeley Journal of Criminal Law* 20 (2015): 75, 112.

62. Sonja B. Starr, "The New Profiling: Why Punishing Based on Poverty and Identity Is Unconstitutional and Wrong," *Federal Sentencing Reporter* 27 (2015): 229, 230.

63. Hamilton, "Back to the Future," 112; see also Baradaran and McIntyre, "Predicting Violence."

64. Starr, "The New Profiling," 230.

65. Heaton, Mayson, and Stevenson, "The Downstream Consequences," 58.

66. Ibid., 59.

67. Fifty-state survey in possession of author. The Federal Bail Reform Act also allows weighing of evidence, although in some circuits – like the 9th circuit – it is the least important factor.

68. See, e.g., *Yording v. Walker*, 683 P.2d 788, 791 (Colo. 1984); *Blackwell v. Sessums*, 284 So. 2d 38, 39 (Miss. 1973) (affirming bail denial where the evidence conflicted on whether the proof was evident that defendant was guilty based on the evidence)

69. *United States v. Salerno*, 481 U.S. 739, 748–9 (1987).

70. Salerno, 481 U.S. at 751.
71. Salerno, 481 U.S. at 752. The Court pointed out that the act provides for all of the following: detainees to have the right to counsel at the detention hearing, the right to testify in their own behalf, to present information by proffer or otherwise, and to cross-examine witnesses who appear at the hearing. While these rights exist in the federal system, they are not respected in pretrial decisions in most states.
72. See Chapter 7, discussing how Judges make determinations of fact not juries.
73. See Rothgery, 554 U.S. 191 (2008).
74. Heaton, Mayson, and Stevenson, "The Downstream Consequences," 59.
75. Ibid., 62; *Coleman v. Alabama*, 399 U.S. 1, 9 (1970).
76. *Gerstein v. Pugh*, 420 U.S. 103, 122 (1975) ("Because of its limited function and its nonadversary character, the probable cause determination is not a 'critical stage' in the prosecution that would require appointed counsel.")
77. *Rothgery v. Gillespie County*, Tex., 554 U.S. 191 (2008).
78. Ibid. at 211.
79. Ibid. at 213.
80. *Bounds v. Smith*, 430 U.S. 817, 821 (1977).
81. *Faretta v. California*, 422 U.S. 806, 834–6 (1975).
82. *Taylor v. List*, 880 F.2d 1040, 1047 (1989).
83. *Bounds v. Smith*, 430 U.S. 817, 828 (1977).
84. *Kane v. Garcia Espitia*, 546 U.S. 9, 10 (2005).
85. See *Jones v. Armstrong*, 367 F. App'x 256, 259 (2d Cir. 2010); *United States v. Taylor*, 183 F.3d 1199, 1204 (10th Cir. 1999); *Degrate v. Godwin*, 84 F.3d 768, 769 (5th Cir. 1996).
86. Martha Neil, "Murder Defendant Loses Jail Cell Computer Over Claims He Worked on Other Inmates' Cases," *ABA Journal* (November 10, 2014), www .abajournal.com/news/article/murder_defendant_loses_jail_cell_computer_ due_to_claims_he_worked_on_other, last accessed August 3, 2017.
87. Natalie Singer, "Self Defense Just Got Easier for Inmates," *The Seattle Times*, April 14, 2006.
88. Pretrial Justice Institute, "Pretrial Risk Assessment 101: Science Provides Guidance on Managing Defendants," www.bja.gov/publications/pji_pretrial-riskassessment101.pdf, last accessed August 3, 2017.
89. *Elimination of Bond Schedules*, Pretrial Justice Institute, accessed March 1, 2017, www.pretrial.org/solutions/elimination-of-bond-schedules/.
90. *Thompson v. Moss Point*, 2015 WL 10322003 (S.D. Miss., November 6, 2015).
91. *ODonnel v. Harris County, Texas, et al.*, No. 4:16-CV-01414 (S.D. Texas, March 3, 2017) (Position of District Attorney Kim Ogg About Bail Bond Litigation Pending in the United States District Court).
92. Ibid. 2.
93. Bail Agents Keen On Defending California's Money-Based Bail System When No One Else Will, CBS San Francisco http://sanfrancisco.cbslocal.com/2017/03/06/ bail-agents-keen-on-defending-californias-money-based-bail-system-when-no-one-else-will/, last accessed August 3, 2017.
94. Compare *Cost of Pretrial Detention in City Jails Takes Bite Out of Big Apple's Budget*, accessed March 1, 2017, www.ibo.nyc.ny.us/newsfax/nws56 pretrialdetention.html (detailing the cost to house a single pretrial detainee in

a year in New York City) with "Pretrial Release Programs Vary Across the State; New Reporting Requirements Pose Challenges" (Office of Program Policy Analysis & Government Accountability, December 2008) (Miami-Dade County supervised 11,101 defendants outside detention facilities).

95. VanNostrand, "Alternatives to Pretrial Detention."

96. American Bar Association, Criminal Justice Section, *Frequently Asked Questions About Pretrial Release Decision Making* 4.

97. Ibid., 5.

98. *Pretrial Supervision & Monitoring*, Pretrial Justice Institute, accessed March 1, 2017, www.pretrial.org/solutions/supervision-monitoring/.

99. Ibid., 12.

100. Mitchel N. Herian and Brian H. Bornstein, *Reducing Failure to Appear in Nebraska: A Field Study*, 11 (The Nebraska Lawyer, 2010), www.pretrial.org/download/research/Reducing%20Failure%20to%20Appear%20(Nebraska%20Lawyer,%20September%202010).pdf, last accessed August 3, 2017.

101. Ibid. The postcard that included the while the "reminder-procedural justice condition" (that the judge would treat defendant fairly) had a 9.8 percent failure to appear rate.

102. VanNostrand, "Alternatives to Pretrial Detention."

103. *Pretrial Services*, Durham County NC, accessed August 3, 2017, www.dconc.gov/home/showdocument?id=20978.

104. Strafford County in New Hampshire has made use of this device and is even able to know where a defendant has been, within thirty feet. Emily Murphy, "Paradigms of Restraint," *Duke Law Journal* 57 (2008): 1321, 1333.

105. Shima Baradaran, "The Right Way to Shrink Prisons," *New York Times*, May 30, 2011, www.nytimes.com/2011/05/31/opinion/31baradaran.html, last accessed August 3, 2017.

106. Maya Schenwar, "The Quiet Horrors of House Arrest, Electronic Monitoring, and Other Alternative Forms of Incarceration," *Mother Jones* (January 22, 2015), last accessed August 3, 2017, www.motherjones.com/politics/2015/01/house-arrest-surveillance-state-prisons.

107. Morris L. Thigpen et al., "Measuring What Matters—Outcome and Performance Measures for the Pretrial Services Field," (National Institute of Corrections, August 2011), www.pretrial.org/download/performance-measures/Measuring%20What%20Matters.pdf, last accessed August 3, 2017.

108. Ibid.

109. ABA Pretrial Release Standards 10-5.3(b). The ABA Standards prohibit financial conditions of release imposed to protect the public's safety. They only allow the imposition of financial conditions of release (other than unsecured bond) when no other release condition would "reasonably ensure" a person's appearance in court. Ibid. at 10-5.3(a). The ABA Standards furthermore request that judges refuse to allow financial release conditions that "result in the pretrial detention of the defendant solely due to an inability to pay." Ibid.

110. Marie VanNostrand, "Alternative to Pretrial Detention: Southern District of Iowa," (Luminosity, Inc. 2010), 11, www.pretrial.org/download/risk-assessment/Alternatives%20to%20Pretrial%20Detention%20Southern%20District%20of%20Iowa%20-%20VanNostrand%202010.pdf, last accessed August 3, 2017.

111. Ibid.
112. Judge Warren Davis, "Should Georgia Change Its Misdemeanor Arrest Laws to Authorize Issuing More Field Citations?: Can an Alternative Arrest Process Help Alleviate Georgia's Jail Overcrowding and Reduce the Time Arresting Officers Expend Processing Nontraffic Misdemeanor Offenses?," *Georgia State University Law Review* 22 (2005): 313, 317 (citing Floyd F. Freeney, "Citation in Lieu of Arrest: The New California Law," *Vanderbilt Law Review* 25 (1972): 367, 367–8).
113. Ibid.
114. Marcia Johnson and Luckett Anthony Johnson, "Bail: Reforming Policies to Address Overcrowded Jails, the Impact of Race on Detention and Community Revival in Harris County, Texas," *Northwestern Journal of Law and Social Policy* 7 (2012): 42, 55.
115. Ibid.
116. "Clarifying the Post-Arrest Process in the District of Columbia: Report, Recommendations, and Proposed Legislation" (Washington DC: D.C. Misdemeanor Arrest & Pretrial Release Project Subcommittee of the Council for Court Excellence, 2013), 5, www.pretrial.org/download/infostop/Clarifying%20 the%20Post-Arrest%20Process%20in%20Wash%20DC%20-%20CCE%202013.pdf, last accessed August 3, 2017.
117. Ibid., 8–9.
118. Johnson and Johnson, "Bail: Reforming Policies," 76.
119. Ibid.
120. "Pretrial Reform in Kentucky" (Frankfort, KY: Kentucky Pretrial Services, 2013), 6, www.pretrial.org/download/infostop/Pretrial%20Reform%20in%20Kentucky%20 Implementation%20Guide%202013.pdf. See also KRS 218A.1415.
121. Ibid.
122. Ibid., 8.

APPENDIX 2

1. "Presumption of Guilt: The Global Overuse of Pretrial Detention," *Open Society Foundations, Justice Initiative* (2014): 17, last accessed December 21, 2016, www .opensocietyfoundations.org/sites/default/files/presumption-guilt-09032014.pdf.
2. Ibid., 20.
3. England and Wales is at 13.8%, Germany is at 18%. Roy Walmsley, "World Pre-trial/Remand Imprisonment List (second edition)," *International Centre for Prison Studies (ICPS)* (2015): 5, last accessed December 27, 2016, www.prisonstudies.org/ sites/default/files/resources/downloads/world_pre-trial_imprisonment_list_2nd_ edition_1.pdf.
4. "Presumption of Guilt: The Global Overuse of Pretrial Detention," 30.
5. "Pretrial Detention and Torture: Why Pretrial Detainees Face the Greatest Risk" *Open Society Foundation,* (2011): 21, last accessed December 20, 2016, www.opensocietyfoundations.org/sites/default/files/pretrial-detention-and-torture-06222011.pdf.
6. Ibid., 17.
7. Ibid., 20.

8. Ibid.
9. Ibid., 30.
10. Ibid., 17.
11. Ibid., 30.
12. Ibid., 17.
13. Ibid., 20.
14. Ibid., 30.
15. Ibid., 17.
16. Ibid., 20.
17. Ibid., 30.
18. Marcelo F. Aebi and Natalia Delgrande, "Council of Europe Annual Penal Statistics, Space 1, Survey 2006," *Council of Europe* (2008), www.ristretti.it/commenti/2007/novembre/pdf/detenzione_europa_2006.pdf.
19. Preventative detention means something entirely different in other countries.
20. George E. Glos, "Bail, Probation and Parole in Belgian Law," *International Journal of Legal Information* 14 (1986).
21. Ibid., 102.
22. Ibid., 101.
23. Glos, "Bail, Probation and Parole in Belgian Law."
24. Ibid., 102.
25. Ibid.
26. Ibid.
27. Ibid.
28. Ibid., 105.
29. Ibid.
30. Ibid., 102.
31. Ibid.
32. Ibid.
33. Ibid., 105.
34. Ibid.
35. Ibid.
36. Ibid.
37. Ibid., 105 n.8.
38. "Prisons in Latin America, a Journey into Hell," *The Economist*, September 22, 2012, www.economist.com/node/21563288.
39. Ibid.
40. Andrea Drip, "Behind Brazil's Arrest First Ask Questions Later Policy," *Insight Crime*, February 24, 2015, www.insightcrime.org/news-analysis/brazil-pretrial-detention-prison-population.
41. Ibid.
42. "Finding Direction: Expanding Criminal Justice Options by Considering Policies of Other Nations," *Justice Policy Institute* (2011): 3, www.justicepolicy.org/uploads/justicepolicy/documents/pretrial_detention_and_remand_to_custody.pdf. last accessed March 1, 2015,
43. Ibid.
44. Ibid.

45. Average for year to 31 March 2014. "World Prison Brief: Country Profiles," *International Centre for Prison Studies,* www.prisonstudies.org/country/canada last accessed March 1, 2015.

46. "By the Numbers: Crime, Bail and Pre-trial Detention in Canada," *Canadian Civil Liberties Association* (2014): 1, www.ccla.org/wordpress/wp-content/uploads/2014/07/2014-07-23-By-the-numbers1.pdf last accessed March 1, 2015.

47. Ibid.

48. "By the Numbers: Crime, Bail and Pre-trial Detention in Canada," *Canadian Civil Liberties Association* (2014), www.ccla.org/wordpress/wp-content/uploads/2014/07/2014-07-23-By-the-numbers1.pdf last accessed March 1, 2015.

49. Ibid.

50. Ibid.

51. Jonathan L. Hafetz, "Pretrial Detention, Human Rights, and Judicial Reform in Latin America," *Fordham International Law Journal* 26 (2002–2003): 1761.

52. Ibid., 1762.

53. Michael Wines, "China Daily Assails Prisoner Abuses," *New York Times,* March 24, 2009, www.nytimes.com/2009/03/25/world/asia/25china.html?_r=0.

54. A Survey on the Rights Protection of Pretrial Detainees in China, Center for Human Rights and Humanitarian Law Peking University (August 2015), tbinternet.ohchr.org/Treaties/CAT/Shared%20Documents/CHN/INT_CAT_CSS_CHN_22154_E.pdf last accessed July 31, 2017.

55. Laura Harmes, "Law Society Calls for 28-day Limit on Police Bail," *BBC Radio 5 Live,* May 28, 2013, www.bbc.com/news/uk-22624648.

56. Data includes Wales. Aebi and Delgrande, "Council of Europe Annual Penal Statistics, Space 1, Survey 2006."

57. Ibid.

58. A.M. van Kalmthout, M.M. Knapen, and C. Morgenstern, "Pretrial Detention in the European Union, an Analysis of Minimum Standards in Pre-trial Detention and the Grounds for Regular Review in the Member States of the EU" (WLP 2009), 950, http://citeseerx.ist.psu.edu/viewdoc/download?doi=10.1.1.194.618&rep=rep1&type=pdf, last accessed July 31, 2017.

59. Ibid.

60. Ibid.

61. Ibid.

62. Bail Act of 1976 c.63 section 4(2).

63. Bail Act of 1976 c.63 schedule I, part I(1).

64. Bail Act of 1976 c.63 schedule I, part II(1).

65. Bail Act of 1976 c.63 section 4(1).

66. Bail Act of 1976 c.63 schedule I, part I(2).

67. Bail Act of 1976 c.63 schedule I, part I(9).

68. Bail Act of 1976 c.63 schedule I, part I(8)(1)(A).

69. Kalmthout, Knapen, and Morgenstern, "Pretrial Detention in the European Union, an Analysis of Minimum Standards in Pre-trial Detention and the Grounds for Regular Review in the Member States of the EU," 953.

70. Ibid.

71. Ibid.

72. Bail Act of 1976 c.63 schedule I part II(2).

73. Bail Act of 1976 c.63 schedule I part II(3).
74. Bail Act of 1976 c.63 schedule I part II(4).
75. Bail Act of 1976 c.63 schedule I part II(5).
76. Bail Act of 1976 c.63 schedule I, part I(2)(A).
77. Number includes untried, convicted but not sentenced, and sentenced but appealing, because France does not report a single number for untried prisoners.
78. Aebi and Delgrande, "Council of Europe Annual Penal Statistics, Space 1, Survey 2006," 37.
79. Ibid.
80. Ibid.
81. "Communique, Pre-Trial Detention in France, Local Expert Group (France)," *Fair Trials International* (2013): 2, www.fairtrials.org/wp-content/uploads/Fair_Trials_International_France_PTD_Communiqu%C3%A9_EN.pdf last accessed July 31, 2017.
82. Ibid.
83. Conserving evidence or material clues, preventing witness or victim pressuring, protecting suspects, ensuring availability, ending the offense, end public disturbance, prevent unlawful collusion between suspect and his or her associate. Article 144 of the French Criminal Procedure Code.
84. "Communique, Pre-Trial Detention in France, Local Expert Group (France)," 4.
85. Ibid., 3–4.
86. Ibid., 4.
87. Ibid., 6.
88. Ibid.
89. Ibid., 5.
90. Ibid.
91. Ibid.
92. John Quigley, "The Tanzania Constitution and the Right to a Bail Hearing," *African Journal of International and Comparative Law* 4 (1992): 178 (quoting Special Criminal Court Act 1979 p. 696).
93. Ibid.
94. Ibid., 178.
95. Ibid. (quoting The Gambia, Constitution, Section 15(5), quoted in *Attorney-General of the Gambia* v. *Momodou Jobe*, 1984 A.C. 689 (Privy Council) n.48, p. 697)(quoting The Gambia, Constitution, Section 15(5), quoted in *Attorney-General of the Gambia* v. *Momodou Jobe*, 1984 A.C. 689 (Privy Council) n.48, p.697).
96. Quigley, "The Tanzania Constitution and the Right to a Bail Hearing," 178.
97. "Finding Direction: Expanding Criminal Justice Options by Considering Policies of Other Nations," 3.
98. Ibid.
99. One study says 12%. Richard S. Frase, "German Criminal Justice as a Guide to American Law Reform: Similar Problems, Better Solutions?," *Boston College International and Comparative Law Review* 18 (1995): 329.
100. "Finding Direction: Expanding Criminal Justice Options by Considering Policies of Other Nations," 3.

101. Ibid.
102. "Appendix 2 Pre-trial Detention Comparative Research," *Fair Trials International*, 11, last accessed July 31, 2017, http://ec.europa.eu/justice/newsroom/criminal/opinion/files/110510/appendix_2_-_comparative_research_en.pdf
103. Ibid.
104. Ibid.
105. Ibid.
106. Ibid., 12.
107. Ibid.
108. Ibid., 13.
109. Frase, "German Criminal Justice as a Guide to American Law Reform: Similar Problems, Better Solutions?" 327.
110. Ibid., 328.
111. "Communique, Pre-Trial Detention in Greece, Local Expert Group (Greece)," *Fair Trials International* (2013): 1, 27, www.fairtrials.org/wp-content/uploads/Greek-communique-EN.pdf last accessed July 31, 2017.
112. Ibid.
113. Ibid., 2, 27.
114. Ibid., 5, 27.
115. Ibid., 4, 27.
116. Ibid.
117. "Greece Report Highlights Misuse of Pre-Trial Detention," *Fair Trial International*, July 30, 2013, www.fairtrials.org/publications/greece-report-highlights-misuse-of-pre-trial-detention/, last accessed July 31, 2017.
118. "Communique, Pre-Trial Detention in Greece, Local Expert Group (Greece)," 4, 27.
119. Ibid.
120. Ibid.
121. Ibid. 2, 27.
122. Ibid., 3, 27.
123. Ibid., 6, 27.
124. Ibid., 5, 27.
125. Ibid., 6, 27.
126. Ibid., 1, 27.
127. Ibid., 3, 27.
128. Ibid.
129. Ibid.
130. Ibid.
131. Ibid., 4, 27.
132. Ibid.
133. Ibid.
134. Ibid., 7, 27.
135. "Report to the Government of Greece on the Visit to Greece Carried Out by the European Committee for the Prevention of Torture and Inhuman or Degrading Treatment or Punishment (CPT) from 17 to 19 September 2009," *Council of Europe*, November 17, 2010, www.cpt.coe.int/documents/grc/2010-33-inf-eng.htm#_Toc259109918, last accessed July 31, 2017.

136. Ibid.
137. Ibid.
138. Ibid.
139. Ibid.
140. Hafetz, "Pretrial Detention, Human Rights, and Judicial Reform in Latin America," 1763.
141. Ibid.
142. Ibid., 1764.
143. Ibid., 1763.
144. This gives 0.7 m² per person. Further, only forty-four of the inmates are sentenced prisoners, the rest are pretrial. Frédéric Gouin, "Prolonged Pretrial Detention Creates Overcrowding in Haitian Prisons," *MINUSTAH/ Office of the High Commissioner for Human Rights*, https://minustah .unmissions.org/prolonged-pretrial-detention-creates-overcrowding-haitian-prisonsla-d%C3%A9tention-provisoire-prolong%C3%A9e, last accessed July 31, 2017.
145. This article is about prisoners, not pretrial detainees; but Haiti is a country that doesn't always separate the two categories of people. So prison conditions should accurately reflect pretrial conditions. "Extreme Prison Overcrowding and Lengthy Pre-Trial Detention Continue in Haiti Despite International Court Order," *Institute for Justice and Democracy in Haiti*, July 3, 2013, www.ijdh .org/2013/07/topics/law-justice/extreme-prison-overcrowding-and-lengthy-pre-trial-detention-continue-in-haiti-despite-international-court-order/ last accessed July 31, 2017.
146. This gives 0.7 m² per person. Further, only 44 of the inmates are sentenced prisoners, the rest are pretrial. Gouin, "Prolonged Pretrial Detention Creates Overcrowding in Haitian Prisons."
147. "Hungarian Experts' Concern Over Pre-Trial Detention," *Fair Trials International* (2013), www.fairtrials.org/publications/hungarian-experts-concern-over-pre-trial-detention-2, last accessed July 31, 2017.
148. "Communique, Pre-trial Detention in Hungary," *Fair Trials International* (2013): 2, www.fairtrials.org/wp-content/uploads/Hungary-PTD-communique.pdf last accessed July 31, 2017.
149. Ibid., 2, 3.
150. Ibid., 3.
151. Ibid., 1.
152. Ibid., 1, 2.
153. Ibid., 2.
154. Agence France-Presse, "Pretrial Detentions Worrying Eastern Europe," *New York Times*, November 19, 2000, www.nytimes.com/2000/11/19/world/pretrial-detentions-worrying-eastern-europe.html.
155. "Communique, Pre-trial Detention in Hungary," 3.
156. Agence France-Presse, "Pretrial Detentions Worrying Eastern Europe."
157. "Communique, Pre-trial Detention in Hungary," 4.
158. Ibid.; see also Article 132(3) of Act XIX of 1998 on Criminal Proceedings.
159. "Hungarian Experts' Concern Over Pre-Trial Detention."
160. "Communique, Pre-trial Detention in Hungary," 3.

161. Aebi and Delgrande, "Council of Europe Annual Penal Statistics, Space 1, Survey 2006," 37.

162. "2010 Human Rights Report: Iceland," *United States Department of State, Bureau of Democracy, Human Rights and Labor*, April 8, 2011, www.state.gov/j/drl/rls/hrrpt/2010/eur/154429.htm, last accessed July 31, 2017.

163. Iceland Const. Artic 67, www.government.is/constitution/, accessed 16 March 2015.

164. Ibid.

165. Catherine Homby, "Italy's Senate Approves Law to Ease Overcrowded Prisons." *Reuters*, August 8, 2013, www.reuters.com/article/2013/08/08/us-italy-prisons-idUSBRE9770HN20130808, last accessed July 31, 2017.

166. Ibid.

167. Ibid.

168. "Italian Law Addresses Excessive Pre-Trial Detention," *Fair Trial International*, August 29, 2013, www.fairtrials.org/press/italian-law-addresses-excessive-pre-trial-detention/, last accessed July 31, 2017.

169. Ibid.

170. "Appendix 2 Pre-trial Detention Comparative Research," 20.

171. Ibid.

172. Ibid.

173. Ibid.

174. Ibid.

175. Ibid., 22.

176. Bail Act, 1997 2 (2)(a)–(f).

177. Ibid.

178. Bail Act, 1997 6 (1)(a)–(b).

179. "Appendix 2 Pre-trial Detention Comparative Research," 18.

180. Aebi and Delgrande, "Council of Europe Annual Penal Statistics, Space 1, Survey 2006."

181. Ibid.

182. "Appendix 2 Pre-trial Detention Comparative Research," 17.

183. Ibid., 18.

184. "Japan 2013 Human Rights Report," *United States Department of State, Bureau of Democracy, Human Rights and Labor*, 6, www.state.gov/documents/organization/220409.pdf, last accessed July 31, 2017.

185. Ibid.

186. Ibid.

187. Ibid.

188. Ibid.

189. Ibid.

190. Ibid., 6, 7.

191. Ibid., 7.

192. Ibid., 6.

193. Ibid.

194. Ibid.

195. Ibid., 7.

196. Ibid.

197. Ibid.

198. Ibid.
199. Ibid., 8.
200. Ibid., 7.
201. "Appendix 2 Pretrial Detention Comparative Research," 23.
202. Ibid.
203. Ibid.
204. Ibid.
205. Ibid.
206. Ibid.
207. Ibid.
208. Ibid., 24.
209. "Socioeconomic Impact of Pretrial Detention," *Open Society Foundation* (2011): 45, www.opensocietyfoundations.org/sites/default/files/socioeconomic-impact-pretrial-detention-02012011.pdf, last accessed July 31, 2017.
210. Ibid., 30.
211. Ibid.
212. Ibid.
213. Ibid., 45.
214. Ibid.
215. Ibid.
216. Ibid.
217. Ibid.
218. Ibid.
219. "Presumption of Guilt: The Global Overuse of Pretrial Detention," 119.
220. Ibid.
221. Ibid., 120.
222. Ibid., 119.
223. "Communique Following Meeting in Poland to Discuss Pre-Trial Detention," *Fair Trials International* (2013), www.fairtrials.org/publications/communique-following-meeting-in-poland-to-discuss-pre-trial-detention/, last accessed July 31, 2017.
224. Ibid.
225. Ibid.
226. Kathy Lally, "Laws to Rein in Russia's Pretrial Detention System are Ignored," *The Washington Post*, November 25, 2011, www.washingtonpost.com/world/europe/laws-to-rein-in-russias-pre-trial-detention-system-are-ignored/2011/11/04/gIQAeNvmnN_story.html.
227. Aebi and Delgrande, "Council of Europe Annual Penal Statistics, Space 1, Survey 2006."
228. Out of the forty-eight reported, not including Russia.
229. Aebi and Delgrande, "Council of Europe Annual Penal Statistics, Space 1, Survey 2006," 37.
230. Aebi and Delgrande, "Council of Europe Annual Penal Statistics, Space 1, Survey 2006."
231. "Medvedev Approves Changes to Economic Crime Law in Russia," *Sputnik News*, April 7, 2010, www.sputniknews.com/russia/20100407/158461749.html.
232. Lally, "Laws to Rein in Russia's Pretrial Detention System are Ignored."
233. Ibid.

234. Will Englund, "Bribery Charge Perplexes Moscow School," *The Washington Post*, October 26, 2011, www.washingtonpost.com/world/europe/bribery-charge-perplexes-moscow-school/2011/10/21/gIQA33vnGM_story.html.
235. Ibid.
236. Ibid.
237. Ibid.
238. Ibid.
239. Ibid.
240. Ibid.
241. Ibid.
242. Ibid.
243. Ibid.
244. Lally, "Laws to Rein in Russia's Pretrial Detention System are Ignored."
245. Ibid.
246. Ibid.
247. Ibid.
248. This distinction has actually prevented her release, as a ceasefire talk has released prisoners of war. Sarah Rainsford, "Nadiya Savchenko: Ukraine Resistance Symbol in Russia," *BBC*, March 6, 2015, www.bbc.com/news/world-europe-31760381.
249. "The Socioeconomic Impact of Pretrial Detention in Sierra Leon," *Open Society Justice Initiative* (2013): 39, last accessed April 14, 2015, www.issuu.com/undp/docs/the_socioeconomic_impact_of_pretria_a7486b030e4a06.
250. Ibid., 41.
251. Ibid., 42.
252. Without regard to how long ago that sentence was.
253. Criminal Procedure Act, N.9 of 1985, n.3, section 5(a)-(d),(f),(g).
254. Quigley, "The Tanzania Constitution and the Right to a Bail Hearing," 174–5.
255. Tanzania Constitution article 15 section 1(a).
256. *Director of Public Prosecutions v. Daudi s Jo Pete*, Crim. App. No.28 of 1990 (Court of Appeal of Tanzania, 16 May 1991).
257. Quigley, "The Tanzania Constitution and the Right to a Bail Hearing," 170.
258. Ibid., 170–1.
259. Ibid., 174–5.
260. Ibid.
261. "Thailand: Tactics of Police Questioned in Investigations of Tourist Murders," *The Associated Press*, October 8, 2014, www.nytimes.com/2014/10/09/world/asia/thailand-tactics-of-police-questioned-in-investigation-of-tourists-murders.html?ref=topics.
262. Ibid.
263. Ibid.
264. Human Rights Watch, *Tunisia: Perils of Pre-charge Detention*, video, run time 7:48, December 5, 2013, www.hrw.org/news/2013/12/05/tunisia-perils-pre-charge-detention.
265. "Cracks in the System Conditions of Pre-Charge Detainees in Tunisia," *Human Rights Watch* (2013): 3, www.hrw.org/sites/default/files/reports/tunisia1113_ForUpload_1.pdf, last accessed July 31, 2017.
266. Human Rights Watch, *Tunisia: Perils of Pre-charge Detention*.

267. Ibid.
268. Ibid.
269. Ibid.
270. Ibid.
271. "Cracks in the System Conditions of Pre-Charge Detainees in Tunisia," 3.
272. Ibid.
273. Ibid.
274. Human Rights Watch, *Tunisia: Perils of Pre-charge Detention.*
275. Ibid.
276. "Cracks in the System Conditions of Pre-Charge Detainees in Tunisia," 37.
277. Ibid., 38, 39.
278. Ibid., 47.
279. "Pretrial Detention and Torture: Why Pretrial Detainees Face the Greatest Risk" *Open Society Foundation,* (2011): 37, www.opensocietyfoundations.org/sites/default/files/pretrial-detention-and-torture-06222011.pdf, last accessed December 20, 2016.
280. Ibid.
281. Ibid.
282. Hafetz, "Pretrial Detention, Human Rights, and Judicial Reform in Latin America," 1762.
283. Ibid.
284. Ibid.
285. "Pretrial Detention in Zimbabwe," ZLHR, *Law Society of Zimbabwe* (2013): 30, www.osisa.org/sites/default/files/pre-trial_detention_in_zimbabwe.pdf, last accessed April 13, 2015,
286. Ibid., 32.
287. Ibid., 30.
288. Ibid.
289. Ibid., 32, 35.
290. Ibid., 33.
291. Ibid., 35.

Index

Index